Figures of Resistance

p. 211 "objects" women as (rainy night scene)

Post-Contemporary Interventions

Series Editors: Stanley Fish and Fredric Jameson

Figures

of Resistance

Language, Poetry

and Narrating

in *The Tale of Genji*

and Other

Mid-Heian Texts

H. Richard Okada

Duke University Press

Durham and London   1991

To my mother and

the memory of my father,

Sueo Okada

© 1991 Duke University Press
All rights reserved
Printed in the United States of America
on acid-free paper ∞
Library of Congress Cataloging-in-Publication Data
appear on the last printed page of this book.

Contents

Contents

Preface

In February 1987 I presented a paper at Duke University that was an earlier version of Chapter 9 of the present study. After a discussant offered generous and insightful comments, the moderator opened the floor to questions. In attendance was Fredric Jameson, widely acknowledged to be the foremost Marxist critic in the United States today. Toward the end of the session, Jameson asked a question that prodded me into rethinking my perspectives on the *Genji* tale and the other Heian texts on which I had been working. He remarked that although what we—one other speaker had delivered a paper on Chinese literature—were clearly suggesting was a sexual politics, we had not addressed it directly, and he asked how we would respond to the issue. The question was directed at the other speaker, but another member of the audience asked me how it applied to the *Genji* tale. As I recall, I stumbled around the question at the time but later began to realize just how pertinent the issue was to practically everything important about the tale and Heian discourse. I therefore set out to reconfigure a major portion of my earlier analyses of the texts and added sections and chapters that explicitly addressed the issue. In the process of rewriting, I began to look more closely at the highly educated and talented Heian women who became the major transmitters and producers of a culture that has not only endured for centuries but has become synonymous with much that is now considered the very essence of the Japanese nation. I also incorporated more of what we know or can surmise about other enabling conditions or contexts of utterance (especially the crucial question of genealogy).

The result is a series of readings of three Heian *monogatari*— *Taketori, Ise,* and *Genji*—readings situated by examinations of other relevant Heian texts, discourses, and various other intertextual circumstances. The three *monogatari* have been canonized in the Japanese tradition and are also accorded prominent places in Western scholarship. As I discuss the issue of reading in the Introduction, I will use the term "close reading" to refer not to the attempt to discover the "true meaning," in any sense of the term, of a text, but rather to a process that can question the possibility of any and all overall meanings. Some readers may not find the thematic closure they expect, but I hope that such readers will follow the analytical strands that run throughout the book. I am concerned with how linguistic, narratological, historical, and sociopolitical discourses, which are my multitiered or polylogic points of focus, can be placed into dynamic relations with each other, with the larger "worldly" situations out of which they emerged, and with present-day postures of analysis, including my own.

In the process of tracing the discourses, I often take sustained issue with aspects of traditional scholarship. Let me state at the outset that I do not intend in any way to negate or belittle scholarship to which, obviously, I am greatly indebted. My aim is rather to call for genuine debate as we continually reexamine our attitudes toward Japan. I do not believe that we are or should be engaged in a contest for the absolute "truth" of a particular methodology but would urge that we always examine the implications of what we do in terms of the situations in which we find ourselves constructed as speaking, writing, teaching, and thinking (gendered) subjects.

This book could not have been written without the help of a great number of people. I wish to thank, first of all, Masao Miyoshi, without whose support, guidance, and criticisms over the years, projects like this study would have been impossible. He continues to provide a powerful example of the critical spirit and energy with which to teach and do research. I am indebted to Edward Fowler, who gave the manuscript a close, critical reading in its incarnation as a dissertation and who has always been an exceptionally sound and cogent critic. I am also grateful to James Fujii for giving me useful and incisive comments on an earlier draft and at a moment's notice.

My Princeton colleagues have been another indispensable source of support. Earl Miner has for many years kindly and freely dispensed much needed encouragement as well as invaluable advice on many matters. He together with my other colleagues, especially Martin Collcutt, Yoshiaki Shimizu, Marius Jansen, and Willard Peterson, have made Princeton a most stimulating and congenial place to work. Outside of Princeton, I have received encouragement and assistance in important ways from Richard Bowring, Janet Walker, Mark Morris, Harry Harootunian, Naoki Sakai, Minae Mizumura, Chieko Mulhern, Brett de Bary, Sumie Jones, Tetsuo Najita, Norma

Field, William Sibley, Sandra Buckley, Susan Matisoff, Anthony Chambers, and Amanda Stinchecum.

I must also mention the scholars in Japan who have given unstintingly of their time and knowledge. The generosity, learning, and energy of Mitani Kuniaki, one of the founders of the Monogatari kenkyūkai (Monoken), are second to none, and I have profited tremendously from our discussions over the years. I have also learned much from discussions with other Monoken members, especially Fujii Sadakazu and Takahashi Tōru, and from the sessions of the group (surely unique among scholarly circles anywhere) that I have had the privilege of attending. I am grateful to Matsuda Shigeho for introducing me to the world of *Genji* studies when he came to Berkeley as a visiting scholar and to Hino Tatsuo for overseeing a lengthy period of study at Kyoto University. I thank Katō Kumiko for her gracious hospitality during visits to Nagoya and the Reizei family in Kyoto for allowing me to participate in a series of their monthly poetry gatherings, which gave me firsthand experience with a traditional way of disseminating poetic techniques. Finally, Katō Tachimitsu was a source of comradeship and lively conversations during a year-and-a-half stay in Sagano.

I also thank Charlene Kiyuna and the McGowan family for their unwavering loyalty. Perhaps my deepest gratitude is to my wife, Tara, who has been a constant intellectual and emotional companion, for proofreading drafts of the manuscript, and for showing great patience and understanding during the stage of rewriting.

A note on the translations of poetry and method of romanization. I have chosen not to follow the accepted practice of translating waka into a strict formal arrangement consisting of a series of four or five stacked, horizontal lines. Because written waka assume various calligraphic forms from one to three or more vertical lines and each of the 5/7/5/7/7 syllabic clusters forms an important unit of each poem, I have used a variable system of three or four horizontal lines with syllabic clusters in the Japanese represented by clearly separated English phrases. By doing so I wish to call attention to the sense of "linearity" that Mark Morris has carefully pointed out and also to highlight when necessary syllabic clusters that "float" syntactically, a configuration that enables the semantic (and incantatory) thrust of the waka cluster to operate in a multidirectional manner. The translations of poetry and other passages found in the study are my own unless otherwise noted. In translating I have punctuated freely in order to create a structure that runs against the grain of modern styles and invokes earlier periods of English usage. Romanized versions of the Japanese terms and phrases taken from the texts are based on equivalences of *kana* orthography as found in modern printed editions or in a reputable classical language dictionary (*kogo jiten*) such as the excellent one edited by Ōno Susumu and published by Iwanami shoten. When referring to words or terms in current use today, I have used a standard modern romanization system (I would thus write *iusoku*, for example, when citing a Heian text and *yūsoku* when referring to its modern use).

Introduction

A book is not an isolated entity: it is a narration, an axis of
innumerable narrations. One literature differs from another, either before it or after it, not so much because of the text as for the
manner in which it is read.
  Jorge Luis Borges, *Other Inquisitions: 1937–1952*

Indeed I would go so far as saying that it is the critic's job to provide
resistances to theory, to open it up toward historical reality,
toward society, toward human needs and interests, to point up
those concrete instances drawn from everyday reality that lie
outside or just beyond the interpretive area necessarily designated
in advance and thereafter circumscribed by every theory.
  Edward Said, "Traveling Theory"

The initial problem is one of perspective.
  Raymond Williams, *The Country and the City*

What are *monogatari* and how should we be talking about them? The
question, with which I began an earlier version of this study,[1] arose
because the term *monogatari* named texts that seemed hopelessly
disparate: (1) collections of poems[2] with "stories" about them (e.g.,
Heichū monogatari and *Ise monogatari*), (2) "prose" works (e.g., *Taketori
monogatari* and *Ochikubo monogatari*), (3) texts (e.g., *Ise monogatari* and
Yamato monogatari) that resembled in part others seemingly of a
different "generic" category (e.g., *Kokin wakashū*), and (4) a single text
that merged or was a mosaic of passages from differing discursive
realms (e.g., *Taketori, Murasaki Shikibu nikki,* and *Utsuho monogatari*).[3]
The continued importance of the term for twentieth-century readers
is evident in the place it holds in the nonfictional writings of one of the
greatest modern Japanese writers, Tanizaki Jun'ichirō (1886–1965),
who during the course of his long and productive career undertook
perhaps the most ambitious and sustained experiment with the
possibilities of narrating, and also from the attention given the term

monogatari in one of the more remarkable books on modern Japanese literature in the last decade, *Nihon kindai bungaku no kigen*.[4] It remains unclear, however, what the term ultimately signifies.

My earlier study explored what it would mean to read *The Tale of Genji* (*Genji monogatari*) and other Heian period (794–1185)[5] *monogatari* texts if we began with the assumption that the language in which they were composed, recited, written down, and received was of serious theoretical concern and worthy of sustained inquiry.[6] In other words, what happens if we view language not merely as an incidental (albeit—with Heian *hiragana* language—a most difficult) obstacle that once hurdled can be abandoned in pursuit of transcendent matters, but as forming, beginning to end, the ineluctable subject of any reading even as it is constituted as subject by that reading? How does the fact that the texts were written in a particular, non-Western linguistic medium relate to or alter existing readings of them, and can contemporary discussions of language, meaning, and form offer any assistance? Such a perspective, I argued, would facilitate the examination of the problems that arise whenever Japanese (both Heian and later) "literary" texts are being discussed.

In setting out to resolve my initial puzzlement, I decided early on that one text, even if it were *Genji monogatari,* would not be sufficient to treat the subject adequately. The Heian texts appeared during a particular period of Japanese history when modern Western categories of discourse (e.g., lyric, diary, prose fiction, literature, history) did not perforce apply. To demand that *monogatari* texts conform to categories and strategies well known to us today, including the isolation of "masterpieces," and then to proceed with analyses as if those categories were self-evident and in need of no further questioning would be to participate in a form of appropriation (even colonization). One step toward an answer to the question "What are *monogatari?*" was to focus initially on aspects of Heian texts that tend not to be articulated in integrative or "polylogic" (as opposed to dialogic) ways: modal-aspectual markers, "tenselessness" of the language, open-ended textual movements, narrators and narrating perspectives (or moments), lack of clear distinction between "first-" and "third-person" narration, quantity of variant texts, and significance of poetic and other citations (in the commonly used "weak" sense of "intertextuality") in which all texts and authors participate.

In the present rereading of the earlier study, I have tried to make coextensive with often extended demonstrations of linguistically oriented narratological readings, which I feel are still necessary at our point in time, another sense of open-endedness: the larger socio-politico-historical intertexts (in the strong sense of the term).[7] I have, accordingly, taken a large hint from contemporary discussions of writing and viewed *monogatari* not as "autonomous" or even as primarily "literary" works as is commonly done, but rather as texts, writings, discourses, or signifying practices.[8] Assuming that notions of narratology and narrative must move beyond formalist or structuralist oriented readings to embrace broader discursive situations and questions of culture, power, and gender, I have sought to rewrite the texts in terms of various intertexts with the aim of discarding the usual essentialist notions connoted by the term "literature" and of examining the texts as scriptive spaces that, rather than "naturally" belonging to universal "generic" categories, can be seen as inscribing particular (historicocultural) discursive (including oral) environments that appropriated, contested, and rewrote other types of existing discourses.

I am not suggesting a wholesale abandonment of issues traditionally associated with the discipline of "literature." Association with and participation in that discipline is an obvious and unavoidably restrictive factor of my own discourse. Even while confirming the impossibility of total abandonment, I want to point toward a way of reading and rewriting whereby the canonical terms and bases of the discussion of what we in the West normally (or normatively) consider the "literary" can be displaced through different modes of inquiry and constructions of "new objects of knowledge."[9] Such "rewrites," then, would enable negotiation of the problematic in a manner that pays attention not only to the totalizing tendencies (thematic, structural, historicist) on which reading strategies have often insisted and that texts and their makers may seem to invite and authorize, but also to the sociopolitical positions of putative authors along with the discursive thresholds, rifts, elisions, and inconsistencies in the texts. In short, I wish to emphasize a strategy that not so much demonstrates how the texts "reflect" the sociopolitical structures of their and their readers' times but attends to the ways in which they construct, appropriate, contest, deny, or assist in altering those structures. I thereby displace my initial question—"What are Heian *monogatari?*"—with the following: How did Heian writers respond to the needs and desires of their specific historical and genealogical situations? How can we articulate the often complex responses found in *monogatari* to other writing already in circulation as well as to other (including our own) "worldly" situations? And how can we do so in a manner that problematizes and keeps contingent readerly temporality and position and, finally, remains mindful of the question of writing subject and enunciative audience?[10]

"Reading" Texts Not of Our Time or Place

Much has been made lately of reading strategies and performances. Rather than espousing particular "reader-response" perspectives with their essentializations of the reader, I pose this question: How does a text arising out of particular historical circumstances, its writer both liberated and constrained by particular sociopolitical and cultural forces, posit its reader (and we must remember that such readers are "gendered" readers) so that she or he is able to "make sense of" or "rationalize" it? The readerly position might be that of a character, a narrator (or "narrating," i.e., the position that emerges when the narrator "speaks" to the reader or audience, who is either an implicit presence or an explicitly addressed interlocutor),[11] the discernible "theme" or assumed "intention," or even the setting in which the story is assumed to have occurred. Many writers have argued convincingly that the act of reading itself constitutes a process of "construction," not simply one of "consumption"; readers do not so much retrieve what is already "in" the text as "re-produce" the text (and its meanings) through interpretive strategies. From such a perspective on the problem of positionality (seen in terms of class, gender, race or ethnicity, and other factors), when we actually engage a text in reading it, we do not simply "receive" meanings (as an antenna receives radio signals) or "discover" truths but to an important and complex degree "construct" those meanings and "truths." And we do so not from any free-floating, neutral point in space and time but from the points of provisional identification the text allows in terms of a reader's historicocultural identities and configurations. The traditional belief in a neutral reading or writing position has been shown to be based on a masculinist (unmarked), Western bourgeois myth, as I shall discuss below.

The particular (though often assumed to be universal) positions of readerly construction, moreover, become moments at which the question of "ideology" enters. From positions always already constructed at particular sociocultural coordinates, the reader "reads," that is, "re-creates," the text and in doing so is apt to merge positions—the ones attributable to the text and the ones offered by the reader's cultural perspective—that may very well be incommensurable and only result from an act of interpretive violence.[12] As Gramsci, Althusser, and others have pointed out, the fact that subjects are constructed within an ideological sphere should not imply any sense of coercion or force but rather collusion; ideology "works" precisely because its mechanisms are erased and the subject takes positions freely and even eagerly.[13] For example, when it comes to reading within a Western cultural sphere texts produced by Heian period women and men who wrote in the presumably "private" native Japanese mode (*hiragana*), in conscious contrast to the officially dominant, "public" Chinese and quasi-Chinese mode (*kambun*), it would seem on the one hand the height of arrogance to assume a congruity of reader-text positions when the controlling perspective is in fact securely situated in a Western male reader's stance (whether actually adopted by male or female) and, on the other, the most naive form of historicism to assume that you can put yourself in the position of a Heian reader and understand the texts as the Japanese of the time understood them. Modern scholar-readers alternate between the two poles, desirous of the latter but left, wittingly or not, with the former.

Let me repeat that I am not advocating yet another version of a "reader-response" approach with either interpretive communities (à la Fish) or interpretive horizons (à la Jauss or Iser),[14] but rather interrogating the relation of constructed "subject positions" to "narrative" (or "narrativity") as problematized by an increasing number of recent writers. Dominant perspectives of reading and interpreting (or noninterpreting) texts in our lifetime—New Critical, structuralist, semiotic, reader-response, Marxist, psychoanalytical—have failed, as their critics have shown, to attend rigorously to aspects of the geopolitical, sociocultural, historical, and sexual forces at work in the production and reception of texts and subjects. Although those perspectives encompass a rich and varied interdisciplinary range, they all fall prey in one way or another to criticisms that question the appropriateness of assuming at crucial moments the operational efficacy of universal or essentialized elements whether couched in terms of humanistic value, form, signification, readerly interpretation, Class, History, or subconscious text (subtext). Their failure to note the displacements that occur when they do not inflect their own analytical stances and procedures for gender, race or ethnicity, class, historicity, contingency, or institutional setting is also vulnerable to attack.[15] Recent scholarship written in the discourse of feminism, poststructuralism, and postcoloniality, in its interrogation of the problems of the body, gender, race, and representation, has been teaching us that modern Western subject positions are deeply inscribed by patriarchal or imperialist-colonialist ideologies. My purpose, accordingly, is twofold: to question, at times implicitly, previous readings of Heian period texts performed in the context of the institutionalized discipline of Japanese literature, or "Japanology," which has sanctioned and maintained practices fully complicit with both patriarchal and colonialist discourse, and to reread and rewrite Heian period texts in order to trace the contours of resistance they present to the employment of Western canonical terms of appropriation (novel, lyric, hero/heroine, [fully rounded] character, plot, first/third-person narration, and so on) deployed in unquestioned and only ironically unmasked strategies of reading.

To assist in interrogating one aspect of the important issue of positionality, let us examine the assumptions underwriting the familiar method of "close reading" we are taught in schools (here I mean American high schools, colleges, and universities), a method that remains the primary pedagogical tool in American institutions of higher learning. The program of close reading, with its roots in I. A. Richards's *Practical Criticism*—the title itself another term by which the procedure is known—was greatly enhanced by the wave of the New Criticism that swept over North America in the 1940s and 1950s. It is, moreover, a procedure that most adherents would claim to be politically neutral, through which undergraduate college students in particular can display their "native intelligence" as they confront texts "directly." One critic, John Barrell, has recently critiqued the method, albeit within a British context:

> It is never possible to speak or write except in discourse; and because all discourses embody an account of reality, they all produce a position from which that account is assembled. Whenever we speak or write we are adopting, whether we know it or not, a specific discourse, one that we feel is more or less appropriate to the topic we are addressing and the situation in which our utterance is being made. All our utterances are therefore political utterances, in the widest sense of being attempts to claim for ourselves particular *positions in language*, which represent us as the subject of knowledge, and represent the world as we, and as those whose interests we assume we share, claim to see it.[16]

Barrell argues for the indivisibility of position, discourse, and politics. An essay written by even the most avowedly apolitical undergraduate student, in other words, since it must be written from a particular cultural "position," demarcated by strictures established in a particular institutional setting, participates in the discourse of that culture and is therefore thoroughly "political."

Barrell's compact and incisive analysis of the problems of close reading, carried out from a position of cultural materialism, touches on such important matters as representation and reference, form and content, the assumption of the value of "full humanity," the valorizing of universals, the resolution of ambiguity through an imposition of the notion of balance, and the neutralization of masculine-subject and middle-class positions of dominance. When the work of close reading is examined, its judgments turn out to be governed by what Barrell calls the ideal of the "fully human," which is "a notion in which the idea of the 'fully literary' is metaphysically and morally grounded. To be fully human is to take on a universal identity, and a permanent one which has not changed throughout the whole of history."[17] Close readers, moreover, firmly believe that their critical method "makes the intrinsic qualities of a text entirely visible, and that, by virtue of this method, they are able to discover exactly what it means to be fully human; they have found a method of distinguishing the essential from the merely contingent" (p. 4). Such a notion of competence has meant that any reader, regardless of gender, race or ethnicity, or class can assume the position of close reader insofar as he or she effaces all that is contingent about his or her own sociopolitical and cultural positions and recognizes that "their political affiliations, and more generally their shifting political situations as defined in particular by class and gender, are somehow contingent to their identity as readers" (p. 4). In order to become certified critics, readers are encouraged to shrug off "certain aspects of . . . [their] complex identities" in order to read a text "*properly*" (Barrell's emphasis), even when the act of endorsing "that kind of position may actually be oppressive." By so doing, the argument goes, they can "become more human and so better human beings" (p. 9).

The "fully human" position, which turns out to be a fully "masculine" one, has always been the neutral, unmarked position and derives, Barrell asserts, from the fact that ideology writes men as generally more "balanced" than women: "If women speak with an uncontrolled 'shrillness' of tone . . . this is the sign of a failure to transcend their femininity—but no male writer ever lost control of his text through a failure to transcend his masculinity" (p. 6). Not only is the judgment that seeks a "balance" between the execution of the text (form) and the ultimate truths to which it must point (content) intimately tied to the dominant masculine reading position, the notion of balance, "a middle point between and above all merely partial and particular situations, bears a close resemblance to a certain ideal construction of the situation of the middle class" (p. 5). Barrell's discourse, then, appears to address the problematics of gender and class.

In response to the traditionalist, institutionalized stance, Barrell notes: "recent critics have denied that there are any qualities that we can identify in human beings that are universal, unchanging, and that constitute a deep ground of identity among all of us. The qualities that human beings express are entirely *culturally constructed*, and furthermore they are *constructed within language* (p. 8; emphasis added).[18] I agree with the implicit claim that we can no longer afford to leave our readings uninflected by historicity and contingency, or leave foundationalist or essentialist moves unquestioned, as also argued by feminist critics,[19] or leave unaddressed the fact that the texts we read as well as our own reading strategies are always (already) situated in specific historical and ideological moments.[20] But what alternatives does Barrell offer? First of all he denies "that there is any one position, from which all 'literary' texts can be read, which is more or less proper or competent than another" (p. 9). After disclaiming any slide into critical anarchy (a relativist "what this means for me" situation), he maintains that we must "identify the available positions from which an effective challenge can be made, which means to read from those generic positions which practical criticism seems to deny: the positions of an oppressed class, an oppressed gender, an oppressed race." And he suggests finally that "it is necessary to identify which of those positions it is appropriate to adopt in relation to each individual text we read" (pp. 9–10).

Although I am generally convinced by Barrell's critique, I take issue with the method suggested above: that you can simply choose from among different positions the one "appropriate" to the text at hand. The act of choosing, of course, presupposes an act of judgment, which presupposes a "place of" judgment. If we are merely choosing among pluralities, the very announcement of that stance of selection has already situated the critic outside the various possible maneuvers.[21] What, for example, is the "generic" position of "an oppressed class, an oppressed gender, an oppressed race," and how are we to adopt it? The terms themselves figure a catachresis that Barrell's formulation keeps concealed. Although Barrell makes the laudatory move of refusing any "exemplary" status for his own readings, he cannot avoid a basically monologic position that groups some readings in opposition to others: "I have tried to do this [criticize an oppressive reading practice] by trying to show that the poems I discuss can be read, and read closely, from some other position than that prescribed to the reader by the discourse of practical criticism" (p. 16). You need look no further than several recent projects to find demonstrations that "oppositional" readings do not of themselves solve problems of representation and narrativity, and dependency on a floating, "Archimedean" stance cannot place the terms of debate elsewhere from that given by the dominant sytem. Writers like Edward Said, Gayatri Spivak, Harry Harootunian, Teresa Ebert, Toril Moi, Tania Modleski, Teresa de Lauretis, R. Radhakrishnan, and Renato Rosaldo have been showing us that the taking of positions is more than a question of armchair choice making, which means an eventual return to business as usual.[22]

Translation and Commentary

In the light of the above I now turn briefly to the situation of Japanese literature studies. Two activities, both related to the program of "close reading" criticized by Barrell, most clearly characterize the history of that area of study in the West. Situated in terms of a methodology, they represent a combination of positivist philology and New Criticism. The former approach encouraged a pseudohistoricist linking of the texts of study to their cultural milieu, whereas the latter fortuitously (or ironically) countenanced the avoidance of wide-angle perspectives (transcultural and intertextual) in order to keep one's interpretative sights trained on the "verbal icon" at hand. While the critics allowed the philologists to devote attention to one text at a time, the philologists could slough off warnings of committing "intentional" or "biographical" fallacies secure in the knowledge that they were engaged in "scientific" endeavor. Having begun their careers as translators, many among the critics found in philology the "discipline" needed to write "commentary" and in

New Criticism the "method" needed to help execute the addendum, usually called the "introduction," to a translation that required the supplying of "background" or "critical" remarks. The actual activity of scholars in the field, however, at times only vaguely resembled the two methodologies. "Philology" too often became yet another act of "translation," not the adaptation of any complex method of philology or text criticism but rather the more mundane (and arbitrary) search for "appropriate" English equivalents to Japanese words. And far from any consistent and rigorous employment of New Critical reading procedures, criticism has meant either summary of Japanese scholarship in terms of historical "background" information and detailed points of descriptive interpretation or an unquestioned (and most often unstated) reliance on the writer's own political and cultural norms for broader interpretive maneuvers.

Theoretical issues themselves have rarely been foregrounded as critical non-self-awareness has kept the analyst in blind obedience to the mandates of her or his cultural (or political) unconscious regardless of how the dictates of that unconscious might be relevant (or irrelevant) to the "object" of study. Indeed a belief in the efficacy of translation virtually seduced practitioners into assuming that cultural others could be objectively interpreted through seamless analogies on every level, from the linguistic to the literary and sociohistorical. Such assumptions, I would insist, are wrong on all counts. The work of linguistic translation involves exclusionary moves similar to those performed at the level of "descriptive" commentary. As I shall be pointing out along the way, in their quest for target-language fluency and readability, translators and critics have often suppressed as marginal precisely those aspects of the native text where its specificity can (and must) be read. In an important discussion of translation, Walter Benjamin touches on the problem using a quotation from Rudolf Panwitz: "The basic error of the translator is that he preserves the state in which his own language happens to be instead of allowing his language to be powerfully affected by the foreign tongue. Particularly when translating from a language very remote from his own he must go back to the primal elements of language itself and penetrate to the point where work, image, and tone converge. He must expand and deepen his language by means of the foreign language."[23] When the prerogatives of the target language are emphasized, they diminish the "spirit of the foreign works."[24] At the level of commentary, as I shall discuss further below, such moves most often take the familiar form of "thematic" readings similarly destined to suppress difference and diminish the "spirit of the foreign works" as they appeal to and manipulate abstractions (metaphors) of "content" and ignore forces of signification that undermine those abstractions. I am in no way imputing sinister motives to highly talented and invaluable scholar-translators. My point is that contemporary discussions of language and representation are addressing the question of how any and all totalizing maneuvers involve exclusions (as well as the erasure of that act) at the very moment of their establishment. Who is doing what to/ for whom, the question of the subject of and constituency for enunci-ation, and his or her position and empowerment, then, become absolutely critical.

Why, it might be asked, impugn a procedure—thematic crit-icism—that, despite dismantling attempts from different fronts in recent years, still persists (even thrives) in all sectors of the academy? First and foremost, because an overriding emphasis on thematic criticism presents in many ways the greatest impediment to extricat-ing Japan studies from an "Orientalist" discourse that is, I hope, unacceptable to all scholars and writers insofar as it certifies an interpretative colonization of the other at the expense of specificity and moments of resistance. As Rodolphe Gasché has put it in a recent study that includes a compelling critique of thematics in the context of literary criticism's differences from the Derridean deconstruction of Western philosophy: "[Theme is] an originary—that is, constituted—unity or substance. As such . . . theme exercises a *totalizing* func-tion with regard to all the signifiers of a literary work. The theme secures the work's unitary meaning, its inner continuity. It is in the logic of thematism to be monistic, monological: therefore, the totaliz-ation to be achieved by a theme can succeed only if there is no other competing theme."[25] Monological "totalization" deprives a work of its specificity and difference, leaving, for Gasché (quoting Heideg-ger), "only this or that dull sense of unambiguous meaning." "What is wrong with literary criticism," he continues, "to refer to Heidegger once again, is that it experiences too little in the neighborhood of the work and that it expresses its already diminished experience too crudely and too literally" (p. 267). Thematic readings, in other words, often either overlook formal and syntactical aspects of texts or deal with them through yet other self-generating thematist moves. The difficulty faced by literary criticism, including its inability to preserve the uniqueness of texts, appears most often as commentary: "As commentary, certainly the discourse of criticism presupposes the works' uniqueness. But as commentary it can only turn that work into an example of a universal truth" (p. 268). Here I prefer to politicize Gasché by recalling Barrell's observation that such universal truths become so only from patriarchally governed, middle-class positions. For the translator-commentators of Japanese literature, the problem becomes not only the turning of objects of study into examples of universal (Western) truths but also the tendency to devalue immediately those works whenever the latter fail to measure up to unquestioned, hidden standards.

The beginnings of a solution (and there can be no simple one) lie not in trying to eliminate "themes" altogether, an impossibility given the necessarily representational (and essentializing) force of linguistic and interpretative activity itself (as my readings will also show) and the institutional requisites of modern scholarly discourse. Rather, to quote Gasché once again, the path lies "through reflecting on the originary unity in which is embedded the differences that organize the literary and critical discourses. . . . Whereas a poeticization of the critical discourse would lead to a mutual overcoming of both in a higher, fuller synthetic unity, and would thus yield to the most elementary telos of philosophical thinking, a reflection on the originary unity in which literature and criticism are embedded maintains their difference and respective uniqueness, while at the same time accounting for this difference" (pp. 268–269). By "originary unity" Gasché refers to those difficult "phenomenologically unthematizable unities . . . that organize and limit the conceptual differences that make up the critical discourse" (p. 269).[26] I would continue to politicize Gasché (and, by extension, Derrida) and add, albeit at a different register, that whether or not we are out to deconstruct the texts we read, we must continually put into question the institutionalized tools of criticism and genealogize their establishment, for those tools often serve to effect precisely those "unthematizable unities" at the very moment when we believe we are accounting for the most important, overarching (universal) levels of the text.[27]

Without venturing further into the issues, which defy summarization, I suggest only that we attend to matters delineated consistently over the past couple of decades in the work of scholars writing from poststructuralist, feminist, postcolonial, and postmodern positions. We must maneuver within various perspectives of critique, position ourselves (or accept our positioning) "elsewhere" to the dominant discourses and ideologies, and beware of reifying any particular position or of unwittingly keeping undeconstructed the crucial notion of "position" ("subject," "narrator," and "author" are a few manifestations) itself. If we work from deconstructive perspectives, for example, we must be mindful of sympathetic critiques (like the one by Gasché cited above, and those by Spivak)[28] as well as the forceful criticisms put forth by writers like Said and Terry Eagleton and interrogate the relevance of the debates to the construction of a critical procedure that will allow us to negotiate new spaces of difference mindful of positionality (especially our own). Unless we do so, we face the prospect of reinscribing the very thematic and cultural dominance we are laboring to disappropriate.

Taketori, Ise, and *Genji*

The present study takes as its main objects three Heian texts: *The Tale of the Bamboo Cutter* (*Taketori monogatari*), the *Tale of Ise* (*Ise monogatari*), and *The Tale of Genji* (*Genji monogatari*). Each of the three parts of the book focuses on a different text. I have chosen the texts for the following reasons: (1) they are often regarded by Japanese scholars as representing the most important *monogatari* texts of the time;[29] (2) the *Taketori* text is cited by the *Genji* narrator as the "parent of *monogatari*," and aspects of the bamboo-cutter story form major pretexts for such important figures as the Akashi Lady, Tamakazura, and Ukifune; (3) the *Ise* text becomes a prime intertextual component (together with *Kokinshū,* also discussed) of poems, situations, and broader narrative linkages, and Narihira stands as a possible inspiration for Genji; (4) many of the historical figures cited or suggested in the texts were victims of exclusionary Fujiwara policies or were close associates of figures who were driven (often exiled) from power; (5) there is a special connection between the texts and members of the Ki family, especially Ki no Tsurayuki, the important ancestor of *hiragana* writing; and (6) since the *Genji* text, to my mind, has not been situated sufficiently in broader discursive networks by Western scholars, it has tended to be overemphasized as an autonomous, practically sui generis, creation. What is crucial for the *Genji* text is its attempt, in privileging *monogatari* over Chinese discourse, to legitimize *hiragana* writing in a manner that repeats the *Kokinshū* legitimization of waka over Chinese poems (and the *Tosa nikki* legitimization of *hiragana* over *kambun* diaries).

I find in the three texts a position of "resistance," a term that I employ as a multivalent emblem for many of the issues with which I deal throughout the present study. In one urgent sense of the term, the Heian texts themselves have almost always presented resistances to their appropriation by both Japanese and non-Japanese readers; the issue becomes even more timely now in the context of cross-cultural readings, interdisciplinary questionings, and postmodern, poststructuralist problematics. In another obvious sense the texts represent or situate figures who openly resist,[30] who assume (or are made to assume) positions of resistance, or who participate in resisting configurations that govern their narrative constructions. And finally, I use the term to gesture toward the question of the resistance of language itself to its own readings, interpretations, theorizations, and totalizations as articulated by contemporary writers.[31]

In addition to the above three texts, I have included in Part I discussions of early discourse and an examination of two narrative suffixes and several pretexts for the bamboo-cutter tale to help situate the *Taketori* signifying practice. In Part II, I have included a discussion of the canonical poetry collection *Kokinshū* that legitimizes waka discourse as appropriate for "public" occasions and sets the parameters of sociolinguistic endeavor in the mid-Heian period. The *Kokinshū* discussion, presenting the case of an imperially ordered collection with clearly designated compilers, complements the discussions of the two private, anonymously compiled collections. The opening section of the private poetry collection of Lady Ise, a forerunner of such celebrated women-in-waiting as Murasaki Shikibu, Izumi Shikibu, and Sei Shōnagon, shows another way that waka find placement into "contexts." It will thus help situate another "private" collection, the *Ise* tale, which Lady Ise is even thought to have compiled and which is radically resistant to readerly appropriation.[32] I shall examine rhetoricopolitical movements of the texts and connect the linguistic and structural ploys found there to questions of genealogy, "fact" and "fiction," and the Fujiwara hegemony.

Part III comprises readings of the daunting *Genji* texts, readings, it must be stated at the outset, that are in no way meant to be "comprehensive" but that interrogate what seem to me some of the important issues raised by the texts. I pay particular attention to the following: a specific feminine authorship and the "marginal" status of *hiragana* writing; the official ranks and genealogies from which such learned salon women as Murasaki Shikibu emerged; the possible relations between narratological representations and gender and rank; the tropological maneuvers and moments that follow from earlier texts and practices and that invert or otherwise complicate distinctions between "fact" (or "history") and "fiction"; and the employment of *monogatari* to trace (and to critique aspects of) the "under or obverse side" (*ura*) of "life" as well as the more complex and difficult-to-negotiate underside of interpretive or reading strategies themselves. I do not seek, then, to highlight, as others have done, such familiar interpretive categories as "plot," "character," or "lyrical moments" as sufficient in themselves to control *Genji* readings, but rather wish to place those and other common terms continually into question. Part I situates *Taketori monogatari* in a larger field of bamboo-cutter pretexts. Part II discusses aspects of "poetic" discourse to amplify moments that are crucial to the *Taketori* narrative and to the socio-political issues it raises. Finally, the first two parts provide pretexts for reading the *Genji* tale.[33] Since we know very little about the historical circumstances of their production, I have read the texts in terms of linguistic, narrative, tropological, and other poetic configurations for the discursive positions they mark and adopt and for their potential contributions to the study of discourse and narrativity (and storytelling). I have elected to omit discussion of *Sagoromo monogatari*, a post-*Genji* text (not yet translated into English) that I included in the dissertation, and to incorporate it into a future study of late-Heian narratives.

Heian *Hiragana* Language

In an informative study of the types of possible phrasal combinations in Heian texts, Yamaguchi Nakami lists two broad categories of combination: phrases simply juxtaposed, one following another, and phrases conjoined by syntactic markers. The latter category embraces three different elements: (1) concessive markers, like *sikaredo* (that being the case, however); (2) pronominal (deictic) markers, like *sore* (that); and (3) repetitions of a word, a topical marker, for example, taken from the previous line.[34] The first general type, interestingly enough, occurs most frequently; the "repetitive" type within the second category the least. Moreover, the first type occurs most often in longer narratives, such as *Genji, Ochikubo monogatari, Yoru no Nezame, Hamamatsu chūnagon,* and *Sagoromo.* Yamaguchi cites an example from the "Aoi" chapter of *Genji:*

> gisiki nado, tune no kamuwaza naredo, ikamesiu nonosiru; maturi no Fodo, kagiriaru oFoyakegoto ni soFu koto oFoku, midokoro koyonasi [The ceremonies, though they are ones usually held for deities, are carried out with great solemnity; during the (Kamo) festival itself, there are many marvelous additions to the official celebrations that offer sights of an unparalleled nature.][35]

Texts in which we might expect to see an overt conjoining of phrases turn out on the whole to comprise units only implicitly linked to each other. Yamaguchi concludes that such phrasal patterns are characteristic of texts written primarily in the native *hiragana* mode, whereas texts written in a Chinese (*kambun kundoku*) style employ more connectives. The so-called poem-tale (*uta monogatari*) represented by the *Ise* tale and *Tales of Yamato* (*Yamato monogatari*) falls somewhere between the two.

In texts where phrases are juxtaposed, where the syntax replays a process of "listing," the cognitive burden falls on the reader, or "audience," since "the audience must ponder the relations between sentences and supply those relations as he or she follows along."[36] The *Genji* narrating constructs extremely lengthy passages that comprise a series of shorter phrases. As the text moves on, narrative focus, grammatical subject, and other referents shift freely within those extended phrases, and it is up to the reader-audience to keep track of the narrating by continually filling in the gaps. Syntactic connectives or anaphoric references are unnecessary, Yamaguchi surmises, because the narrating tends to exhaust one discursive topic before moving on to the next, and the (topical) context prevents the listener from becoming confused (p. 27).[37] *Uta monogatari,* which are thought to have originated in an oral tradition, tend rather to be constituted by shorter phrases linked through a greater use of connectives. Yamaguchi calls such texts "explanatory" (pp. 28–29). As I shall note, however, all *monogatari* texts when tied to oral situations of communal reception are constitutive of an "explanatory" register that does not depend on the presence or absence of sentential conjunctions. In any case, as Yamaguchi's essay suggests, a pattern analogous to one encountered at the narrative level—juxtaposition of narrating moments—can be observed at the syntactic level as well.

Let us remember that equivalent English terms by which we can refer to Heian linguistic segments are not easily found. The notion of "sentence," which might be substituted for "phrase" in the above, for example, is extremely problematic for Heian discourse. As it used to be taught in schools in the United States, an English sentence is characterized as a unit—subject-verb-object (SVO)—representing a "complete thought."[38] In English, which tends to valorize abstract, conceptual discourse governed by clearly demarcated subjects, such "thoughts" grow logically to form transcendent, governing "ideas," a process that highlights the metaphysical impulse of the language and its speakers. Heian Japanese, on the contrary, with its common (S)(O)V pattern, where the burden often falls on the verbal component, tends to elide the "subject" (see below), and rather than "object," we find amplification of a "topic." Discourse thereby always remains "open" and in a particular sense "concrete"[39] with not so much (logical) "thoughts completed" as associative remarks and enunciative contexts in which one participates. "Thoughts" become discursive or textualized moments that respond to a momentarily established topic. The reader-listener realizes or completes them only to have them yield to a succeeding moment that displaces them with another movement similarly constructed. No one group of successive moments necessarily follows "logically" from prior ones.

Robert Brower and Earl Miner note another distinctive feature of the Heian language: its large number of modal and aspectual markers. In their words,

> Few modern languages have such a range of possible inflections for adjectives, few are capable of such subtle verbal distinctions. Japanese verbs of the classical language employed by the Court period do not have our seven so-called tenses, but as many as seven morphemes expressing various kinds of *aspect* combined with as many as fourteen morphemes expressing *mood*. The result of the highly complex system of inflections is a particularly fine adjustment of tone (ultimately beyond the reach of translation) and an instrument especially well suited to exploring states of feeling, mind, and being. The functions of Japanese verbs are indicated by such inflections in agglutinative terminations.[40]

The morphemes referred to are the auxiliary verbal suffixes (*jodōshi*) affixed to verbal stems. The variety of modal markers—which include *mu, ramu, kemu, besi, meri, zi, masi, mazi,* and *nari* (in one of its significations), their meanings ranging from "must," "should," "will," and "seems," to "have heard" and including a few negative counterparts—attests to the "particularly fine adjustment of tone" found by Brower and Miner. Such morphemes also mark the continual emphasis placed on an implied speaker or enunciative position and on the (modal) attitude that speaker or position adopts toward the discourse.[41] The presence of such a powerful modality, however, does not mean that the discourse is "subjective."[42] At the narrative level, then, we find another analogue to a linguistic feature: namely, that a text or narrating moment always suggests a source (hearsay or perception, for example) from which it ostensibly derives, producing a kind of global indirect discourse or narrating.[43] The modal-aspectual markers include ones that signify a type of completed action or state (*tu* and *nu*), those that indicate incomplete action and resultant state (*tari* and *ri*), and two that I take to be (self-legitimizing, or "doubly grounded") "narrative modal-aspectuals" (*ki* and *keri*).[44]

Together with the peculiarities of the syntactic and modal-aspect situation, we must address what is at once the most obvious and the most overlooked (or taken for granted) facet of the Heian language in narrating terms: the language is, by and large, unmarked for tense. The "nonpast," "tenseless" propensity produces an enunciating perspective that gives the illusion that the events being recounted are happening at the very moment of the telling.[45] It does not, accordingly, subscribe to the familiar Western discursive pretense of taking the reader back to a past in order to "represent" events. For Heian narrating, every moment of telling becomes in a sense a "new" and contingent telling, and the events become (always) new "events."[46] The present study seeks to explore and delineate the implications of such a "tenseless" linguistic system for narrative discourse. Although their stance is not clear from the above, I infer from the remarks by Brower and Miner that the question of tense for Heian Japanese is at least to be held in abeyance, and although I agree with that view, I also believe that we ought to be considering the broader ramifications of thinking primarily in terms of aspect and mood (though in ways different from Genette and Todorov) rather than of tense.[47]

Another feature of the Heian language is its "lack" of syntactic subjects (already mentioned), a condition in which the burden of the narrating falls on adjectivals and verbals chosen in accordance with the governing "topic." As Watanabe Minoru states, the phenomenon may only mean that such subjects are not explicitly part of the discourse, since all the reader need do is supply them. The issue, however, is not whether they are implicit or explicit, although Watanabe does remind us of those instances where no "subject" can be found,[48] but rather obfuscation of the distinction between the speaker *of* the text and the speaker *in* the text, between first and third person narration. The syntactic erasure, analogous to the generic (and eroticized) markers *wotoko* (man) and *wonna* (woman) found at poetic moments throughout *monogatari* texts, invites the reader-audience to identify with the discursive perspective and maintain a participatory relation to it.[49] The feature is virtually impossible to translate into a language like English, which insists that proper subjects for each utterance be clearly designated, thus preserving a readerly distance even as it allows psychological identification. Rather than well-defined syntactic subjects, the Heian language relies on an ongoing institution of topical markers to create what I refer to as "narrating moments." A "topic" (the name of a character, a season or month of the year, or a celebratory occasion such as birth, death, or promotion, for example) rules every utterance, and each member or element of a narrating situation uses the currency provided by it to participate in the discursive exchange. The participants do not so much appropriate the topic for an individually interpreted remark or thought as complement it with a gesture toward both the topic and an interlocutor.

Finally, the Heian language positions the subjects of an utterance by an often complicated network of honorific language. By strategic usage of appropriate honorifics, humilifics, or unmarked words and morphemes (prominent in the language to this day) for a speaker's own actions as well as those of his or her listener, socially determined hierarchical relations of great complexity can be designated among the members of a verbal exchange (including a third person referred to by the speaker or listener). The situation becomes even more complicated when the narrator herself or himself participates in the honorific verbal scheme. For example, take a situation in which narrator (N) tells about a character (A) speaking to a second character (B) about a third character (C). N may use an honorific word or suffix for A (to show that A is of higher status than N); similarly, A may use a humilific suffix for herself and an honorific one for B (to show that B's status is higher than A's) and then perhaps a neutral suffix for C (which would mean that A and C are equal in status). Mapping the use of honorific language (the class of honorifics used by the narrator to refer to the Kiritsubo Consort, for example) has led scholars if not to the actual identity of one of the *Genji* narrators, at least to the level of her rank or social class. Although the discovery is by no means definitive, the rank and class noted provide further proof that women related to the "middle ranks" of Heian society form the most important constituency for the *Genji* tale, a constituency that I discuss in Part III.

Reading and Textual Variants

As is well known in scholarly circles, a title like *Genji monogatari* or *Ise monogatari* actually stands as a metonym for its many variant texts. Scholars have spent an enormous amount of energy during most of this century locating, examining, and collating the vast number of textual specimens and providing commentaries for those exemplars judged closest to a Heian "original."[50] Although many felt they were on the track of an "original" text, what we read today are nothing but hypothetical valorizations of a particular exemplar. In the case of *Genji*, for example, that exemplar belongs to the so-called Blue-Cover Texts (*Aobyōshi-bon*), one of three identifiable textual lineages—the others being the Kawachi Texts (*Kawachi-bon*) and the miscellaneous texts known as the "separate texts" (*beppon*). The Blue-Cover Texts derive from the collating work of the celebrated early Kamakura period (1192–1333) scholar-poet Fujiwara no Teika (or Sadaie, 1162–1241); the Kawachi Texts, from the work of Teika's contemporary Minamoto no Mitsuyuki (1163–1244) and Mitsuyuki's son Chikayuki.[51]

Modern institutionalization of the Teika texts arbitrarily solves the textual problem by erasing the questions surrounding the rise of variants, questions which even suggest the Fujiwara-Minamoto relations underlying much of the *Genji* narrating itself. The scholars consulted different available texts (the Kawachi collators seem to have consulted a greater variety with the aim of producing a standard family version. As readers have noted, the Teika texts tend toward a simplified phrasal structure and an altered *kana* orthography based on Teika's own system, whereas the Kawachi texts display a more "explanatory" style. Teika refashioned the text into *cleaner* (though not necessarily *clearer*) patterns; Mitsuyuki and Chikayuki opted for the insertion of commentary or preserved in the texts they consulted those passages that facilitated comprehension. The Kawachi texts, indeed, are criticized for their tendency toward lengthy, run-on phrases in the midst of which the reader can easily lose track of the narrative thread.

It is tempting to ignore modern practices and favor the Kawachi texts, especially since the apparently added on explanatory passages accord well, as we shall see, with the manner in which *monogatari* are believed to have been presented and received. Those who prefer the Teika texts argue that since Teika wrote more tentatively (i.e., more carefully) about his findings than did the Kawachi group, his conclusions must be more faithful to the "original" text and, accordingly, command more respect. Such a position, however, ignores the words of Teika himself, who did not believe it was possible to produce a completely verifiable version: "impossible to erase all doubts [as to the veracity of the text]."[52] The Kawachi collators arouse scholarly suspicion because they claim to have reconstructed a text about which all doubt has been eliminated and are criticized for having been too arbitrary.[53] It being impossible, of course, to assess the arbitrariness of any particular reading, the only measuring stick, lacking an Ur-text (original text), can be another text such as Teika's, which would be subject to similar criticisms.

The two scholarly traditions, in fact, seem to have been motivated by more urgent and private matters than the standards of objectivity assigned by modern readers. They wanted to establish "verified household texts" (*ie no shōhon*), a desire that problematizes the very relation between textual prestige and interpretive power. Suffice it here to note that although both texts attracted important groups of adherents and followers, the Teika texts eventually overwhelmed the Kawachi texts from about the mid-Muromachi period (1338–1573), largely because of the work of the great *Genji* scholar Sanjōnishi Sanetaka (1455–1537).[54]

For the *Ise* text, the version used today is another Teika exemplar, alleged to derive from manuscripts that the scholar himself copied for his granddaughter in the second year of Tempuku (1234). It begins with the "coming-of-age" section and includes a total of one hundred and twenty-five sections. Here too there exist other versions that seriously challenge the supremacy of the Teika texts, most notably the texts thought to have begun with a section (*dan* 69) telling of an Ise Virgin. A complete exemplar is no longer extant but it is mentioned in the colophons of other texts, and parts of it are appended to existing texts.[55] Sometimes referred to as the "Text of the Court-Appointed Hunter" (*Kari no tsukai-bon*), it is also known as *Koshikibu no naishi-bon* for the alleged copyist, Koshikibu no Naishi (daughter of Izumi Shikibu), of one of the variants. The latter receives mention by a monk-scholar of the Rokujō family, Kenshō (1130–1210), who many believe collated a version of the "Hunter text," which he values as highly as the Tempuku texts. This textual "other" is thought to have begun with *dan* 69 and ended with *dan* 11 of the Teika texts, to have contained at least twenty-one poems not in the Tempuku texts, and to have been organized quite differently from the latter.[56] The "final" poem in the Hunter text, moreover, speaks of an eternally repeatable encounter inscribed in the movement of the moon, a fitting end to a text that, as we shall see, refuses closure and replays instead a pattern of continual return.[57] In sum, the *Ise monogatari* reader faces a bewildering textual array consisting of three lines of Teika texts, four lines of "old texts" (*kohon*), three lines of "expanded texts," "Texts of the Lacquered Chamber" (*Nurigome-bon*, also known as "abridged texts," *ryaku-bon*), "texts written in Chinese characters" (*mana-bon*), and the miscellaneous "separate texts" (*beppon*). After thorough study, scholars now agree on two aspects of the *Ise* text: its initial versions were much shorter than the text we read today, and it expanded as a result of accretions by later author-compiler-arranger-editors.[58]

As the above demonstrates, textual problems alone would justify a reexamination of approaches to Heian texts. Aside from the question of the correctness of modern textual procedures, we must not forget what is all too apparent yet almost always brushed aside as marginal to Heian discourse: the extant Heian texts are constitutive of a contingency that arises as much out of the manner in which they were appropriated as out of any vagaries of historical circumstance (such as loss by fire and other calamities or errors by copyists). In other words, textual discrepancies are not necessarily incongruous with the spirit of participatory textual production, and we should take seriously the fact that the term *monogatari* does not denote final, self-identical editions. As the Senshi anecdote with which I begin the discussion of the *Genji* tale suggests, it was possible for copies in different calligraphic hands[59] to appear almost as soon as the initial writer or writers had completed a section of a tale, and the high artistic value that was placed on calligraphic skill meant that persons of all ranks and backgrounds routinely practiced "penmanship" by copying out poems and narratives following accepted stylistic models. During the course of such practice, or at its readings and recitations, a text could easily undergo alteration by any of the components that make up the reader-calligrapher-reciter-audience network.[60] When dealing with the products of such a culture, we must remember that the act of "reading" was a far cry from the passive and individual act it has become today; it was a communally oriented, integrative process that not only required linguistic and poeticohistorical competence but also summoned calligraphic, vocal, and even painterly talent and freely allowed a degree of rewriting, or re-creation.[61]

I

Tales of the Bamboo Cutter

[*Taketori monogatari*] was a work truly appropriate for commemorating the moment when the city [Heian] was divorcing itself from
agricultural villages, and seeking its own free space.
   Saigō Nobutsuna, "Taketori monogatari no
   bungakushiteki ichi"

This era [the Engi era, 901–922] must be called the age of the pivot-
word, and also the age of the rise of the associative-word.
   Onoe Saishō, "*Kokinshū* no shūji"

Individual languages, their roles and their actual historical meaning are fully disclosed only within the totality of an era's hetero-
glossia.
   Mikhail Bakhtin, "Discourse in the Novel"

1

Languages of Narrating
and Bamboo-Cutter Pretexts

For the ancient Japanese, writing could not have been the familiar process it must have seemed to the ancient Chinese or seems to us today when, despite certain obstacles (e.g., writer's block), putting pen to paper or transferring letters from keyboard to computer screen is as intuitive and self-evident as eating or sleeping. As Raymond Williams has noted, "In modern industrial societies writing has been naturalized. It is then easy to assume that the process itself is straightforward, once the basic skills have been mastered in childhood. There is then only the question of what to write *about*."[1]

In contrast to the Chinese mainland where a writing system mated to the phonological demands of a native, basically though not categorically monosyllabic language (i.e., one graph = one sound = referent-idea) developed over centuries, the Japanese, content without written language, found themselves confronting a civilization that began to impose itself not through military aggression but through the medium of written texts. Early attempts to adapt Chinese writing to the Japanese verbal ground must have presented seemingly insurmountable problems given the dissimilarity of the two languages. A writing system suited to the largely monosyllabic Chinese language would a priori be eminently unsuited to the agglutinative and inflecting, polysyllabic Japanese language. As contact between Japan and China (often via Korea and Korean immigrants) increased during the early centuries A.D., texts and other inscription-bearing objects (bronzes, mirrors, coins, and seals) began flowing into the islands. Scarcity of sources inhibits accurate reconstruction of the rise of scriptive activity, but judging from extant sources, Chinese writing seems to have entered Japan as early as the first century A.D.[2] It was not, however, until the fourth or fifth century that Japanese began to write using Chinese graphs and, for the most part, the Chinese language—for the most part.[3] The early specimens offer evidence that the Japanese at the very earliest stages were already disengaging phonetic from semantic values as they used Chinese graphs to transcribe native sounds, especially morphemes that constituted personal names and toponyms.[4] Sometimes referred to as "Japanized (*wa-ka*) Chinese style (*kambun*)," the early practice probably did not extend much beyond transcription of personal and place names. When the first full-blown text as we know it appeared in 712, soon after the capital was moved to Heijō (Nara) in 710 (the Nara period dates from 710–84), the Japanese had been experimenting with writing for several centuries.[5]

Chinese Writing and Japanese Discourse

Assuming its discursive space in diverse ways, the difficult-to-label *Kojiki* (Record of Ancient Matters) text immediately raises issues relevant to Japanese attitudes toward writing and the Chinese language. First of all, in contrast to the later *Nihon shoki* (Chronicles of Japan), *Kojiki* clearly purports to be a written transcription (selected and edited by Ō no Yasumaro at the command of Empress Gemmei) of an orally delivered (by Hieda no Are) discourse: "On the eighteenth day of the Ninth Month of the fourth year of Wadō a command was given to Yasumaro: 'You are to select, record, and present to the throne the old materials recited by Heida no Are'" (p. 23).[6] Are was a young man renowned for his prodigious memory and vocal prowess:[7] "One look and he could recite it aloud; one hearing and it was imprinted in his mind" (p. 22). He had earlier been commanded by Emperor Temmu to recite ("read aloud") selected old texts that recorded imperial genealogies and legendary and historical incidents so that a written transcription could be made for posterity. Empress Gemmei revived the project when it was halted with the emperor's death. Here we see an inextricable connection between writing and orality: on the one hand, the written does not, indeed cannot, come into existence without the oral—the oral authorizes the written; on the other hand, the written becomes a "permanent" document that proves the legitimacy of that which authorized it.

A point of controversy is the meaning of "read aloud" (*yominaraFu*). Some interpret it as signifying that Are somehow clarified the "meaning" of the texts as he recited them aloud. Others argue that, given his performative talents and the common practice of reciting Buddhist sutras, the phrase really meant that Are was commanded to recite the texts *in a particular manner*, using certain patterns of intonation, and that it was a particular oral rhythm (there must have existed other, competing ones) that Emperor Temmu wanted to valorize.[8] To fix the previous discourses into a specific, orally deliverable mode was tantamount to seizing the essence of the texts. The one who performed the act or had it performed became the legitimate possessor and king of all discourses, that is to say, through a topographic metonymy, king of the country.[9] Cognition of the world, channeled through phonic modulations, might have stopped well short of semantic closure, but political power, as it often does, effected another closure. For the Japanese, as we shall see, written discourse does not easily exist separately as a self-contained entity, but is always positioned vis-à-vis a multitude of "intertexts," whether linguistic stimulus (often, though not necessarily, oral), historical "model," genealogical imperative, narrator, and/or reader-listener. If we agree with the above argument that the text was meant to be intoned, we can conclude that for *Kojiki*, the written—at the same time that it accomplished the all-important goal of preserving a specific mode deemed proper to earlier discourses—was ultimately dependent on the oral and that the written text existed only in a contingent state that had to be vocally realized each time.[10]

How did Yasumaro transcribe Are's recitation? Although written with Chinese characters, the *Kojiki* style, whether in phonological or syntactical terms, is not Chinese, which the *Nihon shoki* more closely approximates. By the time of *Kojiki*, proper names and toponyms are not the only items resistant to direct rendering by the Chinese written language; longer discursive stretches, commentary and reading notes, and song-poems are also transcribed in the "Japanized" style mentioned above.[11] Generally called *man'yōgana*,[12] the selected graphs were part of a systematic process of using Chinese characters for phonological value through which the Japanese accommodated Chinese pictoideographs to the specifications of their own language. Take, for example, the opening line of *Kojiki*:

天地初發之時　高天原成神名　天之御中主神　（訓高下天云阿麻）

[When heaven and earth first appeared, the name of the god who went out on the High Plain of Heaven is Ame no Minakanushi.][13]

After the line a gloss (called *kunchū* and found throughout the text) is inserted, instructing the reader to "pronounce the graph *ten* [heaven], which comes after the graph *kō* [high], as *ama*; learn from this as you read on" (p. 26). The sounds /a/ and /ma/ are represented by the two graphs 阿 and 麻

Especially resistant to rendering with Chinese graphs, which tend to specify "meaning," were song-poems, since the incantatory qualities in the actual sounds needed to be preserved.[14] Here is one poem (of 112 in *Kojiki*) considered the ancestor of the thirty-one-syllable *tanka* form:[15]

夜久毛多都　伊豆毛夜幣賀岐　都麻碁微字爾

夜幣賀岐都久流　曾能夜幣賀岐袁

yakumo tatu, idumo yaFegaki, tumagomi ni, yaFegaki tukuru, sono yaFegaki wo (*NKBT*, 89)
[the eight-layered clouds rise, in Izumo, land of the eight-layered clouds, to match the layers of my fence, built to confine my newly beloved; what a fine eight-layered fence]

Each graph, whose meaning is largely irrelevant, represents a single syllable.

As the Japanese continued to experiment with writing, they generated a variety of other phonemic-semantic-graphic combinations. Morphemes such as *tu, mi, ni, ru,* and *wo* in the above song-poem, what today are called "particles" (*joshi*) and verbal suffixes (*jodōshi*), were not represented when the Japanese wrote in a Chinese style. When the Japanese occasionally paid attention to the semantic values of the graphs, the result reads like a "shorthand" notation for transliterating into a Japanese syntactic form a Chinese-like word order. *Man'yōshū* 2845 is an example:

忘哉　語　意遣　猶戀

Only vaguely intelligible to a Chinese reader, the poem requires the following Japanese phonetic realization:

wasuru ya to, monogatari site, kokoro yari, sugusedo sugizu, naFo koFinikeri
[to forget about you, I talk about various things and try to clear my thoughts of you; but, try as I might, I find I end up longing for you even more]

The single graph 語 is given the expanded Japanese rendering *monogatari site*, while the segment 雖過不過 displays the up-and-down word order necessary when reading *kambun* in Japanese.[16]

The above examples represent two ways the Japanese adapted Chinese: the first is a type of phonetic use of Chinese graphs (*man'yōgana*) called *ongana,* where the graph is divorced from its meaning (i.e., *kana* used for their Sino-Japanese sound values); the second is a way of reading the graphs using "orthodox Japanese sound values," *seikun,* where both the Japanese pronunciation and the meaning of the graph correspond to its original semantic value. The Japanese also employed another type of *man'yōgana* known as "native Japanese sound kana" (i.e., graphs used for Japanese sound values irrespective of meaning—*kungana*),[17] with which they experimented at times in radical fashion. Possible combinations include two or three characters pronounced as one syllable or one character pronounced as two or three syllables.

Already evident in the *Kojiki* text and other documents, the use of *kungana* reaches radical proportions in the *Man'yō* collection. When, for example, the syllables *ka* and *mo* (an often-used two-syllable particle combination signifying exclamation) needed to be represented, rather than use two *ongana,* a graph pronounced *kamo* in Japanese was used irrespective of its meaning. A graph frequently so used is one that means "goose." A spectacular example of *kungana* and other *kana* varieties is *Man'yōshū* 2991:

垂乳根之　母我養蚕乃　眉隠　馬聲蜂音石花蜘蟵荒鹿　異母二不相而

> taratine no, FaFa ga kaFu ko no, mayogomori,
> ibuseku mo aru ka, imo ni aFazusite
> [breasts drooping, mother raises silkworms; they spin themselves into confinement, and I, my heart confined, am wrapped in gloom, unable to meet my beloved]

The written version, which contains the three basic ways of using Chinese graphs noted above, can be disassembled into the following components: *seikun* (*tara*) + two *kungana* (*ti* and *ne*) + *ongana* (*no*—the initial segment, *taratine no,* forming a "pillow word" for "mother") + three *seikun* (*FaFa, ka*[*Fu*], and *ko*) + *ongana* (*no*) + *seikun* (*mayo,* mod. *mayu*—here incorporating further graphic play, since the character, which means "eyebrow," was often associated in China with cocoons) + *kungana* (*i*—represented by two characters meaning "horse voice") + *kungana* (*bu*—also with two characters meaning "bee sound"; the pronunciations seem to be onomatopoeic versions of a horse's neighing and a bee's buzzing, thus adding an aural quality to the poet's psychic state) + another *kungana* (*se*, represented with two graphs meaning "rock flower") + *seikun* (*kumo*—like *kamo* above, but here given two graphs meaning "spider") + *kungana* (*a[ru]*—"rough or wild") + two *ongana* (*imo*—written with two characters that mean "different mother," the written version adding another dimension to the poem, since it suggests that the "beloved" in question may be a half-sister or that an actual confinement [by a mother, though not the poet's real mother] has prevented the poet from seeing the woman) + *ongana* (*ni*) + three *seikun* in *kambun* word order (*aFazusite*).

Such extreme instances of linguistic play, which would not appear again,[18] demonstrate that the Japanese, far from despairing over the monumental task of transcribing their language using graphs suited to the mono- (or at times a pleonastic bi-)syllabic Chinese or viewing transliteration simply as a mechanical problem, actually relished the potential in the phonemic-semantic-graphic combinations for extravagant or obtuse modes of expression. In other words, they showed a strong predilection for linguistic experimentation and play—an attitude closely tied to a belief in the spiritual efficacy of words (*kotodama*)—that continued into the Heian period, when simpler forms became available for transcribing the native language. It should be clear from the above that by the late eighth century the Japanese did not employ Chinese writing solely to transcribe their native (oral) language but took full advantage of the linguistic differences and saw in the mainland writing system a distinct and powerful aspect of discourse that took on a life of its own, so to speak, and often resisted easy reclamation by native speakers unfamiliar with the rules of the game. Scriptive anarchy was prevented, of course, since without vocal and syntactic reclamation, the written text was apt to be quite meaningless (the vocal aspect, often in ritualized settings, was emphasized because of the valorization of *kotodama*).[19]

Belief in the magical power of poetry might help explain why a particular poem appears in different ("prose") contexts.[20] We shall see that in most premodern Japanese texts poetic forms coexist discursively with "prose." Prose-poem "hybrids" are not uncommon in the West but discursive or generic boundaries tend to be preserved, and the phenomenon occurs with much less frequency.[21] I wish to emphasize not only that song-poems appear together with "prose" but also that a particular poem or variation often appears in different "prose" contexts. An early example of what I mean occurs in *Kojiki* (*NKBT*, 315):

> On another occasion (*mata arutoki*), the emperor [Yūryaku] climbed Mt. Kazuraki; here (*koko ni*) a great wild boar appeared; when the emperor immediately took an arrow with a whistling tip and shot at the boar, that (*sono*) animal became angry, and charged straight at its enemy [or, alternatively: let out a roar]—read the three characters U-TA-KI for their sound values—thereupon (*kare*) the emperor, fearing that (*sono*) boar's charge, climbed up a *hari* tree; here (*koko ni*) he recited a poem [sang]: Stately ruler of the land, I, an illustrious sovereign, was out hunting; frightened by the charge of a wild boar, a wounded boar, I climbed up into the branches of a *hari* tree, high upon a hill. And thus he sang.
> [yasumisisi/waga oFokimi no/asobasisi/sisi no yamisisi no/utaki kasi-komi/waga nigenoborisi/ariwono/Fari no ki no eda]

The *Nihon shoki* text, couched in its usual *kambun* style, gives a different version of the incident. While the emperor is out hunting, a strange bird signals a warning to the participants. At that moment an angry boar appears, and as the other hunters climb trees in fright, the emperor orders an attendant (*toneri*) to shoot the animal. The attendant also climbs a tree and loses his senses. Meanwhile, as the boar charges at him, the emperor takes his bow, stabs it, and then raises a leg and stomps it to death. The emperor orders an end to the hunt, and as he is about to kill his cowardly attendant, the latter composes the above song-poem and recites it as he faces his death. The empress is deeply moved, and in lofty language persuades the emperor not to kill the attendant. On his way back to the palace, the emperor happily states, "Everyone else hunts birds and beasts; I return home having obtained marvelous words."[22] The *Nihon shoki* version transforms a cowardly (therefore eminently human) *Kojiki* emperor into a wise and benevolent Confucian sage who listens to those around him and favors the acquisition of verbal lessons over wild game. Its *kambun* rhetoric incorporates an impressive array of citations from Chinese texts.[23] Modern scholars rescue the emperor in the former version from a comical reading by claiming that rather than making fun of the emperor, the passage actually praises the *hari* tree for its fortuitous presence.[24]

The examples show the freedom with which a storyteller or chronicler adapted the same song-poem to different discursive contexts. Since emperors and persons of comparable status refer to themselves with honorifics, the poem allows a first-person perspective as in *Kojiki* ("Stately ruler of the land, I, an illustrious sovereign"). In the *Nihon shoki* version the poem accommodates the shift in speaking subject from emperor to attendant. After first referring to the emperor ("Stately ruler of the land, our illustrious sovereign"), the attendant refers to himself for the rest of the poem. After the third-person references to the emperor, in other words, a shift to an "I" perspective takes place, "I" thereby becoming the site at which a number of voices converge to create a verbal event similar to what we find in later poetry. The song-poem was no doubt composed by yet another person, the writer-reciter of *Kojiki* or an earlier source text. The possibility for recycling poems into different contexts will be fully utilized in subsequent poeticonarrative discourse, and the interchangeability of speaking subject (demonstrating again the problems with using strict I/he categories) becomes one sense in which poetic discourse becomes available to appropriation by fictive personae.

The two texts also differ in terms of narrating perspective. The *Nihon shoki* text identifies a definite point in time: Spring of the Second Month of the fifth year (of Emperor Yūryaku), while the *Kojiki* text, employing a narrating pattern that will often appear in *hiragana* discourse, first mentions an unspecified moment. "Again, on another occasion" (*NKBT* 1, 315). Then, in contrast to the *Nihon shoki* narrator, who relates the events as a successive story line with a minimum amount of narrative "interference," the *Kojiki* narrator continually adds deictic phrases to mark moments in the ongoing flow. The often-used word "here" (*koko ni*)[25] appears just twice in the above citation, but other such words are found throughout the brief passage: "thereupon" (*kare*), "that" (*sono*), "immediately following that" (*sunaFati*), and so forth. Called deictics, they are words that are meaningless when divorced from an external context. They do not themselves possess any absolute or stable reference but refer rather to "the fact that language has taken place and that it is something that takes place."[26] Positionality, rather than anything in the "content" of the words themselves, determines meaning. As Jeffrey Kittay and Wlad Godzich put it,

> From the Greek definition "pointing" or "indicating," deixis usually means the function of certain grammatical and lexical features that relate utterances to the spatiotemporal coordinates of the act of utterance. For example, "I," "here," "now," and "you," "there," "then," as well as verb tenses, mean only the "who" and "where" and

"when" of the utterance, which is often given nonverbally . . . their
meaning is determinable only by means of the instance of discourse in
which they occur. . . . Deixis refers to that for which the discourse
has no name but on which it depends; deictic expressions indicate only
what is outside the discourse, but their reference draws one right back
to the discourse.[27]

In the *Kojiki* passage, the deictics suggest traces of an oral narrator
who maintains control over the narration by continually reminding
the listener-reader of his or her extratextual perspective as narrator.[28]

Modal Narrative Suffixes *Keri* and *Ki*

Not previously a common component of "prose" texts, *keri* signals a
new discursive threshold right from the beginning of the *Taketori* text:
ima Fa mukasi taketori no okina to iFu mono ari*keri* (Now it is the past;
there is an old bamboo cutter).[29] In earlier texts *keri* occurred primarily
in song-poems to signify surprise at a previously unnoticed situation
and was written with various *ongana* or, as in *Man'yōshū*, at times in
seikun. It originally marked poetic moments that, as native language
spoken or sung, were especially resistant to "translations" or "trans-
literations" into Chinese. The *Taketori* text represents an early (masculine, it is assumed) attempt to employ *hiragana* writing, the advent
of which means that not only poetry but prose too, no longer limited
by Chinese discourse, could more closely approximate the native
spoken language. It follows then that *keri* signaled something unnecessary or unavailable in texts written in Chinese, at the same time that
it continually re-marked that difference. In other words, a morpheme
whose function had been delimited in *kambun* texts begins to play a
major role in Heian poetic and other kinds of discourse.[30] The use of
keri is less prominent in some *kana* texts than in others, but the
alternative is not discourse predominantly marked by *ki* but rather
discourse "unmarked" by either suffix; namely, the "tenseless"
discourse found in Chinese and Chinese-inspired texts produced in
Japan. In fact, the suffix *ki*, used when reconstituting Chinese into
Japanese, continues to appear in texts written in *kana*, but it becomes
relativized or "framed" by *keri* discourse.[31] The *Taketori* text is a prime
example of the resulting textual "plies," or modal registers.

As Japanese *hiragana* writers, in other words, flexed their discursive muscles and began to infiltrate a territory—prose discourse—

that had been dominated earlier by *kambun* or *hentai kambun* discourse, they did not institute a totally new grammar or jettison completely what they had learned from Chinese, but adopted an apparently "metadiscursive" perspective, a self-commentating, self-authorizing mode employing the native forms previously used to reconstitute *kambun* and *hentai kambun* texts. They thus continued to inscribe traces of the oral, both as a result of a heritage in older poetic discourses, as it had underwritten native readings of Chinese texts, and also as implied in the very syllabic form that was the new *kana* writing. *Keri* was one way of marking that metadiscursive mode. We must remember that there was never simply a question of Chinese "form" and Japanese "meaning" or "sentiment," since questions of form always encroached upon, resisted, and even obstructed the process of meaning production. The Japanese always preserved and marked, as a necessary part of the adaptation of Chinese writing to their own language, a gap between the written text and its "actuation," i.e., the seemingly tortuous method of transforming Chinese phrases into Japanese syntax with Japanese meaning and significance (the *Man'yō* examples). The *Taketori* text not only suggests a different signifying practice, it constructs in the process a stance (or stances) toward Chinese discourse and toward "authority" as well. In a text like *Genji* we see not only a stance toward Chinese discourse, but narrating networks that get continually reconfigured in spatiotemporal and perspectival terms. Modern Western studies of narratology cannot help but benefit from an examination of one of the most complex and interesting instances of the possibilities of narration.

In pre-Heian texts *ki* appears primarily in "descriptive" prose passages (*ji no bun*),[32] whereas *keri* seems generally limited to poetic discourse. As mentioned above, *keri* conveys "surprise" or "exclamation" at a new perceptival or psychological discovery or realization. Take, for example, a song-poem that appears in both *Kojiki* (712) and *Nihon shoki* (720).[33] The *Kojiki* version:

> akadama Fa/wo saFe Fikaredo/siratama no/kimi Fa
> yosoFisi/taFutoku arikeri[34]
> [the red jewel shines even to its cord; but you, who are the white
> jewel, your visage is magnificent!]

The *Nihon shoki* variation also ends with *keri*,[35] which is clearly written in *ongana* in both texts. The primary grammatical mode in these early *kambun* texts was a kind of "tenseless" discourse, to which particles and suffixes were added when they were reconstituted into Japanese. Those supplementary elements include morphemes indicating honorific status as well as the varieties of modal-aspectual markers mentioned in the Introduction. A tenseless discourse (Chinese) is thus modalized (into Japanese).[36]

Instances of *keri* in *Man'yōshū* also occur in poetic discourse. *Man'yōshū* 308, for example, already shows complications:

> tokiwa naru/iFaya Fa ima mo/ari*keredo*/sumi*keru* Fito
> so/tunenakari*keru*
> [Tokiwa: name of things everlasting; the stone hut still exists today; but those who once lived there, were not meant to stay forever]

The first *keri* might indicate that the poet is surprised to discover that the hut still exists (the emphatic particle *mo* further strengthening that awareness), and the final *keri* might be interpreted as renewed awareness of the transience of life. The second *keri*, however, which does not readily allow such an interpretation, might better be read in its "prose" signification: as "hearsay" (those who are said to have lived there).[37] Let us take one final example, *Man'yōshū* 1149, where *keri* occurs together with *ki*:

> sumiyosi ni/yuku toFu miti ni/kinoFu mi*si*/koFi
> wasuregaFi/koto ni si ari*keri*
> [on the road to the land of easy living, Sumiyoshi, I saw yesterday a love-forgetting-shell; its name (I realize now) was only empty words]

The example shows that *ki* (in its attributive form *si*) appears in poetic discourse. The poem further shows that *ki* seems to mark a past moment (in Chinese, "yesterday" would have been sufficient to indicate the "past"), while *keri* suggests that the poet has now realized the inefficacy of the shell.

To read *ki* only as a past tense marker, however, ignores its other functions. Why, for example, is its usage circumscribed in *Nihon shoki* but habitual in *Kojiki*? As we shall see in *Man'yōshū*, *ki* also occurs in nonpoetic passages.[38] When we remember that oral recounting is a common denominator of both *Kojiki* and *Man'yōshū* and that the suffix *ki* was also used to reconstitute such texts as *Nihon ryōiki* and *Fudoki*, which likewise contain oral aspects, it becomes possible that *ki* was added to texts written in Chinese to indicate a "narrated," storytelling situation or that the stories were originally orally transmitted. Once the actual storyteller or reciter is no longer present, the written text compensates by marking a perspective that would have been adopted by the external storyteller. With the advent of texts written predominantly in *kana,* which more closely approximates the native spoken language, a shift seems to have occurred where *keri* comes to be used extensively in prose discourse, becoming the signifier of yet another level of narration external to or apart from (or "enveloping") *ki* narration: the telling of a telling. The usual argument for distinguishing the two suffixes in terms of the two basic categories of "experience" and "hearsay" must therefore be rethought in the light of such signifying practices.

We have seen that in pre-Heian texts *keri* usually indicated (in poetic discourse) a speaker's realization of a situation previously forgotten or unnoticed. Important was the emphasis on the speaker's deictically determined perspective, which I call the narrating perspective. The standard views of the function of *keri* in nonpoetic Heian passages include (1) past tense, (2) "recollection" (*kaisō*), and (3) "hearsay recollection" (*dembun kaisō*), i.e., recollection of something heard. The suffix *ki,* in contrast to the third possibility for *keri,* signifies a kind of "direct recollection" (*mokuto kaisō*), i.e., recollection of something personally experienced or witnessed; in other words, *keri* signifies an orally transmitted tale, whereas *ki* marks the narrator's personal experience. That contrast might explain *keri's* pervasive appearance in *Taketori,* in "tales of poems" (*uta monogatari*), and in other texts bearing the term *monogatari,* but it does not explain its restricted usage in *Ochikubo,* for example, or its appearance in the famous *kana* diaries and in the *Kokinshū* "Kana Preface," or (given its function of "indirect recording") its relatively rare occurrence in *Makura no sōshi* (*The Pillow Book*). Let us examine a few characterizations of the suffix.

Harada Yoshioki, a scholar attentive to temporal matters, has claimed that "*keri* functions to bring the past into the present moment rather than to take the present back to the past."[39] Following Harada, Chiyuki Kumakura states: "The function of *keri* is to indicate that 'the past' . . . 'presently exists.' . . . If we assume that *ki* is the marker of the past, the only logical consequence is that, when *keri* is used, the past is conceived of in some manner as existing at the present moment."[40] In other words, what once existed (*ari*) has come to (*ki,* from *kuru,* "come") exist again or, rather, has been re-presented in an explanatory fashion (e.g., "the fact is that such and such is the case [or happened]"), both readers treating *keri* as a storytelling marker. A phrase formulaic to *Ise monogatari,* for example, signifies discourse that re-presents the fact of a man's existence: *mukasi wotoko arikeri* (Long ago there was a man, as we can reaffirm [restate, reac-knowledge] from hearsay information now).

In the passages examined earlier, however, the use of the suffixes was closely connected to the fact that there were at least two narrating perspectives in question. Harada's weakness lies in his problematic handling of such notions as "past," "present," and "existence." How does language take the present back to the past or bring any past to the present and make it exist there? In Kumakura's case, it is not clear whether he is referring to "tense," as when he speaks of the enduring significance of the *ki* (or "past tense" in his view) component in *keri,* or to "aspect," as in the following: "Primarily, *keri* is an aspect marker just like *ri* and *tari.*"[41] Aspect is usually discussed by linguists in terms of imperfection, perfection, stativity, progressivity, duration, completion, habituality, iteration, momentariness, inception, and termination.[42] Although nouns occasionally take on aspectual fea-tures, verbals (in Japanese, adjectivals as well) are the primary focus, not any reified "past" or "present." If we declare that some "past presently exists," we still must specify whether it is a past event, process, or state we are talking about and, more important, clarify how what seems to be an "explanatory attitude" can be thought of in terms of aspect at all. It is clear that the position or attitude of the speaker toward what he or she is narrating needs to be considered more closely.

Viewing the problem from a different angle, the prominent lin-guist Ōno Susumu has argued that *keri* should be seen in internal-external or inside-outside terms, a situation underlying Japanese thinking even today. In other words, Ōno interprets the *ki* compo-nent of the *ki* + *ari* combination from which *keri* is thought to derive[43] as pointing to a situation in which something that had been external (i.e., not directly verifiable: hearsay or past incident, for example; or, forgotten or external to perception, something unnoticed) to the speaker or to the speaker's in-group has now "come" or been brought "inside" (i.e., reentered his or her sphere or purview of knowledge, perception, or mode of discourse) to be (re-) affirmed, or (re-) ac-knowledged.[44] Ōno's description incorporates the "poetic" function discussed above. The morpheme *ki,* for Ōno, marks discourse that a speaker can affirm with conviction to have been the case, based on some sort of "inside," "direct," or "factual" knowledge.[45]

Ōno's discussion resonates with Takeoka Masao's famous contention that *ki* refers to discourse that lies within the speaker's own world and *keri* to discourse that lies outside the speaker's world, with the difference that Ōno's view brings the "other world," via *keri*, into the speaker's sphere, whereas the location of the speaker for Takeoka would seem always to be an external one. Takeoka's now classic discussion touched off a series of debates as to the significance of *keri*, and many scholars today continue to subscribe to his basic resolution of the issue.[46] To add a further twist to the problem, however, a scholar of *kambun* has argued that *keri* indicates an attitude that displaces events occurring in another world to the present situation (*gemba*), which would accord with my notion of the present "narrating situation."[47]

Neither Ōno's nor Takeoka's solution, convincing for the most part, is completely satisfactory when we consider the complex networks that constitute occasions of narrating. To my mind, *keri* and *ki* are "narrative" or "recitative" markers that also suggest an in-group situation, whereas Ōno's and Takeoka's views do not differentiate among enunciative positions, i.e., narrating perspectives. The situation becomes clearer when we turn to a category of language that most grammarians of the Japanese language and scholars of Japanese literature have neglected, a category under which such attitudes as "must," "will," "should," "can," and "wish" traditionally have been subsumed: modality. Linguists recently have broadened the category of modality to include such notions as "hearsay" and "factuality." A discussion by John Lyons of modality and its relation to tense offers a quotation from St. Augustine that approximates the function of *keri*: "Augustine reconciles these two views [on the existence or nonexistence of past and future] by saying that the past and the future exist only insofar as they are present in the mind: that there 'is a present of past things' in memory, and a 'present of present things' in direct perception, and 'a present of future things' in expectation."[48] Commenting on the first (memory), Lyons goes on to explain:

> What Augustine calls the "present of past things" can be described, in terms that linguists have often used in their discussions of tense, as a past embedded in a present. The semantic plausibility of this interpretation of tense is revealed in such utterances as the following:
> (3) It is a fact (in w_i) that it was raining (in w_j)
> (4) It is a fact (in w_i) that it will be raining (in w_j)
> These sentences may not be exactly equivalent to "It was raining" and

"it will be raining," but they do hold constant the present and the past or future point of reference; and they help us to see what is meant by "a present of past things" and "a present of future things."

Number (3) above is a "modalized" version of the utterance "It was raining" and means "I say here and now (at t_o)—[time zero, i.e., present of narration] it was the case (at $t_i \langle t_o$) that it be raining," where 'it be raining' is a tenseless proposition which the speaker asserts as being true in w_i—i.e. in the actual world as it was at $t_i \langle t_o$ t_i being a point or period of time preceding t_o . . .)" (p. 811). Kumakura's translation of *keri* coincides with Lyons's discussion: "*Keri* does not mean 'I heard that'; it means rather 'the situation is that.'"[49] The former has hit upon part of the significance of *keri*, except that we are in the realm of "modality," not in the realm of "aspect."

Whereas for Augustine a speaker's attitude toward the "past" was closely related to "tense," for the Heian Japanese the attitude involved distinguishable communal modes or registers that are not simply congruous with temporal factors. In narrating transcribed in *hiragana*, at least three narrating perspectives emerge: one that seems a kind of "storytelling" or "communal" perspective ("the fact/ situation we can reaffirm is that"); another that assumes a more direct, "personal" mood, one that does not claim to separate itself from what it relates, although it points to itself as anchored in a narrating moment in contrast to Chinese discourse; and a third perspective (what I call "tenseless" discourse), conspicious from the earliest reconstitutions of Chinese texts into Japanese. Only the first two perspectives produce the cognitive distinctions that some scholars have claimed: *keri* marks indirectness of knowledge or asks for (communal) reaffirmation; *ki* marks epistemological certainty (of a moment prior to the narrating moment).[50]

Finally, usual discussions of *keri* also overlook one other aspect that can help us further connect grammatical considerations to conditions of utterance: the question of discursive legitimation. For writers of *hiragana* the implicit external authority, the imperial (or other hegemonic) sanction accorded *kambun* discourse (with no need to mark a source of information), would no longer have been operative. Non-Chinese writing and storytelling, which meant in most cases discourse of a more "private" or communal nature (such as legends and folktales), would need to disavow fabrication by the teller and appeal to a definite source.[51] In poetic discourse that source was the very fact of utterance, whereas in "prosaic" narrating it was an unspecified text, parts of which were possessed by the writer's "group" as common lore, a kind of narrative or topological deixis. *Keri*, then, represents a legitimizing element of affirmation for *hiragana* discourse through which the discourse grounds itself.

Taketori Pretexts

Although it seems at first glance a simple "fairy tale," *Taketori monogatari* in fact names a discourse that relates in complex ways its extractable "story"—about a tiny creature who turns into a beautiful princess, rebuffs five "eminent" suitors, refuses even the emperor's commands, and finally ascends to the moon. To read the text is also to track the manner in which it resists being tied unproblematically to similar tales surviving throughout Asia and the South Pacific.[52] Rather than unearth particular folkloric or mythic "origins," the task is to situate the *Taketori* text among those tales and among other Heian texts and to ask what it added to Heian discursive practices in terms of new attitudes toward writing and storytelling. That it did signal something new is apparent from the reference in the "E-awase" (A Picture Contest, 17) chapter of *Genji* to the "ancestor (parent) that stands at the beginning of the rise of *monogatari*."[53] Why, we might ask, would an astute reader (as well as writer) like the *Genji* author(s) accord a place of origin to this seemingly modest "fairy tale"? The *Genji* reference suggests that the *Taketori* text shows one manner in which the narrating potential of the native language is realized. For comparative purposes, let us first broaden our parameters and examine some of the important discursive practices related to the *Taketori* text.

A *Man'yōshū* Bamboo Cutter

An early version of the bamboo-cutter story appears in *Man'yōshū*. It stands not as autonomous tale but as pretext for a *chōka* and two *hanka* by an old man and nine *tanka* by nine immortals who appear in the passage (book 16, poems 3791–3802). The brief "tale" goes as follows:

> Long ago there was an old man; he is known as the old bamboo cutter. This old man, when he climbed a hill toward the end of the spring months and looked far out, his gaze fell upon nine women preparing

some sort of hot broth. Their lustrous beauty is beyond compare; their flowery figures know no equal. At this point, the women call to the old man in jest, saying, "Come here old geezer; we need you to blow on our fire." The old man answers, "Okay, okay," and slowly turns toward them, haltingly draws near to where they are, and seats himself cross-legged on a straw mat. Soon the women all are grinning as they poke each other and say, "Who summoned this old man?" The old man then says, "It is completely by chance that I am in the unexpected presence of immortal sylphs; try as I might, I am flustered and unable to restrain myself. I ask that you allow me to offer you a poem as recompense for the transgression I committed of approaching you so familiarly." Now, [here is] the poem he composed along with [two] *tanka*.[54]

The *Man'yōshū* version differs markedly from the two *Hagoromo* tales discussed below and is also quite remote from the *Taketori* text. The focus is clearly the poems, and their value for the old man as repayment for a transgression (his long poem is a cornucopia of words associated with clothing, presumably to entertain and impress the women). Narrating interest lies in the conversational exchanges, which serve as a pretext for the poems. In other words, "story" is pretext for a tale of the production of poetry, a topos we will see later in "poem-tales" (*uta monogatari*). The mocking attitude of the women toward the man and the idea that humans should not mingle familiarly with immortals find echoes in the *Taketori* text.

The Shrine of Nagu

One typical *Hagoromo* version in the *Fudoki* collection concerns a group of celestial maidens who descend to earth in the guise of cranes.[55] A man spies on the group. Realizing they are deities, he is overcome with desire and sends his dog to steal one of the robes, which he then hides. The man marries the robeless maiden who, after bearing him four children (two boys and two girls, all given names), eventually finds her robe and flies back to the heavens. The story ends with two four-character Chinese phrases that resemble "comments" in later Heian *monogatari*: "Alone, he watches over an empty bed; his intoning of song-poems is without end."[56] Apart from the last line and the man's reaction to the women, the thoughts and feelings of the characters are not mentioned. The narrative perspective is stable and unproblematic, more forward-moving commentary than storytelling. There is no dialogue to represent different voices, and we are given no clues that might, for example, explain why the maiden left her earthly husband and children.

Another *Hagoromo* version, "Shrine of Nagu," concerns a heavenly maiden who descends to earth with seven companions to bathe at a spring (called Manawi, in the village of Hiji). An old man steals the maiden's robe (of feathers), thus preventing her from flying away. Forced by the man and his wife to become their child, she lives with them for over ten years, brewing a magical rice wine (*sake*) that cures physical ailments. After gaining great wealth from the wine, the couple suddenly and cruelly throw the woman out of their house. Homeless and without friends or relatives, the woman wanders aimlessly before finally ending up in the hamlet of Nagu, where she becomes the local deity, Toyoukanome no mikoto.[57] The version presents a different discourse where it becomes difficult to identify a "main" story. This brief early example of narrating comprises an amalgam of procedures found in later narratives: (1) the presentation of a well-known story (here the *Hagoromo* legend) that does not stand alone but functions as a pretext for the second part of the narrative; (2) a story of the origin of various toponyms and of a local goddess; and (3) an instance of poetic discourse that divides the two sections.

In the beginning we get a detailed identification of the geographical location of the spring—"the district of Taniha in Taniha no michi no shiri Province; at the northwestern corner from the district office lies the village of Hiji; there is a spring at the top of Hiji Mountain in this village; the spring there is called Manawi Spring; it has long since become a marsh" (p. 466). The text also cites a definite source—"As it states in the *fudoki* of the Taniwa no michi no shiri Province . . ." (p. 466)—that could be either oral or written. Names are then given to the old couple, Wanasa no okina and Wanasa no omina, which perhaps derive from their region of origin.[58] The toponyms mentioned earlier also play a prominent role, here connected to instances of "originary" naming that emerge as the woman wanders from village to village after being banished by the couple. The woman's actions and speech acts become the putative "origins" of the names of the places through which she passes: for example, "again, she reached the hamlet of Nakiki in the village of Taniha and, leaning against the *naki* (tree name and "weeping") tree, wept; thus it is called Nakiki (Weeping Tree) Hamlet" (p. 468). In the early texts it is common for acts of narrative figures—usually deities or emperors who rest at certain places along their migratory paths—to produce the origins of place names, such acts thereby providing divine legitimation for the locale, which can be appropriated through its now specific toponym by those in power.[59]

The *Fudoki* ending adumbrates moments in *Taketori*. After the naming of Naki Hamlet, the following appears:

> Again, she reaches the hamlet of Nagu in the village of Funaki in the district of Takano and immediately announces to the people of the hamlet: "In this place my heart has at last found comfort" [in old legends *taFerakeki*, "feel comforted and at peace," is referred to as *nagusi*]; thus, the woman remains permanently in this hamlet. She is none other than Toyoukanome no mikoto, who dwells at Nagu Shrine in the district of Takano. (p. 468)

A naming thus becomes one way to end a narrative (the death of a person whose life structures the "biographical" sections of official histories [written in Chinese] and most other *monogatari* is another).

Also germane to our discussion is the instance of poetic discourse that divides the two sections:

> plain of heaven   I turn my eyes upward
>   but the haze hangs heavy
> I have lost my way home   I have no place to go
> [ama no Fara/Furisakemireba/kasumi tati/iFezi
> madoFite/yukuFe sirazu mo] (p. 468)

Believed to have been taken from another source, the song-poem the maiden recites shows again the "recycling" process seen above in the *Kojiki* and *Nihon shoki* texts. In *Taketori* we will see how the "fictional" aspect of poems functions in the very instances of naming.

Also noteworthy is the conversational exchange included in some texts (possibly a later addition) between the maiden and the old man. The exchange amplifies attitudes after the latter asks the former to become their child:

> The maiden replied, "I alone have remained in the human world; how could I possibly not obey your wishes? Please allow me to wear my robe." The old man said, "Heavenly maiden, you are planning to deceive me, aren't you?" The maiden then replied, "The hearts of heavenly beings (*ameFito*) are by nature truthful. What reason have you to harbor such doubts and forbid me my robe?" The old man countered, "To have many doubts and no honesty is commonplace in this

human world. Therefore, I was merely following those sentiments when I refused your request." In the end he allowed her [to wear her robe]. (p. 467)

In contrast to tales where the creature returns to the heavens (the man's wariness represents general lore regarding such tales), this maiden remains true to her word and becomes the old couple's daughter only to suffer for her honesty. As it represents conflicting attitudes through dialogue, the narrating is no longer simply "external" to the discourse but begins to stand in complicated relations to it as the differentiation between the voices of the speakers and the voice of the narrator produces contradictory perspectives. The distinction between honesty (of otherworldly beings) and doubt and deception (usual among humans) will form an important subtext of the *Taketori* narrative as well.

The text is written in *kambun* (with the poem in *ongana*), which means that it is basically tenseless, but when it is reconstituted into Japanese syntax, certain forms similar to what we find in *Taketori* are used in the conversational utterances. For example, there is a lexically and syntactically redundant form in which a quotation is introduced with one verb—*iFaku*, "says," or *iFikeraku*, "what he or she says is"— and finished off with the quotative particle *to* plus a second verb meaning "to say": *to iFiki* (said), or *to iFeba* (says, and then). The reconstituted version of the *Fudoki* text supports the contention that the *Taketori* narrative as we know it may indeed have been the result of just such a reconstitution.[60] Take, for example, the passage cited above—"how could I not obey your wishes?"—which closely resembles such *Taketori* phrasing as "whatever it may be, how could I not go along with what you say?"[61]

Finally, from the time the maiden is thrown out of the couple's house, whenever she speaks she appeals to a particular audience: "people of —— village/hamlet" (*sato/mura Fito*). In the *Taketori* text the views of such people, only implicit in the "Nagu" story where it is the reader who is appealed to, will be actualized in "voices" that comment, often sardonically, on the events of the narrative.[62] The last scene is worth a longer citation:

> She said, "I did not stay here because it was in my heart to do so but because you people wanted me to. What has given rise to the hatred in your hearts and your cruel desire to be rid of me?" The old man became more and more angry and demanded that she leave. The heavenly

maiden wept, moved a little toward the gate, and spoke to the people of the district: "For a long time I have been captive in this human world with no way of returning to the heavens. I have no kinfolk here, nor have I any means of survival. Alas, what am I to do? What am I to do?" She wiped her tears in sorrow, and, looking up at the heavens, intoned the following. (pp. 467–468; the poem above follows)

In contrast to the *Hagoromo* legend, the *Fudoki* version represents a more complex narrating instance anchored in the oral-textual voice of the teller-recorder of the local tale and also in the conversations between the characters, with special emphasis on the question of betrayal and the feelings of the victimized maiden. We will see that the *Taketori* narrative also thematizes precisely those questions as they concern the otherworldly Kaguyahime.

The *Konjaku* Bamboo Cutter

Another often-cited version of the bamboo-cutter story is included in *Konjaku monogatari (shū)*, a late Heian (second or third decade of the twelfth century) collection of tales and legends. Since it postdates *Taketori* by about two centuries, the *Konjaku* text might well have been a later version.[63] Parts of it, however, seem to derive from an earlier "folk" version of the tale upon which both the *Konjaku* compiler and the *Taketori* author drew. The longest of the versions thus far examined, the *Konjaku* story consists of the following: the discovery of a child in a bamboo grove by an old man, the wealth that he miraculously gains after finding the child, a series of three suitors and their assigned tasks, the entrance of an emperor, and the woman's ascent to the heavens. Despite the structural resemblances, the two texts constitute vastly different discursive spaces.

Immediately apparent is that not one poem appears. Conversational utterances are given, but the narration tends toward the external commentary variety we saw with the old Ikago version of the *Hagoromo* tale. One feature we did not see in the versions discussed above, however, are passages representing the "thoughts" of characters. Signified by the quotative particle *to* and the honorific verb *obosu* (think), most of the "thoughts" turn out to be the emperor's: "The emperor thought: this woman, I hear, is of unparalleled beauty in the world; I shall go and take a look, and if her appearance is indeed flawless, I shall make her an empress right away"; or, "the emperor thought with joy [after seeing her]: it seems that she intended to become my empress and did not yield to the other men." One final instance of represented "thoughts": "The old man seeing this [tiny person] thinks: I have these many years been gathering bamboo, and now I have found this [person]." The last case is arresting in that the verb "to think" comes at the beginning of the "thoughts," which are not syntactically closed off by the usual quotative particle but merge into the following discourse through its last lexical item (*koto*, an exclamatory morpheme also meaning "fact"), which doubles as the object of the next verb, *yorokobu* (feel joy). Such syntactic merging, resulting in *Konjaku* perhaps from an admixture of sources and discursive modes, will be a regular feature of the *Genji* tale.

Mooring itself in one perspective, the narrative economy of the *Konjaku* version allows for no extended "digressions." It moves quickly from one situation to the next, inserting "simultaneous" events by means of a deictic time phrase, "during this time" (*sikaru aFida*). The tale itself begins by mentioning a specified, but erased, imperial reign: "Now it is long ago (*ima Fa mukasi*): during the reign of emperor —— there was one old man."[64] A crafter of baskets (*ko*), he finds one day a little person (three *sun* in height). His wife places it in a basket. The person grows into a beautiful adult in three months, and her reputation spreads throughout the land. The old man finds gold in the bamboo grove and becomes rich: "After receiving this child into his care (*mauku*), everything goes according to the man's wishes; that being the case, his fondness and caring come to know no bounds." The verb *mauku* (also, "accumulate wealth") is the only example in the tale of the kind of word play that governs the *Taketori* discourse. The suitors are then mentioned:

> Though the woman (*me*) pays no heed to their [high-ranking suitors'] words, they all remain so earnest and persistent that she first says, "If you capture the thunder in the sky and bring it to me, at that time I will marry you." Next, she says, "There is a flower called the *udonge*. Bring it to me, and at that time I will marry you." Lastly, she says, "There is a drum that makes a sound without anyone hitting it. When you obtain it for me, I shall answer you in person." . . . They obey her words, and though the tasks were impossible ones, they ask an old person who knew of ancient matters how to go about acquiring the objects; some (*aruiFa*) leave their houses and go to the oceanside; some (*aruiFa*) abandon the world and go into the mountains; while they search for the objects in this way, some (*aruiFa*) lose their lives, and there are other (*aruiFa*) friends who never return. (pp. 330–331)

The woman (never named) issues three tasks, but the assumption that there were also three suitors is belied by the actual wording. The men (also anonymous) are never clearly reduced to three, and the text itself only gives two directions in which the men go. The word repeated four times, *aruiFa* ("some" or "certain ones"), can refer to more than one person.

The suitors' story is "told" from beginning to end by a narrator who does not adopt different enunciative positions. With the emperor's story, however, the text offers his thoughts and also presents a series of exchanges between him and the woman:

> The emperor says, "I shall take you with me just as you are to the palace and install you as my consort," to which the woman says, "Though it would give me no end of pleasure to become your consort, in truth, my body is not that of a human"; the emperor says, "Then what are you? Are you a demon or a god?" The woman says, "I am not a demon, nor am I a god; however, people from the sky should be coming for me at any moment; please, Your Highness, I must ask you to leave immediately." (p. 332)

The emperor suspects a ruse, but, sure enough, beings from the sky soon arrive and bear the woman away: "At that time the emperor thought, 'Indeed, this woman was certainly no ordinary person,' and returns to the palace." Afterwards, the emperor "constantly thought about the woman and found it difficult to accept, but it was to no avail, and so the matter came to an end." The emperor's "thoughts" are actually only more words the narrator might have uttered, not so much attributable "thoughts" as paraphrase that pushes the story forward. In fact, the emperor's final "thought" turns mid-phrase into a grammatical concessive that becomes the junction at which not only the emperor but the narrator as well give up the matter (meaning the tale itself).[65]

The end of the "story," however, is not the end of the discourse, which actually concludes as follows: "To the end, it is not known who the woman was. Also, what led to her having become the child of the old man? The people of this world certainly consider it a totally incomprehensible matter. Since it is such an extraordinary event, it has been handed down in this manner, or so it is told/recorded" (pp. 332–333). In the last section the narrator no longer narrates a story but provides a commentary or, more accurately, notes the "circumstances" of the tale's derivation. It also distinguishes narrating time from story time and situates the latter in a separate space of telling that corresponds to the moment of the opening phrase "now, it is the past." The combination of text and the commentary that locates the telling constitutes a topos that is found, in different forms, in all *monogatari*.

We must remember that all of the tales discussed above are "anthologized" stories and that such acts of collecting were themselves governed by political and ideological strategies. All most likely derive from existing tales and oral legends subsequently frozen into a particular written form for collection. The perspective from which we read, then, must not erase the "occasional" inscriptions that are the very fabric of the narration that in turn relates to the political acts that enabled the texts' appearance. The *Man'yōshū* text tells the story of an old bamboo cutter, but that story turns into a pretext for the poems that follow; the *Fudoki* story begins with a specific notation of point of origin and provides a variety of further "situational" and originary topoi; the *Konjaku* narrator transforms the "story" into a more generalized "folkloric" tale appropriate for inclusion with other similar tales. It is difficult to resist the conclusion that the collections represent appropriation of discourses by those in power for the purposes of legitimacy and dominance. The *Man'yōshū* and *Fudoki* texts clearly can be so situated. The *Konjaku* collection, too, has been characterized as one produced in response to an imperial command.[66]

A Chinese Bamboo Maiden

Much has been made in recent years about the similarities of a Chinese story to the tale of the five suitors in *Taketori monogatari*. Called "The Maiden of the Dappled Bamboo" (*Pan-chu Ku-niang*), it is part of a long Tibetan tale, parts of which were published in Shanghai in two different editions (1957 and 1961).[67] The tale begins with a lengthy section that tells of the woes of a young boy (of ten), Lang Pa (Tibetan for "son"), and his mother, who raise several species of bamboo and other crops. They discover the maiden in a stalk of a bamboo tree, the prized *ma-chu* variety, after it is rescued by the boy from marauders who are systematically robbing the villagers of their crops. Having become beautifully dappled by teardrops shed by the mother and boy in their sorrow, it had stopped growing when it reached the boy's height. A drop of blood had fallen on it when the mother cut her finger trying to keep the tree from being hauled away.

Exhausted from carrying the tree out of a gorge, the boy falls asleep, only to be awakened by cries coming from the dappled bamboo. When the bamboo is cut open, a baby girl is found. She grows up quickly (like the bamboo) and is named Bamboo Maiden. One day the mother asks the maiden to marry her son, but the maiden, laughing with "the ringing of a silver bell," asks them to wait three years. When five youths, who happen to hear the silver bell of a laugh, are so captivated by the maiden's beauty that they "drool at the mouth like dogs," the tales of the suitors begin. One youth is the son of the head marauder, another the son of a merchant, the third the son of a government official, the fourth an arrogant youth, and the last a cowardly liar. When they come to capture her, the maiden smiles and says, "I'll handle them." She "handles them" by requesting a different object from each youth: (1) a golden bell that won't break when it is struck; (2) a jeweled tree that won't break when it is hit; (3) a fur robe made from a "fire-rat" that won't burn; (4) a golden egg from a swallow's nest; and (5) a crystal from the forehead of a sea dragon. She gives them three years to obtain the objects, meanwhile assuring the son of their failure.

Similarities to the *Taketori* suitors are both numerous and striking. As in *Taketori*, there are five suitors (with particularized identities), and the number three is important—the maiden asks Lang Pa and his mother to wait three years; when the men arrive, the son is away for three days; the phrase "three years" reappears as the suitors' time limit. The objects are either similar or identical (fire-rat-fur robe, jeweled tree [cf. jeweled branch], and golden egg [cf. shell for easy birth]) to those in *Taketori*. Like Kaguyahime, the maiden immediately perceives the first suitor's object as fake and "tosses it away." In both texts the second suitor's trick is exposed owing to his failure to compensate hired craftsmen. There is a discursive difference, however: whereas the *Taketori* narrating provides the "tale" told by the prince, the *Pan-chu* narrator only "mentions" it. The trials of the fourth suitor (the scaling of a height and falling to his death) resemble those of the fifth *Taketori* suitor, and those of the fifth suitor (encountering a storm attributed to the dragon's anger and being washed ashore) resemble those of the fourth *Taketori* suitor.

We must remember that the "stories" of the suitors are only part of the *Taketori* discourse. In contrast to *Taketori* and *Konjaku*, neither old man nor emperor appears in the *Pan-chu* tale, and the suitors are young thieves rather than high-ranking government officials. The son and the maiden, who does not return to the heavens, are the only characters named, whereas the *Taketori* text provides highly suggestive names for most of its narrative figures. The long "introductory" section of the *Pan-chu* tale, with its band of raiders and tale of economic woe, has no counterpart in *Taketori*, the reverse being true for the latter's closing discourse following the emperor's story. The Chinese text includes no instances of poetic discourse or intradiegetic passages spoken by characters. Rather, the narration is similar to the unproblematic, "external" perspective with moments of dialogue and without "thoughts" of characters that we saw in *Konjaku*. Let us now turn to the *Taketori* tale, that "ancestor of *monogatari*."

2

A "Pivotal" Narrative:
The Tale of the Bamboo Cutter

In the *Taketori* pretexts we observed at times a narrating perspective that did not situate itself in a position self-consciously separate from the story it told. What was told was presumably what happened, as it was happening. Of course, everything that could conceivably have "happened" was not necessarily told, but neither did the narration give cause to suspect that what was not told had crucial ramifications. To put it another way, the "enunciation" of the text by its speaker or recorder constituted an "event" that was as much an event of the text as any interpretable "story" event.[1] Conversational passages also moved the story forward without reflexively marking either the utterer's own positions or the broader narrative.

At other times, however, a different perspective emerged. The last few lines of the *Konjaku* text, for example, included an emperor's "thoughts" and the opinion of "people in the world" concerning the verbal event of the preceding text. The text itself ended with an indication that it derived from a source different from its own narrative moment. In the remarkable "Nagu" story several sections were stitched together into one text culminating in the naming of a local goddess. There too (and also in the *Man'yōshū* section) we saw conversational exchanges where a figure questioned a situation, to which another figure responded in dialogic fashion.

What about *Taketori monogatari*? Although its structure resembles that of the *Konjaku* tale, examination of the ratio of discourse to hypostatized pretext (or story) suggests at once vast differences.[2] We shall discover that, given the emphases on the process of "telling," extractable *Taketori* "stories" will rarely relate unproblematically to the circumstances of their narrating. By examining how its pretexts are rewritten and how the disarmingly simple tale is constituted by a wide variety of narrating modes, we can begin to discern why the *Genji* author(s) was (were) led not only to deem *Taketori* originary but also to employ it to underwrite sections of her (their) narrative. The discussion will also introduce problems of authorship, genealogy, and political stance.[3]

Beginnings

The opening section, after its first line, noted earlier, is governed by *keri*:[4] "Making his way continually into the hills and fields, he gathers bamboo, which he puts to use in a variety of ways. His name is Sanuki no Miyatsuko. Among the bamboo is a stalk shining near its roots."[5] Whereas the *Konjaku* text directly related the man's bamboo gathering to the "merits" he received by crafting a specific item, the *Taketori* text activates another signification in the word *ko* (basket): child.[6] The old man discovers "a person about three *sun* in height sitting adorably" (p. 11). The narration, delivered in a tenseless mode and suggestive of oral rhythms, amplifies the discovery; whereas the *Konjaku* man "thought" a similar passage, the *Taketori* figure delivers a speech act:

> "I've learned of you since you are in the bamboo that I see each morning and evening; you seem to be a person who should become our child [*ko*, 'basket']";[7] so saying, he places it in his hand and ends up bringing it home; he puts it in the care of his old wife; they find it exceedingly lovable; since it is quite tiny, she places it in a basket to care for it. (p. 11)

To have a character utter the words of his action is reminiscent of a theatrical performance, a maneuver different from the diegesis of earlier narrators.[8] Speaking and seeing-knowing perspectives are dislocated. The phrasing, including repetitions as in the following, may be a discursive nod to or a trace of oral storytelling:[9] "The old bamboo cutter, as he gathers bamboo, as he gathers bamboo after having found this child, he finds again and again, in the spaces between the nodes, bamboo filled with gold; in this way the old man becomes wealthy"[10] (p. 11). Another reason for allowing the old man to tell us what he knows and how he came to know it lies in his relation to the bamboo grove, a sacred topos appropriate for engendering otherworldly figures. With privileged access to the hallowed space, the bamboo cutter belongs to a class of craftsmen marginal yet necessary to court society, those who can "see" and "know" such alien creatures.[11]

Next we are told, still in tenseless discourse, that the child "quickly" (*sukusuku*, onomatopoeic for rapid growth) turns into a beautiful adult in three months. Traditional coming-of-age ceremonies—tying up her hair and putting on a train—are held,[12] and the child's virtues are further delineated:

> The shape of this child (*tigo*) is of a brilliance unknown in this world; inside the building there are no dark places, light shines everywhere; the old man, especially when he is irritated or troubled, his misery completely disappears when he looks at this child; the anger in his heart is soothed. (p. 11)

The old man eventually gains great wealth and influence,[13] all because of Kaguyahime who, like Hikaru Genji and Prince Sagoromo, is endowed with the quality of radiance and possesses the power to soothe and comfort.[14] After the tenseless "action right before one's eyes" telling, the *keri* suffix signals a reassertion of narrative control, maintenance by the narrator of explanatory contact with the audience.

Mimurodo Imube no Akita is called to give the child a name: "Shining Princess of the Slender Bamboo" (*nayotake no kaguyaFime*).[15] Celebrations continue for three days,[16] and the first section of the text ends as follows:

> All the men of the court, both high rank and low, hearing her praises are perplexed and wonder how they might win, how they might see this Kaguyahime; they come around to her fence and to her door— though it is not easy even for those persons inside the house to see her; unable to sleep peacefully at night, making their way even on dark nights, they gouge out holes and peep through cracks and wander about; it is certainly (*namu*) from that time that they began using the term *yobaFi*.[17] (p. 11)

Some have observed that the rhythms resemble patterns found in Chinese discourse: high ranking/low ranking, how to win/how to see, to her fence/to her door, gouge out holes/peep through cracks, and so on. I prefer to read them on a level with the earlier repetitions, as writing's nod, so to speak, to the oral. In contrast to such discursive amplification, the *Konjaku* version proceeded almost perfunctorily from the mention of the old man's acquisition of wealth to the tasks issued to the suitors by the "woman."

The word play that ends the section constitutes a prominent and recurring feature of the tale: the term *yobaFi* (calling out for [i.e., seeking] a wife) derives from a form of the verb *yobu* (call) and *Fu*, a suffix indicating repetition; configured into a different syllabic combination, the term can also refer to the confused actions of the men intent on winning Kaguyahime: *yo* (night) and *haFu* (to crawl) produce "night crawling." Since in ancient times a man went to the house of a prospective bride and declared his feelings for her by "calling out" her name, "to call" came to mean "to call repeatedly," i.e., "to make an appeal."[18] In a written text the use of a different Chinese graph (*seikun*) would visually mark the change.

Reading the *Taketori* topos as an instance of etymologizing, scholars have located discursive precedents in such texts as *Kojiki*, *Fudoki*, and *Nihon shoki*. Whereas most of the earlier examples concerned the origins of place names (as we saw in the "Nagu" story), the *Taketori* text inserts into a legendary or mythological topos a moment of resistance, an effectively comical signification by means of a "pivot-word" (*kakekotoba*)[19] that initiates a different type of originary topos, one that recognizes its difference in its doubling movement away from presumed monologic reference.[20] As if both to reinforce the moment and to reanchor the discourse to a *hiragana* narrator, the *keri* suffix reappears. We have, in short, a text, perhaps initially written in *kambun*, that replays its own origins beginning with the generation of an alien being whose story doubles as a pretext for an unprecedented play of language, a nativist linguistic moment that generates itself, breaking loose from the graphic and syntactic constraints of Chinese and perhaps also signaling a different attitude toward the notion of *kotodama*. Put differently, *hiragana* discourse now shows off its own proper power to construct prose texts, no longer serving simply as a means of reconstituting *kambun* or of generating monovocal, spiritually charged topoi. Similar passages, forming bamboolike textual nodes, will be repeated throughout the text at the ends of each of the stories of the five suitors and at the final section of the text. The *Taketori* text, it should be clear by now, presents a new signifying practice.

The five suitors, specifically characterized as "men well versed in amorous affairs (*irogonomi*),"[21] are distinguished from less ardent competitors who "stopped coming, thinking that such visitations with no promise of success were useless." In contrast to the *Konjaku* suitors, the *Taketori* five are identified by name and social or official position: Ishitsukuri no miko, Kuramochi no miko, Udaijin Abe no Miushi, Dainagon Ōtomo no Miyuki, Chūnagon Isonokami no Marotari. The first two are "princes," the third a "minister of the right," the fourth a "major counselor," and the last a "middle counselor." Let us examine, at this point, the important names as they form discursive moments different from what we saw in the various bamboo-cutter pretexts.

Name Dropping

Scholars now agree that most of the important names appearing in *Taketori monogatari* coincide with names in historical intertexts. That the five suitors all fail at completing the tasks given them by Kaguyahime and in the process become prime objects of criticism or ridicule offers clues to a narrative stance, as does treatment of other important names in the text: (1) the old man, Sanuki no Miyatsuko;[22] (2) the man who gives the creature its name, Mimurodo Imube no Akita; (3) the woman sent by the emperor to the old man's house, Naishi Nakatomi no Fusako; (4) the man ordered by the emperor to lead a military force against the heavenly beings, Chūjō[23] Takano no Ōkuni, later referred to as Tō no Chūjō; and (5) the man who takes Kaguyahime's letter and the elixir to the top of Mt. Fuji, Tsuki no Iwagasa.

Let us begin with the five suitors. The names of the last three of the five suitors listed above frequently appear together in earlier historical records. The following are the generally accepted correspondences: Udaijin Abe no Mimuraji = Abe no Asomi Mi(n)ushi (d. ?); Dainagon Ōtomo no Miyuki = Ōtomo no Sukune Miyuki (d. 701); and Chūnagon Isonokami no Marotari = Isonokami no Asomi Maro (d. 717). All were active during the time of emperors Temmu (r. 673–686) and Jitō (r. 690–697), and all were trusted retainers of Ōama no Ōji (later Emperor Temmu) as the latter defeated the enemy Ōmi forces by quickly raising an army and seizing control of the government in what is known as the Jinshin Rebellion (Jinshin no ran, 672). Prince Ōama had earlier been passed over by his father, Emperor Tenchi (r. 668–671), in favor of his younger brother, Ōtomo no Ōji, for the position of crown prince (Ōtomo no Ōji committed suicide during the rebellion). In a passage in *Nihon shoki* the three retainers are mentioned precisely in the order of their appearance in *Taketori*,[24] and other sources indicate that the ranks of the three nonprinces given in *Taketori* correspond to their ranks as seen in historical sources.[25]

Regarding the first two suitors, scholars believe that Ishitsukuri no miko corresponds to Tajihi no Mahito Shima, and that Kuramochi no miko corresponds to Fujiwara no Fuhito (d. 720). The former belongs to a family that claims Emperor Senka (r. 535–539) as its founder and whose descendants, accordingly, would have been called "prince" (ō). Although with Shima's generation the family was lowered to commoner status, it is quite possible that, since his father was known as Prince Tajihi, Shima also went by that title. It turns out, moreover, that Shima's wet nurse comes from the Ishitsukuri family, which happens to trace its lineage back to a mutual titular deity, Hoakari no mikoto. Throughout Japanese history such nurses play crucial roles in the upbringing of children and are often accorded the same respect shown the actual mother. Since it was common at the time for a man to be known by his nurse's family name—Shima's father had also taken his nurse's name, Tajihi—he could have been called Ishitsukuri no miko. In the case of Fujiwara no Fuhito, although he was the putative second son of Fujiwara no Kamatari, his real father was Emperor Tenchi, which means that he too could have been called prince. Because his mother happens to come from the Kuramochi family, he indeed could have been referred to as Kuramochi no miko.[26] The two personages also appear in the *Nihon shoki* passage cited above.[27] We now have an intertextual situation in which the names of the five *Taketori* suitors are rewrites of historical figures who ably assisted the victorious Emperor Temmu.

Although all of the men occupy lofty social positions, they are reinscribed into the tale of the bamboo cutter as men accomplished in the art of sexual play (*irogonomi*). Instead of amorous conquests, however, the men are victimized by the impossible tasks put to them by Kaguyahime, and their ignoble ends turn historicopolitical success into fictional amorous failure and ridicule (a situation reversed in the *Genji* discourse). Each becomes the butt of a verbal "joke" that parodies the toponymical processes found in Chinese sources. In *Taketori*, toponyms, through the double tracing provided by the "pivot-word," become narrative place markers or thresholds that engender (fictional) folk etymologies.

What about the other appellations? Sanuki no Miyatsuko, the bamboo cutter, summons Mimurodo no Imube no Akita to name the alien maiden. Since names were usually conferred by the head of a clan (*uji*), it is likely that the bamboo cutter too was a member of the Imube clan. Traditionally, the Imube were responsible for organizing and performing at sacred imperial ceremonies. Akita's name includes the title *mimurodo*, which means "at the side of a deity."[28] The revisionist historical text *Kogoshūi*, compiled by the same Imube clan, for example, tells of the descendants of Teokihohoi no mikoto, the founding deity of the Imube clan of Sanuki famous for crafting bamboo spears and poles. They annually sent, in addition to their regular tribute to the palace, eight hundred bamboo poles. The name that Akita gives the maiden provides a further link to the Sanuki-Imube connection. According to the *Kojiki* text, Emperor Suijin married a princess named Kaguyahime no mikoto, daughter of Ōtsutsukitarine no Ōji.[29] The princess's uncle also appears in *Kojiki*, bearing the suggestive name Sanukitarine no Ōji.[30] Based on the above, it has been further surmised that the bamboo-cutter tale may have been one of the stories handed down by members of the Imube clan of Sanuki and that it was through clan storytellers that the tale became known to members of the court.[31] Although the old man is not directly an object of ridicule as the suitors are, he appears quite silly at times.[32]

Another name, Naishi Nakatomi no Fusako, has been tied to the establishment of the hegemony of the Fujiwara family. The Nakatomi, like the Imube, were supervisors of sacred rites, but they were also the founders of the main branch of the Fujiwara family. It was Fujiwara no Fuhito (659–720) who seized control of the "Rear Palace" (*kōkyū*, i.e., the consorts' quarters to the rear of the main palace), thus depriving the other competing families (especially the Ki and Ishikawa) of the critical feminine power base. Employing a strategy that included lowering in rank already installed imperial consorts from those families, reducing to commoner status sons of those consorts, and otherwise severing their direct ties with the imperial line, Fuhito established a Fujiwara monopoly on children born to emperors and thereby was able to control the candidates for crown prince. It was Fuhito's second son, Fusasaki (681–737), who most aggressively continued his father's political stratagems. Four generations later another Fujiwara, Yoshifusa (804–872), similarly dealt a fatal blow to other competing families (the Ōtomo and Tachibana), when he established the so-called *sekkan* form of government that reaches its apogee with Fujiwara no Michinaga. By referring to the emperor's envoy sent to the old man's house as Naishi Nakatomi no Fusako, the *Taketori* text, it is argued, refers obliquely, through the two syllables *Fu* and *sa*, to those Fujiwara hegemons. The title *naishi*, moreover, designates a high-ranking female attendant whose inability to accomplish her task amounts to a veiled criticism of the descendants of the powerful Nakatomi family.[33] The argument may seem farfetched unless we view the woman as more than a "narrative function." The passage, instead of simply stating that the woman was unable to get a look at Kaguyahime, actually comprises several conversational exchanges involving the *naishi*, the old woman, and Kaguyahime. The following is one example: "I have received an imperial command to come here and take a close look [at Kaguyahime]. How can I possibly return to the palace without seeing her? Can anyone who lives in this world refuse to obey an imperial decree? Do not act so unreasonably" (p. 42). Because she was acting on behalf of the emperor, Naishi's failure to carry out the command is ignominious. The two remaining names have also been linked with other related historical circumstances.[34]

It is not my purpose to reconstruct actual historical situations or appellations per se but rather to explore what such "name dropping" might signify for the *Taketori* discourse. The purpose is not to reify "historical background" or to be concerned with how a text can be read as simply "mirroring" history, but to examine why a narrative should enact a particular reappropriation of "history." The examination of a particular discursive threshold, by allowing a convergence of various intertextual discourses and narrative aspects, can help trace the narratological (and/or ideological) perspectives of the text in a way that neither so-called literary, nor historically foundationalist readings are able to do. The language of the *Taketori* text, which signals the advent of *hiragana* prose discourse as well as its appropriation of poeticodiscursive figures, if carefully attended to, ought to help prevent overdetermined readings on either side.

To summarize the name-dropping situation, we might remember both the originary moments marked by the *Taketori* text, especially the etymologizing and the discovery of the creature in the sacral bamboo topos by an old man bearing the name (Sanuki) of an early storytelling tribe, a name further linked to the man (Imube) who confers the bamboolike name upon the creature, who through that name becomes discursive kin to a figure in *Kojiki*. The backward leap over a century and a half to such early figures, texts, and clans constitutes a conscious nod to a time when written discourse was being appropriated by a centralized authority. The *Taketori* text, by poking fun at the men who assisted in the establishment of that government, enacts two gestures: first, as it seeks to install itself as a legitimate mode of discourse it harks back to another originary discursive moment in history and mimes its movements; and second, it adopts a definite stance toward the figures appearing in the earlier texts, appropriating them for its own linguistic and narrative ploys. The text itself, then, even as it adopts a distinctly critical stance toward the men who supported Emperor Temmu and by extension the growing Fujiwara hegemony, attenuates at the same time the potency of that criticism by remaining true to the centripetal forces of its own linguistic display and power.

Authorship and the Ki Lineage

We might also consider, in relation to the question of names, the text's authorship, which, as is the case with most *monogatari*, is unknown. Expressing a view representative of current scholarship, Katagiri Yōichi points out that based on the text's diction and style, we can only surmise that the author was probably male and that the text first appeared some time after the mid-ninth century, perhaps during the Jōgan (859–877) or Gangyō (or Genkei, 877–885) period.[35] A list of likely author candidates proffered by previous studies includes men like Minamoto no Tōru (822–885), Archbishop Henjō (815–890), Ki no Haseo (845–912), Minamoto no Shitagō (911–983), and even Ki no Tsurayuki (d. 945).[36] Noting the traces in the text of *kambun* discourse, Katagiri and others conclude that the author must have been thoroughly literate in *kambun*, both Chinese and native varieties. Although all the men named above qualify in that regard, one in particular, Ki no Haseo, if not the actual author, is an excellent example of the type of person who could have written the narrative.[37]

A scholar with impressive credentials in *kambun*,[38] *kanshi* (Six Dynasties poets and Po Chü-i), as well as waka discourse, Haseo was one of the most talented and best-known officials of the day. His close friend and mentor, the celebrated Sugawara no Michizane (845–903), decrying the laxity and extravagance found among his contemporaries, declared Haseo to be only one of two men (the other being himself) who pursued the genuine path of poetry. Haseo was also a particular favorite of Emperor Uda. The "fire-rat-fur robe" section of *Taketori* has been read as an implicit criticism of just the sort of excess, accompanied by an unquestioned faith in the power of wealth, that Michizane lamented.[39] Haseo was also a graduate (*monjō no shō*) of the prestigious Heian Academy (*monjōdō*), eventually becoming a doctor of letters (*monjō no hakase*) and head of that institution, and was appointed to positions that required compositional skill.[40] Samples of Haseo's extant writings reveal attitudes congruous to those in *Taketori*: an inclination toward the world abandonment of Taoist immortals (the *Taketori* text is often viewed as an intertextual kin of such

Taoist topoi), a firm commitment to waka, and a concern for the situation of women. The last is one of the remarkable aspects of *Taketori*, manifesting itself both in the old man's worries about Kaguyahime's future welfare after his death and especially in the princess's desire to know a man's true feelings before marriage for fear that his heart may turn fickle afterwards. In a Chinese poem, "Song of a Destitute Woman," Haseo describes the hardships that befall a woman of noble blood who marries a man (chosen from among many suitors) on the basis of reputation. Fooled by a conniving go-between, the parents cater obsequiously to the man, even though he is obviously unlearned and ill-mannered. The man spends all his time and money hunting and drinking. After more than ten years, the man abandons the woman, whose parents are now dead and whose siblings have disappeared. Destitute and full of rancor, the poor woman ends up with no one to turn to for solace. The poem ends with the following four lines,

> And so I say to you high-born ladies of the world:
> If you would select a husband, look well into his heart,
> and do not be taken in by appearances;
> And I say to you parents who have daughters in the world:
> I beseech you to write my words on the sashes of
> your robes [so as not to forget them].
> (Kojima Noriyuki, *Honchō monzui*, 344–346)

Whether or not Haseo actually wrote *Taketori*, the poem's signification is echoed in the actions of both the old bamboo cutter, who is continually fooled by appearances, and Kaguyahime, who specifically voices the concern that she might be abandoned if she yields to a man without "knowing the extent of his feelings."

Returning to the text, we find the narrator focusing further on the persistence of the suitors and on Kaguyahime's response, thus producing a clear difference between a text like *Konjaku* that constructs a story-line and one like *Taketori* that expends narrative energy in representing conversation. The narrator seems to be relishing the newfound freedom provided by *hiragana* writing to render native speech.[41] We are told that although the men are so infatuated with Kaguyahime that they forget to eat, send letters and poems, and make visits, it is all "to no end," *kaFi(nasi)*—a word that will later form another verbal play. The manner in which the text describes the overdeveloped desires of the men prefigures later texts: "since they are men who are overcome with desire even when they hear of a person only slightly prettier than the many who exist in the world" (p. 13).[42] Hyperbolic phrasing also continues: "Though they know that nothing will come of it, they make their way, undaunted, through the ice and snow of the Twelfth Month and the burning sun and roaring thunder of the Sixth Month" (pp. 13–14). The men appeal to the old man but are put off; time "passes,"[43] the men offer prayers, and they become even more ostentatious in their emotional displays.

In a conversation between the old man and Kaguyahime, the former refers to the princess as a "transformed being" (*henge*, i.e., an otherworldly creature transformed into human shape). Kaguyahime denies it and claims that the old man is her parent. The old man then offers a lesson on worldly ways: men and women marry and produce thriving households; women, even *henge*, need backing, which the bamboo cutter, being over seventy, cannot provide for long. When he urges her to choose one of the men, her response recalls Haseo's poem mentioned earlier: "Being one of unseemly looks, I only think about the fact that if I do not know how deep their feelings (hearts) are, and it turns out that their affections were shallow, I shall feel remorse afterwards; they may be clever men of the world, but it is very difficult for me to consider marrying one of them not knowing the extent of their feelings." The old man agrees, and they finally decide on a plan: "the one among the five who shows me what I wish to see shall be the one I deem to possess superior feelings, and I shall place myself at his service" (p. 15). The emphasis on a woman's need for material backing and for discerning "depth of feeling" institutes what will be a recurring concern of *hiragana* discourse, which after all is referred to as a "feminine hand."[44] It is difficult to overlook either the critical climate that would have enabled the placing of a woman in the position of issuer of tasks, not simply as a passive "object" to be acquired, or the discursive situation that again redoubles onto itself since the tasks the princess sets are, in teleological terms, impossible from the beginning and thus generate only an allegory about the impossibility of attainment. In other words, the narrating perspective is in full collusion with that of the princess, a situation that corroborates the view that *monogatari* were written for women. They were not written simply for "entertainment," however, given the powerful parodic force of the historical and political characterizations.

The tasks are then issued to the men, the rhythm of whose actions are mimicked by the narration in phrasing similar to the *Konjaku* tale:

some played flutes, some sang song-poems, some hummed tunes, some whistled, rapping their fans to keep time.[45] As the old man, in the role of messenger (such discursive intermediaries will have far-reaching consequences for the *Genji* text), relays the princess's wishes, the text produces another narrating perspective unseen in the earlier texts: a figure who represents the speech of another figure. The structure—"when I said . . . to her, she said . . . and then I said"—also amounts to a repetition of the previous *henge* conversation (textual event) noted above. The men agree to the terms, and Kaguyahime names the objects, matching object with suitor:[46]

1. Ishitsukuri no miko: the Buddha's stone pot.
2. Kuramochi no miko: a branch of a tree with roots of silver, stem of gold, and fruit of pearls, located on the island of P'eng-lai.
3. Udaijin Abe no Miushi: a robe made from the fur of a fire-rat.
4. Dainagon Ōtomo no Miyuki: a jewel that shines in five colors found in the neck of a dragon.
5. Chūnagon Isonokami no Marotari: an "easy-birthing" shell possessed by the swallow.

Even though the old man protests the difficulty of attaining such objects (protests the princess brushes aside) the crestfallen men refuse to give up and the narrating moves quickly to the first suitor's "story."

The Five Suitors

Five distinct sections tell of the speech-actions of the five suitors. The sections match further, in *engo* (associative-word) fashion, the actions of each suitor to a particular trait.[47] The first three men, for example, are characterized as follows: (1) a man with a calculating heart; (2) a man with a scheming heart; (3) a man of abundant wealth from an illustrious family. In their attempt to perform the impossible, the first two suitors resort to bald deception; the third, relying on wealth, is himself deceived. The last two of the five, after relying on the actions of underlings, personally endeavor to locate the "real thing" but fail miserably. In terms of narrating, each section exhibits characteristics peculiar to itself. The first brief section focuses on poetic discourse;[48] the second, on Prince Kuramochi's made-up tale; the third, on epistolary discourse; the fourth, on another lengthy sea adventure only this time from the narrator's perspective (i.e., "made up" differently); and the fifth, on advice to the middle counselor given by those around him. Besides ending with an "etymological" gesture (like *yobaFi* discussed above), each section also includes public announcements or statements—utterances indicating that the man is about to act or command others to act in some way or has completed some act. Such utterances repeat discursive modes appropriate to officialdom, and also provide an economical means of informing Kaguyahime (and the reader) of an act.

In the first section Prince Ishitsukuri (Stonemaker) announces, "I am setting out today for Tenjiku [India] to obtain the stone pot" (p. 17). Rather than embark on a journey, he goes to a nearby mountain temple, takes a soot-covered pot, and places it in a brocade bag to which he attaches an artificial flower. The princess, like the Chinese maiden, instantly sees through the trick, but before she rejects the pot, the *Taketori* discourse turns poetic:[49]

> over oceans and mountains   I hunted along paths
>   with all my heart and soul [from the moment I left Tsukushi]
> in search of this pot, shedding tears,
>   tears of blood, along the way
> [umiyama no/miti ni kokoro wo/tukusiFate/naisi no Fati no/namida nagareki]

Kaguyahime wonders if the pot emits any light but there is not even the light of a firefly,

> if only the tiniest dewdrop's   worth of light
>   had been lodged inside;
> what did you go in search of   on Ogurayama [Dark Mountain]?
> [oku tuyu no/Fikari wo dani mo/yadosamasi/wogura no yama nite/nani motomekemu]

So saying, she gives it back; discarding the pot at the gate, he sends her this poem,

> in the presence of   Shirayama [White Mountain]
>   its light fades away   with pot [and shame] discarded
>   I still find myself filled with hope
> [sirayama ni/aFeba Fikari no/usuru ka to/Fati wo sutetemo/tanomaruru kana]

The section ends as Kaguyahime refuses even to listen to the prince's reply, and the latter ends up returning home: "ever since the time he continued to make advances after throwing away the pot [his shame], whenever someone shows no shame, it was called 'discarding the pot' (*Fati wo sutu*)" (p. 18).

The prince's first poem is no hackneyed composition but a complex pattern of syntactic and semantic linkages. The place name, *tukusi* (Kyushu), *isi no Fati*, and *ti no namida* are all hidden in the poem. The toponym Tsukushi is embedded in the expression *tukusiFate* (to use up all one's energy), and the final two syllables, *Fa* and *te*, pivot into the expression *Fatenai* (never-ending). *Naisi* can mean "shed tears," which echoes *namida* (tears). The final syllable of *Fatenai* forms a different chain with what follows to produce the word *isi no Fati* (stone pot). As if that weren't enough, the last syllable of *Fati* becomes the first syllable of the phrase *ti no namida* (tears of blood, i.e., arduous labor). The princess's poem responds to "mountain" in the prince's composition (which in turn was metonymical to the object it was attached to) and also associates "dew" with the prince's "teardrops." The text assumes the reader knows that the Buddha's pot was supposed to emit a deep blue-green glow. The prince cleverly cites the princess's brilliance as the reason his pot is dull and includes at the same time the phrase *Fati wo sutetemo* (though I discard the pot [my shame]) that becomes the source of the final comment.[50]

The first instance of poetic discourse, which is the focus of the first suitor's story, replays and greatly expands the earlier linguistic play, bringing rhetoric to bear on the prince's lame attempt at deception. The failure is not simply dismissed, as it was by the Chinese maiden, but appropriated by waka discourse, which then produces another originary etymology. Closure in terms of "story" (as we saw in the Bamboo Maiden tale) becomes discursive dispersal and deferral that laughs as much at its own mechanisms as at the fecklessness of the prince. The section is brief, to be sure, but it is packed with a variety of narrating perspectives: the narrator's discourse, the "thoughts" of the prince, a public announcement, a poem (attached to the object), two responding poems, and a final narrative comment in the *keri* mode. The cleverness of the prince's poetry belies the extent of his willingness to exert himself to gain the princess, but, with failure a foregone conclusion, we realize that *hiragana* discourse is actually valorizing skill at verbal artifice.

The second prince's schemes of construction are more intricate, and, accordingly, the section is longer and more involved. The narrator quickly "tells" us the "story" first, including two announcements of departure, one delivered to the palace and one to Kaguyahime's house. The prince secretly returns to the capital after three days and hires six master craftsmen, builds a thickly walled

storehouse (Kuramochi = "Storehouse Owner"), where he seques-
ters them and himself, and orders them to construct a jeweled branch
to the princess's specifications. We learn later that they spent three
years at their task. When the work is done, the branch is secretly
taken to Naniwa: "He has it announced to those at his mansion, 'My
boat has now arrived back home,' and presents himself looking
exceedingly haggard" (p. 19). The narrating includes other voices:
"When would they have heard of it? They shout, 'Prince Kuramochi
is here with the Udonge [Udumbara] flower'; Kaguyahime, hearing
this, thinks, 'I have been defeated by this prince,' and she is overcome with sorrow" (p. 19). The branch is presented, and Kaguyahime, "desperately heartbroken" (p. 20), regrets having ever
issued the tasks. After the old man prepares the soon-to-be couple's
sleeping quarters, he casually asks a question that proves to be the
prince's undoing: "In what sort of place was this tree located? It is
such a mysteriously beautiful, splendid object" (p. 21).

The innocent question sets the prince off on his own tale, which
forms the major interest of the section. Since it can only be a tale of
deception, it mimes the larger tale as well, and since, by all rights, the
princess has been won, the elaborate tale is pure ornament like the
branch whose "origin" it retells.[51] The prince's longwinded "journey" includes his visit to Hōrai (P'eng-lai) and return, complete with
repeating verbs and phrases that generate momentum: the same
verb, *ariku* (walk, wander) appears four times in the beginning, and
the phrase *aru toki (ni) Fa* (at one point) appears no fewer than six
times to punctuate his trials at sea. Here is an example of the latter:

> *At one point,* the waves turned rough, and I felt we were plunging to the
> bottom of the ocean; *at one point,* we were blown by winds to an
> unknown country where demon-like creatures appeared and tried to
> kill us; *at one point,* not knowing whence we had come, or where we
> were headed, I feared we would be lost at sea; *at one point,* our
> provisions exhausted, we made do with the roots of grasses; *at one
> point,* unspeakably disgusting creatures tried to devour us; *at one point,*
> we gathered shellfish to prolong our lives. (p. 21)

As he nears the island, the discourse turns tenseless, and the prince-
narrator even includes a conversation between himself and a woman
allegedly encountered there:

> Letting our boat go where it will, we drift upon the ocean; about the
> hour of the dragon [ca. 8:00 A.M.], on the five-hundredth day, we see

faintly a mountain in the ocean . . . a woman in the guise of a heavenly maiden, carrying a silver bowl, emerges out of the mountain to fetch water . . . I ask her, "What is the name of this mountain?" The maiden replies, "This is Hōrai mountain"; upon hearing this my joy knows no bounds; the woman asks, "Who are you who speaks thus? My name is Haukanruri," and suddenly she disappears into the mountain. (p. 22)

The prince then lists the wondrous things on the island, claiming to have seen branches far superior to the one he brought back. The old man, completely convinced by the prince's attempt at verisimilitude—his shabby appearance attesting to his return just the previous day—exchanges poems with the prince.

> black bamboo
>> in our gathering of stalk sections over the generations
>> in the hills and fields
> have we ever encountered   the hardships you describe?
> [kuretake no/yoyo no taketori/noyama ni mo/sa ya Fa wabisiki/Fusi wo nomi misi]

Hearing this, the prince replies, "My spirit, beaten down these many days, has finally found peace,"
> the sleeves of my robe   today are dry,
>> the hardships I endured   a thousand in number
>> are but a distant memory
> [waga tamoto/keFu kaFakereba/wabisisa no/tigusa no kazu no/ wasurarenubesi]

The old man's poem is of a complexity far beyond his humble origins. *Kuretake* is a pillow word for *yoyo* (space between the nodes on a bamboo stalk) and also signifies "generations." *Yoyo* is usually associated with *Fusi* (a play on "node of bamboo" and "point that stands out, is remarkable [i.e., the many points of hardship]"). It can also refer to that which affects deeply (the prince's convincing tale) or to the modulations of voice in recitation or singing (perhaps the rhythms of the prince's story?). Both words, *yo* and *Fusi*, are associated with *take*, "bamboo." The resulting associative-words bring the poem to coherence if not into any presumed unity: the poem gestures both to the bamboo cutter's daily toil and to the prince's hardship at the pivotal "points or nodes" (*Fushi*), implying at the same time the *yoyo*, or "segments" of his tale. The prince's poem picks up the word *wabisi* (hardship) and places it between "dry sleeves," which suggest the "wet" ones of his arduous trip as well as the hyperbolic *tigusa no kazu* (the total of a thousand types [of hardships]).

Following the elaborate story and poetic discourse, a sudden reversal occurs when the craftsmen hired by the prince demand payment for their work. They first issue a verbal statement describing their activities over the previous one thousand days, during which statement "the prince can only remain seated, looking dazed and frozen with fear" (p. 24). The text then provides a short "document" restating the prince's promise of reward. Kaguyahime, meanwhile, is delighted: "I was wondering all along if it might be genuinely a tree from Hōrai; since it turns out to be an incredible hoax (*soragoto*, 'empty words'), quickly return it" (p. 24). She then offers a poem,

> thinking it genuine   I listened intently;
>   upon taking a closer look   I found it a jeweled branch
>   adorned only with leaves of words
> [makoto ka to/kikite mitureba/koto no Fa wo/kazareru tama no/eda ni zo arikeru]

Fa or *koto no Fa* ("leaves" or "leaves of words") associates with *eda* (branch). The prince's tale is "retold" yet again, for the branch is no real "branch" but merely one clothed in "leaves" of words, which is all that textual "branches" can ever be. But "leaves of words" already represent a further step in language's attempt to profit from its own figural potential. In the prince's story, however, the process of "adornment" is simultaneously constitutive of the rhetorical mode itself, which means that we are yet another degree removed from the issue of a gaþ between words and things or from static rhetorical expressions and readings. Put differently, the expression "leaves of words" is deconstituted of its conventional rhetorical transparency and allowed to play out its formative configuration.

While the prince slips away in shame, Kaguyahime in her delight rewards the craftsmen. After the prince ambushes the men and robs them of their gifts, the narrator moves to end the section:

> He [the prince] went deep into the mountains; all the officials and servants of the prince searched for him—could it be that he died?—but were unable to locate him; the prince, wanting to hide himself from his retainers, did not show himself for many years; this is the beginning of what is referred to as "losing one's *tama*" [jewel or spirit, *tamasakaru*]. (pp. 25–26)

The narrating perspectives include a further split of the textual perspective: one perspective wonders if he is dead, and another controlling (*keri*) perspective informs us why the prince "disappeared" for several years and offers the etymology.[52]

Appropriate to financial matters, the section devoted to Abe, the third suitor, concerns the problem of monetary exchange. He orders his man, Ono no Fusamori, to pay a Chinese named Ōkei,[53] who happens to be in Japan, to purchase the fire-rat robe. Two "letters" are supplied by the text. Ōkei's reply to the request (which is not given; the text presumably echoes the eliding rhythms of *kambun*) states that the robe does not exist in China but may have been taken to India: "I have heard of it [the robe] but have not yet seen it; if it exists at all, it should be in this country; it is an extraordinarily difficult transaction; if by chance (*tamasaka ni*) it has been taken to India, I may have to pay a visit to a wealthy merchant lord; if it does not exist, I shall have a messenger return your money" (pp. 26–27). The second letter relates Ōkei's difficulty in obtaining the robe: "an item that is not easily found in the world of today or in the world of the past; long ago, a wise Indian sage had brought it to this country [China]; learning that it was in a mountain temple to the west [of China], I prevailed upon a local governor, who was able to buy it by using his political influence" (p. 27). After happily paying the additional sum that Ōkei had to pay the governor, Abe obtains the robe, which comes in an elaborate box. The narrator remarks that "rather than a question of not burning, one first notices its unparalleled beauty." The minister, confident of marriage to Kaguyahime, takes the item to the old man's house. A poem is attached:

> it burns not in flames   the rat-skin robe
>   like the undying flames of my thoughts burning for you;
> its sleeves, now fire-dried   I shall wear it proudly today
> [kagirinaku/omoFi ni yakenu/kaFagoromo/tamoto kaFakite/keFu koso
> Fa kime]

A common word play involves the phoneme *Fi* (fire) in *omoFi* (obsessive thoughts). The last two segments suggest that the minister's sleeves, damp with tears of longing and frustration, are now dry in preparation for the wearing of his wedding robe. The verb *yaku* (burn) is generated out of an association with that fire. The old man exhibits his usual gullibility, but the princess simply asks that the robe be put to the test. Her speech act incorporates the words she will speak if the fur robe turns out to be real: "If this fur robe does not burn though we set fire to it, I shall consider it genuine and do as he wishes; I shall say, 'Since it is an item not of this world, I consider it, without doubt, to be genuine'; in any case, let's try burning it" (p. 29). As she quotes what she will say, she repeats what the previous clause had stated: again, discourse reproduces itself in different guises. Despite the minister's protest, it is tossed into the flames and "it burns to a crisp" (p. 29). Kaguyahime joyfully returns the box with a poem,

> had I known that flames would wholly consume it
>   the rat-skin robe:
> I would have admired it as is
>   and kept it away from flaming thoughts
> [nagorinaku/moyu to siriseba/kaFagoromo/omoFi no Foka ni/okite
> mimasi wo] (p. 30)

As a response to the minister's poem, the last two segments produce another signification out of the fire phoneme in *omoFi:* "I would have kept it out of the fire." When the minister leaves, the text reproduces voices of people of the world. Those "worldly" voices, which we inferred from the "Nagu" and *Konjaku* texts, here perform a discursive role in question-answer form: "The people of the world ask, 'They say that Minister Abe brought the fire-rat's robe and is married to Kaguyahime; is he here?' Someone answers, 'When they tossed the fur into the flames and it fried to a crisp, Kaguyahime would not marry him.' The fact is, after they heard this, they now refer to the inability to attain one's goal as 'no courage' (*aFenasi*)" (p. 30). The word play, mimicking the minister's name, is on "no Abe." Since he never married the princess, hers was indeed a case of "no Abe."

The failure this time derives from too much faith in monetary power and serves as a possible warning against scheming merchants. The two letters from Ōkei appear, through the discursive gullibility of the minister, to highlight the foolishness of the economic transactions of one who believes a merchant—historical sources show that lavish expenditures were a continual problem for the government during the ninth century.[54] We can note also that the text prefers to allow a participant to "speak" from his or her own perspective (the many conversational utterances, the second prince's own story, Ōkei's letters, and so on) rather than from what in the West is known as a "third-person" perspective. *Hiragana* discourse, as it anchors itself in the narrating "now" (self-consciously not "past"), possibly retaining traces of old oral modes, centripetally pulls all voices into an "I" perspective.

The last two suitors, who attempt to command others to procure "real" items, receive ruthless narrative treatment. The next to last suitor, Major Counselor Ōtomo no Miyuki, in his attempt to obtain the jewel in the neck of a dragon, orders a group of men to find and slay the beast ("he assembled every single man in his service"). When the men disappear with the riches they were bribed with, he must set out to obtain the jewel himself. The final suitor, Middle Counselor Isonokami Marotari, takes the advice of attendants and tries to obtain the "easy-birthing" shell from a swallow's nest high up near the roof of a granary. When they fail, he takes matters into his own hands and pays for his foolishness with his life. The major counselor's section begins with an announcement: "In the neck of a dragon there is a jewel that shines in five colors; whoever can obtain it and present it to me shall have whatever he wishes" (p. 30). The middle counselor begins with a request: "Report to me when the swallow builds its nest" (p. 36).

In the first case the major counselor's "journey" consists of narrative statements concerning high winds and lightning, and an exchange between the counselor and the boat captain:[55]

> How did it happen? High winds rise, the sky darkens, the boat is blown in all directions; not knowing which direction they are headed, the boat is tossed about and it looks as if it might plunge right into the ocean; waves batter the boat as if to engulf it; the lightning flashes close enough to come down on top of them. (p. 33)

The phrase "how did it happen" (*ikaga sikemu*) is a common part of the *kana* discursive economy, used to introduce a situation for which one is unprepared. The storm forces an end to the mission. Dazed and seasick after the storm passes, the suitor ends up (in three or four days) on the shore of Akashi, in Harima Province (where Genji is taken by the Akashi lay priest). The counselor is unable to move his body, his belly is bloated, and his eyes are the size of two large apricots (*sumomo*). Upon his return he meets his men, who explain why they disobeyed his orders and ran off. Their speech is marked by *ki* (direct experience); the counselor's by *keri* (metanarration). He rewards them with what is left in his mansion and calls Kaguyahime an *oFo'nusubito no yatu* (great swindler). The last part of the section provides other perspectives:

> Hearing this the former wives who separated from the counselor split their bellies in laughter; the fact is that hawks and crows come and pick at the roof of the house made of thread and carry it all away; the fact is that people of the world remark, "Has that Ōtomo Major Counselor brought back the jewel from the dragon's neck?" "Nope; not at all; he

wound up with apricotlike jewels in both his eyes though." "Ah, hard to eat," they said, and the fact is that ever since then people began using the phrase *ana, tabegata,* "Ah, hard to eat," whenever things go contrary to common sense. (p. 36)

The word *taFegata* in the final phrase also means "hard to bear" or "hard to offer gifts." Rather than an overconfidence in money, the counselor's story displays an overconfidence in brute force. The discourse focuses on conversational exchanges, and at the end, disobedience is rewarded, and the "people of the world" are heard from again. At the major counselor's level, it seems, even facsimiles are impossible to obtain. Or perhaps the lack of a facsimile is associative of the directness of the failure.

Illustrative of the latter case, the middle counselor follows the advice of one Kuratsumaro, a granary official, who suggests that the "easy-birthing" shell can be obtained if one honest man is lifted up to the nest when the swallow gyrates its tail feathers seven times. When nothing is found, the impatient counselor orders himself lifted up in a basket tied to a rope. When he grabs what he believes is the shell, he cries, "I have something in my grasp; lower me now" (p. 39). In their haste the men let the rope slip, and Marotari comes crashing down, face up, onto a large cooking cauldron. When they manage to revive him and he opens his fist, "he saw that what he had grabbed was a piece of old dung the swallow had dropped and cried out, 'All that work, and no shells,' and from that time, when things go contrary to one's expectations, one says 'no shells/no use' (*kaFinasi*)" (p. 39). The play is on *kaFi* ("worth" and "shell"). Instead of ending there, the passage incorporates shells and seeing into the counselor's fear of social humiliation and provides the expected poem exchange, which continues the play on "shells." In response to Kaguyahime's poem,[56] he offers his death verse:

> this [your letter] indeed   was all worthwhile
>   will this life of mine,
> as I now face death   be scooped back to life?
> [kaFi Fa kaku/arikeru mono wo/wabiFatete/sinuru inoti no/sukuFi
> yaFa senu]
> As he finishes writing, he is dead. Hearing this, Kaguyahime felt sorry
> for him. Since then, modest joys are referred to as "having shells/
> having worth" (*kaFiari*). (pp. 40–41)

The counselor's poem activates yet another possible meaning for *kaFi:* scoop. It is no longer a question of success or fake "objects" but of salvaging discourse: the "shell" of an emptiness; in other words, what language and narratives are.

The five failures constitute stories, but they also serve as pretexts for "etymological" moments that re-mark in turn the enabling discourse as a signifier of something other than those presumed stories. When we backtrack and reread the previous discourse in light of the new knowledge of signification, we see that the text is constituted by a wide variety of narrative perspectives that preempt story-lines, now appropriated by discursive anchors. The various perspectives completely fragment the possibility of the monologic or monovocal narrator we observed in our initial discussion of other related texts. The *Taketori* situation thus differs so radically from the other tales discussed above that it becomes impossible to compare them on any simple "story" level. What is more, the *Taketori* narrative is far from finished; there is still over a quarter of the text to go.

Enter an Emperor

The final suitor's story begins with the emperor giving orders to an attendant, Naishi Nakatomi no Fusako, to "take a good look" at the woman. As noted earlier, the *naishi* fails since the princess is determined not to be seen, even at the risk of refusing an imperial command: "If my words mean refusing the command [to serve him] of a king (*kokuwau*), do not hesitate to kill me." When he hears the *naishi*'s report, the emperor is amazed at "the heart indeed of one who killed many men." After a series of exchanges (between the emperor and the old man, and between the old man [acting as intermediary] and the princess), we are told the latter remains firm in her posture of resistance: "Were I to enter court service, I would vanish; you would have your court rank [which the emperor had offered as a bribe], but I would die" (p. 43). The emperor then tries to get a peek at her while pretending to be out hunting. He does manage to look at her face and even take hold of her robe, but when he tries to force her into his palanquin, "this Kaguyahime suddenly turns into a shadow (*kage*)" (p. 45). He realizes that she is an otherworldly being, and she assumes her human shape.

The emperor does what the others could not but ends up just as powerless to possess her. The text repeats the process of sight-knowledge-possession emphasized at the beginning of the tale, only this time the alien creature cannot be captured. As the princess has been throughout, she becomes the pretext for more discourse, the only way she can be "possessed." After the emperor's poem, Kaguyahime recites,

> beneath the crawling weeds   I have spent
>   these many years
> how could I cast my eyes now   upon the jeweled palace?
> [muguraFaFu/sita nimo tosi Fa/Fenuru mi no/nanika Fa tama no/
> utena wo mo mimu]

The term "weeds" (*mugura*) will reappear in *monogatari* texts to signify the topos of an interesting woman hidden from the world.

Separation and Narrative Deferral

Back at the palace the emperor no longer attends to his various women, who pale in comparison to Kaguyahime.[57] Although he could not possess her, their exchange of letters allows the narrative to keep her captive so that she can now become a point of focus vis-à-vis a celestial world. Instead of culminating in the familiar word play, the emperor's story continues into the final section of the tale: "In this manner (*kayau nite*) they consoled each other's hearts for three years; from the beginning of spring, as she noticed the moon's captivating appearance, Kaguyahime fell deeper than usual into sorrowful thoughts" (pp. 46–47). The line contains the first mention of a particular season.

It might help to review quickly the question of time in *Taketori*. In contrast with such texts as *Konjaku monogatarishū*, the *Taketori* text does not place the story in a historical (or historicized) time frame.[58] A primary means of linking sections in *monogatari* texts are the deictic phrases *kakareba* (this being the case), *kayau nite* (in this way), *aru toki* (one time), *sono naka* (among them), *tosituki Fete* (after a period of months and years), and so forth. The suitors' stories, for example, are simply juxtaposed to each other with no temporal linkages.[59] The events of the text are thus always kept anchored to a narrating perspective relativized anaphorically to a previous stretch of discourse. In other words, the constant relativization of time to narrating privileges the spatial-temporal coordinates of the narrating over any references to a time divorceable (or reifiable) from that narrating (or narrator). Points in time had received isolated mention before,[60] but in the last section the text begins to be punctuated by mention of particular days of the month. Representation of successive points in time is now necessary to mark the relation between Kaguyahime's feelings and the phases of the moon prior to her departure.

From "spring" we move to the fifteenth day (a full-moon day in the lunar calendar) of the Seventh Month, then to a time before the fifteenth day of the Eighth Month. The princess finally reveals to the old couple that she is a being from the moon capital who, because of a transgression (unstated), has been doing penance for a time on earth. Now the time of penance is up, and on the fifteenth of the month her people will come for her. She admits to great sadness (emphasized by repetitions of the verb *naku*, "cry") at having to leave now that she is accustomed to the ways of this world. After the confession discursive treatment of Kaguyahime also changes, as honorific expressions, until then restricted to the suitors and the emperor, begin to be used for her as well.[61]

On the fifteenth day the emperor sends a middle captain, Takano no Ōkuni, with an army of two thousand men to guard the bamboo cutter's house. They lock the princess securely in the storage room, where she is cradled by the old woman. The princess warns them that human force will be ineffectual in the face of celestial power. Still constituted by conversational exchanges, the text includes a particularly long utterance by Kaguyahime in which she expresses her sorrow at having to leave the old couple and explains that she was not fated to stay on earth for very long. She ends her speech as follows: "It brings me unbearable grief to leave you having only troubled your hearts; the people of the moon-capital are beautiful and do not grow old; they do not know sadness; the prospect of going there offers me no happiness; it shall cause me no end of longing to imagine you in frail old age" (pp. 51–52). The passage together with the princess's confession and the letters she leaves before departing constitute the lengthiest examples of discourse delivered by a narrative figure. The focus in all the examples is on the complicated feelings generated by imminent separation, that liminal space neither here nor there.

On the same day around midnight (the "hour of the rat"), a spectacle right out of a science fiction movie (e.g., "Close Encounters of the Third Kind") begins:

> Around this time, as darkness fell, at about the hour of the rat, light radiates around the house, brighter than broad daylight; the intensity

of the brilliance is that of ten full moons; you can see the pores in a person's skin; out of the vast sky, people, riding on a cloud, descend and form a line five feet (*shaku*) above the ground; the fact is that those inside the house and out, as if possessed, no longer have the will to do battle; with concentrated effort, they are barely able to take up their bows and arrows, but the strength is gone from their arms, and their bodies go limp; those of staunch will mightily attempt to shoot their arrows, but their shafts are deflected from their marks; instead of fighting fiercely, they only stare at the visitors in a stupefied gaze. (p. 52)

Referring repeatedly to the world as a "polluted place," one of the visitors remarks that the old man was blessed with Kaguyahime owing to accumulated merits. When the old man fails to convince the visitors that they have made a mistake, the doors to her room open of themselves, and she is urged to depart.

The princess twice defers her departure and the putting on of a robe of feathers (*Fagoromo*): the first time she leaves a letter (whose contents the text provides) for the old man in which she states her wish not to leave. She asks the old man to "regard the robe I remove and leave for you as a memento; on nights the moon is out, look up toward me; to abandon you and depart—I feel in my heart as if about to drop from that very sky" (p. 54). The tale of "shells" and words of adornment here finds another emblem: a lifeless robe inscribed in a letter the princess leaves behind. When a member of the alien party urges her to drink an elixir and put on the robe of feathers, she takes a bit of the elixir, then temporizes further by writing the emperor a letter, the text of which is given. In the letter she expresses sadness over her imminent departure and regret at not obeying the imperial command. She also composes the following:

> now, as I put it on,　　the celestial robe of feathers
> 　　at this moment when all will soon be over,
> feelings of longing for you　　well up inside me
> [ima Fa tote/ama no Fagoromo/kiru ori zo/kimi wo aFare to/omoFi idekeru]

She leaves the jar of elixir, finally puts on the robe, and, thus emptied of human feelings, ascends skyward accompanied by one hundred or so heavenly beings.

The tale, however, is still not over. The old couple grieve "to no avail" (*kaFinasi*) and, after reading the letter, refuse to drink the elixir, deeming it "useless" (*yōnasi*), and fall gravely ill. When the emperor reads the letter, he is so grief stricken that he even stops eating, stops all music playing, and asks for the name of the mountain nearest the sky. When someone answers, "The mountain is Suruga—near to this capital and near to the sky," he composes this poem,

> never more shall we meet;   afloat on my flowing tears,
>   for this solitary body of mine,
> what possible use   would a deathless potion be?
> [aFu koto mo/namida ni ukabu/waga mi ni Fa/sinanu kusuri mo/nani ni kaFa semu]

The poem produces another pivot-word in its two possible syntactic segmentations: *aFukotonami* (since there will be no meetings) and *namida* (tears).

Tsuki no Iwagasa is then sent to the mountain with orders to "set fire to them [the jar and the princess's letter]" (p. 57). The text then states, "[The fact is that] ever since he climbed that mountain accompanied by numerous warriors, that mountain bears the name Fuji Mountain. The smoke still rises up into the clouds, or so it has been transmitted" (p. 57). The final etymology inscribes in the name of the mountain a triple graphic word play: (1) "undying," if written with the characters "not" and "die" (the elixir); (2) "an abundance of warriors," if written "wealth" and "warrior" (the warriors that Tsuki no Iwagasa took with him); or (3) "inexhaustible," if written "not" and "use up" (the inextinguishable smoke). The smoke that rises does so out of "words"—the princess's letter and the elixir—and is inscribed in the words of the text. In refusing to drink the elixir, the emperor yields to the helplessness of capturing the alien being. Language does, however, retain traces of the attempt, for as it mimes the princess's ascent, the smoke becomes an emblem for the continual repetition of the narrative itself.

The narrating finally ends, as did the *Konjaku* text, by locating its source in a previous, presumably oral tale, thus distancing itself from the preceding narrative: "or so it has been transmitted" (*to zo iFitutaFetaru*). The reference may be to the toponymic etymology or to the *Taketori* text as a whole,[62] which "originates" throughout in the play of language. The nod to orality must not be taken "literally," of course. Instead of citing any actual oral story, the final phrase might have been a way for the text to found itself in a distinctly non-*kambun* source, thereby echoing the narrating perspective's incorporation of a mode (*keri*) that had initially signified *hiragana* discourse's relation to a legitimizing orality. The *Taketori* text, as I have noted above, represents what may have been the first instance of the appropriation of prose discourse by *hiragana* writing. Instead of only representing different discourses in a monographic *kambun*, the Japanese could now freely give the illusion of different types of utterances and texts—the poems, announcements, documents, letters, adventure stories, reports, decrees, and so on, that appear in *Taketori*—reproduced in a writing better attuned to the requirements of their own language, and it could always incorporate Chinese graphs when necessary or desirable.

The relation of the act of writing to storytelling assumes its most exemplary instances, aside from its conversational plenitude, when the text twice defers Kaguyahime's departure in the two letters she writes before putting on the robe of feathers. Not only are we told she writes the letters, they are reproduced, and, further, her feelings as she composes each text are treated separately: isochrony of "story" (she writes a letter), narrating (the given letter), and reading (we read the letter) is all but realized as the diegetic slowdown reenacts her deferral. In other words, the letters constitute more "words" by which Kaguyahime forestalls her departure, and the text defers the ending of its story, of which the princess is pretext. Being "words," they can only forestall, never having been able actually to present any "thing."

It is characteristic of stories throughout the world to attempt to do just that; "resolutions" of "emplotted" narratives somehow give the illusion of closure and possession, and the reader comes away with a sense of the narrative having been "about" something (often extractable through philosophical or otherwise abstract themes, e.g., variations on love, death, sex, success, goodness, God). Fairy-tale-like stories often close with a "happy ending," some types of novels with a marriage, and detective stories often with clear examples of plot "resolution." By contrast, the *Taketori* text operates as if in full knowledge of the ultimate impossibility for words to produce either oral or scriptive "presence." It continually "ends" its sections as well as the larger narrative with acts of originary nomination (seven in all) that mark the preceding discourse as the main "event" that gives rise to the term in question and amount to an intervention into the process (and possibility) of generating narrative meaning. The terms, however, inscribe word plays that undermine any attempt to garner univocal value for themselves. The discursive focus, lying in the "process" of figural inscription, installs a problematic between the figural and the literal right at the beginnings of *hiragana* discourse. It must be remembered that marks we use today to indicate voicing,[63] though represented by different graphs in *man'yōgana*, were not used in Heian *hiragana* discourse, thus erasing differences between "hati/ hadi wo sutu," "aFe-/abenasi," and "taFe-/tabegata." The last instance takes advantage of the potential for differing graphic representations of a given phoneme that had been common in *man'yōgana* texts.

Taketori and Waka Discourse

The editor of an excellent modern commentary on the *Taketori* text, Noguchi Motohiro, evokes the notion of *kotodama* to observe that at one time "song-poems," which were "genuine speech" (*makoto, koto* meaning "words"), were considered "genuine things" (*makoto*, written with a different graph meaning "things")—the power to move "things" was found in "words." An instance like the "Buddha's stone pot" section shows "'words' breaking away from 'things' and becoming an object of a purely form-oriented interest."[64] With the *Taketori* "etymologies," "words" begin to be manipulated freely, separate from their "representative" function: "In the mind of the writer, events (*kotogara*) are made to conform to an order that derives from the verbal associations; it is here that we can find the key to the formation of *monogatari* literature." Noguchi's comments accord with our observation that "story" often emerges as an effect of a waka, i.e., that waka can serve as pretexts for the prior narrating, which in turn incorporates poetic figures in the redoubling movement of a false etymology.[65]

Finally, the pivot-word is a staple of post-*Man'yōshū* waka poetry, a poetic figure forming a kind of lever that continually enfolds the narration of a story back on to itself as its own originary moment to create a textual situation similar to the movement in the *Ise* tale. The pivot-word has often been cited as evidence for dating the *Taketori* text to the period in which the figure came into vogue (i.e., the latter half of the ninth century), the period of the so-called Six Poetic Geniuses (Rokkasen).[66] In terms of poetic discourse it was a time when the post-*Man'yō* emphasis on composing poetry in Chinese was giving way to a waka revival. It is important to note too that pivot-words should not be read as "metaphoric" moments of recuperation. In its figural movement a waka utterance retains both pivotal facets, each devolving into a signified of the other while at the same constituting that very process. We usually tend in the West to view metaphorical constructs in terms of a "tenor" valorized over a "vehicle," with the latter instantly fading into a trace of the constitutive act. Heian Japanese preferred to retain language's structural ("incantatory") "concreteness," their discourse marked by uneffaced movements where signifiers do not form divisible pacts with their signifieds but rather with other signifiers (in metonymical maneuvers) that allow them to remain both signifier and signified, so to speak, at the same time. When a second signified is retrieved from the redoubled word play, it does not require displacement of the first to stand as an independent "proposition" of the figural instance but functions as an adjacent signification.

We have tracked the following waka moments in the *Taketori* text: first, the instances of pseudoetymology that turned what had earlier been a mythicopoetic topos into a politicoaleatory one (the toponymic plays that subvert the five "historical" figures and historicity itself); second, the manner in which narrative aspects stood in associative (*engo*) relations (for example, Prince "Stonemaker" and stone pot, Prince "Storehouse Owner" and storehouse, and the Shining Princess and the radiant moon); and third, the way that waka compositions punctuate the larger narrative. By its use of waka, *hiragana* "prose" discourse keeps narrative (and readerly attention) tied to the occasions and moments of narrating. The text thus preserves a kind of zero degree, negative space that can be reoccupied by the performer of the text (reciter, copyist, or reader), who in reproducing or varying the utterance participates in an originary narrative act.[67] The moments "represent" that iterability as part of their discursive perspective. Is it a coincidence, we might ask, that a text that installs *hiragana* writing as a viable mode makes continual and definitive gestures toward and appropriates a prime feature of poetic discourse that is also inseparable from that *kana* writing?

Constitutive of the *Taketori* narrative, then, is the realization that "things," being always absent, are fated forever to be reappropriated in the "adornment" of language. The verbal associations and acts dictate narrative events that derive from conditions originating in modes (i.e., waka, *keri, ki,* conversational, epistolary, and so forth) that continually anchor the discourse to a flexible, "present-moment" perspective that distorts or even ignores and undermines the "story" we might have thought it was telling. To the *Taketori* example, I add in Part II a discussion of waka, the ways it was instituted as a hegemonic mode, and the other ways in which the poetic form was appropriated.

II

Waka "Poetics" and Tales of "Ise"

The trope is not a derived, marginal, or aberrant form of language but the linguistic paradigm par excellence. The figurative structure is not one linguistic mode among others but it characterizes language as such.

Paul de Man, *Allegories of Reading*

I situate the point of departure for Japanese literature in the incantatory expressions received from the gods.

Origuchi Shinobu, "Kokubungaku no hassei"

If the genealogist refuses to extend his faith in metaphysics, if he listens to history, he finds that there is "something altogether different" behind things: not a timeless and essential secret, but the secret that they have no essence or that their essence was fabricated in a piecemeal fashion from alien forms. . . . What is found at the historical beginning of things is not the inviolable identity of their origin; it is the dissension of other things. It is disparity.

Michel Foucault, "Nietzsche, Genealogy, History"

3

Constructing a Capital "Poetics": *Kokin Wakashū*

Tanka and *tanka* segments (phrases and "poetic words," *kago*) are a sine qua non of *monogatari* texts, not only marking distinctive thresholds (the *Taketori* text) and serving as important pretexts (the *Ise* and *Genji* tales),[1] but upsetting our notions of what "prose" texts are all about. In the following three chapters I discuss, as a counterpoint (and supplement) to our reading of *monogatari*, three forms in which poetry was "collected" and recontextualized (i.e., appropriated or "narrativized"): the first imperially ordered waka anthology, a private poetry collection, and a poem-tale. Native verses and other religious and folk song-poems that appeared before the compilation of *Kokin wakashū* (Collection of Japanese Poem-Songs, Old and New, ca. 905) were without canonical form.[2] *Kokinshū* installs the *tanka* as the proper poetic form. Compiled at the command of Emperor Daigo (r. 897–930) by four Heian scholar-officials,[3] it contains over eleven hundred poems and includes two "prefaces" (*jo*), one written in *manabun* ("Manajo"), and the other in *kanabun* ("Kanajo"). The prefaces constitute aesthetico-ideological statements that helped legitimize the waka over the different varieties of its counterpart, *kanshi* (Chinese poems). The collection also heralded the establishment at the Heian capital of a new "communal body" (*kyōdōtai*). The first in what was to be a succession of imperially ordered collections over the next several centuries, the *Kokin* collection became the standard repository of poetic inspiration, a source for locating topics,[4] metonyms, and turns of phrase appropriate to season, mood, and occasion. Although only a few managed to commit all the *Kokinshū* poems to memory, familiarity with a large number of its poems became de rigueur for all courtiers, whose everyday lives offered innumerable opportunities, both public and private, to write the notes, messages, letters, and communications almost always accompanied by a poetic composition or citation.[5] The phrase "dark age of national styles" (*kokufū ankoku no jidai*) has long been the accepted characterization of the period between the *Man'yō* and *Kokin* collections, but consensus now holds that although waka might have been excluded from public occasions, it certainly continued to flourish at a private, mostly amatory, register. I am not concerned so much with the quantity of waka found in *monogatari* texts or with judging the quality of individual compositions as with the change in attitude toward poem-songs, poetic language, and the act of collecting, recontextualizing, and legitimizing that new Heian sociopolitical circumstances demanded as well as relations to narrativization in general and to *monogatari* discourse in particular.[6]

Recent Waka Debates

A contemporary Japanese scholar, Furuhashi Nobuyoshi, bluntly states that "poem-songs (*uta*) have been read far too much for their meaning," that they "come into existence for reasons other than meaning alone."[7] He argues that the sounds of the words, *jusei* (incantatory qualities), in an *uta* (or waka, as opposed to poetry composed in Chinese) also played a crucial part in the formation and socially solidifying effects of *uta* selected for *Kokin wakashū*. I begin with Furuhashi's statement as an entry into a discussion of Heian poem-songs found in the *Kokin* collection, a text that has received a flurry of attention in North America in the past few years. Not only are two new English translations now available,[8] but there have appeared in the United States a number of review articles of the translations as well as a monumental study of Heian waka published as a companion to one of the English versions.[9] The translations, the companion volume, and the reviews open up the discussion, long overdue in the West, of Heian waka and of Japanese poetry in general.

In a review of the McCullough translation and companion volume, Edwin Cranston raises an important issue when he contrasts the author's only implicit reference to the ancient notion that he translates as "word-spirit" (*kotodama*) with the work of Konishi Jin'ichi, for whom the notion plays a central role.[10] Cranston doesn't state his own views explicitly, but they can be inferred from his reference to Konishi as a "true believer" in *kotodama*, a scholar whose "analysis of early poetry and song is founded upon the stated premise that any reading that leaves out this magical element is, ipso facto, skewed, ahistorical, and invalid." For Cranston the "premise is particularly controversial in the reading it prescribes for Hitomaro and other poets who clearly show awareness of literature *qua* literature" (p. 315). The remark that poets like Hitomaro "clearly show awareness of literature *qua* literature" reveals Cranston's own biases and is itself a controversial position, as has been shown recently by Gary Ebersole.[11] Like Konishi, Ebersole takes seriously such matters as *kotodama* and other situationally ritualistic aspects and presents a welcome corrective to the general tendency toward overly "literary" readings of Japanese poetry during the age of the *Man'yō* collection, readings that valorize the "individual" and "lyrical" aspects modern readers continue to "find" as they displace the socio-politico-religious situations and motivations for the emergence of the song-poems. Rather than hold to the view that attention to "literature" must necessarily exclude "magical elements" like *kotodama*, what would happen if we revised our modern notions of "literature" and found a way if not to integrate such elements completely into a different attitude toward the poetry, at least to account for their possibility in our readings?

Another voice in the recent debate is that of the linguist Roy Andrew Miller, who has also reviewed the two McCullough volumes.[12] In his thoroughly critical review, language is Miller's primary concern as he first takes philological issue with what he sees as McCullough's often careless handling of poetic and linguistic sources, a situation that results in mistranslations of Chinese texts (written in both China and Japan), and then takes phonological issue with McCullough's neglect of modern reconstructions of the sound values of ninth-century Heian (and also pre-Heian) Japanese. To romanize, as McCullough does, using a system derived from twentieth-century Tokyo dialect is unpardonable in Miller's eyes: "To study any poetry in disregard of the sounds of its texts is to doom the investigation to failure at the outset, if only because such an approach categorically negates the very essence of that which is being studied" (p. 752). Of course McCullough, for better or worse, is simply following the standard Japanological practice of providing Japanese equivalents in their Westernized modern attire. It is her evaluations of certain poems on the basis of alleged repetitive sound patterns, however, that make her failure to address the problem of Heian phonology especially vulnerable to Miller's telling barbs.[13] Moreover, Miller's consistently harsh tone does not detract from the crucial points he raises, and I take his review to be a *cri de coeur* for scholarly rigor as he defines it.

Despite his proper concern with the "sounds of . . . texts," Miller himself, when read against Furuhashi or Konishi, turns out to be oblivious to other, socio-politico-religious, aspects. In that regard Miller becomes in the end an ally of Cranston, who implicitly allied himself with McCullough and thus with accepted Japanological practice. Miller's omissions become even more striking when we find him sounding a radical, Orientalist echo of Furuhashi: "The problem, with her [McCullough's] translations as with her literary analysis, is that she attempts to reduce Japanese poems to ideas that can be communicated generally, in half-approximate paraphrase, to the English-language reader. And that is impossible: these poems *have no ideas*" (p. 757; my emphasis). In Miller's terms, poems "in any language must be a thing of wonder," and the "central business" of literary analysis is the "studying, analyzing, even explaining (if one insists) the how, why, and when of this wonder that infuses every *genuine poem*—and even KKS, for all its limitations of theme and spirit, does surprisingly enough, have its share of genuine poems" (p. 757; my emphasis). Here Miller opens himself up to the charge of unfairness, since he does not tell us what he means by the phrase "these poems have no ideas" (lest it be a wholesale acceptance of the commonsensical but misguided view that poems must not "mean" but "be") and offers no examples of what a "genuine" *Kokinshū* poem might look like. We can be certain from Miller's discourse only that such poems will "have no ideas," and that "ideas" must somehow be different from "themes."

I fully agree with Miller's contention that McCullough operates from a position to which her reader is never privy, that she relies "throughout her second volume in particular, not upon any verifiable body of overt views, opinions, or methods, but rather upon a hidden hoard of criteria and standards," and that a plethora of vague terms are never defined (p. 758), but I must take issue with Miller's basic assumption concerning what constitutes "serious attention to the study of literature." In his words, such attention would mean a study "conducted along the lines of all *other* scientific experimentation and observation": "The results, whatever the field or discipline, are significant only to the extent that they prove themselves *capable of being replicated*. The cardinal question must always be whether or not someone else working with the same materials and under the same assumptions will be able to get the *same results*. Insofar as they represent serious scientific praxis, literary analysis and the reading of texts also incorporate an *identical presupposition of replication*" (p. 758; my emphasis). Yet if anything has been consistently and convincingly questioned in twentieth-century thought, it is precisely the belief that universal, scientific, self-identical results are possible when it comes to studies, including linguistic ones, that involve interpretative moments and maneuvers.[14] What may be for Miller a universal fact of objectifiable procedure ("the same materials under the same assumptions") is actually, as John Barrell has suggested, a local, masculinist, Eurocentric one. I would guess that a great many scholars working in the so-called humanities nowadays would think hard before claiming to be engaged in "serious scientific praxis" (those, for example, working in the revisionist sectors of the disciplines of anthropology, sociology, cultural or intellectual history, or literature, and especially those operating from feminist, third-world, ethnic, poststructuralist, or cultural-materialist perspectives). Miller seems to be trying to subsume all literary analysis under a scientific notion of philological and linguistic practice with which he feels at home.[15] Whether it be in McCullough's arbitrary, impressionistic nonmethod or in Miller's scientific, philological one, I do not see the possibility for broaching the larger questions (which for American scholars the notion of "literature" seems to preclude) of cultural representation and the necessity for sociopolitical readings. McCullough may have failed to live up to Miller's stringent standards, but he himself remains ensnared in putatively scientific webs of his own spinning from which, although he sheds important intertextual light on Chinese sources, no appeals to objective methodology will allow him to extricate himself or to provide neutral criteria for determining what constitutes a "genuine poem."

Whereas Western scholars writing on waka have been unanimous in their reticence to wade into the admittedly treacherous waters of *jusei* or *kotodama*,[16] Japanese scholars these days swim in them easily and often, especially those working from perspectives that follow in the wake of the great ethnologist Origuchi Shinobu.[17] One of the difficulties in working with the terms *jusei* and *kotodama* arises from the differences that exist in Japanese scholarly usage. Furuhashi's treatment of *jusei*, for example, is not the same as Konishi's employment of *kotodama* even though the terms may seem to refer to identical phenomena. The latter argues that *kotodama* gives way by the *Kokinshū* period to the notion of "elegance" (*ga*) imported from China, whereas the former works from a notion of difference between the constructed *Kokinshū* attitude toward language and the attitude found in *Man'yōshū* more than a century earlier.

The case for *kotodama* in *Kokinshū* has been argued by another prolific waka scholar, Katagiri Yōichi. In a book that combines essays and round-table discussion by five leading waka scholars—Katagiri, Fujioka Tadaharu, Masuda Shigeo, Komachiya Teruhiko, and Fujihira Haruo—Katagiri refers to what he calls a "'quality of incantatory technique' (*jujutsusei*) based on the 'notion of word spirit' (*kotodama shisō*) that had been appealed to since ancient times" and that relates to "legends about the spiritual efficacy of poem-songs (*katoku setsuwa*)."[18] During the round-table discussion, Katagiri adds that *kotodama* is closely related to "public poems" (*hare no uta*), those presented before a royal audience or on celebratory, festive, or other official occasions.[19] The passage in the "preface" referred to by Katagiri concerns the material efficacy of poetic utterances, exemplified in the statement "moves without physical effort heaven and earth, makes spirits, both alien and familiar, who are invisible to the eyes, feel pity, harmonizes the relations between men and women, and soothes the hearts of fierce warriors."[20] For Katagiri the passage demonstrates precisely the potency that Heian Japanese believed resided in words configured into phrases and poem-songs,[21] a belief that also requires a rereading of a "poem-tale" like *Yamato monogatari* that has been considered to be of lesser "literary" value.

A question forms itself at this point: is the exclusion from consideration in Western waka discourse of the notion of *kotodama* symptomatic of other exclusions? Among such exclusions might be the political significance of the imperial decision to collect waka; the variable and often fictionalized occasions, conducive to narrative amplification, for waka production (especially "poetry contests" [*uta awase*], "screen paintings" [*byōbu-e*], and the many different ways that poems and other discursive forms were collected and arranged in collections); the authorization of "poetic pillows" (*uta makura*); the relations among rhetoric, "nature," interpretation, and religiopolitics; and the genealogical interconnections among the poets. In other words, the *kotodama* issue subsumes not simply the question of whether or not the Japanese believed in some magical power of words, and certainly not whether there actually could have existed such power—questions that can too easily slip into a "unique to the Japanese state" sort of discourse—but rather the following: what does an accounting for the necessity to institute and preserve such lexicospiritual myths signify for the establishment and authority of the *Kokin* collection and for the later waka tradition and its subsequent interpretations? Let us begin with a consideration of the relation between the Heian attitude toward the incantatory power of words and the various poetic figures that have been identified. The modern tendency has been to consider, primarily from the point of view of "poetics," such figures as devices, thus effectively keeping them cut off from broader, polylogic readings.

"Rhetoric," Orality, and the Reconstruction of a Communal Body

Heian leaders, *Kokinshū* compilers, and other courtiers faced the formidable problem of constructing a new "communal body" (*kyōdōtai*) that could effectively bind together members of court society—members who after more than a century had become accustomed to life at the Heian capital with its public emphasis on Chinese discourse—around a *hiragana* writing based on a practice of waka poetry befitting public as well as private occasions.[22] Furuhashi is silent on socio-geo-political matters, limiting himself to the differences in the circumstances of composition between the *Man'yō* and *Kokin* collections: "In order to resolve this issue [the rise in the number of waka compositions that show a splitting of communal and individual conceptions—his example is Narihira], it would be necessary either to create a new phonological form or superimpose onto the poems an incantatory quality and thus strengthen them" (p. 45). The argument, in part, is this: having been highly irregular during the periods of the so-called Anonymous Poets and the Six Poetic Geniuses (around the mid- to late ninth century; Narihira dies, for example, in 880), waka practice needed to be regulated in order both to appropriate compositions and to counteract unruly or inappropriate tendencies. Furuhashi also argues, interestingly but less convincingly, that the rise of *monogatari* contributed to a valorization of the "meaning" of words and produced a corresponding reduction in phonological emphasis (p. 47). Rather than try to institute a new poetic form, the *Kokinshū* compilers harked back to the moment when poem-songs were believed to have originated (the "age of the gods," *kamiyo*), and in so doing attempted to fortify the existing poetic form by revitalizing the incantatory aspects that were a regular component of the ancient songs.

Furuhashi goes too far, in my view, in identifying "sound" with "communal" aspect and "meaning" with "individual" aspect, but his argument does offer, if yoked to political considerations, a possible explanation of why the *Kokinshū* compilers moved away from the baroque diction of a Narihira or a Komachi (both of whom are well represented in the collection) to the more decorous styles of the period of the compilers themselves, even as they retained older practices: the "pillow word" (*makura kotoba*), the "lead-in phrase" (*jokotoba*), repetition, and the incorporation of what Furuhashi calls a "complementary referral" (he provides two examples, "dream/reality" [*Kokinshū* 658] and "winter/spring" [*Kokinshū* 791].[23] I would add that *Kokinshū* poems also emphasize the possible ways that words referring to things in "nature" and words referring to human and social matters found in the *Man'yō* collection can be interconnected—the deployment of the newer "pivot-words" and "associative-words" to tighten the bonds between the two references might be another symptom of the need to construct a new idea of "nature" for those living at the capital[24]—and that the larger collection is also bound at times by spectacular poem-to-poem linkages. Finally, we must remember that the poems were almost always recited out loud.

With reference to the need to construct a new, capital-based poetics, a note on the function of toponyms, or metonyms of place, is in order. A vast number of such toponymic associations came to be collected into handbooks called "poetic pillows" (*uta makura*) to which poets could refer.[25] Painters relied on them as well, for example, when depicting scenes painted on standing screens (*byōbu-e*). Poets also participated in their construction by composing an appropriate waka for the square area (*shikishi*) left blank at the upper righthand corner of a panel (there were usually twelve panels to a standing screen, divided into six pairs). The viewers of the screens usually composed their poems not as detached gazers at a depicted world, but as figures *in* the scene, making it a participatory mode intimately connected to the reception of narratives. In other words, all you needed to "know" for artistic and narrative purposes were the metonyms appropriate for place and season. As Tamagami Takuya observes, poets could learn about "places" from paintings, a process that precluded actual visits; if a poet knew that Yoshino signified cherry blossoms or that Tatsuta signified autumn leaves, that was all the "knowledge" needed for a poem to be born.[26] In a given painterly or narrative context, therefore, if you knew the relevant metonyms for season and place, you could execute the appropriate painting or "stand in" for the narrative figures. The situation also helps to explain why a "journey" in a narrative often consists only of an exchange of poems or a citation of a pretext to evoke the places "traversed."[27] Here too we find language functioning in a nonrepresentational manner, at least as "representation" is known traditionally in the West. The choice and reestablishment of metonyms, furthermore, also makes operative the incantatory qualities that Furuhashi emphasizes.

Let us examine a few of Furuhashi's examples. To begin with he cites poems that employ repetition. One is *Kokinshū* 74, "Spring II," by Prince Koretaka (closely related, as we shall see, to Narihira):

> cherry blossoms   if you must *fall*, go ahead and *fall*
>   for even though you did not *fall*
> that old friend from home   would still not come to see you
> [sakurabana/*tira*ba *tira*namu/*tira*zu to te/Furusatobito no/kite mo min-
> aku ni]

According to Furuhashi, such repetitions, in the space of a thirty-one-syllable line, display a concern more with the incantatory rhythm itself (in the above poem the repetition of the syllables *ti* and *ra*) than with any putative "meaning."[28] In the case of Koretaka's poem the prefatory note tells us that the prince "composes it for Archbishop Henjō and sends it to him." Given that Prince Koretaka was one of a number of figures during the Heian period who was summarily removed from political life by Fujiwara leaders, we can politicize Furuhashi through a merging of the political and the incantatory and read the poem as a protest against a fate that has forced the poet into a life of solitude and loneliness.

Further support for a politicized reading can be found in the poem's seriate location in the collection.[29] The poem immediately preceding, *Kokinshū* 73, for example, speaks to the fleetingness of the world, in the context of which are placed the falling cherry blossoms. The last two segments of the poem, which juxtapose past and present, are as follows: "we looked, and they were in bloom; now, before we know it, they have all scattered away." The segments permit an allegorical reading that equates the fall of the cherry blossoms with the swift decline of the fortunes of a man like Prince Koretaka. The poem by the monk Zōku that follows, *Kokinshū* 75, mentions in its prefatory note Urin Villa, which was the residence of

Prince Tsuneyasu, Koretaka's step-brother,[30] before it passed into Henjō's management. The resulting links between the Ki family, the princes, the monks, and the political posture cannot be coincidental and make the section, which appears soon after the beginning of "Spring II," especially noteworthy.[31] Zōku speaks of it being "spring" at the branches where blossoms are still attached, in contrast to the "snow" (winter) that falls and stays on the ground. A standard modern commentary,[32] dedicated on the whole to aestheticized interpretations, remarks that the blossoms/snow metonym is a hackneyed usage; yet, it is also possible to read a political transformation within the blossoms themselves as they fall from the "spring" of glory to the "winter" of discontent.

Furuhashi also links incantatory aspects to the practice of the "pivot-word," which we found important in the *Taketori* text. His stance provides a necessary supplement to standard discussions that see it as a play on the puns (available when the medium is *hiragana* rather than Chinese characters whose graphicosemantic nature restricts the rise of homophonous, associative meanings). An anonymous poem, *Kokinshū* 433, has been cited as containing the first instance of the pivot-word:[33]

AFuFi [Heartvine] and Katsura [Laurel],
now you've become   someone only rarely met,
       as rare as Heartvine Festival days;
how could I not consider you   heartless as the laurel tree?
[kaku bakari/*aFuFi* no mare ni/naru Fito wo/ika*ga tura*si to/
omoFazarubeki]

The turn (pivot) occurs at the words *aFuFi* (meeting day) and "heartvine," suggesting the yearly festival of the Kamo Shrine in the Fourth Month, and *katsura* (laurel tree, in the segment [*ika*] *ga tura* [*si*]), also associated with the Kamo festival,[34] the segment then allowing for a syntactic recombination to produce a word meaning "heartless." The poem appears in the *Kokinshū* category "Names of Things," which contains poems inscribed by hidden names. The two florae are not only hidden in the poem but form a locus of word plays; the discovery of the names adds another dimension not in any "metaphorical" sense, but in a "topical" (and incantatory) one. Since the names suggest the Kamo Festival but do not produce any totalizable signification, I refer to such rhetorical processes as "metonymical." We must also keep in mind that pivot-words do not simply play on a dual meaning but implicate both a "natural" and a "human" reference.

Another example of the pivot-word is *Kokinshū* 629, "Love III," by Miharu no Arisuke:

> without expressed design with nothing yet between us
>   our names *rise* in rumors, a *rising* Tatsuta River:
> to refrain now from crossing will not put an end to them
> [aya nakute/madaki naki na no/*tatu*tagawa/watarade yamamu/mono naranaku ni]

The poem pivots at *tatu* (rise, as in "rumors rising" and part of the name of the Tatsuta River) from an explicit concern with rumor into the incorporation of a geographical reference. The phrase "tatutagawa" floats in the middle of the poem, where an implicit syntactic link allows a multidirectional function. In the last two phrases the poet suggests that he might as well "cross" the river (actualize the affair), since refraining from "crossing" would not put a stop to the rumors that have already spread.[35] The poem also relates to Furuhashi's argument in its reference to a toponym with incantatory power (Tatsutagawa), and its repetition of a "negative" morpheme that occurs no fewer than four times—*nakute, naki, watarade,* and *naranaku*—the negations concealing the intensity of the desire for meeting.

The example Furuhashi himself cites is the famous *Kokinshū* 365, the first poem in "Parting," by Ariwara no Yukihira, "Topic Unknown":

> were I to part from you and *go to Inaba* Mountain,
>   and were I to hear that you *pine* for me
>   in the *pines* that grow on the mountain peak
> straightaway would I return to you
> [tati wakare/*inaba* no yama no/mine ni oFuru/*matu* to si kikaba/ima kaFeri komu]

Citing a rendering into modern Japanese, Furuhashi argues that the poem cannot in fact be translated since "it resists meaning" and "does not move toward its [meaning's] construction"; he further claims that the poem works because of its pivot-words *inaba* (the name of a mountain/go away) and *matu* (pine tree/wait) (p. 48). In *Man'yō* poems the poet relies on pillow words and lead-in phrases placed at the head of a poem to preserve or construct ties between a specific sentiment and the communal body; for the *Kokin* poems, the various combinations possible between sound and sense are activated and formalized in the pivot-words. Far from simple lexical play, the doubling takes advantage of the homophonic potential in individual words in order to recuperate an enervated sense (by mid-Heian) of the incantatory power of the poem as a whole.

Furuhashi's attempt to revise modern readings that tend to over-emphasize the "meaning" of Heian waka to the exclusion of their oral or incantatory aspects must be welcomed unreservedly. I also agree that to call such configurations as the pivot-word "poetic device" or "technique" perpetuates a bias that keeps them marginalized and secondary to what is taken to be the poet's "main intent," where readers seek to locate the "universality of a modern humanistic soul" (p. 48). Pivot-words—which may very well have provided the inspiration for a composition (we must rid ourselves of both the notion that "content" precedes "form" and the view that there can be an a priori "human essence" that provides the source for "lyrical" expressions)—link geography to sentiment in a seamless moment in which a cognitive association governs and simultaneously displaces a monological lexical reference.[36] In other words, the poems do not privilege either of the redoubled significations that Furuhashi traces but rather enact its signifying and incantatory processes.[37] A counter-privileging of the rhetorical that has been going on in the West in recent years can now be evoked and read together with the construction of what Furuhashi sees as a phonospirituality that made Heian poets participate and conform to a remythologized communal body.

The reader still might be wondering about the "meaning" of poems such as *Kokinshū* 365 or 433. I would agree that in the former Yukihira clearly suggests continued devotion to a loved one despite the sadness of separation and that in the latter the poet clearly reprimands another person's heartlessness. Doesn't that possibility override the force of both the rhetoric and the incantatory qualities? As in many cases when discussing waka, the answer here lies in the all-important contexts or occasions in which the poem can be situated, providing the metonyms and suggesting appropriate expressions.[38] For instance, the latter poem is clearly a composition on a particular topic: heartvines and laurels, not necessarily as plants but for their associative (communal and incantatory) value and the syllabic possibilities in the patterning of their names that then forms the basis for the other significations. Here emerges a primary *Kokinshū* processual "context": the associative "precedes" other senses. But what are those other senses? Since the poem is anonymous, the poet could be either female (which might be the initial reading) or male. The poet might simply be complaining hyperbolically of inattention (female) or might really be angry (either male or female). In short, there is no single, overriding "other sense": the poem allows various (not infinite) significations anchored in the occasions for which it was composed or collected. I would argue, then, that at this point Furuhashi goes too far in suppressing what he calls the "meaning" of the poems. Poems are not only "about" their incantatory sounds.

The other rhetorical figures that Furuhashi mentions are the "general comparison" (*mitate*, taking one thing as another) and the "associative-word" (*engo*, words, or groups of metonyms, that have come to be associated by convention). He discusses the former, which he calls "the recuperation of incantatory qualities with respect to the meaning of words," by citing two poems, one of which is *Kokinshū* 44, "Spring I," by Lady Ise:[39]

> through the passing year   a mirror for the blossoms
>   the water will become;
> scattering and settling, the blossom-dust
>   they will say, clouds the surface
> [tosi wo Fete/Fana no kagami to/naru mizu Fa/tirikakaru wo ya/
> kumoru to iFu ramu]

Furuhashi refers to the water-as-mirror *mitate*, which leads to the double reading of "clouding over" of a "mirror" by "dust" and covering over of the water's surface by scattered petals, a figure that hinges on the pivot-word *tiri* (scatter/dust), as "the discovery of a new meaning" through a method of "returning the words to their origin (*shigen*), and giving them a different sense" (p. 49).

The notion of *shigen* is problematic in Furuhashi's discussion, since it allows him to claim that practically any polysemic verbal maneuver can qualify as incantatory because it is "returning words to their origin." I would prefer to characterize such moments as originary tropological enactments that aim to reconstruct and preserve the implied communal body in the momentary variation. As for *mitate*, I agree with Suzuki Hideo that it ought to be viewed as a tropological maneuver in which an unexpected metonymic juxtaposition results from a discovery of two references to "natural objects" in contrast to the more general homophonic references to the pivot-word.[40] Suzuki's reading, which rightly emphasizes the purely lexical, associative ground from which the tropes emerge to reconstruct reality (a movement different from the usual tropological logic of "main and secondary" [p. 178], and also "different from the logic of daily life . . . from the beliefs of a communal body, and from mythical conceptions" [p. 179]), must itself be situated, as noted above, in the rarefied atmosphere of the Heian capital, which enabled and required such a lexical focus in the first place, and situated as well in the context of Furuhashi's incantatory problematics and new myth constructions.

Furuhashi discusses the use of the associative-word by citing four poems, one of which is *Kokinshū* 470, "Love I," by the monk Sosei, "Topic Unknown":[41]

> only through gossips   do I hear of you, I am white dew
>   on the chrysanthemums, by night I settle restlessly
> and fade away unable to bear   the fire of a daytime passion
> [oto ni nomi/kiku no *siratuyu*/yoru Fa *okite*/Firu Fa omoFi ni/aFezu
> *kenu*besi]

The associative-words are *siratuyu* (white dew), *oku* (form, or settle on), and *kenu* (evaporate, disappear completely). They are further complicated by three instances of the pivot-word—*kiku* (chrysanthemum/hear about), *okite* ("form," as dew/"wake up, arise"), and *omoFi* ("feel deeply/fire," from the last syllable, *Fi*, which is both "day" and "fire")—and the lead-in to "white dew." According to Furuhashi, the poem does far more than simply articulate a meaning, since the pivot-words depend on the incantatory quality of the lexical items.

As is the case with many poems that inscribe *engo* and *kakekotoba*, *Kokinshū* 470 can be read on two immediately separate levels: as groundless rumor, through the series "hear," "arise with longing," and "feel passionately," or as a reference to natural phenomena through the series "chrysanthemum," "white dew," "form," "day," and "disappear." I agree with Furuhashi that neither series takes precedence over the other and that such examples should not be characterized, as is commonly done, as "richness of expression" (p. 50). In his view the first phrase of the poem and the verb "feel passionately" are sufficient to produce an amatory reading (from a man's point of view), at which point the other natural series "rotates to a position as its trope" (p. 50). I would counter, however, that the position of the poem in the *Kokin* text (as the second poem in "Love I," which begins with a poem series that can be narrativized to tell of lovers not yet seen) also contributes greatly to the amatory reading and that the components of the second series, in any case, are never effaced or simply "rotate to a position as trope." The topic (which is unknown) and the occasion (chrysanthemums = autumn) for which the poem was read would no doubt have activated the chrysanthemum/dew metonyms and provided the impetus for the "sentiment."

Furuhashi ends up endorsing an intent (*kokoro*) behind the words reading that begins to contradict his initial claims. He is saved in part by his attention to the connection between the incantatory aspect of the poems and the need to meld under aestheticopolitical myths a courtier class that had become, in the Heian capital, an abstracted entity no longer tied to tribal villages or ancient communal bodies. The need to construct a new communal body led to a sociorhetorical strategy that aimed to re-create, primarily through verbal means, the long-lost communal body. The so-called poetic devices functioned to allow a practitioner continually to reinforce links with that body, even as they enabled a poet to respond to a given topic in a new and particular way.

The "Kana Preface" and
the Construction of Beginnings

We can now turn to a discussion of the "Kana Preface" itself, particularly in terms of the issues of legitimation, critique, rhetoric, and the installation of waka discourse as a primarily public mode.[42] As I have suggested, a principal aim of the *Kokin* compilers was to reestablish, under imperial sanction, waka (and especially *tanka*) as the valorized poetic form for "public" (*hare*) occasions, *as well as* for private (*ke*) occasions. We have already mentioned the so-called dark age of waka, when the composition of poetry in Chinese flourished in royally sponsored "public" situations, and noted that the term should not be taken to mean that the Japanese stopped composing waka altogether. The "Kana Preface" by Ki no Tsurayuki states: "In our day, ever since the rise of a tendency toward empty ornamentation (*iro*), with people's hearts full of flowery language, there appear only elegantly sensual verses and insubstantial words; poetry is not the preserve of everyone but has become hidden like a log buried at the houses of the amorously inclined (*irogonomi*)." The point being made here is that waka has come to be considered inappropriate for public or official (*mamenaru*) occasions.[43]

The "Kana Preface" represents an attempt to legitimize and recontextualize by continually returning to what it considers to be the roots of waka poetry. The famous first section finds those roots in the human heart, a root (or "seed") that grows into "leaves of words." As we saw above, the mighty power to move things ("heaven and earth," "demons and friendly deities," and "fierce warriors") claimed for poetry was linked by Katagiri to an incantational aspect. The preface tells us further that poetry existed from the time the sky and earth first parted and that it originated in the skies when Princess Shitateru married her visitor Prince Amewaka (Dividing Heaven) to keep him from returning to his celestial home, and on earth with Prince Susanoo, from whose time the thirty-one-syllable poem-song form is said to have arisen. During the prior "age of the gods" the formlessness of the songs made it difficult, we are told, to grasp their import.

After noting the vast number of existent waka accumulated over the decades and the numerous occasions ("praising blossoms," "longing for birds," "being moved by haze," and "saddened by dew") on or for which they were composed, Tsurayuki marks another beginning: the "Naniwazu" poem at the beginning of Emperor Nintoku's reign and the "Asakayama" poem by an *uneme* (palace attendant). He refers to the two as the "father and mother of poem-songs," the ones with which a person begins calligraphy lessons.

Tsurayuki then lists six styles, or types, of poems.[44] In contrast to the "Chinese Preface," which uses the Sino-Japanese term *rikugi* and simply lists the Chinese terms for the six styles, the "Kana Preface" supplies an example for each mode. Received wisdom characterizes the listing in the "Kana Preface" as not much more than an unsuccessful gesture to Chinese precedent, one that, even though it may have effectively secured certification for the status of waka, could only have been a failure, since the categories obviously are neither internally consistent nor appropriate to mid-Heian waka practice. The poems may not fit the categories as employed in texts of Chinese poetics,[45] but they were doubtless selected to fit those categories as they were translated into Japanese practice, and they display a keen awareness of both the rhetoricality of waka language, the interrelationships between words that mark sentiment and those that mark "natural" objects, and, as we have been discussing, the possible sociopolitical (or incantatory) functions relevant to a construction of the capital-based communal body.

There are commentators who take the six modes seriously. One is

Takeoka Masao, who even provides diagrams to help visualize the distinctions between one mode and another. Katagiri too, though he feels that the modes primarily show Tsurayuki's spirit of "play," takes the examples seriously as evincing both a political and a rhetorical aspect (two traditional modes of interpretation). We must also remember that some variant *Kokinshū* texts include interpolations written in by another, unknown commentator whose views contradict those expressed by the author or other writer—particularly in the "Six Modes" section, where even alternate examples appear.

The six modes are as follows:[46] (1) *soFeuta* (indirect style), (2) *kazoFeuta* (enumerative style), (3) *nazuraFeuta* (figurative style), (4) *tatoFeuta* (metaphorical style), (5) *tadagotouta* (correct style), and (6) *iFaFiuta* (eulogistic style). The first mode employs natural references to conceal a sentiment, an admonishment to a prince to accede to the position of emperor (later known as Emperor Nintoku). The implicit sentiment "runs parallel to" (*soFu:* "accompany, run alongside") the "natural" references. The second mode "lists" (*kazoFu:* "count, produce items") the names of three birds, which are actually inscribed as pivot-words hidden in the phrasing, along with two other pivot-words, "illness/arrow" and "shoot/enter." The sentiment hides the listed words. The third mode interconnects, in typical *Kokinshū* fashion, a "natural" reference with a human reference, taking them as "equivalent" elements (*nazuraFu:* "take A and B to be of equal value"); the translation "figurative" does not specify the tropological components. Let us examine the example of the third mode:

> with you here this morning   early the following day
>   if you arise and leave, like frost that leaves the sky
> each time longing overcomes me   I shall fade into
>   constant sorrow
> [kimi ni kesa/asita no simo no/okite inaba/koFisiki goto ni/kie ya wataramu]

The initial segment up to *simo no* forms a lead-in phrase for the pivot-word *okite* ("rise up to leave/settle," like frost), from which the poem modulates into the sentiment of continual longing, with a second pivot at *kie* ("vanish," like the frost, or "die," of sorrow). Those three words are also associative-words. The poem does not simply employ a rhetorical "figure" to enhance a "sentiment" that existed prior to it, but inextricably and equally implicates (*nazuraFu*) the latter in the former, similar to the poems discussed above. The complex time frames add to the indivisibility of the two references: the "present" of the utterance is both "today" and "tomorrow," and the poet surmises a "future" that can exist only hypothetically. Without the lexical base for the metonyms evoked by "frost," the "sentiment," which arises out of (and remains within) the associative-words (we must remember that they participate in a conscious reconstruction and regulation of poetic composition), would not exist.

The fourth mode enacts a "comparison" (*tatoFu:* "take B to explain/ as an example of A") of different parts of the poem:

> my passionate yearnings   no counting can exhaust them,
>   though every last grain of fine sand
> along the rough sea's shore   were counted to exhaustion
> [waga koFi Fa/yomu tomo tukizi/ariso umi no/hama no masago Fa/ yomitukusu tomo]

We are not dealing with a general "metaphor," as the English might suggest. The poet juxtaposes a sentiment and a reference to natural objects through an example. The word repeated twice, *yomu*, which can mean both "count" and "compose"[47] as well as "read," its common modern definition, turns the poem into one "about" its own composition. That repetition joined by another, the word *tuku* (exhaust), becomes a further example of the incantatory dimension we saw in Furuhashi's discussion.

The fifth mode, translated "correct style," is closer to "direct style" (*tada:* "straight, direct")—a poem, in other words, not cast in a particular rhetorical mode.[48] And the sixth and final mode, translated "eulogistic style,"[49] refers not only to laudatory poems but to those that specifically perform an incantatory act in order to protect from harm the person, place, or object in question (*iFaFu:* "invocation [i.e., supplication, to the gods, through appropriate verbal and other gestures] of good fortune, safety, abundance, and so on").

After the "buried log" section cited above, Tsurayuki invokes another beginning. Poems, he tells us, "when we recall their beginnings," initially were not only meant for private, amatory occasions. After a brief comment on emperors who would summon their attendants and have them compose poems on spring mornings and autumn evenings, he then gives a long list of examples that specify which toponyms and other expressions are appropriate to which feelings. To take just a few: "longing for a person by placing an expression alongside (*yosoFu*) smoke from Mt. Fuji; thinking about a friend in the cries of the bell cricket (*matu musi*); feeling a kinship with the pines of Takasago and Suminoe, as if they had aged along with you; recalling the past when you were a man mountain (*wotokoyama*); resenting the brief moment when you were a maiden flower (*womina-Fesi*); you utter poem-songs and find solace in them."[50] As commentators note, each of the examples given in the preface corresponds to a poem or poems found in the collection.

After listing many more examples, Tsurayuki demarcates yet another beginning when he mentions the "Nara reign period" (*nara no oFon toki*), which is thought to refer either to Emperor Kammu, who reigned during the move of the capital from Nara to Heian, or to the next emperor, Kammu's son Heizei.[51] The period marks the point when "they [*uta*] begin especially to be widely composed; [and] the emperor himself understands profoundly the spirit of the poem-songs." Two *Man'yōshū* poets, Kakinomoto no Hitomaro and Yamabe no Akahito, are cited as the most illustrious of the earlier ages,[52] and *Man'yōshū* is also mentioned by name. Tsurayuki stresses that "only one or two persons are left who are familiar with both the events of the past and the spirit of the poem-songs (*uta no kokoro*)" (p. 57). In his brief waka history Tsurayuki next offers the famous short critiques of the Six Poetic Geniuses (Rokkasen): Archbishop Henjō (815–890), Ariwara no Narihira (825–880), Ono no Komachi (fl. 850), Bunya no Yasuhide (fl. 860–879), the (Uji Mountain) priest Kisen (?), and Ōtomo no Kuronushi (ca. 824 or 835–923). As mentioned above, the compilers, in their effort to regulate the parameters of waka composition, found it necessary to criticize rhetorical imbalances in poems by the Rokkasen. Consequently, the critiques show a decided concern with *sama*, which I take to refer to "rhetorical mode," and with the well-known terms "spirit" (*kokoro*) and "words" (*kotoba*), which do not correspond simply to "content" and "form."

Tsurayuki illustrates each critique with a brief but incisive comment. Regarding Henjō, for example, he tells us that, although he had a grasp of *sama*, his compositions lack *makoto*, a term meaning something like "genuine intent," "sincere motive," or "truthful and convincing correspondence," which has continually been valued in Japan:[53] "For example, it is as if he [Henjō] sees a woman painted in a picture and pretends to be moved by it."[54] As for Narihira, "his sentiments are excessive; his words are insufficient; like a wilting flower, without color, whose fragrance lingers on." In other words, the sentiments cannot be reined in and controlled by a diction that is overdetermined. Regarding Komachi, the third (together with the first two just mentioned) most important Rokkasen poet, the critique is striking for its gender marking. First, she is placed within the poetic genealogy of an ancient female poet, Sotohori-hime;[55] then the term *aFare* (deeply moving), absent from the "Chinese Preface," appears: "there is a deeply moving quality to her [and her poetry] that is without strength"; then, "in other words, she resembles a high-ranking woman who is troubled [both physically and emotionally]; it isn't strong because it is a woman's poem-song" (p. 59). Commentators, all male, typically take the woman to be physically ill and take her lack of strength to result from that malady.[56] Tsurayuki, however, seems to be critiquing, in his use of the terms *nayamu* and *tuyokarazu*, which add an ambivalence absent in the Chinese, a focus on a feminine sensibility as it responds to social conditions that produce an affective power arising out of intense grief and longing.[57] I take the lack of strength to refer to a (gender-based) difference rather than simply to an illness. The term *aFare* will become valorized by later women writers, especially Murasaki Shikibu. Here I choose to read it as an inaugural *hiragana* instance of (perhaps self-interested) male empathy for a woman and her condition. The term later becomes installed as a keyword to characterize Heian culture by those very women who became empowered with that *hiragana* discourse. Finally, even the phrasing of the Komachi critique differs from that of the five men. Whereas the latter critiques all end with the *kambun*-like *gotosi* (like, as), the word doesn't appear in Komachi's critique at all (although it does appear in the "Chinese Preface"); Tsurayuki uses instead the native term *nitari* (resembles).[58]

The section ends with another comment on *sama:* there have appeared a great many poets who toss words around, but for them poem-songs are "thought of simply as poems; they do not understand their *sama*" (p. 59). After announcing the present reign period, listing the four compilers, and telling us that they were imperially commanded to present their own poems and those that do not appear in *Man'yōshū*, Tsurayuki finally concludes the "Kana Preface" with another section filled with rhetorical-incantatory moments that emphasize the importance of the four seasons and with auspicious words to guarantee the permanence of waka for the Heian capital as well as for all time. Each comment is made under the auspices of pillow words, poetic pillows, lead-in phrases, and pivot-words. Here are a few: "if they [poem-songs] are willow branches never to be severed, pine needles never to scatter, lengthy vines trailing on to coming generations, and the tracks of birds enduring for a long time, those persons who understand the rhetorical modes (*sama*) of the poem-song and grasp its spirit, how can they not look to the past as one looks to the moon in the vast firmament and feel a profound longing for our present age?" (p. 62).[59]

Time and Other Beginnings

In conjunction with the above discussion, let us examine briefly the poems placed at the beginning of the collection and trace the temporal vectors in the *Kokinshū* composition-recitation-narrativization arrangement. The first poem, much maligned by Masaoka Shiki (among others) as "only an exercise in forced logic," is by Ariwara no Motokata:

> Having been composed on the day on which spring falls in the old year,
> within the year   spring has indeed arrived
>   this one year period
> are we to call it last year?   or shall we call it this year?
> [tosi no uti ni/Faru Fa kinikeri/Fitotose wo/kozo to ya iFamu/kotosi to ya iFamu]

As commentators note, every few years the first day of the new year according to the lunar calendar and the beginning of spring, signaled by the vernal equinox (based on the movement of the sun), did not coincide, thus providing the disjunction marked in Motokata's poem-song.[60] One point of interpretive difficulty has been the word *Fitotose*. Past interpretations include the following (Takeoka Masao's listing): (1) the old year up to the equinox, (2) the period between the equinox and New Year's Day, (3) the whole year to New Year's Day, (4) the day of the equinox itself. After examining various poems which use the word, Takeoka concludes that since *Fitotose* refers to a year period containing only one nodal day (festival, solstice, or equinox), it refers in Motokata's poem to two different years, which can then be referred to as either "last year" or "this year."[61]

We must also address the question of why an allegedly inferior poem, by an inferior poet, is placed at the head of such an important collection. One response is that the compilers were not so much interested in producing a collection of the very best poems available as in constructing a poetic handbook of the possible subtle variations in topic and time, thus providing would-be poets with model poems appropriate for practically any occasion.[62] Some scholars have suggested that the compilers wanted to give a sense of the eagerness with which the courtiers awaited spring. I would also emphasize other considerations: by placing a poem with a temporal problematic at the very beginning, the compilers foreground temporal complexity, which will find repeated demonstration in poems throughout the collection. Consequently, *Kokinshū* 1 not only problematizes the notion of a temporal "beginning," but it links the new beginning to a previous temporal frame, thus marking simultaneously the cyclical nature of the seasons: time does not begin ex nihilo. Furthermore, when we remember that Motokata's grandfather was Narihira himself, the question becomes whether the compilers, by placing an Ariwara poem first, were also signaling a link both to the semilegendary figure who had close ties with the Ki family and to other figures associated with him.[63] Finally, following Furuhashi's discussion, we see that the word *tosi* (year) and its variants are repeated in incantatory fashion no fewer than four times (*tosi, Fitotose, kozo,* and *kotosi*— actually five, if we count the prefatory note), providing an appropriate rhythmical-spiritual opening for the collection. Commentators note the absence of "natural" references, but in the two words *tosi* and *Faru* (spring), we can read an enactment of the intertwining of a "human" temporal construction (the calendrical year) with a "natural" process (the sun's movement) in a move reminiscent of the "rhetorical-incantatory" issue discussed above.

The second poem of the collection, by Tsurayuki, continues the temporal problematic:

> Having been composed on the day spring arrives,
> water we scooped in cupped hands   drenching our sleeves
>   has long been frozen over;
> might the breezes that blow this day of spring's arrival
>   be melting even now?
> [sode Fitite/musubisi mizu no/koForeru wo/Faru tatu keFu no/kaze
> ya tokuramu]

Tsurayuki begins by evoking a time (the previous summer) when someone (the poet or other persona) scooped up water in cupped hands. He then marks the transformation of the water into a frozen state forming a bridge to winter and on into the present new "spring" moment. Thus he also implies a contrast—resulting from the juxtaposition with Motokata's poem—to the first day of the calendrical "new year." Along with the temporal progression, there is a further contrast between the words *musubu* ("tie together," and also "cup hands together and scoop up") and *toku* ("untie," and also "melt"), both words also suggestive of sexual-spiritual tyings and untyings. The poem ends with an indeterminate surmise that leaves the question open-ended, echoing the questioning that ended the first poem.[64] As we read the *Kokinshū* series, then, we not only move from one "associative-progressive" moment to another, but each unit in the series complicates the time scheme in such a way that forces a backward as well as forward reading movement.[65] Furthermore, as if in collusion with that temporal complexity, rhetorical-incantatory maneuvers often result in an interpretive impossibility and undecidability (what I have just called open-endedness) as well.

The last example is the anonymous third poem ("Topic Unknown"):

> the haze of a spring whose start is over
>   where does it rise and drift?
>   on the fair hills of Yoshino
> on the Yoshino hills   the snow continues to fall
> [Farugasumi/tateru ya izuko/miyosino no/yosino no yama ni/yuki Fa Furitutu]

The poet combines both temporal and spatial disjunctions, while adding another link with the two previous poems at *Faru* (spring) and *tatu* (stand, begin). The first segment, "spring haze," can also be read "spring departs,"[66] which immediately confuses the temporal scheme. The first two segments can even be read as a reference to a future moment: when spring ends, for what land will you depart? Otherwise, what ought to be the case in one realm, the "haze" that should be rising elsewhere (cf. "this year" and "melting" in the first two poems), is paradoxical to another realm, the snow that still falls here, where the poetic persona stands (cf. "last year," "frozen over"). For the current series, the coming of spring is apprehended only in conjunction with an awareness of winter and the past. The particle *ya* also reappears to complicate readerly interpretation, and the repetition of "Yoshino" provides another phase in the construction of the communal body. The temporal problematics and linkings in the first three poem-songs continue throughout the *Kokinshū* books, and we occasionally find the compilers consolidating potential poetic links into longer, determinate narrative sequences, as in the Tanabata poems in "Autumn I" (*Kokinshū* 173–183) and the "Love" books.

Engo and Narrative

Engo provides a generative and adhesive mechanism by means of which not only a single poem but a complete narrative (or narrating) moment or sequence might arise. I shall conclude this chapter by discussing the ways *engo* was employed and its relation to the construction of a narrating. Let us take, first of all, a single instance, the anonymous poem *Kokinshū* 675, "Topic Unknown," "Love III":

> all because of you,   my name flourishes, spreads
> it is now the mists of spring
> filling the fields, the hills   drifting into every corner
> [kimi ni yori/waga no Fa Fana ni/Farugasumi/no ni mo yama ni mo/
> tatimitinikeri]

The numerous narrative possibilities quickly become obvious. The words *kasumi* (mist), *no* (fields), *yama* (hills or mountains), and *miti* (be saturated) function as associative-words, and the pivot-words further disseminate the associations: *Fana* ("flower" and "in a flowery [i.e., widespread gossipy] manner"); *no* and *yama* ("fields and hills" and "society"); *Farugasumi* ("mist" and "reputation"); *Faru* also means "to swell," as in the swelling of buds); and the verb *tati* (*tatsu*, "rise, as mist," and "spread" [i.e., gain a reputation]). We also find a lead-in phrase, *Fana ni Farugasumi*, which guides the reading into the last two phrases. The human references in the first two phrases and the natural ones in the last two converge at the end of the free-floating lead-in phrase *waga na Fa Fana ni Farugasumi*, where the poem pivots to initiate the double movement: a name magically turns into a flower that calls forth references to nature. The natural, however, does not supplant the human, nor does the human displace the natural; the natural comes to wear a human face, a kind of prosopopeia, that is carried over from the first two phrases. From these associations it is easy to imagine the poem inspiring a brief narrative, set in spring when the mists hang heavy, about an affair that the gossips have gotten wind of.

Again, the reader might ask: isn't the poet simply blaming someone for damage done to his or her name? And again, the answer lies partially in the placement of the poem. The next to last poem in "Love III," it appears as part of a series of poems that incorporate the same topic: damaged reputation. The figure of birds suddenly taking flight in the immediately preceding poem suggests the spreading of gossip. The last poem of the section, another one by Lady Ise, uses in a similar fashion the figure of dust rising to the sky. So placed, its resonances with neighboring poems take precedence over its status as a solitary verse to be interpreted for general "meaning"; in any case, we can never know its "original" occasion.

In a "poem-tale" like the *Ise monogatari* text, poetic metonyms suggest precisely the short narratives that form "foretexts" for the poem.[67] The first *dan* represents a ritualized foretext (the "man" has just come of age) created out of a poem that supplies the "pretext" for that foretext: place (Kasuga Plain), young woman (suggested by "young purple"), and attitude (confused feelings, especially given his entry into adolescence). The movement of reversal constitutes the *Ise* text itself, which becomes in turn a pretext for a "life" of Narihira.[68]

In the *Genji* tale the narrating of crucial moments often leads to a cluster of metonyms that link a whole series of narrating moments.[69] Let us preview the discussion of the *Genji* text by reading the narration of Murasaki's death, a good example of a narrativized waka moment. The major section, figured around the metonym "dew," follows a scene in which Murasaki hints that her end is near.[70] The passage begins by evoking autumn, which brings welcome relief from the summer heat but also signifies death. Murasaki is better, but it takes little (*tomosureba*) for her condition to grow worse. The narrator tells us "she passes her days with the dew hanging heavy" (p. 489). The empress (the Akashi Lady's child by Genji) comes for a visit followed by Genji, and Murasaki gazes out at her garden "one evening, when a strong wind has started up."[71] Genji is pleased to see "even a slight improvement in her condition" (she has raised herself up onto an arm rest), but it is "difficult for her to bear; how devastated he will soon be, she thinks, and, sunk deep in sadness, she recites." Her poem retrieves the dew metonym and adds another, bush clover (*hagi*):

> you see it form   but for a fleeting moment;
>   at the slightest brush
> of wind it scatters: the dew atop the *hagi* leaves

[oku to miru/Fodo zo Fakanaki/tomosureba/kaze ni midaruru/Fagi no uFa tuyu]

Murasaki compares her condition (through *oku*, "rise up," as of a body and "form/settle," as of dew) to the fragility of the dew before the wind and also echoes the word *tomosureba* seen earlier. After telling us it is a fitting comparison, the narrating gives us Genji's poem:

> at the slightest nudge   we are the dew competing to fade away
>   in this dewdrop world;
> let no time elapse   between the first to go and the last
> [yaya mo seba/kie wo arasoFu/tuyu no yo ni/okure sakidatu/Fodo
> Fezu mogana]

Genji responds to Murasaki's *tomosureba* with *yaya mo seba*, to *oku* with *sakidatu*, and to *Fakanaki* (fleeting) with *kie* (fade away) and repeats the word "dew" to suggest the hope that he does not outlive her. The empress then offers her poem:

> against the autumn winds   it stays not even an instant
>   the dew in this dewdrop world,
> who sees it as simply a matter   of leaves and grasses?
> [akikaze ni/sibasi tomaranu/tuyu no yo wo/tare ka kusaba no/uFe to
> nomi min]

A few lines later it becomes clearer that Murasaki is failing. When the empress takes her hand, the narrator remarks, "it seems she is truly like the dew about to fade away" (p. 492). Then the end finally arrives: "Throughout the night, [Genji] sees to it that everything possible is done for her, but to no avail; day breaks, and she has vanished completely away" (p. 492). By means of metonymic clusters—autumn, wind, dew/tears, bush clover, vanish, scatter—the narrating merges in its incantations a particular situation with the larger Heian communal body, each poem, as well as other phrases used by the narrator, evoking conventional intertexts.[72]

I have attempted to situate the *Kokinshū* text in terms of its reception in Japan and the United States. It is my contention that we must reexamine accepted ways of considering poetry and poetic composition and, by extension, "literature." We can start by taking seriously the incantatory aspects of the poems and asking how they might alter our views of what we tend to consider "poetic devices," "convention," and "meaning," and thus "open up" the text "to historical reality," in this case the Heian "communal body," for which the collection becomes a magnificently constructed emblem. As I have also tried to demonstrate, the "Kana Preface," often read (and written off) as simply a rehashing of the "Chinese Preface," must be reread in terms of the aestheticopolitical circumstances that gave rise to the collection and in terms of the advent of a "public" *hiragana* discourse. The care with which waka were arranged and narrativized into intricately interlaced networks parallels the desire of the compilers to impose order and control over poetic form and composition and at the same time to institute and legitimize the use of *hiragana* for different public occasions. The poems were selected to illustrate the rhythms of "nature" and human sentiment and to provide examples for regulating both public and private arenas. The resulting links between poems offer endless opportunities for readerly input. Sections of the collection lend themselves to reading in a variety of sequential ways, for example, in terms of an extended narrative based on sentiment (a love affair), spatial movement (travel), folklore-based story (Tanabata—seventh of the Seventh Month), or temporal vignettes (seasonal moments). As my reading of the first three poems shows, however, interpretive maneuvers must keep readerly perspective anchored at each poetic moment owing to the need to follow temporal vectors that often move in complex directions. The situation immediately problematizes, of course, any emergent "story" and prevents simple valorization of narrativization itself.

4

An Early Figure of Resistance:
Lady Ise

This chapter discusses the private poetry collection (*shikashū*) of a woman known as Lady Ise (also as Ise, Ise no go, or Ise no miyasu[n]dokoro). Gaining renown while serving in the "salon" of Empress Atsuko (872–907; known also as Onshi, and as the Empress of the Seventh Ward, she was the daughter of the powerful Fujiwara leader Mototsune [836–891] and consort of Emperor Uda [r. 887–897]), Ise is a hitherto insufficiently recognized forerunner of women like Murasaki Shikibu and Sei Shōnagon, who were to play similar roles in similar salons (organized around Emperor Ichijō's consorts Akiko and Sadako, respectively) almost a century later. Her poetry collection *Ise shū* (Ise Collection), especially the thirty or so poems placed at the beginning, provides another example of the way poems were collected and recontextualized (or narrativized), supplementing our discussions of the *Kokinshū* text and the *Ise* tale and also serving as pretext for our discussion of *Genji* and later feminine discourse. Ise is often mentioned in the same breath with the venerable Ki no Tsurayuki, and her "name" happens to be a metonym for the puzzling title of the tale that suggests the life of Ariwara no Narihira.

The Reputation

Although we possess only scant knowledge of her life, the exalted position Ise occupied in the sociopolitical and poetic world of her time becomes apparent in several ways. In *Shinsen zuinō*, an early waka treatise by the scholar-poet Fujiwara no Kintō (966–1041), this note follows a citation of a poem by Ise: "This is a poem that Lady Ise (Ise no go) showed to [her daughter] Nakatsukasa saying, 'Poems should be composed like this.'"[1] Kintō places the poem directly after the Tsurayuki composition that begins his discussion. Ise's poem was prized by later poets as a fine example of how to employ poetic toponyms (*uta makura*, here *Nagara no Fashi*, "Nagara Bridge") and is itself based on a poem in which the toponym functions as a metonym for "aged." The Kintō citation attests to Ise's reputation as one of the most brilliant and highly regarded waka poets of her time, a time when official poetry was dominated by men. Here is the poem (*Kokinshū* 1051, "Eccentric Poems"), followed by the one it cites (*Kokinshū* 890, "Miscellaneous I," Anonymous).

> in Naniwa stands   old Nagara Bridge
>   now it too, they say, is being rebuilt,
> what is left for me to compare   this aging body of mine?
> [naniFa naru/nagara no Fasi mo/tukuru nari/ima Fa waga mi wo/nani ni tatoFemu]
>
> in this world   the things that have aged completely:
>   there's Nagara Bridge   in the province of Tsu
>   and there's myself, that's all
> [yo no naka ni/Furinuru mono Fa/tu no kuni no/Nagara no hasi to/ware to narikeri] (154, *SST* 1:252)

Ise's ability to create new poetic expressions, as in the following, was widely recognized.

> While she was staying at the palace, a man sent, unbeknownst to others, a note saying, "I can't help feeling that you're hiding from me." This was her reply:
> this stream of sorrowful thoughts   that flows unceasingly
>   can I vanish without meeting
> you, whose life is as fleeting   as those very bubbles?
> [omoFigaFa/taezu nagaruru/mizu no awa no/utakatabito ni/aFade kiemeya] (304, *SST* 1:256)

Not found in extant poems previous to the above, the term *omoFigaFa* became a favorite of later poets, especially from the time of Fujiwara no Teika.[2] The two examples indicate that Ise was something of a poet's poet, helping to stabilize the native poetic language by creating new (incantatory) expressions later appropriated by poet-scholars like Kintō and Teika. The latter two poets represent a larger tradition, which includes the *Genji* author (who also cites Ise's poetry),[3] that placed high value on Ise's innovative skill.

Included among the so-called Thirty-six Poetic Geniuses, Ise was the only female poet of note during the age of the *Kokinshū* compilers and the best-represented female poet in each of the first three imperially commissioned waka collections.[4] Of the seventy-four poems by women in the *Kokin* collection, for example, the poems by Ise (twenty-two) and Komachi (eighteen) form more than half.[5] The number of poems by Ise selected for *Gosenshū* is particularly striking. Her seventy-two, only four fewer than Tsurayuki's seventy-six, contrasts markedly with Mitsune's third-place total of twenty-three. *Shūishū* (ca. 1005) includes twenty-five of her waka, putting her seventh overall but only two behind the total of Minamoto no Shitagō (911–983). Moreover, in the case of *Kokinshū*, the seriate placement of Ise's poems in the collection is as significant as quantity. Since as a general rule the editors chose the first and last entries of each of the books with special care, often placing their own compositions at the more important divisions, the placement of four of Ise's twenty-two poems at the ends of "Spring I," "Longing III," "Miscellaneous II," and "Long Poems" shows the esteem in which Ise must have been held. She is also mentioned by name twice in *The Tale of Genji*, each time together with Tsurayuki, whose name appears four times. The famous opening line of the *Genji* tale, "In the reign of which emperor was it, I wonder," is considered a gesture to the beginning of an *Ise shū* variant text.[6] The *Genji* author's debt to Ise is evident in other areas of her narrative as well.

Ise also composed a large number of poems for paintings on standing screens (*byōbu-e*). Often commissioned in conjunction with the activities sponsored for a felicitous public occasion (for example, an emperor or empress's fortieth birthday), screen poems (*byōbu uta*) were formal and demanding compositions entrusted only to the most eminent of poets. Ise's production, which rivals that of Tsurayuki and Mitsune, further attests to her extraordinary reputation.[7] Such screen poems were not always composed simply in praise of a pictorial illustration but often represented the utterances of the figures in the picture. In other words, the poet recited a poem standing in the place of the figure on the screen. Particularly interesting in Ise's case and for our study is the "stance" adopted by the woman in each exchange. Here are two situations.

> The same man arrives and, while loitering by the gate, he hears a *hototogisu* in the orange tree. He composes the following and sends it in:
> is it because he pities me   standing by the gate?
>   the nightingale
> perched in song upon   a branch of the flowering orange tree
> [to ni tateru/ware ya kanasiki/hototogisu/Fanatatibana no/eda ni wite naku]
>
> The reply:
> it takes no notice   at all of you

the nightingale:
to perch on trees and sing   is not that its natural bent?
[nanika tomo/kimi woba sirazi/hotogisu/kinagara naku Fa/saga ni
yaFa aranu] (38 and 39, *SST* 1:249)

In the second situation,

Having heard that she has come out into the autumn fields to view
flowers, the man approaches and recites,
I hear that you have   come out to the autumn fields,
      miscanthus now in bloom,
are you not beckoning me   in secret invitation?
[aki no no ni/idenu to kiku wo/Fanasusuki/sinobi ni ware wo/maneki
yaFa senu]

She replies,
if it knew at all   of your whereabouts
      miscanthus now in bloom,
would it be beckoning   to an empty sky?
[idukata ni/ari to siraba ka/Fanasusuki/Fakanaki sora wo/
manekitateramu] (44 and 45, *SST* 1:252)

The stance adopted in the second poem of each pair, which
appears as part of a series of seasonal poems, echoes the cold-hearted
attitude found in the majority of the poems in the inaugural section of
the *Ise Collection*, discussed below. The group of twenty or so poems
Ise composed for standing screens forms a continuous narrative
thread, and the language resembles sections of a "poem-tale" where
the participants remain simply "the man" and "the woman." The
increasing popularity of the practice of composing poems for screens
is thought to be intimately connected with the rise of narratives and,
more important, the manner in which narratives were received. As
the famous section 147 of *Yamato monogatari* (The Tales of Yamato)
illustrates, a poet composed as if he or she were the figure depicted,[8]
with the same poet often composing both the man's and woman's
poems as in the case above. In other words, in situations where a man
and a woman appeared in a scene, the pictorial suggestion of an
amorous encounter could be transformed into any number of fictive
situations by the poems accompanying the particular screen panel.
The poetic composition by the assigned poet would then be transcribed, as noted previously, onto a section at the top of the panel (a
blank square called the *shikishi*) by a noted calligrapher. Here again
the potential for "fictionalization" becomes an intimate part of the

production process, which is at the same time a component of the overall viewing process. The stylized figures in the painting (they were usually given no distinguishing features) are then reflected in the anonymity of the subjects of the poetic exchange. In narrative texts, however, the reader would know the composer's identity. For example, we know the poets in the *Genji* scenes where only the graphs for "man" and "woman" distinguish the various speakers in the text, and we know that Narihira was the poet constantly being suggested in the *Tale of Ise*. Passages that would normally be read as important "sources" of information about Ise's life inhabit a narrative register similar to what I have described for the screen-painting poems.

Ise's poetic mastery was such that her presence was mandatory at waka poetry contests (*uta awase*), which began to thrive as a result of the renewed emphasis on poems composed in the native language. She was the only woman included in one of the earliest and most important contests, "The Poetry Contest of the Empress During the Kampyō Era" ("Kampyau no oFontoki kisai no miya no uta awase," 893), and she was appointed recorder, a prestigious position, for another contest, "The Poetry Contest Held at the Teiji Villa" ("Teizi-win no uta awase," 913). We know from contest records that judgments for particular rounds often tended to favor Ise's compositions, even when pitted against those of the great Tsurayuki.

> Poem from the left, Ise:
> meetings with you   came to an end long ago
>   from this body of mine
> how many tears, I wonder,   have now flowed?
> [aFu koto no/kimi ni taenisi/waga mi yori/ikura no namida/nagare idenuramu]
>
> Poem from the right, Tsurayuki:
> when my longing for you   has grown to excess
>   try though I may to hide it
> how depressing to think   that others will surely know
> [kimi koFi no/amarinisikaba/sinoburedo/Fito no siruramu/koto no wabisisa] (Hagitani Boku, *Uta–awaseshū*, 63)

Although partial toward Ise's poem, the emperor calls the round a draw after those on Tsurayuki's side complain of biased judgment. Regardless of the specific merits modern readers might choose to find in the poems, the example suggests that Ise was indeed a worthy opponent for Tsurayuki.

The "Life"

Perhaps it is fitting that a woman whose life was so intimately interconnected with poetry should, like Narihira, be viewed primarily through that poetry. Recently, two eminent scholars of Heian literature, Katagiri Yōichi and Akiyama Ken, published in the same year (1985) books entitled *Ise*. As a major component of their portraits of the poet, they present close readings of the first thirty-two (Katagiri) or thirty-three (Akiyama) poems from *Ise shū*. That initial group of poems is usually referred to as Ise's "diary" (*nikki*), after the designation by the Edo *kokugaku* scholar Ban Nobutomo (1773–1846).[9] Akiyama's reading follows Nobutomo in regarding the section as a "diary," whereas Katagiri opts, correctly in my opinion, to emphasize the fictive aspect of the collection, preferring throughout to call it "narrative-like" (*monogatari-teki*).[10]

Before turning to that section and the important questions it raises concerning the relation of poetry to (fictional) narration, a brief account of Ise's family lineage will not only help us situate the poet in the political and social arenas of her time but provide important intertexts for the *Genji* discussion. Ise's father, Tsugukage, was a member of the northern branch of the Fujiwara clan and belonged to the third generation descended from Manatsu (d. 829), who was the older brother of the powerful minister of the left Fuyutsugu (d. 826). Although the northern branch as a whole produced many of the most prominent officials of the day, it was Fuyutsugu's descendants, and in particular men like Yoshifusa, Mototsune, and Tokihira, who suppressed other branches of the clan and rose to the highest political positions. Having been on the losing side in a struggle for power in which Fuyutsugu rose to prominence in 810,[11] Manatsu's line had to settle for lower-ranking posts. Ise's father's rank seems to have been among the lowest, even though he was able to rise to the junior fifth rank. As one of the mid-level officials known as *zuryō*,[12] Tsugukage, much like Murasaki Shikibu's father, Tametoki, spent a good part of his career as a governor of various provinces including Ise, Yamato, Satsuma, and Oki. Ise's sobriquet itself derives from the fact that she entered Atsuko's service while her father was governor of Ise Province. As was often the case with such officials, Tsugukage acquired a strong background in history and Chinese letters at the Heian Academy (*daigaku ryō*) and went on to occupy posts requiring skill in written composition. Ise's grandfather, Muneie, left his mark in history as the founder of Hōkai Temple at Hino, south of the capital, and her uncle and cousin both served for a time as head of the academy (*daigaku no kami*). Poems by Manatsu's fifth son appear in *Kokinshū*, and Tsugukage's cousin was also a noted poet. Having been raised in a family of such prominent scholars and poets, Ise would have benefited from opportunities for learning and resources similar to those of her more celebrated successors.

The presence of such a talented woman would hardly have gone unnoticed by people at court,[13] especially those Fujiwara hegemons always on the lookout for competent tutors for their daughters. Among the reasons advanced concerning why Ise entered Atsuko's service are the following: (1) the usual view that Ise was to be a governess to Fujiwara daughters, an attendant-companion to the empress, or a wet nurse for Atsuko's doubtless soon-to-be-born offspring; (2) the political view that her grandfather took advantage of his close ties with the Fujiwara, especially Atsuko's aunt, and planned early on for her to enter court service; and (3) the view that Fujiwara strategists viewed her as a kind of "saftey valve" in the event that Atsuko failed to perform one of her prime duties as empress and produce a male Fujiwara offspring. The argument summarized by Akiyama is that the court of Emperor Uda differed markedly from the later one of Emperor Ichijō (with Sei Shōnagon and Murasaki Shikibu) in that in the former women from families other than the Fujiwara were able to attain the elite positions of junior or senior consort (*kōi* and *nyōgo*).[14] Political strategy—i.e., the Fujiwara desire that their daughters bear future emperors and other high-ranking officials—eventually led to a virtual monopoly of the highest court positions by their own women. The situation during Ise's time was still fluid and could have accommodated a socially and politically ambiguous situation.[15] Whether or not Akiyama's hypothesis is correct, "literary" language, or rather language itself, often ends up playing by its own rules, and Ise, an adroit wordsmith, used the *hiragana* language with great skill, particularly to reject the advances of those very Fujiwara who sought to profit from her position in the first place. In the fate of her father's lineage lay excellent reasons for such resistance.

Resistance and Male Desire

Once at court Ise became a focus of male desire, and she remained so throughout her long life (she is believed to have been born around 875 and died after 938), becoming involved in a series of entanglements with some of the most important figures of her time. Among them were Fujiwara no Tokihira (875–945, a man destined for notoriety owing to his banishment of the great scholar-official Sugawara no Michizane, 845–903); the poet and well-known lover Taira no Sadafumi (d. 923); and even Emperor Uda himself, whom she bore a son who died in childhood. Her final liaison, with Emperor Uda's brother, Prince Atsuyoshi, produced a daughter known as Nakatsukasa, who inherited her mother's talents and went on to win acclaim as a poet.

Despite the obvious possibilities for fictional re-creations of her life, Ise never achieved the legendary status of an Ono no Komachi or an Ariwara no Narihira. Her reputation as a composer of formal-public poetry, rather than informal-private poetry as in Komachi's case, might have had something to do with it; so might her political status at Atsuko's court. She does not, however, completely escape fictional contagion. Indeed, as I have stated, we can observe an attempt to create within sections of her personal poetry collection a definite fictive "stance." The poetry collection must therefore be seen not as a simple "collection" of poems but rather as a space wherein her "public" poems have been transformed according to a particular attitude. Since the collection is also a major source of information on her life, a reading of it requires that we confront at the same time the problem of biographical "fact" and its relation to waka discourse, a confrontation that the *Ise* tale takes to radical lengths. The real life figure of Ise the "author" does not become the "origin" or "source" of texts bearing her name; rather the texts or textuality "create" the life and the figure of the author. The author becomes, to use a term that has gained great currency, an "effect" of the texts. In other words, since we in fact possess very little verifiable information, what we produce will always be vulnerable to the charge of misrepresentation. As we shall see, however, waka lend themselves to manipulation in ways that always prefigure the possibility of multiple readings (misreadings). If we cannot produce a clear portrait of Ise's life, the attempt nevertheless involves us further not only in issues that lie at the heart of Heian studies but also in matters being debated in contemporary criticism, such as the very possibility of interpretative validity and the discourse of sexual politics as well as the relation between biography and poetic discourse, fact and fiction.

As noted above, the section of Ise's poetry referred to by Nobutomo as a "diary" comprises the first thirty-two poems (actually poems together with the prefatory notes) of her private poetry collection. The collection exists today in multiple textual lineages, a situation common to all Heian period "literary" texts. Akiyama and Katagiri, for example, although they base their readings on different variants, compare their "base text" (*teihon* or *sokobon*) with the other versions whenever appropriate. Three representative versions of the different lineages are included in a volume of the monumental *Shikashū taisei*. The number of poems in those three texts ranges from 483 to 512 to 315. In the following, I present a reading of the initial "diary" section of *Ise shū* using the third variant included in the compendium, since it enables an intertextual reading with the *Genji* tale.

The initial section of the *Ise Collection* commemorates, through interpersonal poetry exchanges and lengthy prefatory notes, moments in Ise's relationships with several, primarily male, figures (the lone exception being Atsuko). The personages that can be identified are, in their order of appearance: (1) Fujiwara no Nakahira; (2) his (and Atsuko's) older brother, Tokihira; (3) a son-in-law of a minister who has been exiled; (4) Taira no Sadafumi (the Heichū of *Heichū monogatari*); (5) Emperor Uda; (6) Empress Atsuko; (7) Sadafumi again; and (8) Atsuko again. The poems address a topic common to all *monogatari*: the relations (most often of an amorous nature) between men and women. The problem, of course, is that the *Ise Collection* is not a *monogatari* or, rather, that it begins to put into question just what waka, waka collections, and *monogatari* are, which raises again the question of "genre." Katagiri's use of the term "poetic narrative" suggests that the text be given a narrativized reading similar to that demanded by *Ise monogatari* and sections of *Kokinshū*. I fully agree with Katagiri's position, and although I cannot delve into all of the problems here, I shall point out a few important aspects.

The derivation of the opening line of the *Ise Collection* has been a subject of controversy due to its similarity to the beginning lines of *The Tale of Genji*. Some, as noted, have argued that whoever wrote the opening borrowed from the *Genji* text. The assumption here will be that the opening to the *Ise Collection* predates the *Genji* opening. Although the line—"In the reign of which emperor was it, I wonder?"—obscures temporal reference, thereby suggesting a fictional time, comparison with other variant texts and historical sources tells us that the figure in question was Emperor Uda and that the empress was Mototsune's daughter, Atsuko. There follow phrases that again exhibit the anonymity we saw in connection with the screen-painting poems as the short narrative goes on to give a brief rundown of the circumstances surrounding an affair (or even marriage?) between this woman and someone referred to only as the brother of the empress: "There was in close attendance upon an empress a woman whose parents were living in Yamato"; "brother [lit., sibling] of the empress"; "seeing this [the man's poem], the woman, despite hurt feelings, is moved deeply." The text, in other words, problematizes referential closure, although most readers of the time would have been able to make educated guesses; it is the "Ise" collection, after all. In contrast to the guise of "fact" worn by imperial poetry collections, however, the *Ise Collection* flaunts the fictive potential constitutive of the brief *tanka* form, whose contexts are susceptible to tampering, and challenges the reader to put the pieces together. Of Atsuko's two brothers, Nakahira and Tokihira, the former is the referent in the present case. Other textual versions give the man's rank as *daishō*, which would have been Nakahira's position at the time. Mention of Yamato Province suggests the governorship of the author's father there (891–894).

The situation depicted recurs in later texts: a talented woman enters the service of an imperial consort; male courtiers soon get wind of the new presence, and begin making advances; an affair ensues. In the *Ise Collection* the initial focus is on a crisis[16] that comes about like this: Ise entered the service of Atsuko soon after the latter became, in quick succession, junior consort, then senior consort toward the end of 888. Word spread of Ise's beauty and poetic skill, and she found herself involved with Atsuko's younger brother, Nakahira. Left heartbroken when Nakahira married into an influential family, Ise resigned her duties and sought refuge with her father in Yamato. The crisis results from Nakahira's marriage to the daughter of a powerful official, a situation reminiscent of the relationship between the author of *The Gossamer Years* and Fujiwara no Kaneie when the latter marries Tokihime. The language of the prefatory note also reverberates with other Heian texts, particularly the phrase, "How did it happen, I wonder?" (*ikaga ariken*), which suggests that Ise and Nakahira consummated their relationship in some fashion.[17] The girl's parents blame the incident on bonds from another life (*sukuse*), a Buddhist belief that often functions as a convenient way of explaining and justifying the commencement of romantic entanglements. We are told of the parents' deep concern for their daughter and of their disappointment at the turn of events.

The first poem in a series of four is composed by the man (*wotoko*) and delivered by a messenger who "arrives [at the residence of the empress] and presents a poem written on a persimmon leaf sporting its autumnal hue." This example of modishly elegant behavior (*fūryū*, the way that young courtiers were supposed to behave)[18] recalls the first section of the *Ise* tale, where the "man" dashes off a poem on a piece of cloth cut from his robe. The *Ise Collection* thus leads off with a man's poem (men usually sent the first poem):

> unknown to others,   to this weather-worn dwelling
>   I made my way; I see
> the time is ripe for weaving   the brocade of autumn leaves
> [Fito sirezu/aretaru yado wo/kite mireba/ima zo momidi no/nisiki ori-
> keru] (1, *SST* 1:246)

Seeing this, the woman, despite her hurt feelings, is deeply moved.

> my tears too stream down   in concert with the passing showers
>   in my old hometown
> the color of the autumn leaves   takes on a deeper shade
> [namida saFe/sigure ni soFite/Furusato Fa/momidi no iro mo/kosa
> masarikeri] (2, *SST* 1:246)

She places her reply in the autumn-tinged leaves of a *nezumoti* branch and sends it to him.[19]

The man had married into another family so the woman doubted that he would have any reason to visit her again; she decides to go to Yamato where she had once lived with her father and stay there a while. The woman,

> the mountain of Miwa   where the gods are said to wait
>   how am I to go on waiting when I know
> that though the years pass   no visitor will appear?
> [miwa no yama/ikani ni mati mimu/tosi Fu tomo/taduneru Fito mo/
> arazi to omoFeba (3, *SST* 1:246)

The forlorn woman wrote this while she was still in the capital, and it moved us deeply. The phrase "no visitor will appear" means that she was put in an embarrassing situation.

> be it the Yoshino mountains   distant as the land of Cathay
>   that you seclude yourself
> I shall not be one   who thinks of lagging behind
> [morokosi no/yosino no yama ni/komorutomo/okuremu to omoFu/
> ware naranaku ni] (4, *SST* 1:247)

The man, deeply moved by the woman's poem, was unable to send a reply and composed the above.

Although the series does not seem problematic at first glance, the elliptical nature of the passage raises readerly problems. It is not clear, for example, in the first exchange, exactly where the participants are. Did Nakahira himself go to Ise's residence (Akiyama's view, p. 47)? Or did he send a messenger (Katagiri, p. 50)? Where was Ise? Was she at Atsuko's quarters (Katagiri, p. 50)? Or at her parent's house (Akiyama, p. 47)? Why does Ise mention the *nezumoti* tree? If it is another name for *nezumimoti*, it would be out of place in an autumn poem because of its evergreen leaves. The difficulties we face here are exactly the kind we face when we read other Heian period texts. Although they are essential components of social exchanges, poemsongs beg for, or assume, extrapoetic information and easily fall prey to strategies that tamper with their contexts. One of the most spectacular examples of such tampering is the *Ise* tale, in which poems by different poets help create a fictive Ariwara no Narihira. The initial sections of *Ise shū* present a similar phenomenon. The first exchange above appears in *Gosenshū* (458 and 459) with this prefatory note: "Coming to an uninhabited dwelling [he] writes [the following] on an autumn-colored leaf and has it taken [to her]." Nakahira is identified as Biwa Minister of the Left, and Ise's name is also given. The location of the house is unclear as are the actions of the inhabitants. Katagiri seems correct in viewing the collection as a fictionalization of the *Gosenshū* poems, with the latter probably representing an earlier version.[20]

Poem two shows a skillful use of two rhetorico-incantatory figures we have seen in poems composed by the *Kokinshū* compilers: *kakekotoba* and *engo*. The morpheme *Furu* in *Furusato* (hometown) contains a pivot-word on "time passing": "old" and "fall, as in rain." The latter joins with *sigure* (autumn showers), *momidi* (autumn leaves), and *kosa masaru* ("hues growing ever deeper"—common lore held that autumn showers caused the leaves to turn) to form an associational pattern. The woman's tears form a semantic bond with the possible meanings in *Furu*: "time has passed and so we both have changed" and "my tears add their power (of sorrow) to the rains and thus turn the colors to a hue even deeper than on the leaves you found so splendid." The season of autumn itself, moreover, plays on its equivalent, *aki*, in the sense of "grow tired of" (i.e., you have grown tired of me).

Poem three, highly regarded by later generations, is included in the following collections: *Shinsenwaka, Kokinwaka rokujō, Kingyokushū,*

Shinsōhishō, and *Sanjū'nisen,* as well as *Kokinshū.* The *Kokinshū* prefatory note is, again, straightforward: "I had been on intimate terms with Lord Nakahira, but he had begun to grow weary of visiting me, so deciding to go to Yamato where my father was governor, I composed this and had it delivered to him." The *Ise shū* passage gives the reasons for Nakahira's estrangement; it is "narrated" and emphasizes personal responses. The poem must be read against its intertextual precedent (*Kokinshū* 982):

> my hut lies   at the foot of Miwa Mountain;
>   if you long for me
> pay me a visit;   it's the gate where the cedars stand[21]
> [waga iFo Fa/miwa no yamamoto/koFisiku Fa/toburaFi kimase/sugi tateru kado]

The suggestion of an invitation, with its mythic undertone, is transformed into resignation in Ise's poem. Her rhetorical question "how am I to go on waiting?" results in a refusal to foreclose toward complete rejection, leaving open the complexity of feeling that involves not only the echoes from the anonymous poem but also the earlier prefatory note where we were told that the woman was "deeply moved" despite her grief-stricken state. The fourth poem also appears in *Kokinshū* (1049), but the compilers attribute it to Nakahira's (and Atsuko's) older brother, Tokihira. The situation resembles *Ise monogatari,* where a poem from *Man'yōshū,* for example, is included in a poem-tale purported to be about Narihira.

Rather than being an exercise in puzzle solving, the *Ise Collection* invites us, in much the same way that *Ise monogatari* and other *monogatari* do, to read a historical presence out of the poetic series even as it defeats any attempt to appropriate the final narrative as one faithful to historical fact.[22] Listed in the "Eccentric Poems" ("Haikai") section in *Kokinshū,* the poem, with its hyperbolic reference to a nonexistent Chinese mountain, was no doubt considered appropriate material for poking a bit of fun at Nakahira. In addition to the possible humorous reading, the fourth poem also raises the issue of the relation of "fiction" to "fact." Although imperial anthologies are usually read as closer to fact than fiction, in the case of *Ise monogatari,* scholars have dated some of its poems to a time prior to *Kokinshū* and argue that the latter's compilers relied on *Ise monogatari* as a source for their selections. The process thereby problematizes the very relation between "fact" and "fiction." "Fact" in this case simply means an attempt at a relatively straightforward, unembellished version of a "fictional" text. More important than either "fact" or "fiction" per se is the question of assumed readerly knowledge. Whereas the *Ise shū* assumes that its readers know that the poem is not by Nakahira and can thus appreciate the underlying humor and contextual disjunction, the *Kokinshū* context places the "fictional" in a different (hegemonic) mode that would not necessarily require prior knowledge.

We can note here a characteristic the *Collection* shares with other types of poem collections, a characteristic that might seem odd to readers accustomed to personal poetry anthologies in the West: the poems in the collection are not confined to those by the poet in question. The initial section of the *Ise Collection* contains no names. A man appears simply as "the man" and Ise as "the woman," if the responding subject is referred to at all. The prefatory notes often do provide sufficient information to enable the reader to identify the interlocutor, but the text reads like passages in *Genji* where the participants in an amorous exchange are referred to in exactly the same way.[23] Keeping in mind such fictive possibilities as outlined above, let us continue to read Ise's "life."

After a series of poems that refer to the trip to Yamato—the time spent there (three months) and the failure to leave this sorrowful world[24]—Ise is summoned back to the palace by Atsuko, and in another lengthy yet elliptical prefatory note, we are told that she (Ise) rejects Nakahira's attempts to renew their affair and that his older brother, Tokihira, begins pressing his own case, asking her to forget about Nakahira and yield to him. But Ise again refuses. The fictional pose of the *Ise Collection* is nowhere near so clear-cut, but the woman continues her unyielding stance (in the poems a reference to the Yoshino mountains reappears). As Katagiri points out, judging from the exchanges between Ise and Tokihira in *Gosenshū*, it could very well have been Ise who pursued Tokihira, even chiding him at times for his womanizing ways,[25] again not unlike the author of *The Gossamer Years*. After the poems dealing with Atsuko's brothers, the collection next introduces another man, referred to only as the son-in-law of a minister exiled following a disturbance at the capital. The son-in-law, too, is banished. The now familiar pose of the woman as a rebuffer of men is maintained, but when she receives a letter from the man, she cannot help being moved to write:

> your earnest words   produce a stream of tears
>   an onrushing shallows

> I find myself willingly   swept away on a tearful current
> [kakete iFeba/namida no kaFa no/se wo Fayami/kokorozukara ya/
> mata Fa nakaremu] (17, *SST* 1:247)

The phrase "being swept away" (which can also mean "begin crying despite myself") can be read as a reference to the man's exile. According to most scholars, the man in question is Minamoto no Toshimi. The possibility of reading the poem as Ise's (or her group's or the editor's) expression of sympathy with Michizane and his followers who were exiled by the Fujiwara is one that reverberates throughout Heian literature.[26] Many Heian texts, *Ise monogatari* being among the most obvious,[27] are subtended by a veiled criticism of the sociopolitical climate of the times, a situation that modifies notions (of an escapist orientation) of what terms like *fūyrū* and *irogonomi* signify. In the case of private poetry collections like the *Ise Collection*, literati were afforded an excellent opportunity for incorporating a double-edged criticism against both the political power structures of the time and the plight of women.

The following section introduces another figure with whom Ise is believed to have been intimate: Taira no Sadafumi, the notorious Heichū of *Heichū monogatari* (Tales of Heichū). The prefatory note again presents a woman who refuses ("not having responded to his letters") the advances of a man "who had been wooing her for some years without making it clear whether in fact he was serious or not." Sadafumi also served Emperor Uda and was a close associate of the *Kokinshū* compilers. The appearance of Sadafumi, the subject of frequent fictionalization and parody himself, further contributes to the fictive process we have been observing. Although not mentioned by name, the poet must be Heichū, since the last poem below also appears in *Heichū monogatari* (section 2). The section continues as follows:

> The year has passed: "Why do you not at least say that you have taken a look at (*mitu*) what I have sent to you?" She answers, "I have looked at it (*mitu*)"; it is from that time that he gave her the nickname Mitsu; the man:
> without an immediate response   stepping its way to you
>   imprinted with the beach plover's tracks
>   would you admit even
> that you had looked at the tracks of my brush?[28]
> [tatikaFeri/*Fumi*yukazaraba/*Famatidori*/*ato mitu* to dani/kimi iFamasiya] (18, *SST* 1:248)

The woman: her reply,
had I no thoughts for you   over the year gone by,
          would I have troubled to preserve the tracks
of the beach plover   to show them to you now?
[tosi Fenuru/koto omoFazu Fa/*Famatidori*/*Fumi*tomete dani/*misu*beki
mono ka] (19, *SST* 1:248)

Summer: on an exceedingly hot day, the same man has composed this,
in the heat of a summer's day   my body is ablaze,
          consumed by hopeless misery;
like the kingfisher, the "bird that longs for water"
          I can only cry out my solitary pain
[natu no *Fi* no/*moyuru* waga mi no/wabisisa ni/*mizuko*F*idori* no/ne wo
nomi zo naku] (20, *SST* 1:248)

The woman offers no reply.

The poems play off the word *mitu* (variously "have taken a look,"
"water," and part of the name of the kingfisher) in the prefatory note.
In poem 19 the woman transforms the word *mitu* into *misu* (show),
which enacts the gesture of "showing" that she had "looked at" his
letter, while simultaneously indicating that she means no more than
an act of reading, offering no hope for realizing an affair.[29] In the
man's first poem, the associative words *Fumi* ("letter" and "step")
and *ato* ("tracks" and "written words") combine with *Famatidori*
(beach plover) and contribute, in a manner we examined in *Kokinshū*
in Chapter 3, to the double meanings inscribed. In poem 20 *mitu*
becomes "water" that is desired on a fiery summer's day as the man
desires the woman (Mitsu). The "fire" emerges out of its homonym
"day": *Fi* in *natu no Fi*. The name of the bird also conceals a play on
Fidori ("incense burner" and "alone") and combines with the associative words *moyuru* (burn) and *Fi*. Although the woman does not reply
to the man's second poem, the *Tales of Heichū*, which only records that
latter, "summer" poem with a series of others, also provides the
woman's reply to it.[30] As Katagiri points out, since the reply poem
appears elsewhere in the collection, it must have been removed from
the initial sequence to strengthen the pose of resistance.[31]

The next passage presents a turning point: the emperor himself
summons Ise to the palace. She obeys and eventually bears him a son.
She continues, however, to serve Atsuko and leaves her son at
Katsura, southwest of the capital. We have here a possible pretext for
the Akashi Lady in *Genji*. Any hint of rivalry or jealousy between the
two women is completely absent (or suppressed), and we get instead

an exchange of poems between the two one rainy day (a setting common in narratives), when the empress consoles Ise, who seems to be longing silently for her child. Ise's reply speaks only of trust in the empress's compassion and protection, the feeling of an attendant toward her mistress frequently found in Sei Shōnagon's *Pillow Book*. Ise's poem also appears in *Kokinshū* (968), but there the prefatory note explains that Ise was at Katsura with her son.

We then switch to poems dealing with the death of the child. Heichū reappears to express his condolences, but Ise remains aloof: "considering him unworthy of her attention, ends up sending no reply." Possibly added to indicate Ise's changed status (mother of a prince, i.e., consort, *miyasundokoro*), the poem still seems a cold-hearted response toward someone who has come to offer sympathy. Heichū's reputation as a philanderer as well as the editor's impulse toward fictional exaggeration seem to be at work here. The construct-edness of the *Ise shū* pose also stands in clear contrast to the *Shūshū* text, which lists the poems in reverse order with no suggestion of any particular attitude of Ise toward Heichū.

After two exchanges with Atsuko, we get a poem supposedly composed in response to an imperial request:

> in the mountain stream I hear its fame resounding
> the palace paved with the hundred stones
> would we could see it once again as we did long ago
> [yamakaFa no/oto ni nomi kiku/momosiki wo/mi wo hayanagara/
> miru yosi mogana] (31, *SST* 1:248)

The unassuming poem again shows Ise's skill at taking a pillow word, *yamakaFa no*, which amplified "roaring spirit" in its *Man'yōshū* usage, and giving it a new twist as a lead-in phrase for *oto* (sound/reputation). She also makes *momosiki* (a pillow word that normally amplifies "grand palace") stand for the palace itself (metonymy to synec-doche). Finally, *mi wo* (body/water route), *Faya* (swift/swift passage of time), and *yamakaFa* are associative-words. According to Katagiri, the poem might have been ordered by Emperor Daigo, during whose reign Ise was no longer at the palace; that would explain the desire to see it again.[32]

The final poem of the section is an expression of grief at Atsuko's death. Since we know that the empress died in 907 and that Ise entered her service in 888, the final poem marks the end of nearly two decades of service. It is believed that Ise then went on to serve

Atsuko's daughter, Princess Hitoko (Kinshi), and that she became involved with Hitoko's older half-brother and husband, Prince Atsuyoshi, who was renowned for his beauty and his love of women.[33] Hitoko dies in 910, and around 912 Ise gives birth to a daughter by Atsuyoshi. From sources that mention the two we know that Ise was an exceptionally talented musician and that the prince was one of her students. The collection includes poems that mark an occasion when Ise lent a seven-stringed zither to Atsuyoshi (poems 356–359).

Final Remarks

Such texts as the *Ise Collection* invite us to read history out of the poetic series at the same time that it defeats any attempt to appropriate the final narrative as one faithful to historical fact. Of the two modern studies of Lady Ise's poems cited above, Katagiri's remains most consistently aware of the fictive process, whereas Akiyama's emphasizes the historical background. The two readings diverge along this fundamental, though by no means strictly drawn, line between history and fiction. The fact that the initial section of the *Ise Collection* can be read as a "third-person" narrative (which is also true for a "diary" like *The Izumi Shikibu Diary*) recalls our earlier discussion of the first and third person narration and further attests to the interrelatedness of (private) "history" and (public) fictionalization.

Finally, the gaps in Ise's story will be filled by the experiences of her literary successors, women like the author of *The Gossamer Years*, with her resolve to keep Kaneie at a distance; or Izumi Shikibu, who loved two brothers; or Sei Shōnagon, whose relationship to Sadako replays the Ise-Atsuko bond. As we have discovered, Ise's collection of poetry has much in common with poem-tales, especially *Ise monogatari*, part of whose title it shares. Although I am not able to do it here, the relation of the act by which Ise is sent to court to the power configurations of the late eighth and early ninth centuries is in need of further exploration. She arrived on the scene at a time when her skill in composing waka allowed her not only the opportunity to commingle with the best male poets of her day but also no doubt (even taking the "stance" of resistance found in the poetry collection with ample grains of salt) to compete with them on an equal footing both on formal occasions and in private repartee. Waka, as a primary medium of exchange, not only provided women a readily available means of contact and expression but, in many cases, allowed them an opportunity to demonstrate powers of manipulation and ensnarement. The security of an empress's protection and favor also guaranteed such women a secure position from which to act and write. Ise was favored by a palace system less structured than the one in which Murasaki Shikibu, Izumi Shikibu, Akazome'emon, and Sei Shōnagon held forth. The text we discuss next, *Ise monogatari*, will place the issues of waka collecting, resistance, biography, and history-fiction in another, extremely problematic, context.

5

Sexual/Textual Politics
and *The Tale of Ise*

The Tale of Ise has proven a mighty riddle to readers throughout the ages. One scholar writes, "Every time I read *Ise monogatari*, I end up confounded by its difficulty,"[1] and another flatly states, "There is no work which presents as many thorny problems to scholarship as *Ise monogatari*."[2] The riddle of the *Ise* text runs throughout its one-hundred-plus sections, or *dan* ("plateau" or "step"), encompassing its mysterious title, its references to Ariwara no Narihira (a tantalizing promise of biographical plenitude),[3] its deferral and deflection of linear movement (there is no temporal or logical arrangement of sections), its number of textual variants (the largest for a Heian text),[4] and its ultimate significance as a cultural product. It takes the act of collecting to radical, contestatory lengths, and it effects for the "private" rewriting of waka what the *Taketori* tale effected for the rewriting of tales. Differences between *Ise* and "poem-tales" often mentioned with it are revealing. The *Yamato monogatari* (Tales of Yamato) text, an amalgam of sections of varying provenance, mentions a wide variety of historical figures with much greater frequency than *Ise* but is not subtended by the life of a single figure; specific names appear at the beginnings of sections, and when consecutive sections tell of a particular figure, "same" (*onazi*) is used—"the same minister," "the same man," "the same woman," and so forth. The sections of *Heichū monogatari* (Tales of Heichū) explicitly refer to the same man (with either *mata* [again] or *onazi*, sometimes giving both—"again, this same man" [*mata kono onazi wotoko*]), but its personages do not resonate politically with its main figure, Taira no Sadafumi.[5] By contrast, *Ise monogatari* transforms the "life" of Ariwara no Narihira into a textual space that accommodates a variety of poetic incidents, many of them situated between fabrication and fact. As we shall see, the text effectively resists recuperation by any and all totalizing and unifying maneuvers.[6]

The *Ise* Title

Post-Heian commentaries, modern studies, and editors of modern editions offer tentative opinions, but all feel that solutions to the title are impossible. Given a lack of verifiable evidence, their despair often stems from a desire for "correct" answers in order to avoid being "unfaithful" to the text. Search for an "author" presence, necessary to validate an "original" or "transcendent" meaning of a "work," derives from a similar desire for verifiability.[7] To read the *Ise* text, however, is to trace a movement that replays the difficulties relating to its title and its potential to unsettle readerly expectations. Let me begin our discussion by listing three classes of possible solutions to the title that scholars have offered:[8]

1. Those solutions that read a reference to a particular person (Lady Ise) believed to have written or edited the text, to a location (Ise Province) where the text was written, or to a group that compiled, wrote, or edited it.

2. Those solutions based on the belief that the title refers to the *dan* that mention an Ise Virgin, especially *dan* 69 in the Tempuku texts. Arguments for the Ise Virgin solution are based either on *dan* placement (the Ise Virgin *dan* was the first *dan* of the "Hunter texts") or thematic weight (the Ise Virgin *dan* are the most important in the text).[9]

3. Those solutions, excluding rather far-fetched conjectures—the author hit on the idea of writing the text while praying at the Ise Shrine, for example—that read a riddle of sorts in the name *Ise* itself. One solution splits the word into its components: *i* (female) and *se* (male), appropriate to a text containing love poems. Another sees in *Ise* a different way of writing (*w*)*ese*, something that is not serious or true, and another gives the phonic variant *yose*, from *yoseru* (to gather, assemble), *Ise* being an "assembled" text. Finally, the first possibility in Ikeda Kikan's list of eleven cites an old adage: "The people of Ise indulge in mischievous behavior" (Ise no Fito wa Figagoto su), a reference to the clandestine "affair" between Narihira and the Ise Virgin that overlaps with number 2 above. Kenshō's *Kokinshū chū* (1191) and Fujiwara Kiyosuke's *Fukurozōshi* (ca. 1158) both mention the adage.[10] Kenshō adds, however, that since *Ise* writes about the affair "as if" it did not take place, it commits a *higagoto*, a term that can mean "mistaken" or "unorthodox," in reference to paths (other meanings are "oblique" and "not straight-

forward"). Kenshō goes on to state that the name *Ise* signfies that the text tends to deviate in some way from the orthodox, turning things upside down. *Ise* speaks, for example, "as if" Narihira's poems were composed by another poet and "as if" old poems were contemporary compositions.[11]

Another commentary, *Waka chikenshū*,[12] also characterized the *Ise* text as one that turns things upside down and alters the order of things:

> What should be placed in the beginning it places at the end; what should be put at the end it places at the beginning; it writes of old events as if they had taken place in the present and writes of present day events as if they were matters of the past; it pretends that affairs at the capital had taken place in the countryside and that affairs of the countryside had taken place at the capital.[13]

The *Chikenshū* author feels that the *Ise* text thus derives from the saying "Ise or Hyūga," which refers to a story of two men from Ise and Hyūga. They die at the same hour on the same day, and one of them becomes reincarnated into the body of the other. The saying applies to matters that make no sense; thus its conferral on the *Ise* text. To take one thing as another, to deliberately alter things, in short, to falsify, dissimulate, pretend—that is what *Ise* might very well be "about."

Related metonymically to texts, titles may or may not correspond to the way texts work. In our day, titles, usually given to a work by its author, are marks of ownership. Since Heian *monogatari* authorship was most often anonymous and since the term ultimately names textual processes rather than static products, titles are neither proprietary marks nor stable fixtures.[14] The solution that links the *Ise* title with *dan* 69 would make sense if one chose the "Hunter text," which begins with that *dan*, as a proto-*Ise* text. But the claim for the Ise Virgin *dan* as the most important remains purely arbitrary. Outside of the biographical gesture mentioned above, the *dan* defy any apparent global linking "principles," being rather independent units that could be freely inserted, removed, or combined to accommodate a compiler-reader's fanciful or ideological impulse. Such acts may account for the sporadic chronological order or the seasonal progressions some have found,[15] and the "group" orientation that emerges from names that either appear or are implied throughout the text.

To view the *Ise* title, then, as a thematic metonym might be a mistake, for the above clues suggest that the title speaks to actual textual movements. Since scholars almost unanimously agree that the text results from several compiler-readers, to read the title as a functional metonym retaining its currency throughout the numerous reader-text transactions and rewrites would be in keeping with the spirit of a text that displays a consistent impulse to dissimulate waka moments and "contexts," to tell tales not only about a hypostatizable "life of Narihira" but also about the materials and circumstances of textual construction itself. Even though he ultimately discards it, Ikeda admits that the *higagoto* hypothesis can be traced back to the Heian period—it was suppressed during the Muromachi period by the Nijō scholars but surfaced again in the Edo period with the monk Keichū (1640–1701), Kada no Azumamaro (1669–1736), and Kamo no Mabuchi (1697–1769).[16] Ikeda bases his own dismissal on a comment by the brilliant Meiji scholar Fujioka Sakutarō, who rejected the hypothesis because it did not conform to the way other *monogatari* titles were derived.[17] Given its peculiarities, it seems entirely appropriate for the text to bear a mischievous title. Whatever the initial reasons, the possibility in the title for a multitude of citational and interpretive schemes reflects the text-making processes in the various *dan* themselves, processes in which we must also participate as we rewrite the *Ise* tale.

Ise Language and One Beginning

Depending on how we qualify the statement, we can characterize the *Ise* text as one that continually begins. Every *dan* except one (*dan* 17) in the Tempuku text begins with the word *mukasi* (long ago), which functions as a rhythmical marker in manuscript texts containing no formal punctuation to indicate beginnings or endings. Sheer repetition means syntactic significance outstrips immediate semantic value, the latter becoming an allegory of the text or "textual perspective" itself: a temporal reference that takes on mythic proportions, recoverable only through the text, which is in the hands of those forever removed from that world. The implied negative view of the past compared to the "now" must also be remembered. In striking contrast to the *Kokinshū* "Kana Preface," which sought to construct a continuity between the past and the present age of the compilers, the repetition of the phrase "long ago" suggests a perspective that can only mark perpetually, as a new discursive threshold, a break with a nostalgic past that can only exist in the narrative "present."

Another word repeated at the beginnings of most *dan* is *wotoko* ("a man," or "the man")—a few *dan* begin with an anonymous woman. Distinct from narratives that begin in the past (however vaguely defined) and quickly introduce main figures, the *Ise* "man" is a flexible, anonymous sign adaptable to various perspectives at which any reader can position himself or herself and rewrite the text. Readers might have been obliged to read the sign as "Narihira," but, again, the constant repetition erodes signified value and shifts the focus instead toward another signification, "point of utterance."[18]

A final recurring element is the verbal suffix *keri*, which is the most conspicuous facet of the text, appearing not only at the borders of discourse, as in *Taketori*, but throughout the various *dan* (except Tempuku *dan* 13).[19] Combined with *mukasi* and *wotoko*, it forms the major *Ise* topos: *mukasi wotoko [ari]keri*, "Long ago: there was a man [as we all know, so it is told, etc.]." The topos is occasionally supplemented by geographic names or poetic (incantatory) terms. Such locative markers appear most often at the beginnings of the longer *dan*, usually providing lexicomythical referents for the poems that inevitably follow. Often the toponyms signify "countryside" or "outlying region," removed from the capital and "other" to the palace, where the unfamiliar is common. Rather than a sense of "real" events in "real" geographical locations, the toponyms become codes to be read primarily for their discursive (i.e., nonrepresentational) potential: if one were in place X, one could compose or recite poem Y, given the metonymic (and other conventional, communal, or incantatory) possibilities in toponym X. The *mukasi-wotoko-keri* triad mentioned above appears in the first *dan* of the Tempuku text:

> Long ago, a man, after putting on the cap, has gone to the village of Kasuga, in the old capital of Nara, to hunt on some property he owns, as the story goes.

Having attained (sexual) maturity, marked by a "capping" ceremony, the man heads for the old Nara capital; he owns land there (or, alternately, has close ties there). We are again in a *keri* narrational mode. The text goes on:

> In the village live two sisters, refreshingly youthful and elegant. The man has caught a glimpse of them through a crack in the fence. It is unexpected, so out of place in this ancient capital; he has become

thoroughly enchanted with them. The man cuts off a swatch from the hunting robe he is wearing, writes a poem on it, and sends it to them. The man is wearing a hunting robe with a *sinobuzuri* design. (*NKBZ* 8:133)

The above topos reappears in later *monogatari* texts: a man leaves the confining palace environment of the capital for the countryside, a signifier of strangeness and freedom; the mode of discovery is secretive and visual;[20] contact is often made by way of a poem. In the present case, the "sending" is transformed into a "recitation," which reproduces the utterance itself:

> on Kasuga plain   this robe of mine rubbed
>   with dye from the young lavender
>   into confused patterns; hides a confused longing within
> that knows no bounds
> [kasugano no / wakamurasaki no / surigoromo / sinobu no mid-
> are / kagiri sirarezu]
>
> He sends the poem without a moment's hesitation.[21]

The poetic instance forms a textual moment that is neither representation nor narration but rather, in a peculiar way, the "thing itself." I do not mean "proposition," extratextual "referent," or reified "meaning," but an utterance textualized or rewritten, made, in a sense, concrete.[22] The poem is marked by the signs of its own creation, and the expectations aroused by the man's encounter with the aforementioned women are thwarted. The poetic utterance appeals to the reader-listener to focus on the verbal act as it integrates the strands of the foretext (the poem may have come first).

The context, for its part, offers a barely discernible "story," its purpose being rather to "mention" words that reappear or are implicated in the poem: Kasugano, "hunting robe," and "confused heart." If the poem did come first, it becomes the pretext for the *dan*. The man's actions are not so much described as "listed" in successive phrases: comes of age, goes to Kasuga, and spies two sisters; heart agitated, cuts off a swatch of robe; writes and sends a poem. The nonpast, *keri* discourse heightens the sense of spatialization and adjacency, as if one were viewing a pictorial representation. The remark "is wearing a hunting robe with a *sinobuzuri* design" shows the intimate relation between the foretext and the enabling, pretextual poem.

The poem offers an exemplary demonstration of the potential

complexity of a thirty-one-syllable poem-song. Of its two parts, the first ends at *surigoromo*. Three nouns are connected by the particle *no*, which may be read as an appositive, possessive, topical, or comparative (the last usually translated *no yō ni/na* in modern Japanese) marker. The first *no* particle in the poem is possessive; the second, appositive—"young lavender grass of Kasuga Plain, this robe, rubbed with [the dye] from the young lavender plant." The three nouns repeat the main strands of the foretext, "young lavender" standing as a metonym for the two sisters. *Koromo*, left hanging in the first part, bonds with the second part only through juxtaposition. The second part completes the echo with the line in the foretext "sinobuzuri no kariginu namu kitarikeru" (the word *sinobuzuri* is split by *koromo*). The first part is normally thought to serve as a lead-in phrase (*jo*) for the rest of the poem.[23] In the poem above, the word *suri* (rubbing) links semantically with both *koromo* and *sinobu*, thus linking the two parts as well. The syntactic distance, however, loosens the semantic area, so to speak, and *sinobu* is freed to connect with *midare* through yet another *no* particle. With *sinobu* we have an example of Heian textual polysemy: a cloth-dyeing process, which is here woven into the fabric of the text, but also either "hold inside, forbear" or "long for (secretly)," both signifiers for "secretive" or "hidden." Thus *sinobu no midare*, the dyed, free-flowing pattern without ordered design, is constitutive of two different interpretations: suppression and longing. Modern scholars usually choose one over the other, most often ignoring the polysemy altogether and simply focusing on the confused feelings. The text allows for either possibility; one alternative cannot dominate the other, nor is it possible to experience both simultaneously.[24] In the same way, "young lavender" is a metonym for the two girls. As stated before in our discussion of the *Taketori* poems, tropological relations in Japanese tend to privilege the syntagmatic movement of metonymy over the paradigmatic, controlling moment of metaphor. The textual strand of the waka is constituted by associative-words that demand a reading straight through to the phrase *kagiri sirarezu*. The girls, curiously, are not the focus of the trope; in fact, they are hardly "there" at all. It is rather the lavender grass—linked with Kasuga Plain, the hunting robe, and the dyed pattern—in short, the process of textualization, that demands our attention.

But the *dan* is not yet over. After the remark, "He probably considered it a situation to be taken advantage of," another poem follows:

> in distant Michinoku
>> where dyes are rubbed in confused patterns
>> whose heart would take on such confused feelings
> for just anyone?　　　certainly not mine
> [mitinoku no / sinobu motizuri / tare yuwe ni / midare somenisi / ware
> naranakuni]

> Such are the sentiments on which the first poem is based; people of old
> certainly had no qualms about acting in elegant ways.

Not the answering poem we would expect, it "comments" on the *dan*,
thus forming a major facet of *Ise* textuality and, together with the
sections of "commentary" in the *Taketori* and *Konjaku* texts, of Heian
hiragana discourse. Such comments, often thought to be additions by
later readers-writers, problematize the preceding text. In the above,
the segment from "He sends the poem without a moment's hesita-
tion" to the end of the *dan* includes the statement "Such are the
sentiments on which the first poem is based."[25] The text provides
what in later Heian poetics will be called the "root poem" (*honka*)
against which a later poem effects a variation. Whereas it would
normally be left up to the reader-listener to retrieve the root poem
from the variant, the *Ise* comment tells the reader outright: read poem
A with the help of poem B; or, poem A was read or recited by the poet
with poem B in mind. The second possibility, not mentioned by
commentators, goes with the last remark in the text, "kaku itiFayaki
miyabi wo namu sireru." *Kaku* (in this way, to this extent) is thought
to refer to the poet's skill in composing the impromptu poem and
impetuously sending it on the textile fragment. The appearance of the
honka would seem to necessitate a further reading for *kaku:* "The way
in which the poet was instantly able to produce a variation on that
stylish poem [is what should be applauded]."

　　The *dan* demonstrates not so much a *honkadori* as a gesture toward
its own reading.[26] We are given, as it were, a reading lesson.[27] By
laying bare its mechanisms, the *Ise* intertextuality openly denies
diegetic movement. Rather than "culminating" points as is commonly thought, poems represent a denial of teleology and a dispersal
of signification. Waka are constituted by signifying networks that
always enable further textual moments.[28] The first *dan* in a crucial
sense rewrites the waka, activating further not only the metonyms
that constitute it but even re-creating its syntactic order: toponym
(Michinoku), person (*tareyuwe ni*), and effect (*midare*). This type of

participation in Heian intertextuality is emblematic of topoi that appear in later *monogatari*.

The "reading lesson" is also a "rewriting lesson," which effects another signifying possibility. The Heian reader would have known that the second poem's author was Minamoto no Tōru, a name that conjures up all that is involved in the term *fūryū* ("modishly elegant behavior," discussed below), of which he was the ultimate embodiment. That pose and the word *miyabi* (elegance appropriate to the capital) suggest further how *Ise* is to be read and recall our discussion of the title. In other words, the "story" is not the (barely) abstractable one of a man who encounters two sisters (there was, we must remember, no actual "meeting") while out hunting, but rather the signifying processes themselves. The text also invites us to read the word "to hunt" (*kara ni*),[29] which in Japanese can also mean "hypothetically," as enacting precisely the fictive, indeterminate *Ise* movement.

Genealogical Intertexts

In light of the first *dan* and to continue our interrogations of genealogy, we must examine the figure of Narihira as another point of entry into issues raised by a text interlaced with pretexts and intertexts and constituted not only by the rewriting of already existent waka,[30] but also by historical texts and legends (such as accounts in Chinese of Narihira's life). On the one hand, acquaintance with possible historical circumstances is presupposed by the *Ise* compilers who alter that knowledge in a movement of dissimulation; on the other hand, the movement is aided by impulses signified by the terms *fūryū* and *miyabi*. I have given common interpretations for the terms above, but I would argue that they authorize the difference of the *Ise* text from other collections inasmuch as the terms gesture to issues far beyond simply elegant or fashionable behavior. *Fūryū*, derived from Chinese, originally meant "style of a past king that lingers on into the present,"[31] and thus, "tradition,"[32] in the sense of looking back to one or more specific predecessors. The component *miya* ("court, palace" or "capital: where the palace is," therefore "deportment proper to the capital") in the latter term, *miyabi* (deriving from a verbal form, *miyabu*), must be read as a specific reference to the Heian capital. As it calls forth its antonym, *hinabi* (countrified), it also suggests a difference from the former Heijō (Nara) capital. Derived meanings for

miyabi include "elegance" and "refinement," but another signification for *miyabi* found in the commentaries is a more active form of
elegance that includes a sense of "amorousness," which activates
itiFayasi (impetuous). The second reading, in keeping with Tōru's
eccentric personality, suggests immediate action when confronting a
potentially amorous adventure and was an ideal of Heian courtly
behavior. In the two terms, then, the *Ise* compilers would seem to be
suggesting a tie with past figures as well as a specific "tradition."[33]

The differences in the terms are precisely what the first *dan*
addresses: a man living at the Heian capital journeys to the site of the
old capital. The term Kasuga Plain becomes oxymoronic with Heijō to
evoke both "spring" (one of the Chinese characters used to write
Kasuga) and renewal. The evocation accords with the "man" having
just come of age, but it also produces a nostalgic counterpoint in
"home," since the name Kasuga appears together with the term *sato*
(village) in the sense of *furusato* (village one calls home). The text
informs us that the man possesses land in the "[old] Kasuga village."
The man's behavior is then juxtaposed with the poem by Minamoto
no Tōru. What, then, does the valorization of Heijō and Tōru suggest
about the *Ise* compiler's aesthetico-ideological stance? To begin to
construct an answer we must examine further the Ariwara genealogy.

Narihira's grandfather was the sickly, poetically inclined Emperor
Heizei (r. 806–809). Born in 774, Heizei had lived in the old capital of
Heijō (Nara) during his youth. Upon abdicating, after less than four
years, to his brother Saga (r. 809–823), he retired to the old Heijō
capital and took Buddhist vows.[34] In 810, soon after Heizei's abdication, there occurred what is known as the Kusuko Incident (Kusuko
no hen), which resulted in the exile to Tsukushi (present-day Kyushu) of Heizei's son (and Narihira's father) Prince Abo. The Kusuko
incident refers to the attempted coup engineered by Heizei's favored
attendant, Fujiwara no Kusuko, and her brother, Nakanari, aimed at
reinstalling Heizei at the old Nara capital. The conspirators were
overwhelmed by Emperor Saga's forces and eventually hunted down
as they attempted to escape. Heizei was brought back to Heijō, and
Kusuko was forced to drink poison. Abo, whose mother's low status
had prevented him from becoming crown prince, remained exiled in
Tsukushi for fourteen years, until 824.[35] After his return, his four
sons—Yukihira, Nakahira, Narihira, and Morihira—received the surname Ariwara.[36]

Born after the prince's return to the capital, Narihira himself never rose to the high positions concomitant with his birth (his mother, Princess Ito, was a daughter of Emperor Kammu), and he ended his career as provisional middle captain of the Right Imperial Guards, and provisional governor of Mino.[37] The official history *Sandai jitsuroku* includes his obituary and also traces his lineage; comments on his good looks, his free spirit, his lack of training in Chinese learning, and his skill at composing "Japanese poem-songs" (*yamato uta*); and lists his official positions. His royal connections with the old Heijō capital, however, cast a different, politically motivated light on the mention of the Nara capital, "Nara no kyō," in the first two *dan* of *Ise*. In other words, the possibility arises that the *Ise* compilers, through the opening gesture, wanted the reader-listener to recall both the Heijō site and the reign of Heizei to suggest an underside (*ura*) to a Fujiwara power structure based at the Heian capital.[38]

Another figure mentioned in *Ise*, a man also victimized by the Fujiwara hegemony, is Prince Koretaka (844–897).[39] The first son of Emperor Montoku (r. 850–858) and his consort Shizuko (daughter of Ki no Natora), Koretaka should have succeeded Montoku but lost out to a Fujiwara-born heir, Prince Korehito. Koretaka had the support of Fujiwara no Yoshisuke, but it was the backing of Yoshisuke's rival, Yoshifusa, that enabled Korehito to become crown prince (later Emperor Seiwa), even though he was only the fourth imperial son. Korehito's mother was Akiko, Yoshifusa's daughter. The ties to Shizuko and Natora produce a kinship situation that links Koretaka to the Ki family and also to Narihira, who is thought to have married a daughter of Aritsune, Shizuko's brother.[40] The once mighty Ki family found itself for the last time on the verge of supplying the maternal grandfather to an emperor.[41] A low-ranking man like Narihira who becomes involved (albeit fictionally) in sexual scandals with members of the imperial household finds an echo in the *Genji* text, though the latter's main male figure rises to the highest ranks.[42] There is no historical evidence that Narihira and Takaiko were ever involved in an affair, but the hint of such an alliance may subtend a desire to undercut Fujiwara power that led to Koretaka's displacement by Korehito.

The flamboyant Minamoto no Tōru, the twelfth (or eighth, depending on the source) son of Emperor Saga, was Narihira's contemporary and one of a large number of Saga's sons and daughters granted the Minamoto (Genji) surname. He served as governor of

Sagami, Ōmi, and Ise and held a variety of offices, including consultant, major counselor, and the exalted post of minister of the left (in 872). He might at one point even have become emperor were it not for Fujiwara no Mototsune, Regent Yoshifusa's adopted son and heir to the position of Fujiwara leadership. Although not the result (as it was with Prince Abo) of overt action, Tōru's ouster, like that of other "Minamoto" men, is analogous to that of Koretaka vis-à-vis Fujiwara power and imperial prestige.[43]

Tōru, moreover, was well known for his extravagantly landscaped garden at his mansion by the Kamo River. The garden, from which his nickname Kawara no Sadaijin (Minister of the Left of the Riverside [Mansion]) derives, replicated a famous seaside area in northeastern Japan, Shiogama, a well-known poetic toponym. Desirous of verisimilitude, Tōru is alleged to have had seawater transported from Osaka so that the salt-making fires of the actual site could be reproduced.[44] The mansion was also a place for a coterie of scholar-officials (a male "salon," including Narihira and Tsurayuki) to gather and was used later by celebrated men like Minamoto no Shitagō (alleged author of *Utsuho* and *Ochikubo*), Taira no Kanemori, and the monk Ampō (Tōru's great-grandson). There is good reason, then, for a poem by Tōru to appear in the first *dan* as a "source" poem.[45]

Fūryū and its lexical relative *miyabi*, as exemplified by Tōru, are also closely connected to "dissimulation"—i.e., something made to seem something else—and Tōru's artificial garden turns out to have much in common with the *Ise* textual topoi. When we remember that the ubiquitous suffix *keri* signals a discursive dissimulation or doubling and its legitimation, the different strands of the textual fabric begin to constitute a conscious design. As scholars have pointed out, *Ise* is not the first text to employ its beginning, since children's stories and folkloric legends often introduced an anonymous main figure with the phrase *mukasi wotoko arikeri*.[46] In the *Ise* text, however, there converge the impulse to tell stories, the growing interest in the potential for dissimulation provided by waka, the textual moment of utterance it represents (when anyone might don the mask of discourse and speak "as if" he or she were the poet), and the desire to implicate historical figures who harbor a desire to participate in a shared stance of resistance.

"Historical," "biographical," and "thematic" readings are ways the *Ise* text invites the reader to "naturalize" (make sense of) the textual significations.[47] Such interpretative strategies, however, always leave a textual residue for which the interpretation cannot account. A better strategy (it is impossible to read without one) would be to read the intertextual strands while being attentive to the relations among the different strands and significations. In such a reading "Narihira," rather than standing for a "person" about whom we can reconstruct a "biography" (i.e., the presence behind the *Ise* writing), becomes a metonym that can be, as is the case with almost all Heian *hiragana* "authors," nothing more than an "effect" of that writing (compare our earlier *Ise shū* discussion), a figure of interpretation, a scriptive trace, a "bio-graphics." The "life" of Narihira provides only an overall scheme, marking a beginning point (coming of age) and an end point (death poem), within which any number of incidents and events can "take place." Consequently, it becomes all the more necessary to position our readings of *Ise* at genealogical intersections, in order to rewrite the complexity and specificity of the text.

Narihira Poetics and *Ise* Textuality

"Narihira" also stands for a particular mode of waka composition. The second *dan* (in the Tempuku texts), for example, presents a Narihira composition that displays his familiar indeterminate movement:[48] "neither awake nor asleep" (*oki mo sezu/ne mo sede*).[49] The *dan* first identifies a transitional (unstable) historical time—"at the time when the capital at Nara had been abandoned and people at *this* capital had not yet settled into their houses"[50]—and then tells of an extraordinary woman ("whose heart, not her appearance, is superior") who lives in the "western sector of the capital" (*nisi no kyau*). The woman seems the object of a number of suitors. The narrator tells us that the genuinely sincere (*mame wotoko*) "man"[51] spends the night with the woman, returns home, and sends a poem the following day. It is the first day of the Third Month, and a soft rain is falling:

> neither quite awake   nor yet asleep
>   watching our night brighten into dawn,
>   I spend the day in longing gaze
>   at the ceaseless rains that come with spring
>   [oki mo sezu / ne mo sede yoru wo / akasite Fa / Faru no mono
>   tote / nagamekurasitu]

Commentators situate the poem according to the two possibilities for joining a poem to the foretext: the poet returned home and a couple of days later sent the poem; or, the poet returned home and sent the poem that day. The latter accords better with Heian etiquette, which demanded a "morning-after" poem (*kinuginu no uta*). Both readings preserve the discrepancy between poem and foretext,[52] and any worry over such discrepancies simply ignores the fictiveness of the *Ise* text. In other words, since Narihira was born in 825, there would be a gap of several decades between foretext (the move to Heiankyō) and poem.[53] The foretext in the second *dan* might be a response to this pretext: given the meeting and the conditions (spring, drizzle), how would the man have composed his morning-after poem? Or, the poem was made the focal point of the foretext. In either case we have another example of *Ise* dissimulation sitting squarely within the Narihira poetic movement, between waking and sleeping and also between historical fact and (con)-textual fancy; in short, sitting on either side of the moments of undecidability constitutive of the text. Again, the woman's response is not given.

The poem for which Narihira is perhaps best known and in which we see an extreme example of his penchant for the rhetorically undecidable appears in *dan* 4.[54] The poetic moment tells of a woman (believed to be the Empress of the Second Ward) once "present" (he was having an affair with her) and now "absent": "on the tenth day of the First Month, she had hidden herself away in another place." He eventually learns of her whereabouts, but she is no longer readily accessible—i.e., she is at the palace. He wanders back a year later on a day commemorative of her departure. The text wends its way to the poem in rhythmical fashion:

> In the First Month of the following year, at the height of the plum blossoms, longing for the year gone by, he goes there; standing, he stares about; sitting, he stares about; but, stare as he might, nothing would resemble the year gone by; sobbing uncontrollably, he lies down on the bare, broken-down floor until the moon sinks low; calling to mind the year gone by, he recites,
>
> is the moon not the same?   is the spring not
>   the spring of long ago?
> this body and this body alone   remains as ever the same
> [tuki ya aranu / Faru ya mukasi no / Faru naranu / waga mi Fitotu
> Fa / moto no mi ni site]
>
> Thus he recites, and as dawn is dimly breaking, he has gone home in tears.

Readings of the poem can only trace its radical undecidability. The interpretations divide into two basic groups: those that take the *ya* in the first two lines as interrogative (*gimon*) and those that take it as rhetorical question (*hango*).[55] The poet is either saying that the moon and the spring are not the same as the previous year or that they are. Further interpretative variations add the question of whether the poet is himself the same or different from the previous year. Commentators who aim for "objectivity" logically assert that "natural" phenomena do not change and hence arrive at the predictable conclusion that *ya* must be rhetorical. But the *Ise* rewriting, "founded" on Narihira's poetic movement, is radically decontextual, not necessarily governed by "natural" laws.

The poem also must be read in its immediate context. *Dan* 4 presents a situation constitutive of an absence that alters the poet's perspective—"he thought the situation [or, the woman] depressing [cold-hearted] as ever"—toward a realization of the impossibility of another meeting. The above foretext emphasizes the difference by repeating three times the words *mi* (look, stare about) and *kozo* (year gone by). In fact, *kozo* becomes a syntactic metonym for the lady, since both are impossible to recapture. What he discovers is that "nothing resembles the year [and the woman] gone by, and he composes the poem with that year in mind" (*dan* 4). As time repeats itself in cyclical fashion, he too repeats his visit, but all he finds is a difference that sits in the suspended space between presence and absence and among fixed interpretations.

To reiterate: as it partakes of the spirit of Narihira's poetic tendencies to dissimulate its politically, genealogically, and rhetorically motivated rereadings and rewritings, the *Ise* text is thoroughly underwritten by the undecidability of particular readings. The figure of Narihira, a trope for a style of poetry and a style of life, linked through Minamoto no Tōru to the emblems of *fūryū* and *miyabi*, becomes a supremely effective way of energizing a discourse that "steps" along, questioning and counterquestioning the cognitive line between "fact" and "fiction." Time and again the collection thwarts, even as it invites, attempts at finding historical correspondences, those politically intertextual positions of its historical, pretextual figures, and adds suggestive complications. What we have is a text that can be, as it most often has been, read under the shadow of a "life" of Narihira even though, as I've argued, it presents a continual refraction from biographical plenitude. Yet, as we had to take seriously the "name dropping" in the *Taketori* text, so we cannot simply dismiss out of hand the *Ise* biographical gesture.[56]

The same poem placed in a different narrative will no longer be the same poem. Given the Narihira ambivalence, even the same poem in the same narrative effectively resists decisive interpretations and self-identical readings. The poem in *dan* 4 appears in the *Kokin* collection, but the prefatory note and the *Ise* foretext are revealingly different. Seeking only to give a matter-of-fact account of the circumstances leading to the composition of the poem and perhaps also to suppress poetic unruliness in a "public" collection, the *Kokinshū* compilers provide a prefatory note that resembles perfunctory paraphrase. Gone are the rhythm and most of the phrases necessary to situate the poem. Instead, the prefatory note grafts a different phrase: "a night when the moon is enchanting." The *Kokinshū* note also destroys the sense of something happening before one's eyes.[57]

Another Beginning

Although terms like "beginnings" and "endings" quickly become problematic, let us now insert a counterpoint to the earlier discussion of the first *dan* and look at the *dan* that opens the Hunter texts, which is *dan* 69 in the Teika texts. It also speaks of a "hunt" and removes the "man" from the capital. Like the first *dan*, the opening topos is a typical one: "Long ago, there is/was a man." What follows not only includes a place name but tends to employ connectives rather than *keri* or other morphological stops, a phenomenon we witnessed at the end of the *Taketori* text.

> The man goes to Ise Province as a hunter dispatched by the court; since the parent of that person [i.e., the one we all know] who is the Ise Virgin has advised her to "tend to this man's needs with more care than you would give an ordinary envoy" and since they are her mother's words, she puts herself wholeheartedly into looking after his needs. (*NKBZ*, 191)

The diegetic foretext, if not of the long, meandering type of the *Genji* text, is much fuller than it was in the first *dan*. Putting "herself wholeheartedly" into the matter consists, among other things, of sending him off in the morning and entertaining him at night. By the second night the man announces suddenly, "I want to meet with you" (fully intending the sexual implications in the word "meet"). Not averse to the proposition, the Virgin waits until everyone is asleep and goes to the man's quarters (situated near her since he was an honored guest) accompanied by a child-attendant. Actually, the Virgin suddenly appears; the narrative does not "take" her anywhere. She stays with him, we are told, for about three hours (from the first hour of the rat to the third hour of the ox—11:00 P.M. to around 3:00 A.M.). A crucial sequence follows: "Before he had told her all that was in his heart, she has left" (*mada nanigoto mo kataraFinu ni kaFerikeri*). The interpretation of the line hinges on whether it was or was not a sexual encounter. Majority opinion holds that it was—after all, she stayed with him for three hours. Others believe that it was not, and still others feel that there is not enough evidence to decide.[58] If the verb *kataraFu* is read as "exchange (physical) feelings," they do not engage in sex; if it is read "speak one's heart, say all of what one is feeling," they do (i.e., they acted before speaking all that was on their minds). The *Ise* compiler seems deliberately to be leaving the question open—a potentially scandalous situation is suggested, and certain kinship ties are evoked (see below), but actual outcomes are left undetermined. The narrator remains at the man's position—"The man, feeling hopeless, ended up unable to fall asleep"—before moving through connectives (*keredo, ba, ba, ni*) straight into the woman's poem:

> you came to me, did you not?   or did I go to you?
>   I am not certain
> is this all a dream? or reality?
>   do I sleep? or do I wake?
> [kimi ya kosi / ware ya yukikemu / omoFoezu / yume ka ututu ka / nete ka samete ka]

> The man recites, in a fit of sobbing,
> in the depths of sorrow,   I am left to wander
>   in the darkness of my heart
> whether dream or reality   find out tonight
> [kakikurasu / kokoro no yami ni / madoFiniki / yume ututu to Fa / ko-yoFi sadame yo]

The text provides only the generic signifier *wonna* (woman), not the particular woman of the *dan*, together with the signifier *wotoko* (man). The topos involving an exchange of poems between a man and a woman appears repeatedly in other *monogatari*,[59] and recalls again those scenes painted on standing screens.[60]

The woman's poem appears in *Kokinshū* (Anonymous, 645) with a prefatory note explaining that when Narihira is out hunting in Ise Province, he secretly meets the Virgin, and "the following morning, having no one to take a message for him, while he sits deep in thought, this is sent from the woman." It is not clear whether the *Kokinshū* compilers took the poem from an early *Ise* version, whether both the *Ise* and *Kokinshū* compilers took the poem from a common source, or whether the poem is really by Narihira.[61] Rather than reply to questions of authorship or "source," the two poems tell the reader to read "as if" the meeting actually took place. *Kokinshū* simply juxtaposes the two poems (645 and 646), separated only with the word "reply" (*kaFesi*).[62] Since most of the poems that appear in *Ise* were existing compositions, the text seeks, through its variations, to surprise, entice, or entertain. Similar to the first *dan*, the foretext stands as pretext: the words of encouragement by the Virgin's mother set the textual play in motion.

The second poem as it appears in many *Kokinshū* texts contains a different final line, "I leave it up to you [reader–listener–people of the world] to decide [which is correct]" (*yoFito sadame yo*),[63] which makes explicit the ambivalent gestures to the reader found in Narihira's poems. Again, it is up to the reader to "rewrite" the poem and the *dan*. The version in the Tempuku text points to what follows, raising the reader's expectations for more discourse, which the text readily provides.

Unlike Genji's fateful meeting with the Fujitsubo consort, the text seems to allow only one "meeting" and thereby thwarts the expectations raised by the poem.[64] The governor of the province learns of the visitor and sponsors a banquet that lasts all night, thus preventing the man from visiting the woman again: "since he must set out for Owari Province at dawn, the man, unknown to others, sheds tears of blood; he is unable to meet her" (p. 193).[65] In the passage changes in perspective that would normally be perceived by a Western reader—as the viewpoint seems to switch from the man, then to the narrator, and back to the man—are not so clear-cut. Since we are dealing with a non–past tense narrating, whether we are in the fields, in the man's "mind," in the space that tells us about the governor, or suddenly at the man's perspective again at the banquet, we are not at a distance that varies all that much.[66]

The *dan* ends with an exchange unique to the *Ise* text. At the banquet, the Virgin offers the man a sake cup, and on its stand she has written the first part of a poem:

> since it is an *en* (creek/bond)   the traveler crosses on foot
>   without getting his robe wet . . .
> [katibito no / wataredo nurenu / e ni si areba]
>
> So she writes, without an ending (*suwe*) to it; taking a charred piece of a pine torch, he writes the ending on the stand, making a link with hers (*kakitugu*).
> again let us cross   the guard station at the meeting slope
> [mata aFusaka no / seki Fa koenamu] (*NKBZ* 8:193)

The two do meet again, *renga* fashion, through a poem. Oddly perhaps, the poem picks up no metonyms from the diegetic foretext, but its references to crossing and dampness, and the pivot-word in *e ni si areba*, "since it is a [shallow] creek" and "since it is a [shallow] bond," repeat important senses from the foretext and leave open two ways for the man to write the ending lines: to meet again or not. The man chooses the former through the play on *auFusaka* (both "meeting slope" and a famous barrier-gate to the southeast of the capital). "Chooses the former" is misleading, since the poem was most likely an existing one, which the *Ise* text severs for its own purposes,[67] splitting apart a waka to demonstrate a rebonding in writing, thereby repeating the earlier "meeting," which was never anything but a textual linkage anyway.[68]

Finally, the last line, taken to be a later addition, provides revealing information, comparable to the end of the first *dan*: "the Virgin, [the one] during the reign of Emperor Seiwa, daughter of Emperor Montoku, younger sister of Prince Koretaka." In nondiegetic discourse, with only a series of nominal phrases connected by the particle *no*, we are given identifications that can be taken as misreadings of dissimulatory gestures or as constructions of another link with earlier genealogical configurations. The note tells us to read the *dan* in terms of a particular Ise Virgin, Princess Yasuko, whose mother was the daughter of Ki no Natora and the woman who bore Prince Koretaka. The resulting tension between fictional incident and "factual" note produces an almost conspiratorial situation: during the reign of the Fujiwara-backed Seiwa, scandalous happenings are going on among relatives and associates of the "true" heir apparent, Prince Koretaka.

Ise and Seriality

The *Ise* sections are commonly referred to by the term we have been using, *dan*. The term is appropriate since it incorporates the idea of "expansion by adjacency," "step." Neither "growing out" of what comes before nor pretending "organically" to affect what follows, each "step" represents a tenseless space of utterance that, with the waka as its emblem, makes irrelevant characterizations such as "chronological development" and "internally structured plot." All *monogatari* texts, similarly constituted by "expansion by adjacency" (parataxis), allow for theoretically infinite expansion.[69] In the words of one scholar, "a work of this type enables any number of additions, deletions, and positional changes."[70]

Not only is *Ise* paratactic, but, as noted above in passing, the same movement appears within individual *dan*. A good example is *dan* 9, the most famous of the *azuma kudari* ("heading east," with its overtones of exile) *dan*. The "journey" to the east turns out to be a series of toponyms. The first is Yatsuhashi (Eight Bridges) in Mikawa. The text simply tells us that the man's party has arrived at Yatsuhashi, and instead of recounting events or describing scenery, the narrating offers an etymology, a focus, as we saw in *Taketori*, on the linguistic event itself.[71] "YatuFasi" sets up the famous *Karakoromo* poem, composed as an *oriku* (lit., bent verse).[72] The poem is a tour de force:

> karakoromo / kitutu nare ni si / tuma si areba / Farubaru kinuru / tabi wo si zo omoFu (140)

Spectacular in its rhetorical density, the poem is constituted by no fewer than five textile associative-words: *karakoromo*, "robe"; *ki(ru)*, "wear"; *nare(ru)*, "become familiar or worn"; *tuma*, "skirt"; *Faru*, "to full (cloth)"; three pivot-words: *tuma*, "skirt/wife"; *nare*, "to be accustomed to skirt/wife"; *Farubaru*, "to full (cloth)/long distance"; and one lead-in phrase, the syllables up to *kitutu*, which lead in to *nare*. The poem, which can be viewed as either pretext to the foretext or woven out of the constructed foretext, is itself a double weave of two types of signification, paradigmatic (the pivot-words, especially "wife" and "skirt"), and syntagmatic (textile/travel). It is also so interwoven with its foretext that one cannot simply "set off" the other.

Translations of the poem, whether into modern Japanese or English, inevitably unravel into simile. Here is a version following the poem's syntax:

> a fine robe   worn to a softness,
>   its skirt as familiar as my wife;
> now, this journey, stretched out like cloth for fulling,
>   fills me with longing for those dear ones back home

The poem modulates between the seriousness of "longing" and the cleverness of "stretching" the textual fabric. The narrating reinforces that duality: "when he has recited the poem, the tears of the men drip down on their dried rice, which has become swelled with moisture." The remark again suggests the ambivalence underlying eccentric elegance (*fūryū*).

Connected only by the phrase *yukiyukite* (go on and on), the next section of the *dan* is not linked thematically with the above. In fact, in one text it appears in variant form as an independent *dan*.[73] Again, we get place names, *Suruga no kuni* (Suruga Province) and the more important *Utu no yama* (Utsu Mountain), announcing signifying strands for the poems that follow. Expecting danger on the dark and ominous road to Suruga, the party encounter a traveling monk, whom they just happen to know. They hand him letters to take back to the capital. *Utu no yama* (also "Reality Mountain") sets up the "dream or reality" moment of the poem:

> in the province of Suruga   near Reality Mountain
>   neither in reality   nor in dream
>   am I able, any longer, to meet you
> [suruga naru / utu no yamabe no / ututu ni mo / yume ni mo Fito
> ni / aFanu narikeri] (*NKBZ* 8:141)

The poem plays on the belief that if your lover no longer appears in your dreams, that person has forgotten about you. The next section, simply tacked on, begins,

> Looking toward Fuji Mountain, though it is only the end of the Fifth Month, we see new snow on it shining brightly.

A poem follows, after which comes an explanation of the shape and size of the mountain, which is compared to Mt. Hiei, at the northeastern corner of the capital. Noteworthy is the deictic *koko ni* (here) in the phrase *koko ni tatoFeba* (if we compare [it to mountains] here). "Here" refers not to Suruga or any spot from which Mt. Fuji can be seen, but to the capital, where the reading/writing is presumably being performed. It is easy to imagine the situation if we think of the *dan* being read or written while looking at a screen painting of Mt. Fuji, which allows both perspectives at once.[74]

The fourth segment of *dan* 9 names a river (Sumida) located between two provinces. The river provides the metonymic pretext for the naming of the bird and also situates the "travelers" on a topo-graphical "seam" (a river between two provinces).[75] The bird the party sees is revealed in its act of playfully catching fish, first by its attributes—white with red beak and legs, the size of a snipe. When the boatman utters the bird's name, *miyakodori* (bird of the capital), this poem appears:

> if that's the name you bear   well, here's a question
> Bird of the Capital:
> is the one I love   alive and well, or not?[76]
> [na ni si oFaba / iza koto toFamu / miyakodori / waga omoFu Fito
> Fa / ari ya nasi ya to]

The last segment, *ari ya nasi ya,* can be read either "be without mishap or not" or "be alive or dead." The latter, with its stronger sense of urgency, is more suitable, since it matches the final line, "everyone in the boat collapsed in tears." The bird's playfulness no doubt con-trasts with the travelers' sadness, but the focus on the word play deflects the reader's attention from such concerns with sentiment to an appreciation of the interweave between the poem and its fore-text.

The semes of separation and longing for home in *dan* 9 are activated by metonymic place names, meaning that they are inscribed in the signifying processes, and should not be reified into autono-mous signifieds. The four segments of the *dan* are four separate "poem-narrations," or "poem-talks" (*utagatari*) that do not privilege the poems but rather, in Barthes's words, show "a serial movement of dislocations, overlappings, and variations." They can also be regarded as examples of "narrating moments" (discussed later), appropriate to poem-talks. Other examples of serialized *dan* are the following: *dan* 21, where an estranged couple exchange sets of poems; *dan* 23, the famous "Izutsu" *dan;* and *dan* 83, which tells of Prince Koretaka. We have seen, then, both in the "steps" from *dan* to *dan* and in the space of a single *dan* the potential for infinite readerly or editorial expansion.

A Writing Lesson

The *Ise* text also expands through observable *dan* "clusters."[77] *Dan* 9 itself, for example, can be grouped with *dan* that specifically mention regions in the east. The cluster begins with *dan* 7, includes *dan* 8, and then comprises *dan* 10 through 15. *Dan* 7 tells us that the man heads east, "it having become a strain to continue living in the capital." The cluster has led scholars to presume the "cause" to be the man's "affair" with the Empress of the Second Ward, Fujiwara no Takaiko, alluded to in *dan* 3 and 6. *Dan* 8 (the compiler does not make definite causal links, but simply juxtaposes the groups of *dan*) continues the "journey." *Dan* 10 finds the man in Musashi, the last toponym of *dan* 9. He is back on the road in *dan* 11, and *dan* 12 repeats the attempted abduction that appeared in *dan* 6, but the topos is now Musashino, which continues the metonymic link. *Dan* 13 also mentions Musashi, while in *dan* 14 and 15 we find another poetic toponym, Michi no kuni, believed to be Michinoku. The "satellite" *dan* assembled around *dan* 9 repeat geographical topoi in the *dan* or contain the seme "outer [i.e., eastern] regions."

Those shorter *dan* may represent traces of the "writing process" inscribed throughout the *Ise* text and may relate to the Heian poetic practice of composing poems on a given topic (*daiei*). We saw an example in *dan* 9, when someone proposed the topic of irises. Similarly, a poet, after (or while) reading a *dan* such as 9, might be reminded of other ways to activate certain toponyms or other related metonyms. *Dan* 13, for example, begins with "Long ago, a man in Musashi" (*mukasi musasi naru wotoko*). The *dan* weaves together the name Musashi with an item, *abumi* (stirrups), produced in the region. The man sends a note (in which we again see a deictic phrase) to his loved one back at the capital: "To speak [of another woman] is to feel embarrassed; not to speak is unbearable." On the outside of the missive he writes, "Stirrups of Musashi." An exchange of poems follows, activating the metonyms derivative of *abumi: kaku* (to hang—of stirrups and of hearts [i.e., to depend on]), and *kakaru* ("hang," and "such; like"). The woman at the capital, upon receiving no further word from the man, recites,

> buckles of Musashi stirrups   hang, come what may
>   so I too keep hanging my hopes on you;
> to hear from you is painful   yet no news is exasperating

[musasi abumi / sasuga ni kakete / tanomu ni Fa / toFanu mo tur-
asi / toFu mo urusasi]

The man's reply,
if I write, you complain,   yet if I do not, you are resentful,
     Musashi stirrups
such are the times   when one shall die of despair
[toFeba iFu / toFaneba uramu / musasi abumi / kakaru ori ni ya / Fito Fa
sinuramu]

In addition to the pivot-words and associative-words (stirrups, buckle, and hang), the "dialectical" movement of the foretext is repeated in the two poems, which also repeat the associative movement of the *dan*. Interestingly, neither poem appears in any other collection. Similar to *dan* we have already seen, the poems in *dan* 13 replay a paradoxical situation that allows no final solutions.

Other well-known clusters include those before and after *dan* 69. We are led into *dan* 69 by three *dan* that mention toponyms: *tu no kuni* (66) and *idumi no kuni* (67 and 68). On the other side of *dan* 69, *dan* 70 to 75 either repeat the name Ise or can be topically associated with *dan* 69. Another cluster begins with *dan* 50, which consists of a short opening note ("Long ago there is a man; feeling resentful of a person who showed resentment toward him") followed by five poems: two sets of exchanges, plus the man's last poem. The seven *dan* that follow all consist of a brief note plus one poem and repeat, in "associative" fashion, words or semes of *dan* 50: *dan* 51 ("flowers," *dan* 50 had mentioned "cherry blossoms"); *dan* 52 ("sweet flags"); *dan* 53 (a bird, the "cock," which echoes "hen" in 50); *dan* 54 ("dew," which is also in 50); *dan* 55 ("be unloved" [*omoFazu*], repeating *omoFanu* in 50); *dan* 56 ("dew," once more); *dan* 57 ("fisherfolk," from "flowing water" in 50); *dan* 57, which does not link directly with *dan* 50 but links up with *dan* 56 through "lodging" (*yado*).

The above clusters are not governed by any overriding organizational principles but display metonymic movements repetitive of those found in individual *dan* as well as in individual waka. The cluster from *dan* 76 to 87 resonates with our earlier discussion of the Narihira genealogy as it hints at historical intertexts. The remarkable list of historical personages that appear includes the following: Empress of the Second Ward (*dan* 76); Emperor Montoku, his senior consort (Takaiko), and Fujiwara no Tsuneyuki, the son of Yoshifusa's rival Yoshisuke (*dan* 77 and 78); Prince Sadakazu, his mother, who was the daughter of Yukihira (Narihira's step-brother), and Yukihira himself (79); Tōru (81); Prince Koretaka and Ki no Aritsune (82); Koretaka (83); Narihira's mother (84); Koretaka (85); and Yukihira again (87). Narihira, sometimes referred to as "old man" (*okina*), appears, of course, in each *dan*. Lastly, a great number of the (mostly anonymous) women who appear in the text turn out, in one way or another (through exalted station, fickleness, cold-heartedness, being simply unresponsive, and so on), to be either unattainable or impossible to remain attached to. I discuss further the implications of such situations of resistance in the section on the *Genji* tale.

Ise and Painting

I conclude by a brief discussion of the relation between *Ise* and painting, especially screen paintings (*byōbu-e*) done in a "Japanese-style" (*yamato-e*). I have already cited Katagiri's remark that *Ise* scenes and their economical action within a proscribed space remind one of Kabuki plays, but he has also claimed that "the scenes in *Ise mono-gatari* are composed in a pictorial manner."[78] As noted in our discussion of Lady Ise, Heian courtiers composed poems for screen painting and on topics suggested by the arrangement of miniature landscapes on a small table: *suhama*. Many *Kokinshū* poems are labeled *byaubu uta* (poems composed for a screen), and such poems constitute major portions of other poetry collections. Particularly noteworthy is a group of poems composed on a screen that depicts a poem popular during the time, Po Chü-i's "Song of Everlasting Sorrow." Five poems are composed "as if" the poet were Emperor Hsüan Tsung, and five as if the poet were Yang Kuei-fei.[79] The poet, though not able to deviate radically from the pictorial design, still had plenty of room to maneuver in a discursive space that demanded variation. An example of the process is section 147 of *Yamato monogatari*, the famous tale of Ikuta River. Of concern here, again, is not the "story" of a girl who throws herself into the Ikuta River, unable to choose between two young wooers identical in every respect (the men die too attempting to save her).[80] It is rather the sequence of poems that suddenly appears in the text, like a strip sewn into the textual seam. The *Yamato* narrator or editor clearly identifies the poems as composed by persons who assume the positions of the characters: "there being a painting presented to the late Empress in which such events of long ago had all been depicted, everyone present composes poems about the three youths buried in the mound, *having changed places with them.*"[81] Ten poems are given, after which the diegesis begins again. The poems are introduced by brief notations: "[composed] as the feelings of the boys," "having become the girl," "having become the girl when she was still alive," "having become one of the boys," "a reply by the girl," and so on.

In the course of written exchanges during the Heian period, it was not uncommon for one person to write poems standing in the place of another (e.g., for one's mistress or master). The *Ise* text presents such an instance when Ki no Aritsune composes on behalf of Prince Koretaka in *dan* 82, and we know that Narihira was often a surrogate poet. The act of writing as if someone else also underlies Tsurayuki's donning a feminine mask in *Tosa nikki*. Waka themselves, as we have repeatedly noted, are always contextualized (in literary and social situations) and constitute enunciating positions at which any reader can perform a new compositional act. That waka are generally unmarked for gender or honorific situation facilitates such acts. The *Ise* text can be considered a global textualization of surrogate writing practices.[82] *Hiragana* writing, marked for aspect and mood, presents a discourse that asserts a difference from *kambun* writing, and legitimizes itself (in its explanatory or communal mode) as it constructs its own deictic narrating positions. The *Ise* tenseless diegesis likewise proceeds "as if" what was being told were taking place right before our eyes on a painted screen.[83] "Storytelling" in a nonpast tense therefore goes hand in hand with the serializing, paratactic tendency of Heian texts (cf. "reading" a picture scroll: scene by scene, left to right).[84] Finally, the valorization of parataxis further relates to the Heian preference for metonym over metaphor.

III

Tales of "Genji"

We must first *overturn* the traditional concept of history, but at the same time mark the *interval*, take care that by virtue of the overturning, and by the simple fact of conceptualization, that the interval not be *reappropriated*. Certainly a new conceptualization is to be produced, but it must take into account the fact that conceptualization itself, and by itself alone, can reintroduce what one wants to "criticize."

    Jacques Derrida, *Positions*

Works composed of written symbols are not *monogatari*. In every case, *monogatari* come into existence at the instant they are read aloud. The written record does not constitute a representation, nor was it intended to. The reason is that *monogatari* meant precisely that which could not be recorded.

    Tamagami Takuya, "Genji monogatari
    ondokuron josetsu"

It may be history, it may be only a legend, a tradition. It may not have happened, but it *could* have happened.

    Mark Twain, *The Prince and the Pauper*

Who speaks and under what conditions he speaks: this is what determines the word's actual meaning. All direct meanings and direct expressions are false, and this is especially true of emotional meanings and expressions.

    Mikhail Bakhtin, "Discourse in the Novel"

6

Situating the "Feminine Hand"

In 975 at the age of twelve, Princess Senshi, the tenth daughter of Emperor Murakami (r. 946–967) is appointed Kamo Virgin (*sai-in*, also high priestess). During an astonishing fifty-seven-year tenure that spanned the reigns of five emperors[1]—En'yū, Kazan, Ichijō, Sanjō, and Go-Ichijō—the princess oversees a literary salon the equal of those at the "Rear Palace" (*kōkyū*). Known as Great Kamo Virgin (*dai sai-in*), she actively encourages artistic activities, establishes such female salon offices as "head of Japanese poetry" (*waka no kami*) and "head of narratives" (*monogatari no kami*), and leaves behind two private poetry collections.[2] According to a famous anecdote in the early *Genji* commentary *Kakaishō*, when Senshi asks Jōtōmon-in (Empress Akiko, or Shōshi) for entertaining stories, the latter in turn commands a talented attendant in her own Rear Palace salon (Murasaki Shikibu) to submit appropriate ones. The attendant makes a pilgrimage to Ishiyama Temple and, recalling from her childhood the story of the downfall and exile of Minamoto no Takaakira, begins writing the chapter ("Suma") that tells of Genji's exile in what is to become the most celebrated narrative in Japan. The well-known story further claims that Murasaki Shikibu wrote the chapter on the back of a copy of a Buddhist sutra (*Daihannyakyō*) and that the famous calligrapher Fujiwara no Kōsei (Yukinari) made a clean copy of it before it was presented to Senshi.[3]

I begin with the above to remind us that apocryphal stories can often help to highlight components and circumstances of old texts, in this case a tale that appeared some time during the first two decades of the eleventh century. The components and circumstances I have in mind include the following: (1) feminine authorship; (2) the existence of artistic and cultural salons composed of highly talented women; (3) the production of writing in response to an imperial (or other) request and the role of sponsorship; (4) the veneration of a "Genji" figure like Minamoto no Takaakira by later generations, and (5) the importance of genealogical and other ties of affinity among former royalty and scholar-officials of the time. We must continue to attend to the cultural and sociopolitical circumstances relevant to the texts' emergence lest we be inspired to read the *Genji* tale primarily as a solitary "literary masterpiece," which still means for many North American readers one enclosed between two covers and thus essentially and cleanly cut off from historical, political, and social concerns. Our now familiar task is to transform attitudes that view such concerns primarily as "background."[4] The following discussion will begin to amplify the components and circumstances noted in the Senshi anecdote.

The "Feminine Hand"

With the *Genji* texts we are in a space quite unusual in world history where women eagerly and skillfully occupied the subject positions of writing in a linguistic medium named for them. Known by the term "feminine hand" (*onna-de*), which signified *hiragana* writing, their discourse employed one of the two types of phonetic syllabary developed to transcribe the sounds of the native language.[5] The term contrasted with "masculine hand" (*otoko-de*), which signified Chinese writing practiced in Japan.[6]

We do not know exactly when *kana* writing developed, but most scholars agree that it came into use some time during the early decades after the capital was moved to the Yamashina site of Heian in 794 from the Nara site of Heijō.[7] The *hiragana* syllabic system functioned as a "private," or supplementary, mode of social communication and artistic expression in contrast to *kambun*, which signified the hegemonic discourse of "public" (i.e., governmental, legal, ritual, historical, and other) constructs. As *hiragana* became legitimized as a feminine mode, it maintained a contingent and potentially subversive aspect even when employed, as it frequently was, by men.[8] The *Genji* text, accordingly, is marked by a stance that attends to the "underside" (*ura*) of life, a stance the following discussions will explore. Male members of the court would not be compelled to suppress the "feminine hand," since their own masculine, Japanese identities would have been deeply implicated in its signification of the private as the native and even, by the early tenth century, the imperial state itself. As we have seen, the compilation of *Kokinshū* at Emperor Daigo's command formally legitimized the displacement of Chinese poetry by Japanese and in so doing elevated the status of *hiragana* writing. A few years prior to Daigo's command, the government, which came to take on an increasingly private, ritualistic cast, discontinued the writing of official histories in Chinese.[9]

As a result of the varied modes of Heian writing, men were not all-powerful but must often have found themselves deeply divided within their own discursive functioning.[10] In other words, male writers may have reserved for themselves the officially sanctioned realm of Chinese discourse but in private, nonofficial, and everyday matters, they were inserted continually into a realm that had become acknowledged explicitly as women's writing, where they were far from being dominant in scriptive terms. The example of Ki no Tsurayuki writing the *Tosa Diary* (*Tosa nikki*, 935) in *hiragana* in the persona of a woman offers, in its self-conscious subordination of a man to a woman's mode, a striking instance of a masculine certification of that mode as well as further evidence of the difficulty of assigning strict gender divisions in Japanese discourse.[11]

Tosa Diary ostensibly names a record kept by a "woman," a member of the entourage of the former governor of Tosa (Tsurayuki), during his journey home—after many delays, often due to bad weather conditions, providing the recorder convenient pretexts for presenting the composition of poetry—to the Heian capital after the expiration of his term of duty. In contrast to the later feminine diaries, it is punctuated by clearly designated months and days. The grief of the woman, perhaps the governor's wife, for a child with whom she had left the capital but who had died in the far-off province, provides a "private" aspect of the "diary," which presumably if written in Chinese would have been occupied with the recording of "public" events. The private sentiment complicates the feelings of the party who are at once happy to be going home to the capital after four years in a remote province and sad, as a result of the devastating personal loss, to leave the land behind. Most of the poems are attributed to certain (*aru*) persons, often a child, on the boat.

The diary is also unmistakably "about" the composition of poems and their appropriateness for given occasions and places. The incorporation into the text of the poem-making process is perhaps only to be expected of the preeminent male writer-poet of *hiragana*. In the context of our earlier discussion of the *Ise* textuality, we must not overlook the references made by the *Tosa Diary* narrator to Prince Koretaka, his Nagisa villa, and Ariwara no Narihira. At one point the narrator mentions both men's names (each prefixed by "the late" [*ko*])[12] and at another Narihira's alone.[13] The *Tosa* text thereby participates in the larger intertextual linkages and lineages established by the *Ise* and *Kokinshū* texts. Other pre-*Genji* texts (*Utsuho* and *Ochikubo*) may have been written by men, but contestatory and political issues are also at stake in claims that their author happens to be a Minamoto (i.e., a Genji) man, Shitagō, a celebrated scholar-official whose political hopes were dashed with the exile by Fujiwara rulers (see below) of his patron (another Minamoto), Takaakira. The latter, interestingly enough, was considered early on to have been a possible inspiration for the figure of Hikaru Genji.[14] The common practice of lumping together tales presumably written by men glosses over the writers' political and genealogical specificity.

Imperial Salons

We must also keep in mind the court "salons," such as Senshi's, Akiko's, or Atsuko's (with Lady Ise), that flourished during the tenth and eleventh centuries. Scholars use the term "salon" to refer to highly organized groups of women attendants clustered around an imperial princess, empress, or other high-ranking woman, a situation notably different from both Chinese and Ottoman practices.[15] Whether located at the palace (or, rather, the Rear Palace) or at private residences and shrines, the salons were spaces *of* and *for* women, though neither distantly removed from nor strictly prohibitive of visitations by men. Here women had "a room of their own," a communal place Virginia Woolf would have envied (for both its feminine communality and the room itself). Heian women possessed, in other words, in addition to their own discursive mode, their own discursive space.[16] One feminist scholar has noted regarding the way women are "devalued" in patriarchal discourse in the West, "Some salons . . . gathered women, culture, and politics in ways that render 'devaluation' too superficial a description."[17] By "devaluation" she means that women have been marginalized as producers of public culture. In Heian Japan women participated actively in the production of (private) cultural conventions (men did so too, of course, but primarily through the "public" medium of Chinese).[18] The views in the *Pillow Book* formulated by Sei Shōnagon under the watchful and sympathetic eye of her mistress, Empress Sadako, represent just such a particularized cultural construction. Maintenance or defense of a particular "group" ("salon" or family line) was often a prime motive for such competitive-minded writers.

When we thus resituate the women into their spaces and their discourse, the tempting characterization of Heian man as "always the reader and woman the read" and the claim that women "can have no power of [their] own until read" requires qualification.[19] In those "rooms of their own," women wrote for each other and for posterity in highly literate and mutually critical and competitive contexts. They were enabled, through their linguistic medium and by their politicocultural space, to speak for themselves and for their men, the latter often existing to be "read" and "written" by women, in a "feminine hand."

Matters Matrilineal

Assertions of male centrality and dominance are also made problematic by the powerful matrilineal emphasis in Heian society. From the famous studies by Takamure Itsue we know that marital arrangements of the courtier classes in Heian times were uxorilocal, duolocal, or neolocal. The early Heian situation, following ancient practices, seems to have been primarily duolocal (the husband commutes to his wife's house, *tsumadoi-kon*) before shifting, during the time of *Genji*, to an emphasis on the uxorilocal (the husband moves in with his wife's family—although the parents might eventually move to a separate residence, *mukotori-kon*). Men did take wives into their own family residences on occasion, but that seems to have been the exception (Izumi Shikibu's move to Prince Sochi's residence and Tamakazura's fictional move to Higekurō's both result in madness in their "principal" wives). The Heian practice afforded women a great degree of stability and support although, as is often pointed out, actual behavior so depended on specific circumstances that generalizations are all but impossible.[20] In conjunction with such arrangements there emerged an often complex (compared to modern-day nuclear family situations) intermingling of the matrilineal and the patrilineal. For example, property was passed on matrilineally to the daughter, while one remained tied in patronymic terms to the larger clan (which dictated the deities one worshiped, where one was buried, and so on). A man who was head of his clan might be supported completely by his wife's parents and might be referred to metonymically by the name of their residence, and that sobriquet might be handed down to succeeding sons-in-law (the politically powerful Fujiwara no Michinaga's residence, the Tsuchimikado Mansion, for example, belonged to his wife, Rinshi, whose father was Minamoto no Masanobu).[21] In *Genji* the status of the mother's family determines a character's fate: the absence of strong maternal backing becomes the Achilles' heel not only of Genji but also of his mother, Murasaki, Yūgao, Tamakazura, and Ukifune. And what has been read as "one long wail of jealousy" by the author of *The Gossamer Years* must be reread in light of the fact that she lived in her own residence where she received her husband Fujiwara no Kaneie (929–990), a situation that surely must have provided the security, support, means, and audience that enabled her to write in the first place.[22] Some feel that the Heian arrangement compensated women for the polygamous social practices of the courtier class, but, at any rate, it is far from a simple case of patriarchal dominance.

Fujiwara political practices necessitated the preservation of matrilineal factors. We know that Fujiwara hegemons retained the emperor as a symbol of authority and opted to exercise de facto control from a genealogically internal position by installing their daughters at the Rear Palace as consorts of crown princes and emperors. As the reigning emperor's father-in-law or, preferably, maternal grandfather (*gaisofu*), they created for themselves the prime positions of regent (*sesshō*) and chancellor (*kampaku*) to the emperor.[23] Two specific cases of *gaisofu* relationship were the tenures as regent of Fujiwara no Yoshifusa (804–872, for Emperor Seiwa) and Kaneie (for Emperor Ichijō), men who greatly stabilized Fujiwara policy. The practice of rule not, as in China, by heavenly mandate, but by genealogical continuity, legitimacy, and exclusion endures throughout Japanese history. As Ivan Morris and others rightly note, the practice depended on, among other things, the production of female offspring, lack of which meant certain defeat. In such cases, the practice of adoption, which remains common to this day, could be crucial.[24]

The "Genji"

The term "Genji" signifies an imperial prince lowered to common (high) courtier status and granted, along with appropriate rank and the charge to establish a new family line, the surname Genji.[25] "Genji" marks a broader gesture to the process of granting surnames to such princes and must not be limited to the "fictional" *Genji* figure. Although other surnames were similarly given to members of the royal family—beginning with Prince Morokatsu, son of Emperor Kōnin (r. 770–781), who was granted the surname Hirone in the year 787—Minamoto, in particular, comes to be considered a "sacred" (*seinaru*) surname.[26] The practice of forcing princes to take the Minamoto surname begins in 814, when four sons and four daughters of Emperor Saga are made "commoners." A first-generation Genji was the most revered and of the most ambivalent status—no longer royal, yet not really a commoner—whereas the status of a second-generation Genji, like Yūgiri, would not differ that much from the Fujiwara situation noted earlier (in fact, the Fujiwara usually welcomed marriage to a Minamoto daughter). Although a few such men were able to return to royal status and even become emperor, for the vast majority (and there are scores of such cases) the change in status was irrevocable.[27] Daigo was the last emperor to grant the Genji surname.[28]

The "demotions" initially took place owing to economic reasons—it took less to support nonroyal courtiers who occupied government posts than princes and their entourages who did not—but in some cases the move was politically motivated, as in the *Genji* narrative. It is in the latter cases that the experiences and interests of *zuryō* (provincial governor) class women and Genji men can coincide to engender strong feelings of mutual compassion: the two groups not only shared a bond of learning, as the demotion of princes sometimes led to their entering the Heian Academy (from which *zuryō* members often graduated, see below)[29] or preparing themselves in other ways for public office, but they were also liable to harbor a common grievance against Fujiwara injustices, feelings that they transposed—given the impossibility of overthrowing their adversaries—into an acceptance of their fate.

For the Genji resignation and melancholy often led to a retreat into amorous pursuits revolving around waka composition. Traces of their often bleak political fortunes, however, formed a powerful undercurrent of resistance throughout their subsequent poetic and narrative compositions, as the *Ise* text showed. The extent to which "aesthetics" and politics intertwine continues to be a crucial problem for the *Genji* text, one largely ignored by Western *Genji* commentators, for whom what we encounter is overdetermined at the level of the "aesthetic," the "lyrical," or the "beautiful."[30] The term *irogonomi*, for example, often taken to mean simply sex for sex's sake, or lust, or even love, must be viewed, in the mid-Heian context, not in terms of escapist or romantic tendencies but rather in terms of the imperial attitude toward sex for political and genealogical purposes. For the ancient emperors, sexual conquest of a local shaman meant symbolic subjugation of the region of her origin. In the context of the palace, having sexual relations with the highest-ranking consorts meant keeping the imperial line supplied with qualified candidates for succession.[31] First-generation Genji courtiers, recently severed from royal privilege, were given license to engage in polygamous acts as if activating the vestiges of imperial prerogative derivative of their genealogical origins. As some scholars argue, the practices of such courtiers must be distinguished from those of nonroyal Fujiwara hegemons like Kaneie or the fictional Kaoru, who, as the son of a royal mother-turned-Genji, seems to be unavoidably affected by his ambiguous status. That Genji secretly fathers an emperor (Reizei, a situation that prompted a remark by Ivan Morris about the "illegitimacy of the imperial line") powerfully motivates that ambiguity.[32]

Minamoto no Takaakira

Now let us examine more closely the "Genji" who appears in the Senshi anecdote, Minamoto no Takaakira (914–982). Cited in such early *Genji* commentaries as *Okuiri*, *Kakaishō*, and *Shimeishō* as an inspiration or "model" for the Genji figure, Takaakira was born to Emperor Daigo and one of his junior consorts (*kōi*, the rank of many such mothers, including the fictional Genji's), Minamoto no Shūshi. He was even known to his contemporaries as the "Shining Genji," having been one of five sons ordered to take the Genji surname in 920. The incident in which he became embroiled was the Anna Incident (*anna no hen*) of 969, merely one in a series of effective ploys instigated by Fujiwara leaders over an almost two-hundred-year period, beginning with the Kusuko Incident (*kusuko no hen*) in 810 (discussed earlier), to eliminate potentially influential members of other families as well as other Fujiwara colleagues who posed threats to dominance.[33]

To sketch briefly, the Anna Incident occurs on the twenty-fifth day of the Third Month in the second year of Anna (969) as the result of a "leak" by two men, Minamoto no Mitsunaka and Fujiwara no Yoshitoki, of an alleged plot against Prince Morihira, fifth son of Emperor Murakami. Morihira, who had become heir apparent when his brother Norihira became emperor (Reizei, r. 967–969), would be replaced with Prince Tamehira, favored fourth son of Murakami and Takaakira's daughter, and Reizei would be forced to abdicate to Tamehira.[34] The information leads to the arrest by the Imperial Police (Kebiishi) of Tachibana no Shigenobu, the monk Remmo, and other "coconspirators." During their interrogation it comes to light that another figure was involved in the plan, none other than the minister of the left, Minamoto no Takaakira. The police quickly surround the minister's residence, and a decree is issued announcing Takaakira's appointment as Dazai no Gon no Sochi (provisional governor-general of the Dazaifu, in present-day Kyushu). Tantamount to being sent into exile, the appointment was the kiss of death for a Heian official.[35] It is recorded that on the first day of the Fourth Month all of the buildings, save two or three miscellaneous ones, at Takaakira's residence burned to the ground. The coconspirators are exiled to various regions. Takaakira is reported to have taken Buddhist vows at the time.[36]

Takaakira's career illustrates possible permutations in the ambivalent and uncertain status of a talented "Genji" official. In Takaakira's case, that status made him the prime target of a Fujiwara frame-up, as scholars believe the Anna Incident to have been. An able scholar-official,[37] he was a favorite of the powerful and sexually prodigious Fujiwara no Morosuke (908–960) and married two of Morosuke's daughters, one of whom was the younger sister of Yasuko (Anshi), the influential grand empress. He was also on good terms with Emperor Murakami, who was also sexually active, as evidenced by the extraordinary number of consorts at his Rear Palace,[38] as well as with Yasuko herself. The political climate changed dramatically, and with it Takaakira's fortunes, when Morosuke and Yasuko die (in 960 and 964, respectively), the latter after giving birth to Princess Senshi (the Great Kamo Virgin in our story above). Takaakira managed to marry one of his daughters to Prince Tamehira, the other focus of the incident, in 966. In clear opposition to customary practice, the ceremony was held at the Shōyōsha, one of the apartments at the palace.[39]

Alarmed by the sudden establishment of an intimate genealogical tie between Takaakira and the imperial family that could eventually lead to Takaakira becoming the maternal grandfather of a future emperor (a kinship position the Fujiwara, as noted, had always jockeyed for with great success), the Fujiwara leaders began touting Prince Morihira as the legitimate heir apparent. Murakami's death the following year (967) effected another downturn in Takaakira's career, as it removed his final source of viable support. The Fujiwara moved quickly to install Morihira as crown prince at the new court of Emperor Reizei. When Fujiwara no Saneyori (900–970) became both regent (*sesshō*) and great minister (*dajōdaijin*), Takaakira, although promoted to minister of the left, stood an isolated figure. The man believed to have been the prime mover behind the frame-up of Takaakira was Minister of the Right Fujiwara no Morotada (920–969), who died several months after the incident, on the fifteenth day of the Tenth Month of 969,[40] as if in retribution for his treatment of Takaakira. There immediately ensued an intense struggle for power among the Fujiwara leaders. His political career shattered, Takaakira was allowed to return to the capital two years later.

The incident was not only crucial to the machinations of the Fujiwara, who once again eliminated a threat to their customary position as guardians of the imperial line, but it also profoundly affected court society at large, in part because of widespread belief in Takaakira's innocence. *Nihon kiryaku*, a late Heian historical source, records that "the capital was thrown into great turmoil, similar to the terrible rebellions of the Tengyō Era."[41] *Eiga monogatari* records Takaakira's fate as follows: "Takaakira's banishment was the most distressing event of the era—far worse than anyone's death, for death is, after all, a natural occurrence. Everyone was shocked and indignant that such a tragedy should have struck down a man who bore the Minamoto surname and was the first son of the wise and saintly Emperor Daigo." It further invokes the most celebrated exile in Japanese history: "Long familiar with tales of the exile of another great minister, Sugawara Michizane, and now dazed by the same cruel blow, they [Takaakira's wife, daughters, and sons] wept and lamented in pathetic fashion."[42] The *Ōkagami* narrator, in a revealing passage, tells us,

Although Prince Tamehira ought to have succeeded Emperor Reizei as crown prince, he was passed over in favor of his younger brother, just because the Lord of the Western Manor [Takaakira] was his father-in-law, a situation that led to some curious happenings. Since power would have shifted to Takaakira's family if Prince Tamehira had become emperor, and the Genji would have been the ones to prosper, the prince's ever resourceful uncles, acting in a manner that went against all propriety, installed his younger brother ahead of him as the heir apparent. Nobody inside or outside the palace had any way of knowing what the men were up to. Everyone thought the nomination would go to Prince Tamehira, who was next in order of birth. But all of a sudden the youngest prince's nurses were told to dress his hair; then, Kaneie put him into a carriage and he entered the palace by way of the north guard quarters. You can imagine the feelings of those who had supported the rightful candidate. Prince Tamehira even had to stand beside the throne [a humiliating posture], although plenty of other princes were available in those days, and there were other roles he might have played. Those who witnessed the spectacle told how deeply they were moved to pity by it.

And as for the Lord of the Western Manor, how it must have rankled in his heart! Thus indeed did some dreadful and heart-rending events occur. This does not do justice to the subject, but it is too presumptuous for humble folk to talk about such things publicly, and I must stop. Bringing up old stories is a bad habit of mine.[43]

The incident was not only of momentous import for the writers of the *Eiga* and *Ōkagami* texts (the so-called historical narratives, *rekishi monogatari*), but it is also given lengthy mention by the author of *The Gossamer Years* herself. Although married to Fujiwara no Kaneie, who had much to gain by Takaakira's removal, the woman known to posterity as the mother of Michitsuna (*Michitsuna no haha*) writes:

> Whatever sort of grave offense caused it, there irrupts under the heavens (*tenge*) a tremendous commotion about people being ex- iled. . . . Around the twenty-fifth or twenty-sixth day [of the Third Month of 969], the Minister of the Left of the Western Manor is banished. With everyone wanting to take a look, the world (*ame no sita*) is in an uproar, and people race wildly toward the Western Manor. I listen for news, thinking about the dreadfulness of it all and am told that the minister has slipped away without making an appearance. I hear that after more pandemonium caused by the manhunt—around Mt. Atago, then Kiyomizu Temple—his whereabouts are finally dis- covered and he is exiled. Knowing it's useless, I still feel devastated— even someone like me, who knows little of what actually happened. Among those who realize what it all means, there will be none whose sleeves are not soaked [with tears].[44]

The *Gossamer* author's inclusion of the initial escape, manhunt, and subsequent capture intensifies the pathos surrounding Takaakira. She goes on to mention the minister's many sons, their distant regions of exile, the pain of separation, and the taking of Buddhist vows. After stating that the incident occupied people's minds for some time, the author explains: "Though it is a matter that I ought not enter in a diary concerned only with my own affairs, since I am one of those who was deeply saddened by the events, I hereby record them" (*NKBZ* 9:207). Later, after she hears of the distress of Takaakira's principal wife when the Western Manor is destroyed by fire, she is again overcome with sadness and, as an outlet for her feelings, composes a "long poem" (*chōka*), an archaic form practically extinct by her time, and sends it to the woman under an assumed name.[45]

As the above shows, Takaakira's sudden demise shocked court society. It was viewed by later generations as marking a turning point in Heian history. The *Ōkagami* narrator, for example, remarks that the ascendance of Reizei meant the end of an age: "With the advent of Reizei's reign, though it may have been the reign of a new emperor, the world is cast into implacable darkness; it is from that era that the world begins its decline."[46] The feeling that the world had fallen into an age of decline and that the eras of Daigo ("wise and saintly" in the quote from *Eiga* above) and Murakami had been a golden age of rule by sage-kings (an age that produced Fujiwara ministers like Morosuke, who formed amicable alliances with the Genji and the imperial family) becomes the prevailing sentiment at the time of the *Genji* narrative.[47] I have discussed the Takaakira incident and its treatment in various Heian texts neither to establish a historical "ground" for the *Genji* tale nor to argue for a particular "model," but to underscore the importance of attending to what might be called a historicogenealogical or sociopolitical intertextuality.

Women, Writing, and Resistance

The Senshi anecdote made reference to an empress who commanded a talented attendant to present an interesting tale. We have seen that such attendants lived, while at court, in lively Rear Palace salons conducive to cultural production, and, perhaps most important, we have seen that such women possessed a discourse gendered (nonexclusively) as feminine. The following will examine one more aspect of such writers, their "middle-rank" (*zuryō*) status, and how that status affects our reading of their texts. In particular the ways in which it relates to the stance of "resistance," read in its full polysemy, form a prominent feature of their discourse.

The term *zuryō* comes to designate officials dispatched on successive (and sometimes exceedingly lucrative) tours of duty as provincial governors. They often derived from scholarly families known for learning and poetic skill, which they painstakingly transferred to their offspring—primarily to sons but often (by chance, as in Murasaki Shikibu's case) to daughters as well. Those officials included such men (the daughters will be discussed below) as the following: (1) Kiyowara no Motosuke, Sei Shōnagon's father, who descended from an illustrious line of poet-scholars and was a compiler of the second imperially ordered waka collection, *Gosenshū* (951); (2) Ōe no Masamune, Izumi Shikibu's father, whose family name was one of the most respected and whose younger brother, the famous Ōe no Masahira, was married to Akazome'emon, a noted poet and salon associate of Murasaki Shikibu; (3) Fujiwara no Tomoyasu, the father of the author of *The Gossamer Years;* and (4) Fujiwara no Tametoki, Murasaki Shikibu's father, who was also a member of a family of celebrated poet-scholars.[48]

Belonging to such families, women, if so inclined, had ready access to a tremendous fund of scholarship and, if fortunate enough to be chosen as attendants for an imperial "salon," were further blessed with the material and psychological benefits of royal sponsorship and protection necessary to become producers of cultural discourse. Their positions in the salons were highly uncertain, however, ever vulnerable to the winds of political change that arose from the private and arbitrary (and even at times self-undermining) practices of the Fujiwara rulers (Sei Shōnagon's tenure at Sadako's salon presents precisely such a case).[49] Such situations of uncertainty may account for the popularity of Buddhist practices and the strains of melancholy that run throughout *hiragana* discourse.[50]

Figures of discursive resistance recur throughout the various *hiragana* texts, beginning with the otherworldly "Shining Princess," who resisted all of her suitors, including the emperor, and even, in a decidedly unfilial manner, gainsaid her aged "foster" father (and mother). The language of the text, especially its poetic moments, also resisted thematic recuperation. The *Ise Collection* began with an initial section that read like a combination poem-tale, poetic diary, and poetry collection, thereby resisting generic categorization, and its author figure consistently adopted poses of resistance vis-à-vis her suitors. The *Ise monogatari* text also enacted resistances to commonly accepted ways of collecting poems (public and private): it created and moved within an eccentric poetic space that self-consciously destabilized such notions as biography, history and fiction, and poetic authorship.

The famous diaries written by the *zuryō* women include similar situations that have proven "resistant" to readers. First, there is the *Gossamer* author and her calculated poses. She resides in her own private residence and is thereby able to lock out her husband, Kaneie, whenever she wishes; in fact, the instances of male visitors knocking on her gate punctuate the text.[51] She possesses the wherewithal to go off (seemingly at will) on religious retreats, which were a primary means of feminine escape from the trials of the capital. She takes great pride in the fact that Kaneie turns to her for assistance in composing poetry for special occasions, and she brandishes her discursive skill with particular enthusiasm, especially when she becomes preoccupied with narrating the tales of her son's wooing of the woman of Yamato (*yamatodatu Fito*) and the Yatsuhashi woman, tales that take up more than half of the third section of the diary (modern editions usually divide the diary into three sections). Such aspects attest to a writer supremely aware of both her enunciative and economic positions, and the power of the *hiragana* medium. Much, if not most, of the "diary" also has the decided feel of a "poetry collection," or "poetic tale," a feature that again complicates generic categorization.[52]

Second, there is Izumi Shikibu, whose "diary" also reads like an expanded poetry collection (à la *Ise Collection*),[53] and who is represented as anything but a passive female victim of masculine dominance. She continually acts the part of the aggressor: the one apt to send a poem first, the one able through her poetry to entice the prince into paying a visit, the one who gets the better of him in poetic repartee, and the one who confounds his thoughts with the rumors surrounding her allegedly fickle behavior (as in the *Gossamer* text, the prince occasionally finds himself locked out). Although some have considered her an exception,[54] I would emphasize those aspects she shares with her sisters-in-writing.

Third, there is Sei Shōnagon, whose *Pillow Book* contains a fascinating mélange of confident, even conceited, and elaborately configured lists, preferences, judgments, and narrations. The author evinces an irrepressible pride in the scope of her learning (excepting the actual composition of waka) and her ability to handle the men who invade her quarters, even humiliating at times the unwary visitor. It is all played out, moreover, under the loving but ultimately vulnerable sponsorship of her empress, Sadako.

Fourth, Murasaki Shikibu's *Diary* is exceptional for the many representations and critiques of the women in her world. The diary, along with her poetic "memoirs," also contains "locking out" incidents, the most famous being her rebuff of the great Michinaga himself.

Such texts as those of Sei Shōnagon and Murasaki Shikibu can be and often have been given a "documentary" reading for the glimpses they allow us into the many close-knit clusters of women organized at the Heian capital, but they show just as powerfully that those salons enabled women to represent their world with a great deal of freedom, skill, and, often, humor, an act of representation that raises at the same time that it resists questions of verisimilitude.

Finally there is the *Genji* tale, filled with women who disrupt masculine schemes, from the Aoi Lady, Genji's principal wife, to the Rokujō Lady, to Asagao, to Tamakazura, to that supreme resister, Ōigimi, in whose construction figures a significant sexual politics (she is the daughter of Genji's younger step-brother, the Eighth Prince, whose side happened to lose out in a struggle for political power). The text itself, as I hope to demonstrate, continually resists attempts at appropriation (colonization) by means of modern Western literary categories.[55]

Narrating the *Genji* Text

Let us begin once again with the Senshi anecdote. Not only can the worlds of the imperial salons suggested there help us situate mid-Heian women writers like Murasaki Shikibu in their discursive environments, but they also enable a further move wherein we can mark a strong correlation between the salons in which the women actively participated and the narratological questions that the *Genji* text inevitably poses. By the latter I mean questions involving socio-linguistic aspects of Heian Japanese: its "tenselessness," its tendency not to make subject positions explicit (e.g., through an avoidance of pronominals), its use of "honorific language" (*keigo*), which produces constantly shifting configurations of speaker-hearer-referent nexes, its extensive incorporation of poetic (waka) utterances, its citations and references (often only implied) to other texts and situations, its relation to calligraphy and painting, and its built-in "commentary" feature, which we saw in the earlier texts discussed above but which now becomes a striking feature of the text. It is immediately evident that the problem of "narrating" in *Genji* requires a broadening of the parameters of what is commonly considered to be the proper study of "narrative."

For modern Japanese scholarship, narration itself does not become an explicit item of interest until the 1970s, with the work of such writers as Mitani Kuniaki, Takahashi Tōru, Fujii Sadakazu, and Noguchi Takehiko, but the problem of narration has always been a topic of discussion in the long and respected tradition of commentaries on the text.[56] In fact, one of the trademarks of the medieval *Genji* commentaries is a propensity to demarcate stretches of textual utterance, including those that refer to an extratextual voice, that of the putative "author," Murasaki Shikibu, and to label them with categorical terms. The term most often used now for what is believed to be that author's voice is *sōshiji*—i.e., the ground (or ground level, *ji*) of the text (*sōshi*).[57] One contemporary student of such *Genji* passages points out that the famous linked-verse poet Sōgi (1421–1502) was the first commentator to use the term, although different terms had been employed previously to mark similar passages.[58] A noteworthy predecessor is the well-known commentary *Kachō yosei* (1472), by the great scholar Ichijō Kanera (1402–1481).[59] Kanera identified twelve instances—using such phrases as *monogatari no sakusha no kotoba* (the words of the author of the *monogatari*), *monogatari no ie* (the house [meaning not clear] of the *monogatari*), and *monogatari kaku hito no kotoba* (the words of the person who writes the *monogatari*)—that would come under what scholars today call *sōshiji*.[60] Sōgi's consolidation was in turn adopted by later commentaries such as *Mōshinshō* (1575), and terminological consistency was achieved with *Sairyūshō*, whose practices in turn found their successor in the valuable Edo period text *Kogetsushō* (1673), by Kitamura Kigin (1624–1705).[61]

A narratological watershed was achieved by the Edo period text *Genji monogatari hyōshaku*, an unfinished commentary by Hagiwara Hiromichi (or Kōdō, 1813–1863). Displaying a fine ear for narrative nuance, Hagiwara made suggestive references to the various narrative perspectives. His reference, for example, to comments by the "author" (*sakusha*) as "words of the recorder" (*kisha no kotoba*) established a basis for distinguishing between the act of "authoring" and that of "writing" or "recording," distinctions that become decisive in a seminal twentieth-century discussion of *Genji* narration, the famous "Reading Aloud Proposal" (*ondokuron*) by Tamagami Takuya (discussed below). Moreover, Hagiwara realized the difficulty in distinguishing passages that could be read either as the thoughts of a character or as the words of the author, and his comments contained an implicit distinction between the biological "author" and the "narrator": "What are called *sōshiji* are not the thoughts or words of a character in a *monogatari* but those places which seem to be comments delivered from somewhere else (*hoka yori*); these are the words of the author (*sakusha*) transformed into the words of the person who narrates (*monogatari kataru hito*)."[62]

When modern Japanese scholars began turning their attention to the specific problem of narration, they were able, then, to draw upon an illustrious tradition of commentary for terminology and method. Besides *sōshiji* the commentaries contain such terms as *kaiwabun*, (conversation), *naiwabun* ("internal speech," also related terms like *naigo, shinnaigo,* or *shinchūshii*), waka, and *ji no bun* (description),[63] all suggesting a productive propensity to read the text as a mosaic of different voices, styles, and discourses. The last term, *ji no bun* ([back]ground writing), which scholars frequently use today, refers to those passages that in the West might be termed "description," although the latter is a problematic term at best.[64] *Ji no bun* designates, in the context of the present discussion, what remains after the passages that fall under the other categories listed above are subtracted. Although a renewed interest in *sōshiji* was already underway when Tamagami's "proposal" appeared, not only did the proposal have a great impact on later scholarship, but Tamagami's discussion encompasses many of the social "intertexts" noted above.[65]

In 1950 Tamagami Takuya introduced his famous and controversial "Reading Aloud Proposal" (*ondokuron*).[66] Taking seriously the fact that "silent reading" is a modern phenomenon,[67] Tamagami attempted to explain those *sōshiji* in *Genji* as presumably the voice of a narrator who seems to take the stage and speak directly to her audience. He paid special attention to those *sōshiji* that evaluated a character or event for the edification of what he believed was the primary audience for the tale.[68] The earliest narratives, his argument goes, were written by men, who monopolized the "public" written language of *kambun*. Tamagami classifies those early texts by a term, "old tales" (*mukashi monogatari*), found in the texts. *Genji*, which he calls "genuine" *monogatari*, represents a time when tales begin to be written by women who had gained a fundamental competence in *kambun*,[69] women who were born into families where Chinese scholarship was dominated by male descendants. Tamagami claims that the shift in *monogatari* authorship from *kambun* scholars to "women-in-waiting" (*nyōbō*) was possible because the latter were from the start the readers (or rather the "reciters") of *monogatari*, their primary audience being their mistresses, imperial princesses and consorts who usually looked at illustrations while the women read the text aloud:[70] "*Monogatari* come into existence at the moment they are read aloud by *nyōbō*."[71] During such sessions the reciters would often ignore their (presumably Chinese) texts and freely embellish, expunge, or otherwise alter their stories as they responded to the needs of the occasion. The *Genji* text represents a stage in the development of *monogatari* when such female attendants took up writing brushes and began composing tales themselves. In doing so, they put into the text comments that had formerly been left to the reciter's discretion. The often lengthy *sōshiji* found in the *Genji* text appear because it is the written version of a woman reciting the tale: "When a woman read [the text] aloud, it would come alive again as the tale of a former lady-in-waiting."[72]

The process leading to the appearance of the *Genji* text can be outlined as follows:

Stage 1. Chinese text (Tamagami uses the term *manabun*, a variety of Chinese incomprehensible to the Chinese themselves as well as to many Japanese, who could, however, make out the gist of the passage from the meaning of the individual characters).[73]

Stage 2. Performance of a Stage 1 text by a woman.

Stage 3. Written version of Stage 2 by a female scribe.

Stage 4. Recitation (performance) of a Stage 3 text for reactualization.

In other words, *Taketori* and other pre-*Genji* narratives derived from an encounter between a *mana* text, consisting of a basic (or basically intelligible) story outline, and its reciter, a woman who read the texts aloud and in her own words. Since many additions were necessary during such a performance—passages not actually in the "text" and those that needed modification to accommodate a particular occasion—the *mana* texts, in Tamagami's view, left almost everything to the reciter's discretion. Since a narrative might therefore differ radically from one reading performance to the next, the process also explains the numerous variant texts that exist today.[74] There is much to be said for conceiving of artistic creation as a social "performance," something other than a solitary activity undertaken by an isolated individual, and Tamagami's "literal" reading of textual evidence also helps to concretize those real world narrating situations that analyses tend to efface. But his identification of narrative comments with particular authorial personages, however influential it has been in leading many to make similar identifications, goes too far in hypostatizing the various comments.[75]

For all its suggestiveness, Tamagami's own failure to pursue implications contained in his "proposal," especially concerning the issue of orality, reduces its impact. First of all, his emphasis on the oral versions of the narratives suggests nothing less than a valorization of a kind of "performance." *Monogatari* signified oral performance, not "texts" per se: "Works composed of written symbols are not *monogatari*."[76] Second, his statement that the *Genji* text could be and was written down, albeit this time in *kanabun*, not *manabun*, figures a contradiction: those things which, by definition, could not be "re-presented" by scriptive means not only become texts that can be written down after all but are also further re-presented if and when they are read aloud. A perceptible slippage—from *monogatari* as (only) speech to *monogatari* as (scriptively recreatable) text—has occurred. At this point we can pose two questions: Once we have one scribe's version of a text, isn't that sufficient? And what determined whether or not a text was to be written down? The process described would seem even to stifle the propagation of variants, unless the women were always at liberty to amplify the texts according to mood and audience. Rather than concentrate so heavily on linking the *sōshiji* in *Genji* with oral performance, Tamagami might have viewed the comments as components integral to any Japanese narrative, written or oral,[77] thereby avoiding the obvious tautology: *monogatari* contain *sōshiji*, thus they were read aloud; they were read aloud, thus they contain *sōshiji*. Textual variants resulted perhaps less from verbatim recordings of oral performances than from the fact that they were constitutive of the writerly (or performative) *monogatari* mode, whether at the hands of copyist, reciter, or scribe. The inscription of the performative meant that the texts were dependent not on any particular recitation but on *any* act of reading, writing, or copying. We can revise Tamagami's hypothesis to include the various ways that texts were appreciated (or appropriated) and collapse strict distinctions between reading aloud, copying, and reading silently to oneself. It cannot be emphasized too strongly that for the Heian Japanese reading often meant an act not qualitatively different from writing, i.e., from composing.[78]

I find Tamagami's study especially valuable for its attempt to integrate the larger sociopolitical and discursive contexts: the impact of Chinese literary styles, the situation of reading texts aloud in feminine salons, the role of scholarly families, the education of women empowered to write in *hiragana*, and the narrative comments. The most remarkable aspect of Tamagami's position, however, may be his valorization of orality: "The reason that written [texts] were referred to by that term [*monogatari*] was the fact that they were read aloud."[79] Lack of evidence that *monogatari* were actually composed to be read aloud weakens Tamagami's argument somewhat but doesn't detract from the force of what I take to be the main point of the essay: "Works composed of written symbols are not *monogatari*. In every case, *monogatari come into existence at the instant they are read aloud.* The written record does not constitute a representation, nor was it intended to. The reason is that *monogatari* meant precisely that which could not be recorded."[80]

Tamagami based his reasoning in part on a hint taken from a famous scene in the "Azumaya" (Eastern Cottage, 50) chapter of *Genji*. In the scene, which remains as one of nineteen extant *Genji* picture-scroll illustrations, one of the three main female figures of the final ten "Uji" chapters ("Hashihime" to "Yume no Ukihashi," 45–54), Naka no kimi, is having her hair combed while her half-sister, Ukifune, looks at pictures coded (we assume) to the calligraphic text that an attendant is reading aloud to them.[81] Taken together with the tenseless flow, Tamagami's statements engender a situation typical of all *monogatari*, one I refer to variously as "narrating instance," "narrating moment," or "narrating."[82] "Tenseless narrative" means that the narrating valorizes each of its moments or instances, rather like a picture scroll or slide show, viewed frame by frame, matched with a running commentary, each moment susceptible to extensions and amplifications and also appropriate elisions. The situation is also reminiscent of those narrator-commentators known as *benshi*, who once held forth at silent movie theaters throughout Japan.[83] In either case, the events described seem to happen even as they are being told.[84]

As a result of the amalgamation of linguistic features, performative situation, and the suggestions of visual representations, the *monogatari* narrating effects a series of discrete moments, without, moreover, "internal" temporal controls other than those provided by notations of ritual or seasonal time and heuristic biographical schemata. It is not incumbent on what is prior to function as a logical "cause" for what follows, and practically anything can be substituted for anything else in the seriate current.[85] I must emphasize that tenseless narrative does not mean "present-tense" narrative. The narrating easily refers to prior moments, but they are always anchored to the spatiotemporal coordinates of the particular moment in question. What happened once has relevance not as an always already reified, abstractable past point in linear time, but as the narrating continually re-presents it in a deictically determinate now.

In the above context, we might recall what Genette has called "simultaneous narrating," which he defines as "narrative in the present contemporaneous with the action."[86] Such narratives are, he claims, "in principle the simplest, since the rigorous simultaneousness of story and narrating eliminates any interference or temporal game."[87] He also cautions that the merging of the two can produce two distinct types of texts—emphasis may fall toward the story or toward the discourse—and he characterizes the two types as either "objective," where the narration becomes transparent to the story, or "subjective," which is a type of "interior monologue" where the action "is reduced to the condition of simple pretext, and ultimately abolished."[88] The qualifiers demonstrate the Eurocentric limitations to Genette's analysis, for when we confront a *monogatari* text, we find that although it is similar to what I have characterized as the *monogatari* narrating situation, such terms as "objective" or "subjective" are not particularly useful. Rather, it can be argued that *monogatari* narrating constitutes a mode that privileges the narrating *without* becoming "subjective" (in the strong Western sense, "subjectivity" being an extremely difficult issue East or West), confining ourselves to the two terms. If the assumptions underlying Tamagami's proposal were followed further, the claim would emerge that narrative discourse itself, the performative event, becomes an important, perhaps *the* important, "story." When we reconstruct the text within the deictics of its performative situation and yoke it to the pictorial possibilities as mentioned above, it becomes clear that the narrating register never really disappears even when a character's "internal thoughts" are given, and whether or not the "consciousness" of a character takes over becomes a nonissue. Viewed in those terms, "story" remains in a particular way the pretext for or the effect of "discourse."[89]

Tamagami has had more than his share of critics.[90] Their aim, it must be remembered, was to demonstrate to literal-minded colleagues that "author" and "narrator" are not identical, as Hagiwara had suggested more than a century earlier. I agree completely on the need to speak in less anthropomorphic terms. At the same time I view the issue in terms of the relations between narrating (or what can even be called "general writing") and what consequently ends up being narrated as well as the further, unexplored question of how either comes to be possible in the first place rather than as a question of any specific narrator, omniscience, point of view, or even consciousness.[91]

In the end, Tamagami's proposal remains most difficult to displace, since it allows for the dynamic yet contingent interaction between text, reading (performance), and real world (salon, or storytelling) situation and also helps explain the rise of textual variants. As every recitation or copying of a *monogatari* would differ from every other one, the same would hold for every recitation or copying of a *waka*. Such a perspective also recalls contemporary notions of how the act of reading constitutes the text being read and of how one "reading" cannot be either self-identical to another or the text self-identical to itself.[92] The oral aspect of Tamagami's proposal might be viewed as an obverse component and narrative effect of every written (version of a) text. As Fujii Sadakazu writes, "The early writer was not free of the limitations of [the] oral transmission [form]."[93] Instead of combing textual traces for clues to the "origins" of *Genji* variants, instead of a nostalgia for any "genuine" text, we must try to eliminate speech versus writing binarisms and accommodate the "textualizations" that occurred when acts or performances based on voice, calligraphy, and painting converged in those close-knit salons at the Rear Palace and elsewhere, producing the interconnections among reciter, reader, writer, scribe, copier, and text, interconnections in which no one element precedes nor supersedes any other but only finds its construction as the others' effects.

Fujii also links diachronically, in ways that both help broaden the scope (as I too am attempting to do) and demystify the *Genji* text, the narrators' comments in the *Genji* texts with analogous topoi in earlier texts like *Kojiki*, the *fudoki*, and historical texts where we often find a deictically oriented, abbreviated commentary on the events narrated. In other words, an "explanatory" (*kaisetsu*), narrating register, similar to the end of the *Taketori* segments and the end-of-*dan* comments in *Ise*, appears in all Japanese narratives. What in other languages has been referred to as "authorial aside" represents a common procedure for Japanese. It is not, therefore, because the *Genji* texts result from an author's "genius" or represent a "higher" level of "development" that the mechanics of their narrating are complex. Rather, they were created out of a distinct moment when women, empowered with a self-legitimating discourse marked for them (*onna-de*), found themselves gathered together in culturally stimulating sociopolitical groups that themselves rested upon the always changing mid-Heian configurations of rank, status, and power.

In the chapters that follow I have chosen certain sections and passages from the *Genji* text to initiate readings that negotiate the issues discussed above. Of the remaining six chapters, four (7, 8, 9, and 11) focus on individual *Genji* chapters and two (10 and 12) on matters better addressed by a wider-ranging coverage. Chapters 7 and 8 read two "beginnings" ("Kiritsubo" and "Hahakigi," often characterized as initiating, respectively, the "main" and the "ancillary" chapters). I connect the question of sociohistorical circumstances and feminine authorship to problems of narrating pace, "history," and representation. Chapter 7 traces the *Genji* narrating as it establishes its own tenseless maneuvers and raises simultaneously the question of "history" and "fiction" as they are located in the domain of the "private." I also focus on Genji's mother's lineage, which turns out to prefigure the all-important Akashi line. Chapter 8 extends the discussion of narrating in a "feminine hand" to the issues of representation (and its objects), critique, judgment, and Genji's "education." The "seed" for the Tamakazura narrating, moreover, is planted in "Hahakigi." Chapter 9 examines a major "figure of resistance" (Tamakazura) whose "story" grows from that "seed" and whose narrative construction is linked in important ways by means of poetic conventions to the earlier situation. The chapter also discusses the status of *monogatari* narrating as an unstable construct implicated in sexual-rhetorical maneuvers at the same time that it privileges *hiragana* writing over official histories written in Chinese. Chapter 10 examines critiques of the arts and attempts to situate the discussions in terms of a sexual politics and a genealogically governed authority and their relation to discourse arising out of a particular Rear Palace salon. Chapter 11 reads a third "beginning" of the tale to establish the "seed" for the Akashi "story" and to demonstrate how the narrating is constantly reconfigured by movements of complementarity. I take up the problem of the "marginal" in narrating terms in order to examine the introduction of the Akashi family and the staging of the fateful meeting between Genji and Fujitsubo, both interposed in a chapter ostensibly devoted to Murasaki. I also discuss the problems of "substitution" and "origin" relevant to the "marginal" *hiragana* mode. The final chapter ("introduced" by the previous one) traces the narrative "life" of the Akashi family to show how the fortunes of one family are inextricably tied to the fortunes of the tale's main "Genji" figure, a construction of convergences that requires a further negotiation of the linguisticonarrative, sociopolitical, aesthetic, and genealogical aspects introduced in the earlier chapters. The Akashi "stories" provide crucial moments of intersection for the "Genji," the *zuryō*, and the imperial in terms that also interconnect the social status of the presumed *Genji* author or authors to their larger intertexts.

I reiterate that I do not aim for "comprehensive" coverage of the formidable texts, especially coverage based primarily on "thematic" appropriations,[94] which end up instituting necessarily exclusionist moves unable to account for cultural specificity at either the macro or micro level.[95] The following readings, in their attempt continually to resituate themselves in relation to the reconfigurations and displacements effected by the *Genji* narrating, will simultaneously complement and critique existing readings of the *Genji* text and mark their own perspectives as polylogic and contingent (in their resituating).

7

Narrating the Private: "Kiritsubo"

The following continues to rewrite the Senshi story by focusing on a seemingly "marginal" moment in "Kiritsubo" (Paulownia Court). I must begin, however, at the famous beginning:

> In which/whose reign [might it be/have been]? Among the many senior consorts (*nyougo*) and junior consorts (*kaui*) in attendance stands one not from the highest ranks and blessed far more than the others with the emperor's affection. The various women who have harbored high hopes for themselves from the beginning of their tenure at court look down upon the amazing upstart with feelings of resentment; even more restless are those junior consorts equal in rank to her or lower. As she goes about her duties day and night, she only incites the hearts of those women. Was it because she had to bear the brunt of all that rancor?—she falls seriously ill and, apparently plagued by strange feelings of despondency, begins to spend more and more time at her own [i.e., her parents'] house; the emperor becomes further moved to pity by her plight and finally can think of nothing else; so, paying no heed to the remonstrations of others, he behaves toward her in a manner that must surely set a precedent for all the world.[1]

As the narrating cites, *in medias res*, an already established, ongoing situation, we are given no information about the emperor's identity, when he ascended the throne, or how he met the Kiritsubo (Paulownia) Consort, a name taken from a tree planted in the garden of her Rear Palace apartments. The focus, rather, is the narrating itself, which continually locates us in its tenseless moment without any pretense of offering a detached, representational account of past events.[2] The opening phrase, *idure no oFontoki ni ka*, which elides a fuller syntactic form—for example, *idure no oFontoki ni ka ariken*, found at the beginning of one of the *Ise shū* variants—challenges the reader-listener as it figures an undecidability: are we to take it as a "literal" question (anticipating a specific answer) or a "rhetorical" question (it doesn't matter whose reign it was, or it matters and we all know which it was)? The question of referentiality is posed only to be taken away; we are told that what is now being narrated might really have happened but also that its referent is not accurately determinable, in marked contrast to the *ima Fa mukasi* and *mukasi* openings already encountered.

To the question of historical reign another factor is immediately added: it was a reign notable for the many senior and junior consorts (*nyōgo* and *kōi*) installed at the Rear Palace. Among the many imperial consorts, one who is of lower rank and from a lower-ranking family has monopolized the emperor's affections and, consequently, is the object of intense jealousy and vilification. Under normal circumstances an emperor was obliged to parcel out his affections (and sexual energies) according to the rank of each woman.[3] The larger situation is crucial for, as Tamagami Takuya notes, the narrating does not focus solely on (i.e., in no way romanticizes) the relationship between the emperor and his ill-fated consort, but suggests the strained relations that have come to exist among the many women who resent his singling out a lower-ranking junior consort.[4] Immediately after the opening section translated above, the narrator refers to a famous Chinese pretext: Yang Kuei-fei, loved to excess by the T'ang emperor Hsüan Tsung, an ominous precedent that would have been on the minds of all courtiers.[5]

The opening lines gesture to a particular historical situation in a manner that inscribes history within a general rhetorical and fictional movement that carries the history forward as an integral part of its narrating momentum, continually questioning it as it proceeds. The early medieval commentaries, quick to notice possible historical intertexts, read "honorable reign" (*oFontoki*) as a direct reference either to Emperor Kammu (r. 781–806), the first Heian emperor, or, more convincingly, Emperor Daigo, Takaakira's father, whose Rear Palace (even more so than Murakami's) was populated by numerous consorts.[6] Many parallels have been found throughout the text to the reign of Daigo—the emperor known to posterity as a major revitalizer and champion of waka through his sponsorship of public events (such as poetry contests) and his encouragement of poet-scholars like Ki no Tsurayuki. Later generations commemorated Daigo's reign as a time when actual authority resided with the emperor, especially after the death, in 909, of Fujiwara no Tokihira.[7]

A comparison of the above version with Edward Seidensticker's now-standard English translation will highlight important textual features:

> In a certain reign there was a lady not of the first rank whom the emperor loved more than any of the others. The grand ladies with high

ambitions thought her a presumptuous upstart, and lesser ladies were still more resentful. Everything she did offended someone. Probably aware of what was happening, she fell seriously ill and came to spend more time at home than at court. The emperor's pity and affection quite passed bounds. No longer caring what his ladies and courtiers might say, he behaved as if intent upon stirring gossip.[8]

The past-tense markers and the clipped cadences of the latter translation take the reader back to a represented, "once upon a time" world that the narrative recounts. In the Japanese that world is coextensive with the narrating at every moment, always anchored to that narrator and her narrating situation from the moment she utters "in which/whose reign?" (a phrase that is [must be?] suppressed in the standard version);[9] employs context-specific honorifics; and conjectures continually. Seidensticker's version gives the commonly desired impression of a neutrally detached, third-person narrative long characteristic of Western novelistic discourse.

Other matters eliminated or altered in the standard version include those having to do with historical and cultural specificity: (1) it omits the specific, crucial mention of two important ranks of imperial consort, *nyougo* and *kaui* (the text clearly places Genji's mother in the latter category), and presents instead a general world of "ladies" and "love," thus losing the references to the particularized setting—the women's Rear Palace quarters; (2) the phrase "probably aware of what was happening" not only sounds a bit offhand but suggests that the woman's illness results from her own awareness (or even conscience), whereas the Japanese, again, foregrounds the narrator who surmises to an audience about the powerful, spiritual forces believed to be omnipresent, a situation obtaining in many close-knit societies where a look or a word can kill;[10] and (3) in the last sentence of the Seidensticker version, in place of the clear reference, repeated several times in the chapter, to the establishment of (historical) "precedents" (*tamesi*), with its polyvalent references not only to "gossip" but also to different aspects of *Genji* itself (not to mention its anticipated and actual impact on later *kana* discourse), we find the more domestic "stirring of gossip." The ambiguity in the term *tamesi* will inform much of the *Genji* text: a narrative constituted by "gossip" destined nevertheless to establish "precedents."[11]

After the initial situation discussed above, the narrator "begins" again and fills in the *kōi*'s background: her father was a major counselor, now deceased and her mother a well-bred woman descended from an old family lineage. The consort, we are then told, gives birth to a child: "Is it that their bonds from a previous existence are deep? A baby boy, brilliant as a jewel not of this world is [i.e., has been] born" (1:94).[12] The event enables a new context that raises the question, how can such a remarkable creature exist in the world? The narration, instead of focusing on the new arrival, immediately places it into another situation by comparing the new child to the first prince (the future Suzaku Emperor), born to the most powerful *nyōgo*, Kokiden: "Overcome with anticipation, the emperor quickly orders the child brought to the palace; upon gazing at it, he sees that it possesses a beauty rarely seen in the world." The very next line brings that first-born prince into the situation: "As for the First Prince, born of a senior consort who is the daughter of the minister of the right, a prince backed by powerful people and esteemed by all as the next in line to the throne; nevertheless, he cannot compare with the new arrival's radiance; so even though he [the emperor] regards him [the First Prince] with proper displays of respect, it is this [new] prince, especially, on whom the emperor lavishes unbounded affection, thinking of the child as his private possession" (1:95). The words "private possession" (*watakusi mono*), like "precedent" above, have a proleptic significance far beyond the immediate situation. The "public" sphere implied in the status of the older son, soon to be crown prince, and the "private" sphere now monopolized by Genji together participate in a public-private relationship the *Genji* text will explore throughout its countless incidents and narrating moments. Although in keeping with its *hiragana* discursive mode it ultimately privileges the "private," it does so, as we shall see later, in a manner that continually traces the complex, mutual dependency of the one upon the other.

Yugei no Myōbu

The narrating begins yet again after the birth by describing anew the emperor's scandalously immoderate affection for the Kiritsubo Consort and the resentment growing ever more intense among his now neglected other women. Unable to withstand those debilitating pressures and forces, the consort soon dies.[13] At this point, there appears what seems, if considered from the point of view of "story" or "plot," an inordinately long section (it occupies about one-third of the chapter), which narrates the emperor's dispatching of an attendant,

Yugei no Myōbu, to the home of his dead consort's mother to persuade the old woman to return to the palace with the baby. The very length of the section, which is also constituted by a public-private difference, tips us off to the locus of narratorial interest, and the section is worth examining in some detail. It also exemplifies the flexibility of voices and registers possible in *kana* narrating.

The passage, which shows how the *Genji* text plays off waka conventions, begins with the narrator telling of the devastating effect the death of his beloved consort has had on the "Kiritsubo Emperor" and reminding us that it is autumn, the most poignant season: "even for those who look after him, it is a dew [and tear] filled autumn" (1:102). The emperor sends a close attendant, called Yugei no Myōbu, to the house of the consort's mother, where the new baby is also staying: "at dusk, when winds suggesting an autumn storm rise, and one suddenly feels the chill on the skin, memories flood his thoughts more than usual, and he dispatches one called Yugei no Myōbu" (1:102). The narrating then remains with the emperor, telling us that he recalls his dead consort's skill at playing stringed instruments and at poetry composition, and, though he has visions of her being there before him, "they are inferior, after all, to the 'reality of the deepest darkness'" (1:103). The emperor's words form a citation to an anonymous "Love" poem (*Kokinshū* 647):

> the reality of [an encounter in] the deepest darkness
> > dark as leopard-flower seeds
> > surpasses not in the least
> I see, the visions   of a vivid dream
> [nubatama no/yami no ututu Fa/sadakanaru/yume ni ikuramo/masarazarikeri]

The *Genji* intertextual moment reverses the *Kokinshū* sentiment, which calls the vision in a dream more distinct than the reality of darkness. For the emperor, it was fleeting enough when the *kōi* was alive; visions of her now are certainly no better. Meanwhile, the Myōbu's "journey" has occurred:[14] "she arrives at that place and, as soon as her carriage is pulled in through the gate, the impression is deeply moving (*keFaFi aFare nari*)" (1:103). After quoting a statement she heard from an earlier messenger (a Naishi no Suke), the Myōbu transmits verbatim, or so we assume, the emperor's words, adding her own comments about the latter's condition. We are then given part of the text of the emperor's letter, which expresses concern for the child's well-being and a desire to have both the child and the grandmother come to the palace so that the emperor can share his grief: "Think of me as a memento of one who used to be, and come [to the palace]" (1:105). In Japanese, the phrase "think of me as" (*nazuraFete*) forms a rhetorical figure from the verb *nazuraFu* (consider A as B, taking them to be of equal value), which also appeared in the "Kana Preface."[15]

The grandmother replies, with references to Chinese texts,[16] that she appreciates the imperial concern but that she has no intention of going to the palace, and although it may be natural for the infant prince to return, the thought of separation doesn't alleviate her sorrow. Then in a transitional pause the narrator tells us that the prince has retired for the night. The Myōbu asks to see him but, given the late night hour, quickly makes ready to leave.

Instead of a departure, however, the narrating turns to the grandmother once again. Almost as an afterthought (and as we shall see such seemingly "marginal" passages of temporal discrepancy often provide crucial narrating clues) she expresses a desire to unburden her sorrow and asks the Myōbu to visit again "privately" (*watakusi ni mo*). She then begins to speak of her daughter (in *ki* discourse):

> From the time she was born, she was one on whom we placed all our hopes; the former major counselor [the *kōi*'s father] up to the very end would tell me repeatedly, "Do not fail to carry out our plan to have this person enter court service; do not abandon hope, what a waste that would be, just because I have died"; though I was apprehensive about how she would fit in without powerful backing, my immediate concern was not to go against those dying words [of his], and I sent her to the palace; the kindnesses His Majesty displayed were far beyond what we could have expected, and our gratitude was unbounded; yet, though she tried to get along with others while hiding the embarrassment at not being treated like them, their resentment grew, and she was tormented by an increasing number of unbearable incidents until things ended up as they have, most unnatural to behold; I now fully realize just how painful august blessings can be; this too is because of *the darkness of a confused heart*;[17] she could say no more, and as she went on sobbing, the night hour has grown late indeed. (1:106)

During the private, unofficial part of the encounter, between comments about the lateness of the hour, the grandmother reveals her husband's fierce determination to have their daughter received at court. Such ambition will be repeated later in the Akashi family line, when a former provincial governor and lay priest sacrifices his daughter to achieve the success the *kōi's* father had hoped for. That the Kiritsubo Consort met with a tragic end is, we learn, partly to be blamed on family ambition. The Myōbu then transmits, through the narrator, the emperor's words, which express the "private" side of the situation:

> "His Majesty would agree completely: 'Though I am speaking of my own feelings, that I cared for her so much as to startle others to such a terrifying degree was owing to my having realized that we would not be together for long;[18] now, the ties to that person certainly remain painful ones indeed; although I tried to make sure that the feelings of those around me would not be offended even in the slightest, because of this person [the *kōi*] I had to bear the ill will of those who would otherwise wish me no harm,[19] and after all is said and done, I am abandoned, with no means of consoling myself, afraid of what others will say; a complete eccentric. I wonder about our former life'; he repeats such phrases over and over again and is constantly given to tears"; her words know no end, and, in tears herself, she says, "Since the hour has become very late, I must deliver an answer before this night is over," and hurriedly goes to the palace.[20] (1:107–108)

The emperor realizes the consequences of his actions but claims that the death was not so much his fault as due to ties from a previous life. At that point the Myōbu still has not departed, and we are given an exchange of poems between her and the grandmother in a passage that tells a veritable poem-tale:

> The moon about to sink over the hills; the sky perfectly clear as far as one could see; the wind now quite cool; almost able to imagine tearful faces from the cries of the insects in the grasses, truly an abode among the weeds difficult to leave behind:
> like the bell crickets   though I were to cry
>   until my voice gave out
> the long night would not be time enough
>   for my endless tears to fall
> [suzumusi no/kowe no kagiri wo/tukusite mo/nagaki yo akazu/Furu namida kana][21]
> She is unable to force herself into [the carriage]:
> in the deafening sound   of insects raising a chorus of cries
>   the dewy-tears lie heavy on the reeds [in this ruined garden]
> yet more dew falls from above the clouds
>   where that person dwells

[itodosiku/musi no ne sigeki/asadiFu ni/tuyu okisoFuru/kumo no uFebito][22]

I might end up blaming everything on you; she had her words delivered [to the Myōbu]. (1:108)

In its suggestion that a visit from the court only brings more sorrow, the grandmother's poem reveals both her grief and her deep displeasure at the emperor's unforgivable behavior.

While the Myōbu is (presumably and finally) returning to the palace alone, the narrating focuses on the emperor's response in another important section that includes references to the historical Emperor Uda (867–931, r. 887–897; he is referred to metonymically by the name of his retirement villa, Teiji-in, see below), to Po Chü-i's "Song of Everlasting Sorrow,"[23] and to the important waka poets discussed earlier, Ki no Tsurayuki and Lady Ise. The passage announcing Myōbu's return from her mission begins with a long phrase containing two *keri* suffixes, the first affixed to her discovery that His Majesty is still awake and the second to her finding him in the garden conversing with "four or five of his female attendants." In both cases the suffix signifies discovery or realization, as in the latter example: "[The emperor] is engaged in conversation [with them], and I/she discover/s it now." As is often the case, it is difficult to distinguish the narrator from the character, here the Myōbu.

Next the narrator tells us how the emperor has been passing his lonely hours: "These days he looks, morning and night, at the depictions of scenes from the poem 'The Song of Everlasting Sorrow,' the ones painted by the Teiji Villa Emperor, complete with poems commissioned from Ise and Tsurayuki; all he does is make the comments on that [Po Chü-i] story, either in Yamato diction or Chinese verse, his pillow talk [i.e., his sole topic of conversation]" (1:109).[24] The emperor then requests a detailed report from the Myōbu. When he sees the letter from the *kōi*'s mother, he comments on the father's dying wishes and on the mother's obeying those wishes and sending her daughter to court:

"[The mother] not gainsaying the testament left by [her husband] the deceased major counselor and realizing the high hopes he had for her to enter court service; as an expression of my joy, I [the emperor] had planned all along to reward them; what use are such words now?" So saying, he is deeply moved as he imagines how [the grandmother] must feel. He continues: "Nevertheless, when the young prince grows up, I'm sure there will arise occasions for appropriate action. Let us hope that she is patient and lives long enough to see it come to pass." (1:110–111)

The emperor's words suggest that he will endeavor to repay the *kōi's* family by ensuring a successful career for the prince. Again, for comparison, here is the Seidensticker version: "He had hoped to reward the grandmother's sturdy devotion, and his hopes had come to nothing. 'Well,' he sighed, 'she may look forward to having her day, if she will only live long enough to see the boy grow up'" (p. 12). The latter erases historical and textual specificity, omits the crucial references to the husband (the "deceased major counselor") and his testament, which echoes the exchange between the Myōbu and the grandmother,[25] and overemphasizes instead the old woman's "devotion." It also passes over the emperor's thoughts about the future. The emperor's hope for the grandmother's longevity proves futile, and her death leaves the child alone in the world with only the emperor's affection and his own beauty and considerable talents to sustain him. As I have noted, an ambition similar to that expressed by the *kōi's* father will later characterize the head of another crucial family, the Akashi lay priest.[26]

Though it may seem desultory, the Myōbu section forms a high point of the chapter *in its very desultoriness*. It is easy to imagine the attendants in Akiko's salon listening with particular interest to the story of an attendant like themselves conversing with a grandmother similar to one of their own or that of an acquaintance about matters having to do with the motives and desires of figures in the world. Among the historical personages cited, Emperor Uda, Daigo's father, represents a case of a prince who initially took the Minamoto surname (Minamoto no Sadami) but later became emperor.[27] Moreover, not born of a Fujiwara mother, he actively supported a formidable Fujiwara rival, the brilliant minister Sugawara no Michizane, and was able for a time to keep the powerful ruling family at bay until the latter managed to exile the minister in 901.[28] The period of Uda's rule is referred to as the "Glorious Kampyō Rule" (*kampyō no chi*), analogous to Daigo's rule mentioned above (*engi no chi*). Without neglecting the composition of Chinese poetry, Uda managed to spend a great deal of energy advancing the cause of native waka composition and native culture in general. One of the most celebrated poetry contests, for example, was held in 913 at the Teiji Villa under Uda's sponsorship, with the emperor also serving as judge. Uda not only encouraged such poets as Tsurayuki and Lady Ise but was sexually intimate with the latter and, as noted earlier, even had a child by her. He is also believed to have been a behind-the-scenes influence on the *Kokinshū* project, and he is particularly remembered for a text, "The Kampyō Testament" (*Kampyō goyuikai*), which consists of advice and admonitions concerning court practice and etiquette, written at the time of his abdication for his son and successor, Emperor Daigo.[29] A final indication of the reverence with which Uda was held by scholar-writers is *Yamato monogatari*, a text that begins with the words "The Teiji Emperor" (*teizi no mikado*).[30]

After the grandmother's death, important incidents are told in quick succession. First, the narrator notes the child's intelligence and natural talent, which make him a big hit among the emperor's bevy of women, including even his mother's rival, the Kokiden Consort. Next, on the pretense that he is the son of a controller (*daiben*), he is taken to Kōro Mansion (Kourokwan) where a Korean soothsayer, believed to be a member of a Korean delegation, pronounces the first of the three governing prophecies in the narrative: "He has the mark of one who will become an ancestral founder of the nation and rise to a rank equal to that of a king; to see it from that angle is to see possible chaos and sorrow; to see it as the mark of one who becomes guardian of the public [imperial] realm and serves the interests of the state is also to contradict its significance" (1:116). As if to inscribe further his historical intertext, the passage makes mention of Emperor Uda's "admonition" (*imasime*) that foreign dignitaries should not be received at the palace.[31]

Astonishment at the child's destiny quickly gives way to practical considerations—Genji's lack of strong political backing—and after also consulting native fortunetellers, the emperor chooses to avoid potential conflict with the Kokiden Consort's faction and sets his second son on a course of learning and governmental service. Accordingly, he changes his status to that of nonprince: "He [the emperor] has decided to make him a Genji" (1:117).

Fujitsubo

The third incident, which occurs in the next narrating section, provides yet another beginning (although by now the reader will have long realized that the notion of "beginning" itself is not a functionally linear one for Heian texts) by introducing the Fujitsubo Consort. The fourth daughter (*si no miya*) of a "previous emperor" (*sendai*),[32] the princess piques the emperor's curiosity when a trusted attendant, an assistant handmaid (Naishi no Suke) who had served that previous emperor (actually, "had served during three reigns"), vouches for her remarkable resemblance to the dead Kiritsubo Consort: "She is called Fujitsubo [Wisteria Court]; her face and features amazingly recall [Genji's mother]" (1:119). Genji will be unable to forget the following remark, which he overhears: "She certainly looks a lot like her [the Kiritsubo Consort]" (1:120). The princess's mother, remembering the fate that befell her daughter's predecessor, harbors serious misgivings but dies before reaching a decision, whereupon the daughter's guardians, with the approval of her older brother,[33] quickly decide it would be in her (and of course their own) best interest if she entered the Kiritsubo Emperor's court. The narrator immediately invokes Genji's mother, comparing the new consort's royal status with the former's unrecognized one: "this one: of superior rank, which in itself commands respect; and, since no one can humiliate her, the emperor can act as freely as he chooses; as for that one: without the consent of his court, his desires certainly took an unfortunate turn; he does not forget her, but his feelings change in spite of himself, and he seems to gain special comfort from her [Fujitsubo]—how deeply affecting are the ways of the heart" (1:119). Although the final phrase can be read as Seidensticker (and many modern commentators) reads it—"So it is with affairs of this world" (p. 16), which emphasizes a distant, even negative tone (i.e., the narrator turns a matter-of-fact eye to the easy transferral of imperial affection)—the narrative comment also permits a different, positive reading: something as accidental as resemblance can and often does arouse strong emotions (in both emperor and reader). The second reading better coincides with the prior narrating instances we have seen: the artibary world of *sekkan* Fujiwara politics that encouraged the harboring of ambitions with no guarantee of success. The Kiritsubo Consort just happens to have been of low rank and Kokiden of high, their statuses thus sealing the fates of their offspring; Fujitsubo just happens to resemble Genji's mother, thus she can enjoy imperial favor without fear of immediate reprisal.

The foregrounding of the accidental at the heart of the originary creates an initial metaphorical movement, but since it is a movement that continues to pay its dues, so to speak, to its founding maneuver (accident), instead of the usual displacement and subsequent stabilization we might expect of metaphorical totalization, the originary situation keeps open the possibilities for future accidental linkages, thereby instituting a lateral motion that continually contravenes the establishment of hierarchically formed (tenor-vehicle) pairs. The movement is similar to what we witnessed in the various tropological configurations of poem-songs.[34]

An important ritual event, Genji's coming-of-age ceremony, takes place when he reaches the age of twelve.[35] What comes to pass on that outwardly auspicious occasion institutes a disruptive source for the first nine chapters: Genji's marriage, now that he is a nonprince, to a high-ranking commoner, the daughter of the minister of the left. The incident plays on the Fujiwara desire to marry daughters both into the immediate royal family and also to formerly royal Genji men. The bride, who becomes Genji's "principal wife" (*kita no kata*), will later be referred to as the Aoi (Heartvine) Lady. The situation is notable for its juxtaposition with the introduction of Fujitsubo, thus becoming inextricably associated with it.[36] As the reader discovers, Genji will never warm up to his first wife who is a few years his senior. Unwittingly implicated in the staging of a political (public) act, she cannot displace either the strong (private) attachment the youth already feels toward Fujitsubo or will later feel toward Murasaki, Fujitsubo's niece. Each woman (the *kōi*, Fujitsubo, and Murasaki) is usually seen as a "substitute" for the succeeding one, although such configurations cannot ultimately remove the male Genji from a position of centrality vis-à-vis those substitutes.[37] The situation will be the first of many similar cases of the unhappiness that almost inevitably arises from such "arranged marriages" between men and their "principal" wives, situations implicitly critical of public, external matters as against private, internal ones.

The chapter nears its end with the revelation of Genji's feelings for Fujitsubo and the Aoi Lady:

> In his heart of hearts, thinking only of the peerless figure in the Wisteria Court [Fujitsubo]; if he/I could just marry someone like her; she is totally unlike anyone else; the minister's daughter appears to have been blessed with the most careful upbringing, but she does not find a place in his heart; his only concerns are the feelings of his childhood, a source even of pain to him now. (1:125)

Genji's feelings toward Fujitsubo might be thought to arise naturally—i.e., because he misses his mother and he sees her as a surrogate—but they are also helped along considerably by the emperor himself. The latter had taken Genji along with him on his visits to his women, and Genji had, we are told, ample opportunities to get a peek at the Fujitsubo Consort. Also, as the mother of the Ise Virgin in *Ise monogatari* counseled her daughter to grant the Imperial Hunter every favor,[38] so the emperor advises Fujitsubo to do the same for Genji: "Do not treat him as a stranger; I feel in some odd way that I am bound to compare (*yosoFu*) you to her [Genji's mother]; do not consider him rude, but be responsive to his charms; since he resembles his mother in every feature, it would not be unbefitting to regard you as that other person [*kayoFu*—exchange her for you]" (1:120). The pivotal words are *yosoFu* (compare/see a likeness, pretend that X is Y) and *kayoFu* (exchange X for Y [and vice-versa], commute). The emperor/narrator here transforms (the term used for the trope in Japanese is *mitate*) a "natural" and accidental resemblance into an explicitly tropological one. The gesture exemplifies the manipulation of the possibilities of a coincidence of resemblance and continues the privileging of the "beautiful" for "private" ends. Although the Kiritsubo Emperor is forced to remove Genji from the political reality of imperial succession, he sees to it that the potential for the realization of a powerful and necessary bond is firmly in place. Only subsequent events can bear out the success of his efforts, but the existence of the bond itself forms a proleptic moment that already suggests a degree of certainty as to outcome. As if to emphasize further the bond, the narrating juxtaposes the two: "Everyone calls him the Shining One (*Fikaru kimi*); Fujitsubo takes her place beside him, and with the Honorable [the emperor's] Feelings divided equally between them, she is spoken of as the Princess of the Radiant Sun (*kagayaku Fi no miya*)" (1:120). The emperor's counsel thus brings together the rhetorical and the political in a configuration of mutual complicity and signals a movement that will remain at the heart of the *Genji* narrating.[39]

We are told near the end of the chapter that Genji's mother's house (*nizyau no win*, now emptied of its former inhabitants) is renovated into a grand mansion with a magnificent garden with the requisite flora, hillock, and small lake, and we are also given Genji's reaction to the new residence: "In a place like this, if only I could install someone like the one that obsesses me; he was continually preoccupied with such sorrowful thoughts" (1:126). Again, we can hear a question in the words: who will Genji end up installing in his newly rebuilt mansion reerected in the memory of his dead mother? Who will be that someone who is like the Fujitsubo Consort and therefore also like his mother? The following comment, reminiscent of the end-of-*dan* comments in *Ise* and end-of-tale comments in *Konjaku*, finally recuperates the chapter for the narrating mode: "The name, The Shining One: granted by the Korean visitor as an expression of praise—thus, indeed, has it been transmitted to us" (1:126).

As the narrating moments fall into their places, the frequent gestures to historical intertexts construct precedents and prophecies that will govern future moments. The obsession of the Kiritsubo Emperor for his *kōi* finds repetition in Genji's feelings for Fujitsubo, feelings that the emperor actively encourages. Such obsessions, as they embrace the Rokujō Lady and Oborozukiyo,[40] ultimately mean sorrow: death for his principal wife and exile for himself. The *Genji* text tells of a "private" (*ura*) side of life, but that side too is only a part of the larger "world" to which the text occasionally makes suggestive references. Among the items in that world are the Rear Palace and its intricate balance, the *kōi*'s father's ambition and her mother's sacrifices, the former emperor, the Naishi no Suke who served three reigns, and the Korean delegation. In the following chapter I discuss another "private" side of life, women from the "middle ranks," and the narrating complexities of their representations in the "rainy night critique of ranks."

8

Feminine Representation and Critique: "Hahakigi"

It is often asked whether "Hahakigi" is really the second *Genji* chapter. Calculating a five-year gap in Genji's age after "Kiritsubo," scholars have posited a missing chapter, "Kagayaku hi no miya." The observation may be "thematically" or "temporally" apposite, but in narrating terms it ignores the fact that the very first words of "Hahakigi"—"The Shining Genji, splendid in name only"[1]—refer directly to the last line of "Kiritsubo." Since the question of chapter organization is closely connected to "Hahakigi," a few remarks on the organization of *Genji* chapters are in order.

"Secondary" Chapters

"Hahakigi" represents another beginning insofar as it is believed to inaugurate a chapter series, or cluster, that takes off in topical directions different from those in "Kiritsubo." Such chapter clusters, generally referred to as *narabi no maki* ("chapters in a row," or "lined-up/lateral chapters"),[2] focus on characters from a social status (the "middle ranks," as we shall see) different from those of the other ("main") chapters, which deal with "influential upper-rank ladies."[3] Such clusters include "Hahakigi" followed by "Utsusemi" (The Shell of the Locust, 3) and "Yūgao" (Evening Faces, 4); "Wakamurasaki" (Lavender, 5) followed by "Suetsumuhana" (The Safflower, 6); "Miotsukushi" (Channel Buoys, 14), followed by "Yomogiu" (The Wormwood Patch, 15) and "Sekiya" (The Gatehouse, 16); "Tamakazura" (The Jeweled Chaplet, 22) followed by the nine chapters from "Hatsune" (The First Warbler, 23) to "Makibashira" (The Cypress Pillar, 31); and "Niou no miya" (His Perfumed Highness, 42) followed by "Kōbai" (The Rose Plum, 43) and "Takekawa" (Bamboo River, 44).

The lateral chapters are also marked by temporal disjunctions. When temporal flows are plotted, as commentators have meticulously done over the centuries, discrepancies far more radical than the five-year gap between "Kiritsubo" and "Hahakigi" arise: "Suet-sumuhana," for example, begins before the time of "Wakamurasaki" (which precedes it) and ends at a point after it; "Yomogiu" backs up to a point near the end of "Akashi" (two chapters preceding it) and, together with "Sekiya," concludes at a point before the end the chapter they both follow, "Miotsukushi"; "Tamakazura" reverts after its opening lines to a period traceable to "Hana no en" (fourteen chapters earlier) and ends at a point simultaneous to "Otome" (which precedes it); and so on. The structural and temporal anomalies result perhaps from the attempt by the narrating to produce the fuller account (in comparison to historical chronicles) mentioned in the "Hotaru" discussion of *monogatari*.[4] They also show the effects of a narrating movement weighted deictically to its own situation, which intersects with salon settings in which different occasions demanded different narrating sections. The result is a narrative attitude that shuns temporal linearity and keeps alive the potential for "open-ended," multidirectional extension, meaning again that concern with "story-level" consistency quickly becomes irrelevant.

Being moored to narrating moments and occasions partially explains the predominance of *sōshiji*, which tend to congregate at the beginnings of the lateral chapters.[5] The "Hahakigi" chapter provides an excellent example:

> The Shining Genji, splendid in name only; liable to having that name extinguished for his many alleged improprieties; how dreadful of those rumormongers to have passed along even secret incidents he had kept to himself, since they would give him a reputation for frivolity if later generations were to hear of his amorous affairs; in fact, to the extent that he worried about what the world might say and adopted a sober profile, he certainly would have been laughed at by the likes of Lesser Captain Katano for not becoming erotically entangled in any amusing adventures. (1:129)[6]

The self-legitimating narrator incorporates vectors of past ("he had kept secret") and future ("if later generations were to hear") anchored to its ongoing movement. The other deictic phrase, *"these* secret incidents," indicates the narrating to follow, although it can also refer to stories the gossips have already bandied about or ones the audience already has heard (in the so-called missing chapter?). The narrating makes ostentatious use of gossips, relays of information, and reputation, at the same time it criticizes gossips for revealing secrets. It also suggests that its story will set something of a precedent: Genji will be a man who does not take relationships lightly, who will not simply pursue women for the thrill of it, like Lesser Captain Katano.[7] Though we are given hints that he is far from innocent (could those "improprieties" refer to his later affair with Fujitsubo, and have they already had one erotic encounter?),[8] Genji will be constructed as a courtier not particularly constricted by fear of gossip who will turn out nevertheless to be a somewhat serious-minded lover. The implied question of the ambivalent manner of narrating the sober figure is already partly answered in the very ambiguity that characterizes the position that figure assumes (in contrast to previous tales, presumably written by men, that dealt with characters like the Katano lover) and in the complexities noted in the "Kiritsubo" chapter.

The "Hahakigi" chapter, then, initiates a series of lateral chapters governed by instances of *sōshiji*. In establishing a basis for structural and narrative "anomaly," it begins to spin narrative threads that will be woven further in later chapters, one such thread being the introduction, through Tō no Chūjō's storytelling, of a woman later known as Yūgao. She and her daughter (later known as Tamakazura) play vital roles in the *Genji* text, implicated not only in rhetorical, genealogical, and critical links throughout but also situated at thresholds of diversion or amusement that ultimately involve stories of failure, resistance, and even death. The so-called Hahakigi line of chapters, in other words, forms an "obverse (private) side" (*ura*) to the Kiritsubo line, just as the *Genji* text itself forms an obverse side to the offical chronicles. Whereas the "Kiritsubo" chapter relies on citations to historical pretexts and intertexts, the "Hahakigi" chapter forms itself the pretext for much of the rest of the *Genji* tale, especially as an intertextual "source" for the impulse that drives Genji to seek out women from the class of middle-rank officials, the *zuryō*. In pursuing further the topic of narrativity and subject construction in "Hahakigi," I focus on the section that consists of the remarkable series of staged narrating moments known as the "rainy night critique of ranks" (*amayo no sinasadame*).

The Rainy Night Critique of Ranks

After situating Genji as a middle captain (*tiuzyau*), telling us in the *ki* (personal experience) mode of his reluctance to visit the house of his father-in-law,[9] and citing a poem from the first *Ise dan*,[10] the narrating wends its way to the rainy summer night (around the Fifth Month) when three courtiers—Tō no Chūjō (head chamberlain middle captain), the experienced Hidari no (M)uma no Kami (director of the Left Imperial Stables), and the scholarly Tō no Shikibu no Jō (the Fujiwara secretary of the Ministry of Ceremonial)—discuss the merits and demerits of women. The latter two suddenly appear, deliver comments, and then disappear just as suddenly. Genji, who never narrates, is at once the hypostatized audience and object of instruction (and male-female desire), even falling asleep (or pretending to) at one point before becoming the subject of narrating in the last section of the chapter.

Occupying a good three-fifths of the chapter, the narratings discuss how women of different ranks qualify as objects of desire. The pretext is a ritual pollution (*monoimi*) at the palace that requires abstinence and strict seclusion.[11] As often happens, overt "public" circumstances provide an opportunity for revealing the covert "private" world beneath (or behind) the scenes, for focusing on the question of "underside-frontside" (*ura-omote*) relations constitutive of all aspects of Japanese writing and the "life" constructed therein. The "prologue" to the section introduces Genji's lifelong companion and rival, commonly referred to as Tō no Chūjō, here called "middle captain born of a princess" (*miya bara no tiuzyau*). He is the son of the minister of the left and is Genji's brother-in-law. His mother, the "princess" later known as Ōmiya, is the Kiritsubo Emperor's younger sister.[12] We are told that he and Genji often exchange notes on their amatory adventures. The captain appears as a good-natured, gullible youth eager for tales of amorous conquest.

The initial context is a conversation concerning letters received from women. Genji at first refuses to show those he has received, and the narrator concludes that he must be keeping letters from high-ranking women tightly hidden away.[13] When he agrees to show his letters if his friend will do likewise, a switch to the main topic occurs through a strategy common to the text: "'I'm sure I don't have any that you would find worthwhile'; so he speaks, and while he [the captain] is on the subject" (1:132). "While he is on the subject" (*tuide ni*) may sound like the announcement of a topic of marginal importance, but it in fact signals that the narrating is now turning to its "main" topic. The strategy accords well with the *Genji* storytelling mode itself, a nonserious and nonofficial writing that dissimulates the serious and is itself always a *tuide*-type (in both its senses of "occasionality" and "marginality") of telling that destabilizes primary-secondary topical axes.

The captain introduces the topic of discrimination when he asserts that it is impossible to find women who are without flaw and remarks on the difficulty of obtaining reliable information since dissimulation is apt to be operating. On the surface a woman appears talented, but she puts on airs and is critical of others; those of tender age are hidden from the world, and their personal traits are closely guarded by doting parents. The rumors are intriguing, but if you pursue the matter, you are usually disappointed. The captain's remarks are ostensibly based on "experience": "I have gradually come to realize" (1:132). When Genji asks about women with no redeeming features, the captain is unable to imagine anyone being so gullible.[14]

Genji's companion then distinguishes three ranks in proper society: "Those high-ranking ones (*sina takaku*): they are cared for so thoroughly their faults are often concealed, and everything about them naturally sounds fascinating; the middle ranks (*naka no sina*):[15] that's where the manner each woman adopts in accordance with her feelings is visible, where differences needing to be distinguished are certainly numerous; when we come to the bottom grades (*simo no kizami*), it is definitely not worth an inquiry" (1:134). In other words, while those women belonging to the loftiest ranks indulge in dissimulation, and those at the lowest are not worthy of notice, those of the middle ranks are at once approachable (i.e., knowable) and worth knowing in all their particularized variety. Duly impressed with his friend's knowledge, Genji asks about distinguishing (*kedime*) between those formerly of high rank who fall on hard times and those who begin at mediocre rank and rise to high status. Before the captain answers, the other two men, who are experienced lovers and skillful talkers, arrive. The captain, we are told, "is ready to dispute with them the distinctions and determinations (*wakimaFe-sadame-arasoFu*) of ranks; much of the discussion will be of a rather startling (*ito kikinikuki*) nature" (1:134).[16] With that narrative disclaimer, the captain launches into an answer to Genji's question,[17] and the "rainy night critique of ranks" begins.[18]

After noting that those risen from the lower ranks who suffer from defective lineage (*sudi*) and those of good lineage who have fallen on bad times should both be placed in the middle ranks,[19] the captain mentions a specific group of officials: "Called *zuryō*, they involve themselves in managing the affairs of remote regions; even among those whose ranks are determined, there are still finer gradations (*kizami kizami arite*); these are times when one should choose appropriate women from those ranks" (1:135). He also mentions the many highly successful and wealthy families of the fourth-rank *hisangi* ("not yet consultants," i.e., those of the fourth rank soon to be promoted to that office) with interesting daughters raised with great care. There are, he adds, "many examples of [women] going off to enter court service, and meeting with unexpected good fortune" (1:135). When Genji laughingly remarks, "it all depends necessarily on a person's assets" (1:136), the too-serious captain ignores the comment as inappropriate.[20] The director's comments follow immediately.

Let us consider briefly Tō no Chūjō's remarks, as cognizance of their implications is crucial for the *Genji* text. As the term by which the section is known suggests, the narrator and the participants take up the problem of *zuryō*-class women in terms of a "judgment" or "critique" (*sadame*). Other closely related terms are "distinction" (*kedime*) and "grade" or "gradation" (*kizami*). As the term *sadame* suggests, the middle ranks necessitate judgments and distinctions, in contrast to the highest and lowest ranks, where character is predictable. Accordingly, the chapter raises the following questions: How does one choose a wife from among the many likely candidates?[21] And what does it mean to choose from the middle ranks in the first place? For our study it is important to question as well the audience at whom the section is directed. As the "critique" sets out to establish "objects" of (narrative) desire for the male Genji, himself an object of attention, it also delineates differences among women of the middle ranks and their families. Since women are the writers, representers, and narrators, the middle-rank women, and especially those *zuryō* daughters, must be read as objects constructed for themselves in a sort of narrative fold.[22]

Fine (and ever-changing) distinctions characterized much of Heian court society. The apparatus included levels of official ranks—senior, junior, upper, and lower (e.g., senior fourth rank lower grade); group designations like *kugyō, tenjōbito, kandachime*, and *jige*;[23] and special or provisional offices, like the sixth-rank chamberlains, the fourth-rank consultants, and the so-called provisional (*gon*) offices that were created out of exceptional (extra-code) circumstances. The present chapter illustrates the finely sensitized discriminatory powers that the innumerable permutations among rank, office, and social status demanded.[24] Families are viewed as constantly changing units buffeted by the winds of political change and uncertainty, a situation in which original status (birthright) became secondary to current circumstance and rank. The "Hahakigi" narrating serves, then, to introduce to the *Genji* reader-listener a major obverse aspect of the text (and of Heian society), an introduction necessary, first, in immediate, narrative terms, because Genji was still a high-born neophyte in such matters and, second, in historical terms, precisely because the "middle ranks" had, by the time of Murasaki Shikibu and the Ichijō Court, come to represent the most unstable section of officialdom, populated, consequently, with the most interesting personages.

The clear thrust of the discourse thus far has been the valorization of the middle-ranking families and their daughters. Genji's apparently teasing remark refers to the real opportunities for accumulating tremendous wealth enjoyed by middle-ranking provincial governors. Many women from such families, as Tamagami notes, attained lofty status and brought prestige to their lineage. The "Hahakigi" narrating attests to the diversity of women at the middle ranks, making those women and the level of society itself the real "heroines" of the text. Their complex relations to the upper levels constitute areas of major narrating focus, treated in a manner analogous to the relations of the Hahakigi line to the Kiritsubo line.

The Director's Discourse

The figure responsible for the bulk of the discussion is the Uma (or Sama)[25] no Kami (the director), the most skilled and prolific storyteller. Several years older than Genji and Tō no Chūjō and a man of the world whom the latter regards with a kind of gaga reverence, the director displaces the outclassed captain and delivers lengthy speeches punctuated by remarks by the general narrator. Both the captain and Tō no Shikibu no Jō (the secretary), a scholar risen from the lowest ranks, later offer their own stories, but Genji will remain the listener and learner throughout, functioning as the reader-listener's stand-in and the object of conjecture by the general narrator. Many of the experiences related by the three speakers in "Hahakigi" reappear in variation later in the text, as if to underscore the undeniable significance (far from minor, or ancillary) of the chapter and prove what a good listener and learner Genji really was on that rainy night.

The director immediately dismisses women from the highest

ranks, because they offer no possibilities for interesting disjunctions: if they meet one's expectations, that's nothing new; if they do not, it's an acute embarrassment. He then mentions two other possibilities: the well-known *mugura no kado* woman, the treasure hidden away behind a weed-choked gate,[26] and the woman who belies the coarseness of her easily observed (because lower-ranking) father and brothers, and possesses a degree of talent and pride.

The narrator, meanwhile, focuses on the positions of the secretary and Genji. When the director pauses to glance at the secretary, the narrating tells us, "Whether or not he [the secretary] is wondering if the [latter] remark is meant to refer to his own younger sisters' distinguished reputations, he says nothing" (1:137). It then switches to a conjecture about Genji—"'Well, well. Even among the highest ranks (*kami no sina*) that kind of woman [with no faults] is difficult to find,' he must be thinking" (1:137)—following it with another comment: "He is wearing layers of soft white singlets under only[27] a loosely slung, informal court robe and has left his collar ties dangling; lying on his side in the lamplight—most beautiful, one would want to see him as a woman" (1:137). The phrase "want to see him as a woman" (*wonna nite mitatematuramaFosi*) has important ramifications. The standard interpretation ("wish to turn him into a woman and look [with sexual implications] at him" or "look at him as if he were a woman") reads the phrase as an instance of the famous Heian valorization of the feminine, which here becomes a case of feminine reversal underwriting male desire. Tamagami notes, however, that the passage has also been interpreted as "want to be a woman and meet with him, sleep with him," which situates the primary perspective squarely with the narrator.[28] Seidensticker's translation—"his companions almost wished that he were a woman"[29]—misses the transformative force and the fact that the narrator and her own audience are also major participants in the scene. The narrator's presence is discernible in *besi*, a suffix of conjecture: "so he [Genji] would no doubt be thinking" (*kimi Fa obosubesi*) (1:137).

The act of representing Genji in terms of the beauty (and sensibilities) of women becomes another mark of the *hiragana* representational perspective. It accords with other nonbinary pairings found in the *Genji* text, ambivalences (his part royal–part commoner "Minamoto" status, for example) at the heart of his construction. Those ambivalences cannot be coincidental to the fact that a woman (or women) authored the tale.[30] Most commentators read the "critique" in terms of "literary" concerns—for example, the romanticized motif of the *mugura no kado* lady—but such paradigms, needless to say, appropriate the section only from the masculine "gaze," or subject position.

The director next addresses the difficulty of choosing a wife whom one can entrust with household affairs. He compares the process to the difficulty in selecting good officials to govern a country. In the latter case, many officials assist each other in a hierarchically determined bureaucracy, but the wife must bear alone the burdens of domestic responsibility. We hear in his words both a hyperbolic valuation of the domestic and yet another emphasis on finding a woman of compatible temperament whom one doesn't have to retrain or teach.[31] Since no one is perfect, if one compromises and perseveres for the sake of appearances, people will imagine the union to be a happy one. The director notes that in the case of such highborn men as Genji and the captain, the choice becomes even more difficult.[32]

Becoming subtler in his discriminations, the director refers to the advantages of choosing a childlike (*ko mekite*) woman. She may be lacking in some respects but seems eminently teachable.[33] Such gentle and malleable women, however, cause anxiety since they cannot make decisions on their own, whereas cold and forbidding women are apt to handle situations superbly. The narrator then adds: "Even in his expansive coverage, he has difficulty making judgments (*sadamekanete*) and is quite depressed" (1:141). The director then stresses the finding of a woman one can trust throughout one's life:[34] if a woman happens to have talent, it's a blessing; if not, you shouldn't demand it; and if she remains faithful and doesn't give in to jealousy, she'll come to acquire a style of her own. The director also suggests that women are able to influence the course of their marriage: "Always be calm . . . when an incident makes you resentful, drop little hints that you are aware of his misbehavior; on occasions when you really feel like censoring him, express your feelings subtly so as not to arouse resentment; if you do that, his fondness for you will certainly grow deeper (*aFare mo masarinubesi*); in most cases, it depends on the mate (*miru Fito*) whether or not one's unsettled heart [*waga kokoro*, i.e., the husband's] can be pacified" (1:144). Here too one reads, in the purported advice to women, the construction and guidance of male desire: look for the woman you can trust and don't be taken in by appearances, a sentiment already expressed, with the gender of the participants reversed, in the *Taketori* text. The director agrees that a man's (woman's)[35] ways can be mended if she (he) shows trustworthiness, fidelity, and forgiveness, and he advises women "to persevere quietly in the face of trouble" (*tagaFubeki Fusi*) (1:144). What we might tend to read as an example of chauvinist behavior designed to keep women docilely in their places takes on a different cast when we remember that it is a woman (or women) as writing subject who represents, in a feminine hand, a man mouthing the words. Awareness on the women's part of a masculinist prescriptive would not, of course, obviate the negative force of the passage; it does, however, complicate any interpretation of it.

In the next narrating section, the director mentions impatient and impulsive women. He relates in some detail a (no doubt typical) tale (*monogatari*) that he overheard as a child.[36] The tale concerns a woman who leaves her husband because of his infidelity. Intending at first only to test his feelings, she eventually finds herself unable to turn back. She even takes Buddhist vows but bitterly regrets doing so in the end. The director admits to being moved to tears by the story although he now realizes how contrived it was. Here we find, in another act of self-legitimation, the representation of a narrator who narrates a story and comments on it. The *Genji* tale, by extension, will also tell stories that move the reader-listener to tears yet will not resort to such obviously contrived and manipulative devices.[37]

The narrating then turns immediately to the captain's sister, Genji's wife: "He [the captain] feels that his own sister, the Aoi Princess, fits their critique (*sadame*) perfectly; he is then disappointed and irritated to see Genji napping and not adding his own comments" (1:144). As seen here and as noted above, the speeches of the characters are constantly redirected toward the participants and their narrating situation. The captain hints at an awareness of Genji's treatment of his sister; Genji, only pretending to be asleep, is no doubt fully aware of the captain's insinuation.

The narrating then casts the director's speech in a humorous light: "The director of horses, having become a doctor of critique (*monosadame no Fakase*), sits whinnying away (*FiFiraki-witari*); the middle captain, eager to hear his reasoning to the end, plays the addressee, concentrating with all his might" (1:145). The humor defuses readerly resistance to the director's speech but also further legitimizes it. As will be the case for the *monogatari-ron* (defense of narratives), that which at first appears trivial ("whinnying speech") is precisely what the *Genji* narrating mode asks the reader-listener to take seriously.

In the section that follows (Genji stays "asleep" through it), the director compares choosing a wife to the problems of discrimination within the arts—carpentry and crafts, painting, and calligraphy. His narration concerns a distinction between creations that are fresh and without fixed patterns and those marked by an enduring mastery, where "true substance" (*ziti*) can be discerned, and concludes that one should not trust those clever only at outward displays of affection. The director may be implying that the distinction between the immediately appealing and genuinely worthwhile is analogous to the distinction between previous *monogatari* and *Genji* as well. The comments, however, do not simply divide the new and the old, the superficial and the substantive, into binary pairs. The freshness of the new, deriving from freedom of conception, will be exactly what is valued later in the "Picture Contest" chapter when Genji's Suma sketches win the day. And the reliance on prescribed forms will be grouped with things professional, often of Chinese origin, that the narrating almost always denigrates. The difference may be that the "Hahakigi" narrators are specifically male.

The section ends with the narrator's comments: "He draws near [the others]: Genji awakes; the middle captain, sitting opposite [the director] with his chin propped in his hand, believes everything; it might seem odd, this feeling that you're in the presence of a priest about to unravel the laws of the world, but on such occasions (*kakaru tuide ni*) none of the men is able to keep hidden his most intimate stories" (1:147). The comment might be taken as a spoof of Buddhist sermons and not merely a continuation of the uncharitable characterization of the thoroughly gullible Tō no Chūjō.[38] *Kachō yosei* notes that the structure of the critique follows the tripartite style of presentation found in the *Lotus Sutra*, in its three divisions of *hōbenbon*, *hiyubon*, and *kejōyubon*. Buddhist sources, earlier *monogatari*, and other mythical and legendary tales no doubt furnished models for discussion and argumentation (as well as satire) and also provided structural hints to the *Genji* narrator.[39] The comment may indeed be a parody of Buddhist practices, but it also suggests the importance of the *Genji* tale—the "defense" in the "Hotaru" chapter will also echo Buddhist sermons. That Genji has been a less than interested listener underscores his role as stand-in for the audience, who most likely would not share the captain's unbridled enthusiasm for such disquisitions. His waking up now signals that the interesting part of the critique, the "real" stories are about to begin.

The series of narratings that follow find legitimation again in their being based on personal experience. They continue to attest to the rich variety of women in middle-rank families. The director begins by telling a tale of subtle reversals concerning a jealous, talented woman who bites his finger (another reference to *Ise monogatari*) and then of a skilled musician whom he discovers to be entertaining another lover. He becomes a veritable *monogatari* narrator as he intersperses his tales with poems and many citations. The captain then tells of the woman, known later as Yūgao,[40] of a gentle, yielding disposition, who was frightened away by his principal wife. The captain's narrating also contains citations and poems. The final participant, the secretary, is, we are told, a *monzyau no syau*, a graduate of the Heian Academy, as were many of the *zuryō* fathers. He tells a hilarious story about a serious and proper Chinese scholar whom he finds one day reeking of a garlic potion she has ingested to cure an illness. Unable to stand the stench emanating from behind her screens, he leaves hurriedly, her quick repartee to his parting poem ringing in his ears. The secretary's "comrades think the story outrageous (*asamasi*) and burst out laughing, calling it a complete fabrication (*soragoto*)." The tale no doubt also had the learned Murasaki Shikibu and her companions roaring with laughter.[41] The sections are excellent examples of the narrating flexibility made possible by a *hiragana monogatari* mode that easily accommodates double or triple narrating layers or registers (compare the Yugei no Myōbu section discussed earlier), each register itself continually anchored to the now-familiar self-legitimating, deictic ground of the general narrator's oral storytelling. Each narrator inserts the requisite poem exchange, poetic citations, and syntactic ploys.

Tō no Chūjō's Tale

Let us now examine, as a link to the next chapter, the captain's story. We learn that his secret visits are infrequent, even though he has become her (the woman later known as Yūgao) sole support (her parents are dead). Since she never shows resentment and is always congenial (if a bit too diffident), the captain keeps assuring her that she can continue to depend on him. With his visits growing ever more rare, there occurs an incident of which he only later learns. Someone near his principal wife utters cruel and unpleasant remarks that reach the woman. A great deal of time passes without a visit and the captain, unaware of recent events, receives a letter from her. The captain narrates in the *ki* mode:

"She was [it is said] completely downhearted and dejected: since there was also a little child with her, she was at a loss as to her course of action; she broke off a *nadeshiko* blossom and had it sent to me"; tears come to his eyes as he speaks; when Genji says, "Come now, give us the words of the text": "Well, it was certainly nothing special,

a mountain rustic   close to ruin though her wall may be,
        I ask that you cast
a dewdrop's worth of kindness now and then,
        to the *nadeshiko* blooming there

[yama gatu no / kakiFo arutomo / woriwori ni / aFare Fa ka-keyo / nadesiko no tuyu][42]

"Being thus reminded of her, I paid her a visit: as always, there was no sign of duplicity (*ura mo naki*), yet her face showed the strain of despair; I looked at the rundown house, covered with dew; the atmosphere in which human cries vied with the cries of the insects seemed to me like something out of an old *monogatari*.

of the various flowers   all in bloom together,
        the best is difficult to discern;
yet, for me, as always,   nothing surpasses the *tokonatsu*

[sakimaziru / iro Fa idure to / wakanedomo / naFo tokonatu ni / siku mono zo naki][43]

"Putting aside the *Yamato nadeshiko* [Japanese pink], I seek to assure the mother's heart, as in the saying, 'even a speck of dust.'[44]

the sleeves I use to wipe it [the dust] away   now damp with tears;
        upon the *tokonatsu*   a storm rages in concert
and fall comes too,
        a time of falling out of favor

[utiFaraFu / sode mo tuyukeki / tokonatu ni / arasi FukisoFu / aki mo kinikeri][45]

"She pretended to speak nonchalantly, betraying no hint of deep resentment and, though she could not help the tears from falling, she hid them with obvious embarrassment, desperately afraid of letting on that she was affected by [my] coldheartedness; I felt relieved and again didn't see her for a while; it was during that time that she vanished without a trace." (1:158–159)

The captain then sums up his feelings for the woman in the *keri* (current narrating) mode.

The passage is constituted by the captain's recollective *ki* narration, his *keri* narration, and the narrator's basic register (remembering the problematic distinctions between a "first" or "third" person narration), which is particularly noticeable between the second and third poems. The section forms a synecdoche of the chapter as a whole and functions as a self-validating, proleptic "source" for the rest of the narrating. The "poetic" words found in the above exchange (showing how the narrating appropriates the waka tradition) will reappear when we learn about Yūgao, the red-nosed princess (Suetsumuhana), and the child (Tamakazura).

As well as a series of "personal" accounts, the narratings also become examples of a general *Genji* narrating mode, which they simultaneously confirm and enact. By including actual examples of narrating based on "personal" experience, marked by *ki* endings, and the requisite poetic exchanges, the general narrator takes full advantage of the linguistic means at hand for convincing the reader-listener of the validity of the tales; they are trial instances to prepare the ground for the later *Genji* narratings. The lessons of the chapter, then, are for the edification of reader-listeners and also of Genji, who continues to recall the critique the following day when he visits his wife (the Aoi Lady), and they go on to become the subject of narrating as Genji encounters for himself the woman from the "middle ranks" known as Utsusemi.

Subjects and "Judgment"

The extended focus on the middle ranks in the critique and in the "Hahakigi" line of chapters as a whole effects, as I have noted, a reorientation of the locus of narrating from the palace compound (where the "Kiritsubo" chapter and the "critique" itself take place) to that arena of Heian life most difficult to categorize owing to its constantly changing and changeable character, an arena where the old families who fall in the world converge with the lowly who rise. Scions of the highest social levels like the captain and Genji, moreover, spend much of their youth at the upper middle ranks, thus for a time easily interacting with members who belong hereditarily to a more modest rank. The middle ranks therefore not only offer the richest material for *monogatari* narrating but also implicate factors that contribute to narrating complexity as they activate connections with other levels of society, particularly that group of marginalized royalty, the so-called Genji. The textual strands set in motion by the "Hahakigi" chapter will find an ultimate interweaving when the middle ranks and the Genji converge in what is arguably the most important intertext of the tale: the Akashi family.

The "Hahakigi" narratings also construct several different subject positions. As Genji and the overzealous captain learn about middle-rank women (primarily from the more experienced director), they come to view them as prime objects of desire. Since the stories also demonstrate that they can assume the position of pursuer, such women thus constitute "objects" of desire never fixed or predictable. Consequently, the men often find themselves floundering in situations without behavioral precedent or form (*kata*).[46] As often as not they end up unable to make judgments (*sadame*) and fail miserably, humorously, and tragically to achieve their amatory goals—the *Genji* narrating is as notable for presenting the failures as the successes of its main figures.[47] Despite the director's wealth of experience and verbal skill, "judgment" (*sadame*) itself never takes place, for it cannot really ever take place: that is both the allure and the exasperation of women from the middle ranks; their tales can be told but only as a tale of the failure of action and the impossibility of precise judgments due to the absence of precedent or unimpeachable evidence.

The female attendants at the Heian court no doubt thoroughly enjoyed constructing themselves in all their variety as such elusive prey: mysterious and surprising, pliant and prideful, self-effacing and talented, jealous and loyal. The self-representations, then, create objects of narrative (and male) desire but also offer guidelines for choosing and obtaining those objects.[48] Together with the creation of "precedent" underlying the "Kiritsubo" chapter, we read the problematizing of "judgment" in "Hahakigi" as testimony to the fact that even as the *Genji* tale continually reinforces its self-legitimating maneuvers, it also takes on a powerfully didactic (even argumentative) cast. With the ever-present narrating positions keeping utterances anchored to a deictic present, the reader-listener is "taught" how to regard everything from the arts to previous *monogatari*, genealogical ties, rituals and celebratory occasions, vengeful spirits, and household management. Genji's own desire to teach the Murasaki Lady reverberates with the director's comments in the "critique," making it an example of the didacticism subtending the text. The fact that the putative authors were selected partly as tutors for their mistresses no doubt made such emphases unavoidable.

An ideological corollary to the above lies in the mystique surrounding the imperial that casts a continual shadow over the narrating. Women like Murasaki Shikibu and Sei Shōnagon were deeply indebted to their sponsors (Empresses Akiko and Sadako, respectively), and the "salons" provoked intense rivalry even as they fostered fierce loyalties. In Genji's case, such middle-rank women might arouse intense curiosity and desire, but their inevitable inadequacies would only strengthen his passionate feelings for his stepmother (and cousin, if the former Emperor is the Kiritsubo Emperor's elder brother), the Fujitsubo Consort, whom he comes to view as perfection personified. That a particular group of women were constructing the subject/enunciating positions is of absolutely crucial significance and has been too long overlooked in *Genji* studies.[49]

The director closes the "critique" with remarks that continue to address a feminine position: "To be thoroughly acquainted with the path of learning, by studying the Three Histories and the Five Classics,[50] would most certainly result in an absence of charm; yet is it right, just because one is a woman, to let oneself be totally ignorant and unaware of worldly matters, whether public (*oFoyake*) or private (*watakusi*)? Although it is not necessary to devote oneself to study, for a woman with even a modicum of intelligence, there are many things naturally seen and heard" (1:165). After the statement come examples of unrestrained and insensitive feminine behavior: filling a letter, even in *hiragana*, with Chinese characters so that when read aloud it is stiff and unnatural (women of high rank, he adds, are particularly susceptible); or becoming engrossed in poetry to the point of inserting citations to old poems from the very first line and sending compositions at the most inappropriate or awkward times. As the director advises women not to put on airs or try to act stylish, the narrator reveals Genji's thoughts: "Regarding what [he, the director] says, Genji continues to reserve in his heart feelings for that one honorable figure (*oFon'arisama*); in this context [*kore ni*, i.e., the director's conclusion][51] there is nothing lacking, nor is there anything excessive in her behavior [i.e., the Fujitsubo Consort fits the conclusion perfectly]; his heart pounded as he thought how exceptional she was" (1:166–167).[52]

The conclusions on women and feminine behavior are far from categorical, since everything depends on sensibility, a quality that cannot be guaranteed, predicted, taught, or controlled by logical discrimination. Safe behavior, as the director states it, pertains primarily to those who want for discriminatory powers, an issue raised at the beginning of the chapter and one central to Heian aesthetics. The "rainy night critique" focuses on women who resist reification into types, since each instance redefines the grouping and no description or judgment can ever be exhaustive or final. The critique also stages and signifies its own narrating processes as each storyteller accommodates moments basic to *hiragana* representations: the poetic exchanges and figurations that form a major aspect of *monogatari* telling.[53] The stories are not narrative "summaries" but reproduce (that is, present) the actual "events" that are also the events of the telling.

The narrating that follows the "critique" will continually refer to it, and Genji will soon (at the end of "Hahakigi") spend the night with a woman from the middle ranks. Predictably now, the affair ends in failure, as will his more dreadful and tragic encounter with Yūgao, the "Evening Faces" woman. The next chapter takes a thread of Tō no Chūjō's tale told above and traces its realization in the figure of Tamakazura, a figure born out of a telling and fated to tell the tale of its narrating.

9

A Figure of Narrating:
Tamakazura

The *Genji* narrating stages itself in its most spectacular guise in telling of Tamakazura, whose "story" of desire and resistance takes up most of the Ten Tamakazura Chapters (*Tamakazura jūjō* 22–31), a group of "lateral" chapters. Her "story" recalls Tō no Chūjō's narration in the "rainy night critique of ranks" and links with Genji's subsequent fleeting affair with Yūgao. I focus first on the "Hotaru" (Fireflies, 25) chapter and the famous "defense of narrative" (*monogatari-ron*), which argues for the displacement of *kambun* histories by *monogatari*. The "setting" of the "defense" is Genji's palatial residence, completed at the end of the "Otome" (The Maiden, 21) chapter and known as Rokujō-in.[1] The mansion consists of four residential wings, which house four of Genji's most important women. The four are matched cosmologically and poetically to season and direction (and floral patterns) in four resplendent gardens: Akikonomu (autumn-southwest), Murasaki (spring-southeast), Hanachirusato (summer-northeast), and the Akashi Lady (winter-northwest).[2]

We learn about Yūgao's child long after "Hahakigi," when the narrating tells us at the beginning of "Tamakazura" what transpired after Tō no Chūjō's principal wife had made life miserable for the mother. Yūgao's father was a third rank middle captain,[3] making both her and Tamakazura women of the upper levels of court society. With her mother dead and her father ignorant of her whereabouts, however, Tamakazura is taken by Yūgao's wet nurse to Tsukushi (Kyushu) when the latter's husband is appointed senior assistant governor-general (*daini*) of Dazaifu. What is important from the perspective of the *zuryō* backgrounds of Heian women writers is that Tamakazura is raised there as the *daini*'s granddaughter, much as a *zuryō* daughter might have been.[4] Dazaifu easily evokes thoughts of exile (remember Takaakira's fate), and scholars have read an instance of feminine exile in Tamakazura's being sent to the distant region.

Two pretexts that have been cited as inspirations for Tamakazura are *Sumiyoshi monogatari* and the *Taketori* tale. The former is thought to have told about a woman who is banished by an evil stepmother, barely escapes abduction, and is the focus of a series of suitors. It is a tale Tamakazura herself mentions during the course of the "defense," as she compares her narrow escape from the grasp of the Higo wild man to the fate of the *Sumiyoshi* woman. The *Taketori* tale, which has been read as the "exile" to earth of a heavenly maiden, forms a pretext for other aspects of Tamakazura: her sudden appearance in the capital; the rapidity with which she "grows" up (she is four when the chapter begins and, after only a few lines, twenty-one when she arrives at the capital); the reference to her as a jewel with the attribute "dazzling" (*kirikirisi*);[5] the concealment of her real identity; the many suitors, including the emperor, who vie for her hand, and the emperor's inability to win her; the references to bamboo;[6] Genji's reference to himself as "old man" (*okina*); and, like Kaguyahime, Tamakazura's sudden removal from her foster parent's presence.

There are also clues to another connection. Tamakazura, as mentioned, did not reside with her mother when Genji visited. We learn at the beginning of "Tamakazura" that she was living with Yūgao's wet nurse in the "western part of the capital" (*nisi no kyō*). Taken together with the "exile" to Tsukushi, the term *nisi no kyō* would no doubt have called to mind for *Genji* readers memories of the exile of that previously mentioned Lord of the Western Manor (*nisi no miya dono*), Minamoto no Takaakira. The Ten Tamakazura Chapters themselves provide another clue to a possible Takaakira connection as they trace a determined movement through each of the four seasons punctuated by the staging of elaborate occasions of private, poeticized ceremony and ritual. Scholars have likened the movement to a series of "monthly" (*tukinami*) standing screens (*byōbu*), with motifs appropriate to each month painted on twelve separate panels. Such events as occur in the chapters, moreover, would have been governed by precedents often written down by a family member (the head of the family, for example) for the benefit of that genealogical line. The "testament" left by Emperor Uda to his son, Emperor Daigo, is only one example of such writings. In the "Hatsune" (The First Warbler, 23) chapter, for example, Genji makes the following remark, after hearing the voice of a captain: "His [voice] doesn't seem in the least inferior to Ben no Shōshō. How odd that these are times when those who excel in precedents of protocol and etiquette (*iusoku*)[7] appear one after another; many among the people of old seem to have been truly outstanding in matters of learning; as for the *lineages* of matters pertaining to the emotions (*nasakedatitaru sudi*), however, they cannot surpass people of today" (3:153–154). Relevant to the present case is that the exiled Takaakira was famous, as mentioned previously, for his scholarly learning, which he put to excellent use in writing the *yūsoku* text *Saikyūki*.[8] Any staging of private ritual would have required familiarity with *yūsoku kojitsu*.

The Jeweled Chaplet

The discovery of Tamakazura, in the chapter by that name, forces the reader-listener to link a series of former moments in the text: the "Suetsumuhana" chapter (6, where the "red-nosed" lady—whose father was a prince and also a provincial governor—was sought after by Genji as a possible substitute for Yūgao),[9] the "Yūgao" chapter (and the death of the mysterious woman who refused to reveal her identity), and Tō no Chūjō's narrating in the "Hahakigi" chapter. The references by Tō no Chūjō to the mother as a *tokonatu* and to the child as a *nadesiko* and the word "dew" (*tuyu*, also "slight quantity") reappear in the present characterization of Tamakazura together with other terms associated with her jewel-like sobriquet. When Ukon, Yūgao's former attendant (and daughter of her wet nurse), now in Murasaki's retinue,[10] discovers Tamakazura, she uses the word *tama* (jewel) in the phrase *tama no kizu* (flaw in the jewel), referring to the possible adverse affects on her character resulting from the experience in distant Tsukushi. Ukon earlier had called her *Fujiwara no ruri* (*ruri* means "lapis lazuli").[11] And when she later informs Genji of her find, she makes the association explicit: "We have discovered the link (*yukari*) to the dew on the evening faces that so helplessly vanished" (3:114). The "link" in this case is a mother-daughter one, but we can read in it an echo of the aunt-niece connection underlying the Lavender "link," which is also implicated again since Ukon now serves Murasaki.[12]

Delighted at the discovery, Genji decides to keep his find a secret from Tamakazura's father, Tō no Chūjō, and pretend that she is his own daughter.[13] Since it is difficult, given his exalted position, to engage personally in amorous activities, he sees in Tamakazura a perfect way to add excitement to the Rokujō-in.[14] She will attract young men and thereby provide a welcome diversion. More specifically, Genji's intention is to "take special care with her" so that she can become, in his words, a *kusaFai*—written with the character that

usually means "seed," "kind," or "species" and which, as pivot-
word, can also mean "cause," "source," or "material"—with which
he can tantalize those youthful courtiers always on the lookout for
new conquests.[15] He wants her to be a lure, an ornamental magnet.
As he once tutored Murasaki on how to be the ideal wife, so he will
attempt to teach Tamakazura how to be the ideal seductress, and as
she provides entertainment for Genji and others at his mansion, she
will also form the entertainment of the narrating.

Remembering all too well his disappointment with Suetsumuhana, Genji sends Tamakazura a letter to determine her suitability, to
be certain that she is without any fatal "flaw," a concern that recalls
the difficulty expressed in the "critique of ranks" on evaluating
middle-rank women. He includes the following poem, which plays
on the key word *sudi:*

> unaware though you be ask and you will learn:
> like the line of rushes at Mishima-e,
> the lines of our destiny are not at an end
> [sirazutomo / tadunete siramu / misimae ni / oFurumikuri no / sudi Fa
> taezi wo] (3:117)

> Her reply:
> of no consequence to anyone, a poor rush, by what
> sort of line did I
> take root and remain like this in a swamp of a gloomy world?
> [kazu naranu / mikuriya nani no / sudi nareba / ukinisi mo kaku / ne
> wo todomekemu] (3:119)

Later, after Genji has brought Tamakazura to his mansion, he recites
a poem from which her sobriquet derives:

> my longing strong as ever continues for the other;
> this jeweled garland;
> in pursuit of what lines has it come calling on me?
> [koFiwataru / mi Fa sore naredo / tamakadura / ika naru sudi wo / tad-
> unekituramu] (3:126)

The term *tamakadura* forms an "associative preface" for *sudi*, *tama*
being a purely ornamental suffix used to highlight *kadura*, a vine used
in hair ornaments. The ornamental function of *tama* in the poem
corresponds to the function Genji wants her to fulfill at the Rokujō-in,
but the twisted, "vinelike" (*kadura*) "course" (*sudi*) of her textual
lineage will upset those initial plans. The reference to his continued
longing for the mother resonates with the configurations of the

Fujitsubo Consort–Murasaki pair in that both the daughter and the niece come as bodies already displaced from themselves insofar as desire for the aunt and mother will always circumscribe any possibility of pure desire for their descendants. In the "Kochō" (Butterflies, 24) chapter, where Genji's erotic display startles Tamakazura, he recites a poem that tropologically merges mother and daughter through evocation of "orange blossoms" (*tatibana*), that fragrant signifier of recollection:

> to those sleeves once fragrant   with the scent of orange blossoms
>   I compare yours [I think of you as your mother]
> no difference in your bodies   presents itself to me
> [tatibana no / kaworisi sode ni / yosoFureba / kaFareru mi to
> mo / omoFoFenu kana] (3:177)

Genji makes the (sexually charged) comparison through the word *yosoFu*, the same word with which the Kiritsubo Emperor compared the Fujitsubo Consort to Genji's mother.[16] Heian poetic training would immediately have brought to mind the anonymous *Kokinshū* "Summer" poem (139), which itself enacts recollection:

> it awaits the Fifth Month   those orange blossoms,
>   in their fragrance I detect
> just that scent of the sleeves   of someone long ago
> [satuki matu / Fanatatibana no / ka wo kageba / mukasi no Fito no / sode
> no ka zo suru]

Genji transforms the addressee into a double of that "someone long ago" and suggests through the word *mi* ("body," also "fruit") the "substance" beneath the robes (here arising synecdochically from "sleeves"). A similar movement occurred when he rhetorically merged the Fujitsubo Consort and the Murasaki Lady.[17]

We can also reinvoke the term "dew," a common metonym in Heian poetry for *tama*, as exemplified by the famous *Gosenshū* "Autumn" poem (308) by Bunya no Asayasu:

> pure white dew   blown ceaselessly by the wind
>   over the autumn fields,
> beads not strung completely together   scatter in disarray
> [siratuyu ni / kaze no Fukisiku / aki no no Fa / turanukitomenu / tama
> zo tirikeru]

Such a rhetorical construction as displayed by Genji is not unlike the broader concerns constitutive of the marginalized *hiragana* writing itself (merely fiction, merely for entertainment, merely for women, and so on), of which the narrating will have more to say shortly. Similarly, the new addition to the Rokujō-in will be a supplementary accessory (repetitive of the *tama* in Genji's poem) to the already complete (in sexual-rhetorical terms) world of Genji's imposing mansion. Having no designated place of her own,[18] Tamakazura is given a room in Hanachirusato's summer sector, whose garden happens to be populated with metonyms characteristic of the former's textual lineage: *tatibana* ("orange blossom," a poetic evocation of the textual past, her mother, and the "rainy night critique of ranks"); *nadesiko* (the term used in the "critique" to refer to her); and *kuretake* ("black bamboo," suggestive of the *Taketori* pretext).

The narrating is also explicit as to the room she will occupy in the northeast quarter: a library that has been cleared of all its books. Again, in a noncoincidental announcement of her status, a textual displacement is enacted that signals at the same time the beginning (or rather the continuation) of her own unprecedented "textual" lineage, a lineage that emerges from a prior narrating incident found in the "source" chapter of the lateral series. Now rediscovered but marked as surplus, in a reenactment of the desires constructed in the "critique" (and also in the *Taketori* pretext), Tamakazura will be the focus of a series of suitors. As all new characters do, Tamakazura will enable further textual production, but in her case, unlike the others, the manner in which the narrating itself proceeds must always be a partial (re)tracing of her very figuration. And though that figuration seems to indicate superfluousness and marginality, the actual originary importance of Tamakazura (and poetics) to the broader narrative will invalidate any such hasty judgments, as we now know to be the case whenever judgments of women of the middle ranks, both as narrators and fictional figures, are involved. Keeping the discussion anchored to the constant intervention of the narrating, let us now turn to the fourth of the ten Tamakazura chapters, "Hotaru," in order to read the "defense of narrative," a conversation first between Genji and Tamakazura and then between Genji and Murasaki regarding *monogatari* and fiction.[19]

Fireflies and Fiction

The debates themselves don't begin until about halfway through the chapter. The first half of the chapter, which would seem at first to be the most important part, tells of a little trick Genji plays on his brother, the "Fireflies" Prince Hyōbukyō (*hotaru hyaubukyau no miya*). Genji suddenly releases a swarm of previously gathered fireflies while his brother has an audience with Tamakazura. The ploy allows the prince a peek at the latter's face, thereby further fanning the flames of an already heated desire. The incident also gives the chapter its title and the prince his nickname. Here again, what might seem at first glance, or in "story" terms, to be the focus of the chapter (but is practically forgotten in later discussions) is actually an introduction to a conversation about fiction situated in a seemingly desultory exchange rife with seductive overtones.

The chapter opens with the narrator mentioning Genji's powerful ("weighty," *omo'omosi*)[20] position in the world and adding that the lives of all those who depend on him (his several women) were peaceful and secure, just as they had hoped.[21] All those, that is, except one: "The lady in the [west] wing (*tai no Fimegimi koso*),[22] of course; poor thing, what with that completely unexpected worry added to her troubles, she seems totally at a loss as to what she might do" (3:187). That "completely unexpected worry" refers to the advances Genji had made to her in the previous chapter.[23] She realizes that compared to the boorish Gen who wooed her in Tsukushi, her present situation is a vast improvement, "yet that events could take such a course (*kakaru sudi*) is something that people would not even dream of, so she suffers quietly, regarding his [Genji's] behavior as bizarre and wanting nothing more to do with it" (3:187). The word *sudi*, "line" or "lineage" (in textual and kinship terms) and thus "course of events," plays a crucial part in the constitution of the "Jeweled Chaplet."[24]

After the mention of Tamakazura's woes in dealing with Genji, a foster father who poses as a real father, the narrating switches to the latter's perspective (*otodo mo*). We are told that confession of his desires has brought him not relief but more suffering.[25] Waiting for moments when her women leave her side, he continues to "give her subtle hints of his extraordinary feelings." At that point, in a typical move, the narrating switches from Genji to Tamakazura in midphrase: "[Fearful that he will not restrain himself] her heart pounds through her chest." Not wanting to reject him outright, she tries to pretend nothing is happening. The narrating remarks that since she is cheerful and congenial by temperament, she tries to behave with propriety, which only makes her "radiate more of a charming and captivating air."

When Genji's brother sends a letter asking to be received at close quarters, the fireflies incident begins. As in the "Hahakigi" critique, it is the Fifth Month, the month of recollection, when sexual relations between men and women were proscribed. It is often a time of incessant monsoon rains, suggestive of frustration and brooding.[26] Not at all opposed to the prince's request,[27] Genji, the ever-ready tutor, advises Tamakazura on how to answer the prince's letters. But she refuses. We learn that her women, who could be counted on in such instances, do not come from good families. There is one blood relative, however, the daughter of Tamakazura's uncle, a former consultant (*saishō*) whose family had fallen on hard times. Known as Saishō, the woman writes an acceptable hand and is dependable, so Genji summons her to write a reply, as he dictates it, to the prince.[28]

The lack of talented women around Tamakazura emphasizes her solitary position in the world and suggests why she had to become a quick learner in order to survive, as survive she certainly does. For though Tamakazura refuses to respond to the prince's letter, she is rapidly mastering the ways of the world and of men. Though she is not particularly taken by the prince, we are told, she sees in him a way out of her difficulties with Genji. In a startling twist on the *Taketori* text, a foster daughter's interest in men (in other words, the emergence of her womanhood) arises out of a desire to avoid the advances of her supposed "real" father and the sorrow deriving from her singular position.

The incident begins when the prince arrives quietly one evening. Unaware that Genji is orchestrating the whole affair, the visitor is led inside one of the doors (*tsumado*) to a cushion near Tamakazura, who sits behind a portable curtain. The narrator comments that even though Genji is not her parent but an exasperating meddler, he has taken extraordinary care to make sure that everything is just right. As commentators note,[29] the narrating seems to be taking great delight in telling the reader-listener how Genji finds it necessary to pinch Saishō (who has quite forgotten her duties as messenger in the heat of the moment),[30] how the atmosphere is highly charged, and especially how the air is heavy with incense wafting about both from Tamakazura's room and the prince's robes. Completely enchanted, the prince pours out his feelings, and Genji is satisfied.

Switching to Tamakazura's perspective, the narrating tells us that she had already retired (we don't know exactly when) to an inner room, leaving the prince talking to the air. When the Saishō comes in to relay the prince's words, Genji follows right behind her and advises Tamakazura to be less formal and speak to him directly. Afraid that Genji might use her disobedience as an excuse for sneaking in himself behind her screens, she moves again to a spot between the main rooms (*moya*) and the space near the veranda (*tumado no ma*) where the prince is sitting. We are then told that while Tamakazura hesitates, unable to reply to the prince's long-winded speech,

> [Genji] draws near, and as he lifts over a length of the portable curtain—a sudden light: has someone brought out a candle? [She is] startled; earlier that evening, [Genji] had bundled a number of fireflies in thin cloth and had wrapped it again to conceal the light; pretending to be rearranging things here and there [he uncovers the fireflies]; she is horrified, and the glimpse of her profile as she hides her face behind a fan appears extremely beautiful. (3:192)

The narrating then gives us Genji's thoughts: if the light were strong enough, the prince would surely have looked; he's interested only because he thinks she's my daughter; still, he couldn't have anticipated how beautiful she really was; what fun to throw complications into his amorous inclinations. The narrator adds somewhat sardonically that Genji would not have behaved so with his real daughter.

Genji leaves, and the narrating repeats part of the incident from the prince's vantage point, quickly modulating into a poetry exchange focused on fireflies. The narrator sends the prince on his way with appropriate Fifth Month phrases and citations, including a *sōshiji* ("finding it bothersome, I didn't ask about it [whether there were poems on the *hototogisu*]"),[31] and ending with comments by the attendants. One adds the feminine side of Genji's foster parent status: "Last night [Genji] played the role of the mother (*meoya datite*) in making all the preparations; unaware of his real feelings, they are moved to pity and admiration" (3:194). The narrator thus makes explicit the disjunction between inner feelings, her own enunciating position, and the knowledge possessed by the attendants. Genji, it seems, has been discreet.[32]

The narrator then brings the incident to a close with a further elaboration on Tamakazura's reactions: "My sorrows are due to my own lot in life," she thinks, thereby emphasizing again her solitary fate shared by many from the middle ranks. She doesn't dislike Genji; in fact, she could even imagine becoming his wife if only things could be "normal" (i.e., if Genji were not posing as her father): "a situation unlike anyone else's; I'm sure it will end up a favorite subject of the gossips (*yogatari*)" (3:194). Then we are back with Genji: he doesn't want to marry her off to just anybody, and although he has had to keep in check his amorous feelings for the Akikonomu Empress (the Rokujō Lady's daughter and another of Genji's foster daughters), with Tamakazura, who is approachable and up-to-date (*imamekitaru*), he finds it difficult to restrain himself. Even so, "he shows inordinate control in keeping his yearning to himself, and despite it all they do seem suited to one another" (3:195).[33]

The narrating is constructing complicated and ambivalent paths of desire, restraint, and reputation: Tamakazura is attracted to Genji but is unable to countenance the dissemblance; Genji polishes his jewel for others but is much too desirous of it himself; the suitors are unaware of the game so that we find brothers, like Tō no Chūjō's son Kashiwagi, wooing their sister, and a nonbrother, Yūgiri, believing himself disqualified; and there is continual fear on Tamakazura's part that the secret of her identity will be exposed. Most striking, perhaps, is the overwhelming presence of a narrating perspective that maintains firm editorial control of the various perspectives, stopping, starting, backing up, commenting, and offering comments through those textual doubles who attend the different figures. Everything is "told" (in a manner that differs from modes of discourse that primarily seek to "describe," "show," or "represent"). Even the commonly held notion that the narrative consists of static "scenes," thereby forming the scriptive counterpart to picture scrolls, becomes problematic.[34] As seen before, the narrating seems suspended in its own enunciating moments, partly because the narrator does not "represent" a consistent world in time or space but freely yields to the powerful deictic links constitutive of narrative configurations.

On the fifth, the Day of the Iris, Genji pays Tamakazura a visit on his way to an archery meet (another *tuide* moment) and, contrary to his elaborate machinations of the previous day, warns her to beware of the prince.[35] Genji, the reader-listener realizes, was simply enjoying a prank and is not interested in her marrying his brother. Soon thereafter, Genji spends a rare night with Hanachirusato, and they discuss briefly Genji's brothers—the Fireflies Prince and a Prince Sochi.[36] Genji also is reminded of the General of the Left (Higekuro), considered one of the brightest prospects of the day, although not by Genji as a son-in-law.[37] Here the celebrated *monogatari-ron* appears.

In reading it, we must keep continually in mind Tamakazura's full textual "lineage" (*sudi*), originating in the "rainy night critique" and now wrapped in Genji's sensual connivances.

The "Defense": Genji and Tamakazura

The narrator begins by again sounding the seasonal note and incorporating the topic of entertainment: "With the long rains, more severe than in other years, and with no prospect of clearing, the various women spend their days and nights absorbed in drawing and copying tales [or copying illustrated tales, *we-monogatari*]" (3:202). The Akashi Lady's skill at drawing is mentioned (she sends samples to her daughter in the Murasaki Lady's quarter). Then, juxtaposed to it: "At the western wing, since she [Tamakazura] was of an experiential lineage (*koto no sudi*),[38] which makes them [picture-tales] seem to her by far the most startling, she spends her days and nights busily drawing and reading" (3:202). Tamakazura is unable to find examples to match her own experience; her life exceeds what is depicted in the old tales, in particular a *monogatari* about the Sumiyoshi Lady.[39]

Genji enters at this point and, seeing the illustrated tales strewn about, chides Tamakazura for believing everything she hears: "Women are born to be easily deceived; there is precious little that is genuine (*makoto*) in these stories; knowing that, they lose themselves in such incessant babbling (*suzurogoto*) and fall right into the [storytelling] traps; they copy them out unaware, in the oppressive heat of the Fifth Month rains, that their hair has gotten all tangled up (*kami no midaruru*)" (3:202). In the repetition of the word *midaru* we can read a sexual-poetical convergence of season, the woman's obliviousness, and Genji's lustful thoughts. He does admit, however, that such old stories are necessary for relieving boredom: "Surely, without old stories [*yo no Furugoto*] like these, how could we possibly comfort ourselves for having nothing with which to while away those long empty hours" (3:203). The function of tales is to divert, as marked here with the verb *magiru*, a verb to be noted in "Wakamurasaki."

Now warming to the occasion, Genji declares that among such "lies" (*ituFari*), there are those stories

> that strike one as truly probable, that unfold in a convincing manner, and though one knows they are of trivial value [*Fakanasigoto*], one's feelings are stirred nevertheless; to see adorable ladies sunk in sorrow-

ful thought cannot but capture part of our attention; or, again, there are those incidents we know to be preposterous and yet, even as we watch, we are amazed at the exaggerated and contrived manner with which they are constructed; each time we hear them again quietly we do find them unimpressive,[40] but there most certainly are stories that provide instant pleasure, and unabashedly so. (3:203)

Genji then remarks that he had overheard attendants reading to his daughter and has concluded that "ours must be an age of clever talkers; I am led to feel they [the stories] issue from the mouths of those quite accustomed to telling empty lies (*soragoto*); isn't that right?" (3:203).[41] Tamakazura responds pointedly: "How right you are; only someone accustomed to telling lies (*ituFari naretaru Fito*) would take it in such an odd way; I cannot help thinking that they contain the genuine events (*makoto no koto*)" (3:203–204). Fed up with Genji's game playing and deception, Tamakazura (and the narrator) appeals to the "truth" in the "fictions" she reads to counter Genji's remarks. The narrator had earlier noted that Tamakazura found in the tales nothing resembling her own experiences; now she labels those tales as truthful. The "lies" she must tell are inscribed by the truth of the disjunction between her life and the fictional tales, and between an alleged "truth" of the *Genji* narrating and the "lies" of earlier *monogatari*.

Genji switches, with a laugh, from a derogatory to a laudatory pose: "How insensitive of me to have put down those tales; they have recorded the affairs of the world ever since the Age of the Gods (*kamiyo*); texts like *Nihongi*[42] tell only part of the story; it is in these [tales] that we find the most useful learning (*mitimitisiku*) and the details of life" (3:204). The remarkable reversal has caused many readers to tie Genji's remarks (and those that follow) securely, if misguidedly, to Murasaki Shikibu and the question of authorial intention. He continues:

"It is certainly not a matter of speaking out about the events of a person's life exactly as they occurred (*ari no mama*); what happens is that as you find it impossible to keep those events locked in your heart, you begin to preserve in speech the features, both elegant and vulgar, of people who make their way in the world, all those incidents (*Fusibusi*) that you never tire of observing, and want to hear more about, and pass on to later generations; when you want to speak of elegant things, you exhaust all of the best incidents, and when you want to obey the dictates of others, you collect those startling incidents of a vulgar cast; whichever the case, you never speak of things not of this world." (3:204)

The emphasis on expressive impulse recalls the "Kana Preface," and the desire to pass on stories to later generations accords with what we've seen regarding the establishment of genealogical continuity and the establishment of precedent (*tamesi*). Observations of the world, Genji (and the narrator) seems to be suggesting, validate by themselves the stories one tells, although one may also feel obliged to attend to the interests of reader-listeners: those observations, moreover, are not reproduced "exactly as they happened" but according to the storyteller's selections based on personal response and desire. He also reiterates what we've been tracking as the "supplementary" function of *monogatari*: they fill in the details, provide an underside (*ura*) of life that the official histories neglect. The word *mitimitisi* is a topic of debate among scholars, but it seems a clear reference to a "way" (or "ways") of behaving that is just as valuable as anything found in the "official" texts. We can recall the "Hahakigi" director comparing the choosing of a wife to the choosing of capable officials.[43] Genji continues in an especially difficult (partly because of textual variants) passage:

> "The way stories are constructed in other courts [i.e., China], based on their own learning, is different; when it comes to this same Yamato land, old differs from modern-day; there is indeed a distinction (*kedime*) between the deep and the shallow; to conclude that they are all empty lies (*soragoto*) gainsays the heart of the matter (*koto no kokoro*)." (3:204)

Nearing the end of his speech, Genji introduces a Buddhist note:

> "The laws (*minori*) that the Buddha, with his virtuous heart, has revealed also contain what are called parables (*Fauben*); the unenlightened will even be suspicious of what seem to be contradictions here and there; the Mahayana scriptures contain many such instances, but in every case, if you follow its gist to the end, you arrive at a single objective; the gap between enlightenment and confusion is on the order of the difference between the good and the bad in people; put in its best light, it turns out that all things, no matter what they are, do not amount to nothing," and thus he spoke of *monogatari* as being consciously crafted to a purpose. (3:205)

Given the hyperbolic cast of the comments and the fact that they arise out of a play of instruction and seduction enshrouded in a genealogical fiction, it is difficult to disentangle the motives from their utterance. The didactic force behind Genji's sexual impulse that had taken precedence in his treatment of Murasaki now gets used for other purposes. In the first (Murasaki's) case, to teach meant the construction, via the "rainy night critique," of a tailor-made object of desire. Such a woman could be entrusted with the management of private matters including the caretaking of the Nijō mansion, which Genji seems eventually to hand over to Murasaki.[44] Genji plays a further teaching role as a foster parent to the Akashi princess. In Genji's tutoring of Tamakazura there is didacticism in the service of ornament and play—that is, in the service of matters that will always exceed attempts to establish the demarcations and distances necessary for teaching. The more the quick-witted Tamakazura (taken together with her textual linkage to Yūgao) learns from her tutor (as well as father and mother figure), the more desirable she will become; thereafter, desirability for its own sake will continually threaten to expose the impossibility of maintaining the surrogate status as the figural reaches a precarious stage poised for an imminent fall into the literal.

The "defense" comprises the notions that *monogatari* supplement official texts (written in Chinese), guide and edify as well as entertain, and employ strategies similar to those of Buddhist teachings. The comparison of *monogatari* to Buddhist parables, in particular, should alert us to the possibility of reading a globally applicable discursive reversal and alterity: words are not, can never be, what they seem, including of course the "words" of Genji's speech. It is not a case of narrating events "exactly as they occurred" (*ari no mama*), which, as many writers have been arguing, would be impossible; rather, what a writer selects out of affective impact that is self-validating must also always be given a differential reading. We face here an exemplary instance of an allegory of a reading process, an indication that *monogatari* and especially the *Genji* text, which is always the self-valorized text as distinguished from earlier tales, is not "groundless, empty talk" (*soragoto*) but must be read in a manner that pays attention to the underside (the intertextually grounded and ungrounded acts) of its own reading, writing, and reciting.

Immediately following the didactic passage cited above, Genji continues to take advantage of the unprecedentedness of his situation with Tamakazura and play on the paradoxical potential of fictive illusion. He switches to a mode that, together with the expected poetry exchange, brings us closer to the issue of reading than the segment of the "defense" usually privileged:

"Are there among these old tales (*Furugoto*) any stories (*monogatari*) of well-meaning fools like me? I'm sure that even among those extraordinarily aloof princesses none is as cold-hearted and perfunctory as you. What do you say we create an unprecedented tale and tell it to the world?" then, he draws near her as he speaks: she pulls back her face, and says, "Even were we not to do so, this unusual affair[45] will most certainly become the talk of the world (*yogatari*)," to which Genji replies, "Do you think it unusual? I really have never before felt this way"; he has drawn closer, acting in an extremely suggestive and playful manner. (3:205)

The verses that the two exchange poeticize textuality, continuing to play on the difference between Genji's reading (Tamakazura's behavior is unparalleled) and Tamakazura's (Genji is an unprecedented parent). Genji's poem:

> in a time of excessive longing,
>   I search my way through   textual traces of the past
> yet a child who gainsays its parent   is nowhere to be found
> [omoFiamari/mukasi no ato wo/tadunuredo/oya ni somukeru/ko zo taguFinaki]

Genji alleges that she is being unfilial and that such behavior would be proscribed by Buddhist law. Reluctant at first to respond, Tamakazura becomes sufficiently irritated (when Genji strokes her hair) to offer the following:

> through the ancient traces   we search, and truly
>   none is to be found
> in this world, in this way   a parent with a heart like yours
> [Furuki ato wo/tadunuredo geni/nakarikeri/kono yo ni kakaru/oya no kokoro Fa]

Tamakazura's ambivalence perhaps can be seen in the fact that although she repeats many of the words in Genji's poem, she matches them to a different reading. As she equates "this world" with the world of the "old texts," her reply prevents Genji from losing complete control of himself, and the narrating provides the deictic comment for the reader-listener: "Given *this* state of affairs how will it all turn out?" (3:206).

The dynamics of the passage involve one perspective, Genji's, that reads figuratively (tales are lies but have a larger purpose) and, even while scolding Tamakazura for being a bad "daughter," tries continually to act on the knowledge of the deception; and another, Ta-makazura's, that reads literally (tales are true even though they do not match her own experiences), so that she can only read Genji's deception for what it is, as a "true" deception that must be accepted as such—namely, even though such "fathers" exist neither in texts nor in the world, the subsequent false status must be taken literally. Genji's behavior is unprecedented partly because it is founded on the assumption that it can use the reality hidden inside the fiction as a basis of action, while Tamakazura, in order to escape the trap, appeals to the unmovable fact of the socially accepted falsehood. Both perspectives effectively mark the difference of the *Genji* fiction from earlier tales, but we can also read another assertion, reminiscent of the *Ise* tale: the interplay between the "figural" and the "literal" is constitutive of fiction itself in its constant and contradictory (or mutually undermining) interplay. It is an interplay that must recall the figural from its traditional banishment into the margins, as mere ornament, as *kusaFai* and *tama*. When the figural reappears, however, as Tamakazura does, it is not simply as one pole of a binary relation between two terms of distinctive value but as a full participant, so to speak, in an ongoing process of reversals in the manner we have been observing. The process of reversals in the Genji-Tamakazura fiction demonstrates what can occur when it is no longer possible either to ignore the figural and opt for the "literal" (now rewritten as one mode of the figural) or to keep the figural relegated simply to the status of ornament.

In Genji's machinations, what began as a desire to fill a lack gets confused with a desire for the "object" that was only supposed to be a "means" of filling that lack. In linguistic terms the apparently seam-less relation between the grammatico-syntactic structures of the "defense" and semantic totalizations (as in assertions of what the chapter is "about") must get permanently upset. The result is that what might be considered the "literal" must now be continually remarked and recast. A situation emerges that also puts into question any notion of a readily assumable "context," since a reading of the fictional would no longer provide the monadic basis upon which its metaphysical translation "content" can rest. The latter is also effaced in the moment that it becomes other to itself, i.e., a trope. Through such a reading we are able to begin to demystify the representational force of the "defense," which, as we now discover, had already effaced that same force in its very constitution.

The "Defense": Genji and Murasaki

The narrating modulates, following the comment above, into a discussion between Genji and the Murasaki Lady on selecting appropriate texts for the Akashi Princess's education. The passage, which forms a counterpoint to the above discussion, begins with the topic "the Murasaki Lady too," demonstrating the usual lack of concern with representing figures in spatiotemporal terms. We then get a comment by Genji on his sobriety: "I must after all set a precedent (*tamesi*), for in terms of patient and deliberate[46] feelings I am unlike anyone else" (3:207). Echoing the "rainy night critique of ranks," the narrator then remarks: "Indeed, he certainly has collected affairs of his choosing that are of an uncommon variety" (3:207).[47] In marked contrast to his conversation with Tamakazura, Genji warns Murasaki to keep *monogatari* dealing with amorous affairs away from the princess.[48] The following connects with the previous passage: "What discrimination! Or so the lady in the wing [Tamakazura] would cry if she heard [his remarks], which would most certainly put her on her guard" (3:207). The surrogate Tamakazura, whose function is to entertain, is juxtaposed to Genji's real daughter, who is being readied for life at court.

Revealing an explicitly didactic view of *monogatari*, the Murasaki Lady comments on the types of unacceptable models: the woman who quickly imitates figures found in tales and a woman like the "Fujiwara Lady" (Fujiwara no kimi) in the *Utsuho* tale, who deserves praise for not yielding to her many suitors,[49] but who speaks too directly and whose behavior is unfeminine. Here, again, we can detect a valorization of the feminine, not only the feminine that men desire, but one that women (have learned to) desire as well. Genji's response further highlights differences as he emphasizes the "individualistic" aspects of people who find it difficult, given the "disparities among what each person establishes as his/her aspiration," to act in appropriately elegant ways. The conflict of wills Genji refers to coincides with both the rise of ambition we have noted and the nature of the middle ranks. It is the parents, after all, who will be held responsible for the shortcomings of children (especially daughters) whose only redeeming feature turns out to be a childlike (*komekasiki*) quality. Although a person should behave according to his or her status, since the order of social ranks is never fixed but always contingent (another unmistakable "Hahakigi" echo), stories do not all follow hypothetical rules and thus require careful selection. He notes that troubles arise when people (attendants) lavish praise on a child only to have the subject belie it in word and deed.[50] The narrator ends with a comment on old tales about wicked stepmothers (*mamaFaFa*), explaining that Genji wouldn't want the princess to think that all stepmothers (i.e., the Murasaki Lady) are the same.

In a final section, beginning with the topic "the middle captain," the narrator tells of various persons who yearn for Tamakazura,[51] including Tō no Chūjō, now the palace minister, who remembers a long-lost child (*kano nadesiko*). He consults a soothsayer about a dream and is told that he will meet such a child, at present someone's foster daughter. What he discovers, however, is not Tamakazura but the hilariously inept Ōmi Lady. In addition to forming a clear link to "Hahakigi," the minister's comments cast further light on the present chapter in their revelation of the rarity of foster daughters: "It practically never happens that a girl (*womunago*) becomes someone else's child; what sort of situation can it be?" (3:212). We realize the narrating has taken a novel genealogical occurrence and made it a crucial part of the *Genji* configuration.

The Tamakazura lineage shows how the *Genji* text appropriates poetic tropes and implicates them into its narrating. Our discussions have shown further that we must not universalize either the "critique" or the "defense" and turn them into self-standing "arguments" or controlling metaphors of the tale. They form arguments, but the intertextual forces keep them pulled in specific directions related to class, gender, and genealogical concerns.

10

Aesthetics, Politics,
and Genealogy

Our discussions of the "rainy night critique of ranks" and the "defense of narrative" found a distinct focus on women from the middle ranks and a privileging of *monogatari* over *kambun* histories. Rather than being monologic disquisitions by narrator or character, both the "critique" and the "defense" incorporated multisubjective storytelling moments (anchored to the variable, deictic narrating) inscribed by vectors of desire, judgment, politics, aesthetics, learning, and didacticism. If we think once again of the salons of Akiko and Sadako and of the significance of the *hiragana* mode itself—a sign of the non-Chinese and the nonmasculine—we begin to discern a particular aesthetics that emerged from one such collective environment: the Akiko salon and Murasaki Shikibu's family genealogy. In the great expanse of the *Genji* text, in which other cultural matters— painting, poetry, music, calligraphy, the seasons, textile patterns, and incense—are discussed, what form did a particular "feminine" concern take regarding such matters? The following narrating moments, implicating questions of aesthetics, culture, politics, and genealogy, supplement the two earlier discussions.

The "Picture Contest"

"E-awase" (A Picture Contest, 17) offers a lengthy discussion of painting and drawing, which, we discover, are considered incidental accomplishments with respect to calligraphic skill. The chapter stages a cultural event—a contest over the excellence of paintings. Like similar events in other chapters, the contest is firmly embedded in the politicogenealogical and gender configurations of the participants (especially the late Rokujō Lady's daughter, Akikonomu, for whom Genji acts as foster father) and becomes nothing less than a key determinant of power configurations. The chapter appropriates for women a "public" event, a "contest," staged in their own (private) quarters. The event, which actually spans two separate occasions, rewrites the many different types of intertextual "contests" (*awase*) popular during the Heian period.[1]

The chapter begins with the former Ise Virgin (Akikonomu) entering the Reizei Emperor's Rear Palace. Suzaku, the former emperor, had courted her, but Genji had prevented the liaison; Genji, for his part, had refrained from installing her at his Nijō mansion out of deference to his stepbrother.[2] A potential problem is immediately adumbrated by the narrator: the Reizei Emperor, born of Fujitsubo (she had taken Buddhist vows in the "Sakaki" [The Sacred Tree, 10] chapter but had been promoted to the rank of "empress," *chūgū*), feels more affection for a consort who had earlier entered his Rear Palace, Kokiden, the fourth daughter of the provisional middle counselor (who was formerly Tō no Chūjō).[3] The consort's sobriquet is that of the counselor's mother who, we remember, was the enemy of Genji's mother. The presence of the new arrival (and competitor for imperial favors) unsettles the counselor, who had planned on his daughter's becoming empress. After the narrator emphasizes the new consort's beauty and the fact that two consorts are all the emperor can handle—bad news for the daughter of Prince Hyōbukyō (Fujitsubo's older brother, Murasaki's father, and a constant loser)— the contest begins. The two consorts (both *nyōgo*) become the foci for the two competing sides.

A crucial pretext for the event is the Reizei Emperor's love of pictures and his own artistic skill, inherited from his "real" father, Genji.[4] Since Akikonomu[5] also happens to be an excellent artist (inheriting her skill from the Rokujō Lady), their mutual talents and interests magically transform the nature of their relationship ("his affections transfer themselves to her" [2:366]), thus further unsettling the counselor. Determined not to let his daughter lose her standing, the counselor orders pictures from the finest artists in the capital. As subjects for the paintings he selects interesting scenes from tales (*monogatari*), which provide the best topics, and supplies poems himself. Here we mark a convergence of aesthetics, politics, and genealogy: aesthetics (in this case, pictorial art) becomes a primary means of gaining a powerful political victory, since capturing the emperor's feelings is tantamount to guaranteeing the future success of a family line.

Irritated by the counselor's secrecy, Genji orders the best paintings, old and new, brought out from Nijō, and he and Murasaki select appropriate ones.[6] Paintings depicting "The Song of Everlasting

Sorrow" and "Wang Chao-chün,"[7] heart-rending though they may be, are deemed inauspicious. Genji also brings out the diary he kept during his exile at Suma and Akashi, and shows it to Murasaki for the first time. We are given Murasaki's (and the narrator's) reactions, while Genji's own thoughts turn to those who helped him achieve success: Fujitsubo (their secret liaison being a major reason for his self-imposed exile) and the Akashi family. The counselor redoubles his efforts, and both sides collect a great number of paintings. The Umetsubo (Akikonomu) side assembles illustrations of ancient tales of the highest pedigree; the Kokiden side, those of a uniquely modern kind. The phrasing used for the latter recalls language employed in the "critique": "in the sense of seeming novel and flashy to the eye, they [the latter] are immeasurably superior; the emperor's attendants, all of those who knew anything about painting, made it part of their daily routine to pass judgments amongst each other (*sadamea-Feri*) about this or that one" (2:369). Also present is Fujitsubo, who divides the women into two groups and assumes the role of judge. Such details as the names of the women are given, with a comment that they were all thoroughly versed in protocol and etiquette (*iusoku*).

The texts for the first round are *Taketori* (left)[8] and *Utsuho* (right) and for the second *Ise* (left) and *Jōsammi* (a no-longer extant tale, right). The commentaries supplied by the two sides address aspects of the tales rather than the quality of the paintings; the narrator also gives detailed descriptions of the materials used in their construction. Tamagami notes that the text presents here the first mention of a "picture contest" and reminds us that, since the main focus of attention normally would have been the poems, it is exceptional for the contest to focus on *monogatari*, things considered appropriate only for women and children.[9] We can read in the incident an attempt to legitimize such tales by situating them in a "public" context (a "contest") displaced to the "private" Rear Palace. In other words, the passage offers yet more evidence to support the claim that the legitimization achieved for waka by the *Kokin* collection and for *nikki* by the *Tosa* diary is now being achieved in turn for *monogatari* by the *Genji* text and its producers. Here too names of historical personages (a painter and a calligrapher) appear to accentuate the maneuver: Kose no Ōmi and Tsurayuki (for *Taketori*), Asukabe no Tsunenori and Ono no Michikaze (for *Utsuho*) and, interestingly, Ariwara no Narihira.[10]

The right wins the first round ("the left had no counterargument") and also the second, although we are told that a clear decision was not forthcoming (*mata sadameyarazu*). During the latter round Fujitsubo's powerful presence rescues the left from those on the right who disparage *Ise* and Narihira. When the trendy paintings that strike the eye put forth by the right seem on the verge of carrying the day over the left's older paintings with their lofty pedigree, Fujitsubo offers as her critique[11] a poem that echoes one by Hei no Naishi about disparaging Narihira and plays also on the difference between novel conceptions and true mastery:

> to the cursory glance   most likely will it seem timeworn,
>   now the years have passed;
> that fisherman of Ise:
>   must we watch his name sink below the waves?
> [mirume koso / uraFurinurame / tosi Fenisi / Ise wo no ama no / na wo ya sidumemu] (2:372)

The poem presents an intricate pattern of associative-words woven together with pivot-words: *mirume* (seaweed-glance), *ura* (bay-concealment), and *sidume* (sink down–disparage). The first two segments can be rendered as follows: the seaweed that has grown old these many years by the bay. "Fisherman" refers to *Ise monogatari*, for which Narihira is the metonym, and *ura* suggests that "behind" the appearance of being timeworn lies genuine substance. Fujitsubo criticizes artworks that merely create an immediate impact and favors those objects that derive from an established lineage. Note that "genuine substance" is by no means a universal term but refers to a particular lineage that Fujitsubo (and the *Genji* narrator) are valorizing. We are thus served a reminder that aesthetic preference is both closely interconnected with Fujitsubo's previous decision to support Genji and Akikonomu and with the *Genji* narrator's own inferable allegiances, as seen in the construction of the link between her text and the *Ise* "man."[12]

Genji soon arrives and suggests that the proceedings be moved to the emperor's presence for a final judgment (*katimaki sadamemu*). Having readied them for such an eventuality, he now adds his Suma and Akashi scrolls to the collection of the left. Though Genji had forbidden the commissioning of new works, the counselor, foolishly ambitious as ever, again secretly orders new paintings. The retired Suzaku Emperor, learning of the counselor's behavior and unable to forget his longing for Akikonomu, sends over paintings from his own collection.[13] Among the depictions of the annual observances (*seti-we*) painted by the old masters is one containing commentary in the hand of Emperor Daigo himself (*engi no oFontedukara*) and another the retired emperor had commissioned from Kose no Kimmochi depicting Akikonomu's departure for Ise.[14]

The contest is rescheduled and held in the "ladies withdrawing rooms,"[15] in the emperor's presence, with Genji's brother, Prince Sochi, as judge.[16] Fujitsubo is also in attendance. The activities, marked by lively discussions, extend into the evening. For the last round, the left submits Genji's Suma paintings: "the work of such a master, expressing every nuance of feeling in his heart, executed with such clear and calm composure, knew no equal" (2:377). Although it had also saved its best for last, the right is thoroughly routed, and all the participants are moved to tears. The narrator tells us that the sketches vividly reproduced what Genji actually experienced and felt and that he had also added passages, including waka, written in "grass-style *hiragana*" (*sau no te ni kana*), in contrast to the public diaries written in Chinese that primarily record details. The result: "People can think of nothing else; the interest that the numerous other paintings had attracted is now completely transferred to this one, so moving, so exciting; all the others give up, and the left achieves a total victory (*hidari katininarinu*)" (2:378).

The narrating next presents a conversational moment between Genji and his brother where we learn that during his boyhood training received from the Kiritsubo Emperor, the emperor had warned him not to get too involved in academic study (i.e., the nonfeminine, Chinese learning) since it didn't usually lead to a long and happy life and since those of high birth can manage without it. Artistic skill is referred to as "natural talent" (*honsai*) and opposed to learning, or "acquired talent" (*saigaku*). Capable in both areas, Genji had felt a special affinity with painting and wished for the leisure to paint to his heart's content. His exile, as it happened, gave him precisely that leisure.

The conversation then turns to artistic mastery. The prince remarks that some arts can be taught but others cannot. Painting and Go belong to the latter: "[A] person's spirit/soul (*tamasiFi*) manifests itself; there appear lazy people,[17] seemingly without any rigorous training, who can paint a perfectly acceptable picture or play a passable game of Go" (2:379). He then recalls that the emperor took

special pains with Genji's artistic training and lists the more important arts: letters (*monzai,* Chinese poetry) and musical instruments,
headed by the seven-stringed koto (*kin no koto*), followed by the flute
(*yokobuwe*), the lute (*biFa*), and the thirteen-stringed koto (*sau no koto*).
Especially interesting is the following comment on painting: "As for
painting, I had thought all along that it was an extraneous accomplishment, something you did to amuse yourself while practicing
calligraphy" (2:380).[18] Here again, we find the marginal (in this case,
an "incidental" accomplishment dependent on natural talent) becoming the concern of the moment. Genji's painterly skill (a "marginal" accomplishment), then, enables solidification of the all-
important shift in the Reizei Emperor's affections from Kokiden to
Akikonomu (which means a shift in power to Fujitsubo and Genji's
side), thus producing a crucial victory that will profoundly affect
future power configurations at court (and pave the way for the
Akashi Princess).

After we are told again of the counselor's anxiety over his daughter's losing all claim to the emperor's affections, the following comment on precedent appears: "To those annual observances (*seti-we*)
Genji had intended to add precedents that later generations would
hand down as having begun during the present reign; he made sure
that even those fleeting amusements of a private nature (*watakusi-
zama*) were realized with the most extraordinary conceptions
(*medurasiki sudi*); it was an exceedingly glorious era" (2:382).[19] The
mention of the "private" sounds a now familiar *monogatari* note, and
the chapter ends with Genji's thoughts of taking Buddhist vows and
his equally serious (and contradictory) worry over the education of
his children. The genealogical concern arises out of other issues
raised by the contest: the inextricable relations among aesthetics,
politics, and sexual preference; the partiality toward the "incidental"
over the established (painting in relation to calligraphy, poetry, and
music; *hiragana* in relation to Chinese; women's activities in their own
quarters in relation to traditionally "public," male-dominated events,
and so on); the importance within that feminine connection of ritual
precedent (*yūsoku*); the valorization of Narihira, in whose general
sphere must also be included, as we have seen, Tsurayuki (and other
members of the Ki family as well as Emperor Daigo); and, finally, the
recurring emphasis on complementary change as one of the primary
determinates in life.[20] We have seen thus far how the *Genji* narrating
integrates strategically placed discussions of the interconnections

between the subjects of writing, their genealogical relationships and sociopolitical situations, the larger significance of the *hiragana* mode, and the issues thereby represented. The following situates narrating moments that discuss incense, calligraphy, waka, and music.

Incense

The passages on incense and calligraphy appear in "Umegae" (A Branch of Plum, 32), the chapter following the last of the "ten Tamakazura chapters." Situated as in "E-awase" in a politically crucial moment, the discussions, here involving the Akashi Princess, arise out of conversations between Genji and his brother, Fireflies Prince Hyōbu. As has been noted, the narration seems unaware of the incidents pertaining to Tamakazura (who had recently been abducted by Higekuro) as it focuses on the ceremonies surrounding Genji's daughter by the Akashi Lady: her coming-of-age ceremony (*mogi*) and her installation (which doesn't actually occur in the chapter) at the court of the crown prince (the Suzaku Emperor's son), whose own coming-of-age ceremony is also narrated.[21] During a lull in regular (public and private, *oFoyake watakusi*) ceremonies (usual for the end of the First Month), Genji announces an incense-blending contest (*takimono awasetemaFu*). He wants to gather the best fragrances for his daughter's entrance at court (3:395). Of the samples he has received from a vice-governor of the Dazaifu (the famous place of exile), he remarks that in such things as incense, damask, and brocade, newer products are no match for the familiarity and delicacy of the old, and he orders materials from his Nijō storehouse. He asks everyone to create two blends, a request that prompts a bustle of competitive activity among the Rokujō-in women. We are told that Genji has somehow learned the recipes for two blends that Emperor Nimmyō (r. 833–850) had forbidden to be taught to men (another valorization of the matrilineal), while the Murasaki Lady possesses recipes handed down by Nimmyō's son, Prince Motoyasu (known as the Shikibu Prince of Hachijō), who himself had carried on the incense tradition of his father. At this point Genji's brother, the Hyōbu Prince, arrives.

After we are told of the Asagao Princess's entrance and poem and Genji's (surmised) reply,[22] the latter explains that the furious activity involving the blending of incense, capricious as it may seem, is actually to secure the future for his only daughter. Genji asks the prince to judge the entries,[23] and the narrating begins with the now-familiar line "taking advantage of this occasion" (*kono tuide ni*), which refers to the general preparations at the Rokujō-in for Genji's daughter's coming-of-age ceremony.[24] Genji's brother singles out for comment the entries by the Asagao Princess, Genji, and Murasaki. The other Rokujō women, the Summer Lady (Hanachirusato), and the Winter Lady (Akashi) also submit blends. The latter in particular is the subject of a brief but intriguing reference: "She hit upon the idea of using the splendid recipe for the 'scenting robes incense' (*kunoekau*), the Hundred Paces recipe that the emperors [Daigo and Suzaku] had copied from the former retired emperor Suzaku (*saki no Suzaku-win*) and that Lord Kintada had chosen and blended for presentation" (3:401). The identity of the "former retired emperor Suzaku" and the subject of the following verb (which I have rendered "copied" [*utu sasetamaFite*]), consisting of the highest level of honorifics appropriate to an emperor, have been read differently by modern commentators. To my mind, most scholars correctly take the first reference to be to the historical Emperor Uda, who lived at the Suzaku villa and was thus referred to by that name, but err in taking the subject of the following verb to be the fictional Suzaku Emperor, Genji's brother. Most older commentaries and the *Nihon koten bungaku taikei* text read a reference to the historical emperors Daigo and Suzaku.[25] Lord Kintada (889–948), a grandson of Emperor Kōkō, was a "Genji" official who served during the reigns of Daigo and Suzaku and is known to have possessed exceptional talent in the matters of scent and taste. What we have, in other words, is a *zuryō* daughter, the Akashi Lady, turning to recipes belonging to a lineage important to the producers of the *Genji* text in order to compete with the other Rokujō women. The prince pronounces it "possessed of an understated, sensuous elegance unparalleled in the world."

Calligraphy

The discussion of calligraphy is also connected to the upcoming installation of Genji's daughter, who is scheduled to live in the now thoroughly renovated quarters that Genji's mother had occupied (the Shigeisa, another name for the Kiritsubo Court). The pretext for the discussion involves the princess's "box of books" (*sausi no Fako*). The narrator tells us that Genji "orders the selection of those [texts] that would be suitable as they are as models for calligraphy practice and that there are [he possesses] many masterpieces from an earlier era that are famous to this day" (3:407). Genji then launches into a critique of calligraphic modes and styles. First, he discusses old and new, remarking that the new is usually inferior to the older specimens and that items produced in his own lifetime have generally become shallow;[26] there is one exception:

> Only in the area of kana (*Firagana*) has the present age achieved an unsurpassed excellence; the old traces (*Furuki ato*) constitute predetermined styles (*sadamareru yau*), styles that do not feature an expansive sense of creative freedom; they all follow the same paths (*Fito sudi*); it is precisely during our age when people have introduced styles that are fascinating and splendid;[27] at the height of my serious training in the feminine hand (*wonna-de*), among the many outstanding models I had collected, I happened to acquire not more than a line or two, written most casually in a running style (*Fasirigaki*), and not intended for any particular occasion, by the mother of the empress;[28] I was struck by how uncommonly fine it was; thereafter my behavior gave rise to awful rumors that damaged her good name. (3:407)

Genji's comments reveal that the Rokujō Lady's calligraphic skill incited his infatuation, a revelation that, as Tamagami notes, tells the reader-listener that she wasn't simply a substitute for the Fujitsubo Consort.[29] After a comment on Akikonomu's hand (delicate but lacking in refinement), he discusses Fujitsubo, Oborozukiyo, the Asagao Princess, and Murasaki and in the process establishes a vocabulary of aesthetic critique. Fujitsubo's was a "line full of great depth and sensuous beauty (*ito kesiki Fukau namamekitaru sudi*), but it had a frailty to it and was especially deficient in tonal richness (*niFoFi*); the principal handmaid [Oborozukiyo] to the retired emperor [Suzaku] is one of the masters of our age, but her style is too showy and leaves the impression of being stilted (*soborete kuse zo soFita[n]meru*); still, she along with the Asagao Princess and you yourself are the masters" (3:408).[30] Murasaki's hand is deemed "exceptional for its tendency to suppleness with a compelling sense of intimacy (*nikoyaka naru kata no natukasisa*)" (3:408). Genji then adds, "When one progresses in writing Chinese (*manna*) styles, incongruous characters seem to infiltrate one's kana writing" (3:408). We are being presented with a subtle, informed argument not only for the superiority of *hiragana* but also that the present age has been able to raise it to an art form.[31]

Desirous of the best texts for his daughter, Genji, as he did with the blending of incense, sends out requests, especially to his women, for calligraphic samples. He orders work done in the "reed hand" (*asi-de*) and asks for "poem pictures" (*uta-we*).[32] As he did with the incense contest, he secludes himself in his part of the mansion and concentrates on executing the different Chinese and Japanese styles.[33] His brother arrives with his own samples of superior old poems, and we find that he has selected those that display a bias for arranging poems individually into three vertical lines, written with a minimum of Chinese characters. The two then review Genji's work. The first example, the "grass" style,[34] executed on stiff Chinese paper, is judged splendid and auspicious. The feminine hand done on softly intimate, delicately textured Korean paper receives this comment: "The colors [of the paper] were not flashy; his work had a sensuous beauty (*namamekitaru*), written in a relaxed feminine hand, displaying exquisite concentration (*uruFasiu kokoro todomete*); absolutely unparalleled" (3:411–412). The highest praise is reserved for poems written on the more flowery paper produced in Japan, poems "appropriate for the wild grass style (*midaretaru sau no uta*),[35] executed in a randomly disarrayed manner (*midaregaki*), letting his brush run free; it is a work limitless in its interesting aspects; its fanciful flights possess a magnetic charm; wishing he could gaze at it forever, [the prince] does not give the other entries a second glance" (3:412).[36] The other styles are no match for native (free-form) style on native paper.

Entries by a guards commander and Yūgiri are then briefly discussed, the former's criticized for being mannered, the latter's praised for its skill in the "reed hand" and its sudden stylistic variations. At that point the prince sends his son to fetch some old examples to offer the princess, and the son returns with a copy of four scrolls (*maki*) worth of selections taken from the *Old Man'yōshū*[37] in Emperor Saga's hand and from *Kokinshū* in Emperor Daigo's. The latter manuscript is the one that the narrator, predictably, describes in detail and refers to by the now valorized term for the feminine, "sensuous beauty" (*namamekasi*). The passage ends with Genji praising the old manuscripts: "People these days pride themselves on only one facet [*katasoba*, compared to the overall splendor of the works by the emperors]" (3:413). The import of the comment is not completely clear, since Genji had begun the discussion by praising the modern age for its excellence in *hiragana*. He might be accommodating his brother's kindness to his daughter (and the fact that the calligraphers are emperors) or suggesting that earlier men displayed a wider range of talent; or he may be indicating that a certain feminization had taken place around the time of Daigo, whose work is to be distinguished from Saga's, corresponding with other concerns we have been discussing. In any case, he commissions manuscripts from the most brilliant calligraphers regardless of official rank. Only the finest specimens, treasures considered rare even in foreign courts, will be good enough for his daughter. Paintings too are included. And as for his Suma diary: "He wants to pass it on to his descendants so that they will learn about it [his exile]" (3:414), but he decides to wait until the princess is a little older. Reading once more a suggestion of a link between Genji's fortunes and that of Takaakira, especially following the mention of Daigo, it is possible to conclude that the *Genji* text itself, inclusive of the Suma exile, seeks to suggest and transmit to later generations the sorrows of the "Genji" man Takaakira.

The critique of calligraphy in all its facets is underwritten by a valuation of the feminine hand, especially those styles like the "reed hand" that are not governed by predetermined form. The *Genji* text, written in *hiragana*, the signifier of the native language, also exists without predetermined forms and formulas (compared to texts in Chinese). It appeared in an age when *hiragana* writers were in the process of determining what patterns and models they needed and selecting them from earlier texts, an age when (women) writers were adapting and expanding on earlier tales (like *Taketori*) or working variations on poetic texts (like *Ise* and *Kokinshū*). As we saw in "E-awase," however, aesthetics is never divorced from the broader politicosexual maneuverings and allegiances, in this case the installation of Genji's daughter as the crown prince's (and eventually the emperor's) consort. As the discussion demonstrates, calligraphic talent was valued highly, and, accordingly, for a prospective consort to count magnificent manuscripts among the items in her trousseau offered another guarantee not only of her own success but also of that of her family (and of their lineage).

Waka

Next come the critiques of waka and music. The former appears at the end of "Tamakazura" (22), after Genji receives a reply poem from Suetsumuhana; the latter in the "Tokonatsu" (Wild Carnations, 26) chapter, involving the interplay between Genji and Tamakazura. A later discussion appears in "Wakana II" (New Herbs: Part Two, 35).

The discussion of waka emerges out of the narration of Genji's request that Murasaki select appropriate robes for the women installed at the Rokujō-in and raises again the question of form and genealogy. Among the women, who all send answering poems, is Suetsumuhana, the Safflower Lady (still "living in the Eastern Mansion," i.e., Genji's old Nijō dwelling). Her reply becomes a pretext for the waka critique: "to receive such gifts is to deepen my sorrow,

> putting it on to see its fit I find resentment overcoming me;
>   this Chinese robe
> I return to you dampened sleeves and all
> [kite mireba / uramirarekeri / karakoromo / kaFesiyaritemu / sode wo nurasite]
>
> The lineage (*sudi*) of the hand tended toward an older, unassuming (*auyori*) style.[38]

Murasaki wonders why Genji is so intrigued by the lady's style. After a few lines we are given Genji's critique, which is generally taken by commentators to be negative:

> "Poets of older times are unable to leave off mentioning Chinese robes and drenched sleeves to express resentment; I too certainly belong to that company; to cling to one line (*Fito sudi*) and not be taken in by newfangled phrasings is, I must admit, quite admirable. When in the midst of others, at annual observances or at poetry gatherings organized in the presence of the emperor, the three letters ma-do-wi [sitting in a circle] should never be far away;[39] and when challenged by the composition of a response to one's lover, it helps to insert the five letters a-da-bi-to-no [fickle person] at the pause [i.e., caesura] to effect a smooth connection between the other phrases"; Genji smiles as he speaks. (3:131–132)

Genji's "smile" (or "laugh") is usually read as an indication of negative criticism but, as we saw in the "Hotaru" discussion, laughter can also belie serious intent. Genji continues:

> Let's say that one is very familiar with the handbooks (*sausi*) and poetic pillows (*uta makura*), has read through them carefully, and selects phrases from them: the compositional line (*sudi*) one comes to take should not change that much; the lady once sent me a handbook that belonged to her father, the Hitachi Prince; it was a book using our

native paper, on which he had written down his thoughts on poetry; it was filled to the edges with poetic exegeses (*zuwinau*), and all the illnesses [*yamaFi*, "proscribed expression"] one should avoid; those are things I've never gotten the hang of, and it did not seem that they would allow me any more freedom of movement; too difficult, I thought, and returned them; for someone who is familiar with such matters, the lady's reply here is quite ordinary. (3:132)

The negative view of "form" implied in all of the critiques continues in Genji's waka discussion. Too much attention to form inhibits "movement" (imagination). But he also criticizes those who simply imitate new fashions and aligns himself squarely with those who value the older ways. The seeming ambivalence derives from the enunciatory positions of the participants involved: Suetsumuhana is old-fashioned, but that should not mean wholesale abandonment of poetic scholarship and rules; a certain degree of form is necessary but, as with all art, that form must also be linked to the relevant genealogies.

The waka discussion modulates into a concern for the education of Genji's daughter, the Akashi Princess, a concern that resituates an "aesthetic" concern within a didactic one, again involving the Akashi family. When Murasaki expresses regret that Genji returned the book on poetry, since it could have been used for the princess's education, Genji remarks it "would be of no use for the princess's study (*oFongakumon*)." "Putting too much effort into one area," he warns, "is ill-advised, although to be unfamiliar with anything at all would also be regrettable; not to waver but to know calmly one's own mind and heart (*kokoro no sudi*), to give the appearance of congeniality, is the most appealing" (3:133). The difference between the comments here and those in the "Hahakigi" narrating lies perhaps in the difference between a *zuryō* woman and a princess. That women are well advised to cultivate an inner toughness undoubtedly derives from experiences in the imperial salons, and the unwillingness to rely excessively on predetermined forms becomes an important factor in their very survival.

Music

The two passages on music or, more specifically, on the various stringed instruments known as koto concern Tamakazura (in her difference from the Akashi Princess) and the Third Princess and hinge once again on a form-formless or foreign-native problematic. The first passage appears in the "Tokonatsu" chapter and the second, in "Wakana II." In "Tokonatsu," Genji, who has been spending more and more of his time at Tamakazura's quarters, remarks one autumn evening as he casually plucks a Japanese koto (*wa-gon*): "I have been disappointed in the fact that you seem to have no affinity (*sudi*) for such instruments" (3:221). He goes on to discuss the Japanese koto:

> During autumn nights under the cool rays of the moonlight, at a spot not far inside the house [on the veranda], when it is played in concert with the voices of the insects, there is an intimacy to it, a pleasing modern sound; lacking the solemn tunings required for official concerts,[40] it can be handled informally; with this instrument you are able to match the sounds of many other instruments and rhythmical patterns; truly marvelous; referred to as *yamatogoto*,[41] it gives off an air of insignificance, but it is actually constructed with the utmost skill; thought to be perfect for women who aren't familiar with foreign instruments; I think you should . . . work at it diligently by playing along with other instruments; there isn't anything particularly intricate about playing it, but to truly master it is most difficult."[42] (3:221–222)

The absence of predetermined form, the hallmark of the Japanese koto, places great demands on its performer. In such cases, where the modern is also the nonforeign, the old does not take precedence over the "modern." Although the instrument is suited to women, the best performer at present, Genji adds, is Tamakazura's real father, now palace minister (*uti no otodo*). Genji ignores her request to hear her father play by simply showering more praise on the Japanese koto. Using its alternative appellation "Eastern koto" (*adumagoto*), he notes that, at least at the Japanese court, where the emperor always summons it first, it is referred to as the "parent" (*oya*) of all instruments. The reference to "parent" again evokes Tamakazura's own (i.e., the minister), and Genji assures her that she will eventually be able to hear his artistry and even take lessons from him. He then plays a tune himself, and she is awestruck—"she had never before heard such a modern and wondrous sound"[43] (3:223)—unable to believe that anyone can surpass Genji's playing.

As in the "defense," the exchange conceals an ulterior, narrating purpose: the staging of another erotic scene between "father" and "daughter." Although Tamakazura refuses to try her hand at it, her eagerness to hear more of Genji's koto playing draws her physically (and emotionally) near him, and he is enchanted: "The way she tilted her head as she listened intently made her seem most captivating in the torchlight" (3:224). The koto discussion occurs at a point when Genji is at the height of his self-conceived quandary regarding whether to continue with his ruse of using Tamakazura to lure others, to take her himself, or to devise some other plan. The musical instrument, from that point on, becomes a convenient pretext for Genji's visits, a musico-erotic situation that can be stated as follows: what is incidental (the Japanese koto in relation to the more formal instruments) itself becomes instrumental to something else that is also incidental (Genji's play acting with Tamakazura as opposed to the education of his real daughter, the Akashi Princess). In the revealingly marginal *monogatari* mode, the attention men are encouraged to pay Tamakazura also serves to keep interest deflected from and prevents potential problems concerning Genji's own daughter.

The final discussion concerning koto mastery (especially mastery of the seven-stringed koto [*kin*]) appears in "Wakana II," in a conversation staged between Genji and his son Yūgiri. The narrating is thoroughly marked not only by an immediate concern with musical matters—the seven-stringed koto, unlike the *wa-gon*, does have accepted forms (*ato*) and is supremely difficult to play; in ancient times people spent years in strange lands acquiring its secret traditions (as in *Utsuho monogatari*)—but also by a concern for mastering a subject and passing that mastery on to a new generation. In wording reminiscent of the opening lines of the "Kana Preface" (see Chapter 3), Genji speaks of the instrument's transformative power: "to subdue the heavens and earth, soften the hearts of demons and gods, the sounds made by all things that obey its sound;[44] those who are deep in sorrow are moved to joy, the lots of the base and the poor are raised to the upper ranks of society; they are saved by great wealth and are recognized by the world" (4:189). He then acknowledges that those who can teach the true traditions have almost disappeared,[45] that he practiced the esoteric pieces by himself with hardly any instruction, and that his ability pales in comparison to the masters of old: "It is indeed unfortunate that there are so few in the later generations to whom the little that I have learned can be taught" (4:191). Comments on the degeneration of the world (the previously mentioned belief that the world is entering the age of the "Latter Law") are presented insofar as it infringes on koto instruction. The focus of Genji's pride at his instructional ability in the "Wakana II" section is the Third

Princess, who is scheduled to play the seven-stringed koto in the presence of her father, the retired Suzaku Emperor, at his fiftieth birthday celebration.[46]

We can recall briefly, in closing, the short critiques that followed the director's "whinnying" in the "Hahakigi" chapter, where the director made a distinction between the new formlessness and old configurations in which predetermined forms existed. Presented as analogies to the judging of women, the first concerns crafting with wood; the second, painting; and the third, calligraphy. Of particular interest in the first is the following:

> As he [a craftsman] creates many items according to the whims of his heart, there are times when he might be called upon to make playful objects for a specific occasion, objects for which prescribed models [*ato*, also "trace," "mold," "paradigm"] have not been determined (*sada-maranu*); in appearance they may be very stylish and may make the viewer realize that objects can be crafted in such a manner; successive occasions would produce further transformations, the styles striking the eye as up-to-date; they can be splendid indeed.[47] (1:145)

To the above is contrasted the crafting of items for which patterns are available. The controlling term of the section is *sadame*. The critique concerns the construction of those things close to the everyday and the familiar, which present the most challenging tasks for the true artist. The same considerations are noted in the very next example, painting. There are many skilled painters, the director notes, in the Bureau of Painting, and for each product by those artists selected to draw the ink line sketch (*sumigaki*, i.e., the initial and most important step, entrusted only to a master),[48] it is difficult to make distinctions (*kedime*) between the superior and inferior. He distinguishes the painting of imaginary places and things ("Mt. Hōrai, the forms [*sugata*] of terrifying fish in wild seas, the shapes [*katati*] of savage beasts in foreign lands, the faces of demons") based on "the whims of the heart" from the native and mundane:

> The contours (*tatazumaFi*) of everyday mountains, the flow of water, the facades (*arisama*) of human dwellings close to the eye,[49] all of it is presented in a manner convincing to the viewer, with intimately rounded forms serenely interspersed; and with mountains—not the precipitous kind,[50] thick with trees and multilayered to give the impression of remoteness from the world—and a woven fence in the foreground to suggest a garden.[51] (1:145–146)

Whereas the first is easy to do adequately, the second demands "a master's brush strokes," and in "many cases . . . the mediocre artist cannot measure up" (1:146). Implicit in the form-formless construct is a comparison between Chinese painting (*kara-e*) and Japanese painting (*yamato-e*), between the latter's more difficult construction of verisimilitude in contrast to the depiction of stereotypical objects not of this world.[52] The calligraphy discussion also involves a distinction between superficial writing where "at first glance the result might seem skillfully and tastefully done" and "those cases in which the genuine line [*makoto no sudi*, 'stroke,' and also 'lineage'] has been executed with great attention to detail: the brush strokes, at superficial glance, may appear faint, but when examined once again alongside the other, the work of substance (*ziti*) will inevitably be preferred" (1:146).

The director distinguishes objects that immediately captivate the eye from those that seem ordinary and familiar at first glance but actually possess "substance" born of breeding and long training (precisely the distinction valorized in the "defense"). The director then relates his comments to the judgment of women: "If such is the case even concerning trivial matters,[53] how much more so is it when we come to human feelings and intentions: those who put on airs according to the situation at hand, whose shows of affection are for the eyes only, I cannot put any trust in them at all" (1:146). The concern for substance over superficiality and the emphasis on the skill of a true master (which becomes apparent in dealing with the common and everyday rather than the novel or unearthly) coincide with a concern for the difference between prescribed forms and nonprescribed forms. Working within the former, the master manages to make them convincing. As seen in the "defense," subjects are taken from everyday life ("you never speak of things not of this world"), and it is up to the writer (master storyteller) to make them come alive. *Monogatari* thus supplies the "substance" ("the details of life") felt to be lacking in official discourse and does so based on an ability to make "distinctions (*kedime*) between the deep and the shallow."

The critiques demonstrate that the question of "aesthetics" in *Genji* (the acquisition of artistic skill and its transmission to later generations) must not be disengaged from the question of "politics" and genealogy (especially Emperor Daigo's lineage as it subtends the families of the Rokujō and Akashi ladies), and it is the task of future

Genji readings to continue to trace such relations. Moreover, questions raised in the discussions of "form" and "nonform," ancient and modern, Chinese/foreign and Japanese, and natural and learned skill relate in their various configurations directly and intimately to the *hiragana* mode itself and, by extension, to the broader parameters of *monogatari* discourse as instituted by the *Genji* text. As the narrating moments clearly demonstrate, discussions and critiques of aesthetic or cultural matters form sites of convergence among the represented arguments, the specific lineages of the participants (including the inferable narrator and her audience), and the scriptive mode itself. To put it yet another way, the critiques must not be taken as universalized, disembodied disquisitions on any notion of "aesthetics" pure and simple but themselves form discursive thresholds where the larger intertexts can be retraced. In the final two chapters, I turn to the Akashi family line, the genealogical line that underwrites the greater part of the tale. I take up first its "introduction" in "Wakamurasaki" (5) where it must be read in conjunction with the narrating of the fates of Murasaki and Fujitsubo, and then its role in the larger narrative.

11

Substitutions and Incidental Narrating: "Wakamurasaki"

We have noted how the "Wakamurasaki" line of chapters contrasts with the "Tamakazura" line, and how the construction of such chapter lineages corresponds with other nonlinear aspects of the tale.[1] Furthermore, the "three Hahakigi chapters" of the "Tamakazura" line seem of a different world from the former line since its characters, with the exception of the Fujitsubo Consort, do not appear in "Wakamurasaki" (5). It is clear that thematic consistency (in terms of characters) will not form a reliable basis by which to judge chapter orderings in a text whose narrating moments demand readerly reconfigurations with each new instance. "Wakamurasaki" introduces not only Murasaki, who forms a link with Fujitsubo, but also the Akashi Lady, linked to both the Myōbu narrating in "Kiritsubo" and the "Hahakigi" critique. The chapter also gestures to *Ise monogatari*,[2] and it is the source of Fujiwara no Kintō's famous question to Murasaki Shikibu.[3] The embedding of the Akashi introduction and the Fujitsubo affair in a chapter ostensibly "about" Genji's encounter with Murasaki (also ultimately a marginal figure) are further examples of the intricate conjunctions in the *Genji* tale (a narrative complementarity analogous to the temporal complications in the first three *Kokinshū* poem-songs). In the following, I discuss the two introductions and Genji's fleeting sexual encounter with the Fujitsubo Consort.

Let us begin with the opening lines: *waraFayami waduraFi tamaFite*. Seidensticker translates: "Genji was suffering from repeated attacks of malaria."[4] The Japanese phrase marks a polyvalence far beyond physical malady. It refers to "malaria," but the first word also suggests its pivotal components, *waraFa* and *yami* ("childhood" and "illness"), that is, "inflicted with an ailment as [or from the time one is] a child." The opening thus reverberates, in incantatory fashion, back through "Hahakigi" to "Kiritsubo" and to Genji's ever-present fixation, the Fujitsubo Consort. It also gestures to the first *Ise dan*, situated, as Genji will be, away from the capital. The initial pivot signals a complex narrating moment as it figures a question: How will

Genji be cured? Since the usual prayers and incantations have been ineffectual, he is to consult a sage in the northern hills well known for curing ills: "Taking four or five of his close attendants with him, he sets off just before daylight."[5]

What Genji finds, however, goes far beyond physical cures. The narrating continues in the *keri* (discovery) mode: "It is a place (*tokoro narikeri*) somewhat deep into [the mountain]; since it is toward the end of the Third Month, the blossoms in the capital have passed their peak (*suginikeri*)." We are told that since Genji's activities are normally strictly circumscribed, the flowers and dense mountain mists all "strike him as startlingly new" (*medurasiu obosarekeri*). The narrator then mentions the sage, who immediately gives Genji a potion to drink and sets about performing spells and incantations while "the sun has climbed high [in the sky]." The stage thus set, the narrating quickly addresses its main concerns: Genji's discovery of the dwelling where he will espy Murasaki and his learning about the Akashi lay priest.

Akashi

In the first instance, Genji walks out a few steps, looks out over the mountain, and notices among the monks' quarters clearly visible below him a particularly elegant dwelling surrounded by a wattled fence. He learns that a certain priest has been in seclusion for two years. He then notices several little girls offering water and flowers to the Buddha. His attendants wonder why a priest would be in the company of women and, upon investigation, report an elegant feminine presence.

Then, retracing its steps,[6] the narrating begins again: "As he (*kimi*) goes about his prayers and as the sun is rising high, he worries about his condition; [the attendants] say, 'Do something to distract yourself; it is best not to think about it'" (1:275).[7] This time he "walks to a mountain behind him" (*siriFe no yama ni tatiidete*) and looks out toward the capital: "The haze hangs far in the distance; the tips of the trees in every direction are smoky masses trailing here and there, 'so very like a painting' (*we ni ito yoku nitaru kana*)" (1:276). The narrator's speech seems to switch to or merge with Genji's at the comment on painting.[8] In this way the narrator sets up, by means of two spatially juxtaposed passages—temporally simultaneous (note the position of the sun) and grammatically parallel (note the repetition of the verb *tatiidete*)—introductions of two women, the future Murasaki and Akashi ladies. In the Murasaki Lady's introduction, the situation emerges from the visit to the mountain, a location away from the city, marginal to the capital, where the "Hahakigi" discussion has taught that an unexpected encounter is apt to occur. The situation in the Akashi introduction emerges out of advice given to Genji to "distract himself" (*magiraFasu*) from thoughts of his illness; i.e., the marginal, so to speak, within the marginal.

The introduction to the Akashi Lady occurs first. When Genji remarks of the environs that anyone surrounded by such beauty would want for nothing, one of his attendants responds, "This is quite ordinary; if we could show you the shapes of seas and mountains in other regions, how exceedingly splendid your paintings would become," and some mention "the Fuji Mountain and that other peak" (1:276).[9] The men manage to "distract him in various ways" by speaking of the bays and shores in the western regions. At the second mention of "distraction," we are introduced to the eccentric Akashi lay priest in a long monologue by one of the attendants. The length of the speech attests again to the function of such "distractions" within what at first seemed the main point of the chapter, Genji's physical cure. The attendant, Yoshikiyo,[10] singles out Akashi Bay in Harima as especially fine. Although it has nothing in particular to recommend it, its vistas are like no other place. The uniqueness of the locale happens to match the spirit of its erstwhile governor, who has built a splendid residence. Lately turned a lay priest, he lives with his wife and a daughter they have raised with the greatest care. Yoshikiyo narrates in strict *keri* discourse:

> It is said that he is descended from a minister (*otodo*), and is one who ought to have risen in the world (*subekarikeru Fito*); an odd sort, preferring not to mix with people at court, throwing away his office as a middle captain of the guards; though it [the governorship] was a post that he requested, he was not taken very seriously by the local people and saying, "Have I brought any honor to myself that would allow me to return to the capital?" he ended up shaving his head; yet he does not live up in the mountains but has settled right by the sea; it seems perverse, but when you think about it, though there are places farther inside the province where one could seclude oneself, such remote areas would feel so desolate, and the young mother and child would find them unbearable; besides, it is a place where his heart can freely roam. (1:276–277)

Yoshikiyo's account continues, as he tells of a recent visit to the priest and of the latter's magnificent lifestyle. Having achieved worldly success after a troubled career in the capital, the priest can now live out his life in unparalleled luxury. His attitude having completely changed as a result of taking vows, he now prepares for the next world with the devotion of a holy man.

But the speech is still not over. One particular item, predictably, catches Genji's attention: "Well, what about that daughter?"

> "I hear that her looks and temperament are not at all of a pedestrian sort. A succession of provincial officials over the years have gone to great lengths to show their interest in her, but the man has not accepted a single offer; I hear he is constantly admonishing her: 'It is bad enough that my own life has sunk (*sidumeru*) to nothing; you are the only child I have, and I am hoping for wonderful things for you; if I die and my hopes are not fulfilled, if the fate I have decided for you turns out differently, throw yourself into the ocean." Thus Yoshikiyo speaks, and Genji listens with great interest. (1:277–278)

Speculative comments by the attendants follow. They fear that a daughter fit to be the consort of the Dragon King of the Sea (*kairiuwau*) would be too haughty and troublesome a partner.[11] We learn from further comments that the mother must be of especially high birth (*FaFa koso yuwe arubekere*) since a dazzling array of beautiful and talented attendants have been recruited to wait on her daughter. Genji adds: "What sort of hopes would drive his thoughts so deep to the bottom of the sea?[12] The seaweed [*mirume*, 'eyes that see,' i.e., public opinion] at the depths would be sorely put out [others will be put off by the thought]" (1:278–279).[13] Genji is deeply affected by the Akashi story, and his attendants are sure that, given his inclination for the unusual (*moteFigamitaru koto*),[14] he will most certainly not ignore it.

As we have seen, the narrating has taken great pains (representing the speech of an informed observer, Yoshikiyo, and including critical comments by Genji and his other attendants) in introducing the Akashi priest and his family. The lay priest, a former provincial governor (and *zuryō* class member), fits perfectly, as it happens, the middle-rank emphasis in "Hahakigi." His wife's family lineage also seems high enough to bode well for the daughter's breeding, despite the rustic surroundings. The man appears to harbor the highest ambitions for his daughter. Read in conjunction with the earlier comments by Genji's grandmother (the *kōi's* mother) about the ambitions of Genji's grandfather and the focus on the middle ranks in "Hahakigi," the above passage not only more firmly establishes the importance of a certain sector of Heian society for the *Genji* text, but must also be read proleptically—Genji will remember the story, and the reader-listener must do the same.

The strong sense of anticipation created raises simultaneously the question of how the Akashi family will figure in Genji's life. The Akashi priest's actions, as he tries to control the fate of his family, embeds the question: Can any *zuryō* official be that powerful? The rhetorical force of Genji's query serves to direct readerly attention to the priest's as-of-yet unfathomable ambitions.[15] A seemingly incidental part of a chapter ostensibly devoted to the young Murasaki takes on important dimensions that belie its concealment in an attendant's speech designed simply to "distract" Genji.

Murasaki

The narrating now introduces Murasaki. Noticing that their master's illness seems to have subsided, Genji's men want to return to the capital immediately. The sage, however, prevents Genji's departure: "He [Genji] seems also to be under the spell of a possessing spirit [*mono no ke*]; let us have him continue his prayers quietly tonight and leave tomorrow" (1:279).[16] Delighted at the chance to stay away from the burdensome capital, Genji announces: "Well, then, we leave tomorrow at daybreak." The malevolent *mono no ke* presence, the terrifying power responsible for Yūgao's death, keeps Genji in the hills so that he can discover, almost immediately thereafter, the young Lavender.

The passage begins with another mention of free time, which also invokes distraction: "The day being quite long,[17] and with time on his hands: distracted[18] by the dense twilight haze, he takes a walk toward (*tatiide-tamaFu*) that wattled fence"[19] (1:279). Accompanied only by Koremitsu, he peeps into the western side of the house and sees a nun offering prayers to her personal Buddhist statue.[20] The narrating enforces, through the use of *keri*, an atmosphere of discovery and merges with Genji's position: "The one at her devotions to the Buddha placed before her is [none other than] a nun (*ama narikeri*); with the blinds slightly raised, she seems to be offering flowers to it" (1:279). Genji guesses her age to be over forty and, as he gazes at her unusually refined figure, he is deeply moved (*aFare ni mitamaFu*).

The narrating then introduces the main figure: "Among them [the children at play] is a girl who has come running in—is she about ten or so? She is wearing a white singlet and a well-worn robe in the yellow rose (*yamabuki*) combination. She doesn't resemble any of the other children: her lovable (*utukusi*) looks, which will clearly only become more so in time; she stands there, her hair swaying as if a fan were opened, having rubbed her face until it has gotten all red" (1:280). The cause of the tears is the loss of a pet sparrow. The narrator's gaze is Genji's gaze; verbals are governed by aspectuals; "motion" is halted. The comment about the girl's future (*oFisaki*) will be repeated as a suggestive part of Genji's assessment of her.

After the nun comments on the girl's childishness, we are given the child's features: "Her face seems lovable (*rautage*), the fuzzy outline of her eyebrows, her forehead with her hair pulled back in a charming way, her hair perfectly adorable—a person who makes one curious to see how she will grow up; his gaze is fixed on her; in fact, he realizes that he can't help staring because of a remarkable resemblance to the person he yearns for with all his heart, and his tears stream down" (1:281–282).[21] The nun then refers to the girl's mother, a "late princess" whose father had died when she was about ten. At that point the narrating presents two poems, one by the nun and another by an attendant:

> without knowing how they will fare these young grasses
> as they grow to adulthood;
> the dew that must leave them behind
> has no space in which to vanish straightaway
> [oFitatamu/arika mo/siranu/wakakusa wo/okurasu tuyu zo/kiemu sora naki]

> as long as it knows not what the future holds in store
> for these first grasses growing,
> how can the dew even think of vanishing?
> [Fatukusa no/oFiyuku suwe mo/siranu ma ni/ikade ka tuyu no/kien to suramu]

The poems gesture to *dan* 49 of *Ise*, in which a brother and sister exchange poems, and hint at the later Genji-Murasaki bond.[22]

The bishop arrives and informs the women of Genji's presence, referring to Genji as the "Genji Middle Captain," and also as "Hikaru Genji." A conversation between the nun and the bishop follows, Genji leaves, and the narrating then merges with the latter's thoughts: "What a fascinating person I have seen! That's why these amorous fellows are constantly on the prowl, cleverly managing to discover women not normally seen; even setting off (*tatiiduru*) on one of my/his rare outings[23] has been sufficient to produce an encounter completely unexpected—he is amazed" (1:282). Genji's thoughts eventually return to the Fujitsubo Consort: "And yet what a genuinely adorable child! What sort of person can she be [i.e., what is her background? her lineage?]? As an exchange for that honorable person (*oFonkaFari*), to comfort me day and night; if only I could keep her by me—so thinking, in his heart he has become completely obsessed by the idea" (1:283–284).

The intensity of feelings derives from the unexpected discovery, and the fact that the child is adorable[24] and will likely grow into a charming woman, but, most important, she resembles the Fujitsubo Consort, whom Genji would have known as a child only a little older than Murasaki.[25] Genji's thinking recalls the Kiritsubo Emperor's desire to remake the Fujitsubo Consort into the Kiritsubo Consort;[26] now Genji has a notion to substitute the child for his first obsession. The latter displacement differs since the Fujitsubo Consort is still alive. Instead of the former vertical (metaphorical) replacement, so to speak, of life for death, it becomes a horizontal (metonymic) one, the constant association serving to console an ultimately unfulfillable desire that nevertheless has been and remains realizable.

Genji gathers more information on the girl when he visits the bishop's quarters soon after the above passage. Vividly recalling the "visage of that afternoon" (*Firu no omokage*), Genji suddenly inquires about the women who live there, pretending that his question relates to a recent dream.[27] The bishop informs Genji that "there once lived an inspector major counselor (Azechi no Dainagon); it has been a long time since he died, so you probably don't know him; his principal wife is my younger sister; since the inspector's death, she has turned her back on the world" (1:286). Genji then asks about a daughter, taking care to assure the bishop that he speaks "not with amorous intent but in all seriousness." The bishop replies:

> "There was [*ki* mode] only one daughter; it will have been over ten years now since she died, I think; the former major counselor, possibly with an eye to offering her to court, had treated her with the greatest care; but he died unable to carry out his true intentions; while the nun was taking care of her by herself, whatever sort of person [attendant] it was who set it up, Prince Hyōbukyō began secretly visiting her; his principal wife, being of high birth, caused the daughter no end of

anguish; overwhelmed by sorrowful thoughts, she eventually died; I saw at close quarters how sadness can lead to illness"—he spoke of other matters as well; so the girl is that person's child, Genji thinks, putting the pieces together. (1:287)

It all makes sense now: "She is of princely lineage, and that explains the commonalities with that person—so he thinks, and is deeply moved and wants her for his own" (1:287). Genji (as well as the reader-listener) realizes that more than a resemblance to "that person" is involved. The bishop's narrating has produced, in his niece's (Murasaki's mother's) situation, a repetition of the fate suffered by Genji's mother, whose father was also a major counselor (*dainagon*) with similar ambitions for his daughter.[28] We learn later that Fujitsubo is Prince Hyōbukyō's sister and therefore Murasaki's aunt.

The narrator tells us that Genji finds "her bearing refined and beautiful with no hint of impudence; how wonderful it would be to make her mine and teach her however I please as she grows up" (1:287). To make absolutely sure of her identity, Genji asks if the union produced a child, a "memento" (*katami*). When the bishop confirms Genji's suspicion and speaks of the nun's worries about the future of a motherless child, Genji immediately offers to be her guardian. The narrating then moves into a section where the bishop and the nun try to convince Genji that the girl is much too young to be the object of what they take to be a sexually motivated proposal.

Several factors can be reconstructed from what we have read thus far of Genji's discovery of the child: first, Genji's obsession with the Fujitsubo Consort thoroughly affects his view of all the women he meets; second, the "rainy night" judgments continue to determine his evaluations of women; third, the narrating reweaves (reconfigures) textual lines into increasingly complex strands of relations staging the important incidents (which, as incidents of "speech" and narrating, are valorized over the illusion of extralinguistic "events") in its by-the-way or seemingly marginal mode; and fourth, the growing complexity embraces questions of politicogenealogical ties, social status and official rank, and the ongoing rhetorically and intertextually constructed modes of judgment, substitution, and desire.

In regard to the second point above, the emphasis on Genji's desire to teach the girl[29] as he wishes (*kokoro no mama ni*) seems to derive directly from the "rainy night critique" and relates to the didactic attitude noted earlier. One characteristic of the middle ranks, we recall, was the difficulty in determining desirability and the highly valued "trustworthiness," and one way to guarantee those qualities was to fashion a woman, Pygmalion-like, to fit one's own preferences. According to the director, the best sort of Galatea was the lovable, teachable woman, although one drawback was that such women often cannot be entrusted with important responsibilities (for example, while one is absent from home). As if attesting to Genji's skill as a teacher, the Murasaki Lady will prove her mettle when the latter leaves her in charge of all domestic matters while in exile at Suma. The question of teaching also reverberates genealogically, raising as it does the question of establishing a personal line, which Genji's being made a first-generation Minamoto would have required.[30] In the child, then, genealogical ties, the desire for an appropriate wife and companion (and surrogate mother), and the requirements pertaining to the establishment of a personal lineage all deflect the emphasis the girl's guardians continually place on the sexual and participate in driving Genji to abduct her just before she is to be returned to her father, Prince Hyōbukyō.

The question of substitution—or, more precisely, a kind of "associative substitution"—that Genji's discovery of the child raises has long been an important topic in *Genji* studies. In Japanese the terms most often used to name substitutions are *yukari* (affinitive link) and *katashiro* (substitutive form), although they are often joined by such related terms as *hitogata* (substitutive human form, effigy), *nademono* ([talismanic] figure to be rubbed), *katami* (keepsake), and *mikotomochi* (imperial mouthpiece). The terms, which can be read to be analogous to the movement of *engo* in poetic discourse, are usually applied to the "lavender" series we have been tracing—Kiritsubo, Fujitsubo, Murasaki, (and later) Third Princess—and to the women of the "Uji" chapters—Ōigimi, Naka no kimi, Ukifune.[31] In order to orient the terms and the movements they signify in *Genji*, it is also necessary to consider briefly the question of beginnings and origins, and their relation to repetition or, rather, iteration.

One difficulty with analyses involving substitutions is that the first member in the series inevitably comes to stand as a self-identical "origin" for what follows: the Kiritsubo Consort and the Kiritsubo Emperor, for example, so stand to the later women and emperors. The successive members, as a consequence, unavoidably get marked as secondary and fall into a substitutive alignment. Furthermore, if they happen to be invested with humor, they can easily be marked as "parodic" as well (for example, Gen no Naishi and the Ōmi Lady). In response to such traditional interpretations, I would reiterate that reading the *Genji* narrating involves not least a mindfulness of the following: (1) its pretexts and intertexts, which include the "Song of Everlasting Sorrow," with the pair Hsüan Tsung and Yang Kuei-fei, as well as the earlier Uda and Daigo courts; (2) its narrating mode, which always "begins" with narrating moments that are polyvalent and is therefore always already insinuated into any "representational" maneuver; and (3) its *hiragana* mode of writing, which stands as supplementary—to the hegemonic *kambun*, to the earlier *hiragana* writing, as well as to presumed oral storytelling modes—and whose very strategies, as we have noted, are constitutive of that marginalized position.

I would argue, then, that we must be wary of essentialist, self-identical notions of "origin" and "substitute," and instead explore different formulations that will help us avoid lapsing further into or remaining content with variations of the origin-substitute binarism. Contemporary discussions of the notion of repetition and iteration can be of assistance inasmuch as they explore ways of articulating substitutive and repetitive moves that enable us to address what has been termed a general condition of writing itself before the necessary and predictable emergence of binarisms. In the case of Genji and the Murasaki child, for example, it would help to think what Jacqùes Derrida has called "original repetition," a repetition that "already divides the point of departure of the first time,"[32] where, in a remark that is especially apropos of *hiragana* writing, "everything 'begins' . . . with citation."[33] Such a notion of repetition, to be distinguished from the usual view of repetition as moving from "an already constituted entity, moment, instance, or the like,"[34] Derrida terms "iteration," a structure originarily constitutive of all writing and its signification of absence. The "origin," in its very positing, is thus already contaminated by the possibility of repetition: "The time and the place of an *other* time must from the outset affect the *first time* if the latter is to be susceptible to repetition as a first and unique moment, whether or not such a repetition actually happens."[35] In the case of the *Genji* tale, "repetitions" do happen and keep on happening, and the figures of the Fujitsubo Consort and the Murasaki Lady only reinforce the instability at the "origin" by announcing their own status as "supplement,"[36] which, in an unavoidable inversion, recon-

stitutes the prior identity into an "effect" of the subsequent position.[37] The following moment, which presents Genji's second encounter with the Fujitsubo Consort, will pose the question of "origin"
in a slightly different way.

Fujitsubo

As a respite (another "incidental" insertion) during the lengthy
negotiations between Genji and the nun and her brother, the narrating stages, with Koremitsu and a Nurse Shōnagon acting as intermediaries, Genji's fateful meeting with the Fujitsubo Consort. The
meeting occurs almost exactly in the middle of the chapter. To signal
the momentous occasion, the narrating announces in a topically
governed manner similar again to a "poem-tale": "The Fujitsubo
Princess." The prior passage had ended with Genji feeling "unsettled" about his prospects with the child, and now with the sudden
mention of the object of his obsession comes this qualifier: "There
being matters about which she is distressed (*nayamitamaFu koto arite*),
she has retired to her own home" (1:305).[38] The usual interpretation is
that she is ill, but *nayamu* has a range of meanings broader than
physical ailment. Its component *yamu* can even be read as an incantatory echo of Genji's *waraFayami* that began the chapter.

Mimicking in its rhythms Genji's agitation, the narrating quickly
takes us to the moment of intimacy, only to skip right past it:

> [He is] greatly touched by His Majesty's fretful and sorrowful counte-
> nance; still, feeling that at least on these occasions [he must meet her],
> he wanders listlessly about as if his spirit had left him; nowhere,
> nowhere at all does he feel like going; whether at the palace or at home;
> during the day he idles away the time in a daze, and when it grows dark
> he presses Ōmyōbu to assist him; how did she manage it? Even after
> going to such unreasonable lengths, while he is with her he has no
> sense that it is real: how sorrowful! (1:305)

Eliding the sexual act,[39] the narrating then switches to the consort's
perspective, which suggests an earlier meeting, before ending with
Genji's perspective:

> For the princess too, to recall that shocking incident has been a constant
> source of anguish; she had firmly resolved to have that be the end of it;
> and now with gloom hanging heavy in her heart, she seems devas-

tated; yet, for him, [she is] someone who inspires longing, so adorable, even though she is never too familiar, and her thoughtful behavior puts him to shame, a person after all like no one else; how is it possible that she is without even the slightest flaw? He even hated her for it [being so perfect]. (1:305)

The Fujitsubo Consort is clearly unable to reject Genji, who has been ably assisted by her attendant (Ōmyōbu) and no doubt by Koremitsu as well. Her resolve not to allow a repetition of the earlier meeting seems based mainly on fear of gossip and does not lessen her feelings for him (feelings, we must remember, openly encouraged by the emperor). Most striking, however, is Genji's reaction both to his father's obvious suffering and to the consort's equally obvious pain. Assuming a masculinist perspective often found in the text, Genji is aware of the consort's feelings, but he still seizes the opportunity to force a meeting with her. And although he sees that his actions have caused her great distress, that very condition only heightens her appeal—Genji reacted in a similar way to Yūgao's fears, and he will react similarly to Murasaki's profound distress about his marriage to the Third Princess. The narrating, though seemingly predisposed to construct Genji in a positive manner (not as the run-of-the-mill fickle courtier-lover), is also ready to find in that construction, at crucial moments, an inescapable blindness to a woman's suffering, which can be used simultaneously to fuel and to excuse his own uncontrollable desires. The narrating instance we are examining concludes with the expected exchange of poems:

> He seemed to want to take up lodging at the Mountain of Darkness [Kurabu no yama—to be able to remain together],[40] but, it being an unfortunately short night [early summer], he felt it cruel and unfair,
> together now, yet   so rare those dreamlike nights to meet again;
>   would that this body of mine
> find camouflage directly   in a world of dreams
> [mite mo mata/aFuyo marenaru/yume no uti ni/yagate magiruru/ waga mi to mogana][41]

> He was choked with tears and, despite the situation, her heart was overcome with pity,
> the sensation of our time   will people talk thus of it?
>   though I place this body of unknowable sadness
> into a dream from which   no one ever wakes
> [yogatari ni/Fito ya tutaFenamu/taguFinaku/ukimi wo samenu/yume ni nasite mo]

> Overwhelmed by thoughts, as is quite to be expected, her demeanor is imposing;[42] the Myōbu has gathered his robes and other apparel and brought them to him; back at his quarters, he has spent the whole day crying in bed. (1:305–306)

The disjunction that emerges from the exchange produces the gulf that keeps the two apart. For Genji, dreams offer escape and concealment and a way of prolonging the moment; for the consort, whose behavior reveals depth of feeling but, predictably, a greater concern for reputation and propriety, dreams offer no escape or protection from almost certain notoriety. Profoundly disquieting for both, the incident leads to the consort's pregnancy and the birth of another prince (regarded by the world to be the emperor's). As if aware that he and Fujitsubo have had their final sexual encounter, Genji directs his energies toward gaining possession of Murasaki.

At this point the reader realizes that Genji's obsession with the Fujitsubo Consort results in no small part from a prior meeting: "that shocking incident." The prior situation explains the constant references in "Hahakigi," "Utsusemi," and "Yūgao" to Genji's inability to put her out of his mind. The second meeting, however, playing on the momentary "was it dream or reality" mode of *dan* 69 of *Ise*, makes him realize the futility of his desire and also strengthens the consort's resolve to put an end to indiscreet behavior. Moreover, the child that she bears is marked as a "big secret" of the text, a secret suggestive of taboo and transgression although, strictly speaking, no sociopolitical taboos have been broken.[43] The following configurations, fostered by the fictions at the heart of the *sekkan* imperial genealogical structure, can be extrapolated from the incident: Genji sleeps with his (step-) mother, who is the age of a sister; that (step-) mother-sister bears him a son who is believed to be his (step-) brother.[44] The transgression deeply affects the participants (Genji and the consort are beset by guilt and fear of exposure, and the future Reizei Emperor, shocked when he discovers his true parentage, tries unsuccessfully to abdicate to Genji) but produces no cataclysmic results.[45] It is rather the narrating of the event, in its customary mode revelatory of the underside (*ura*), that will transmit the tale to future generations. The fear expressed by the consort will prove to be unwarranted, since it is a "private" secret, but the narrating manages to insure that the royal figure and the incident will not be forgotten. The narrating of the union, in accordance with the maneuvers of the chapter itself, legitimizes itself through more gestures to the *Ise* text, this time the *dan* that deals with the Imperial Hunter and the Ise Virgin.[46]

The Ōmyōbu's role (along with that of Koremitsu) in the fateful meeting must not be overlooked. Genji was completely at her mercy for the arrangement of the encounter, and later her inability to repeat her performance drives him to dispair. The Fujitsubo Consort, too, was a victim of such manipulation. Recall that it was a close attendant to the emperor who initially recommended the Fujitsubo Consort and also that it was no doubt a scheming attendant who helped Murasaki's father, Prince Hyōbukyō, gain entry to her mother's quarters. The crucial functioning of such intermediaries, whose most intimate thoughts and actions would have been second nature to the likes of Murasaki Shikibu, is a prime focus of interest for the *Genji* narrator (who would have occupied a similar position to such figures as Genji) as well as for her reader-listener.

After noting the birth of the prince and the misery of the two participants, the narrating returns to the negotiations between Genji and the nun for guardianship of the child. The reader-listener will have anticipated that Genji eventually gains possession of her (he does so by force), but it is also important to remember her father's position. Prince Hyōbukyō's principal wife made life unbearable for the child's mother and drove her to death. The correspondences to Genji's own mother's and Yūgao's (with Tō no Chūjō) cases cannot be coincidental. In abducting the child, Genji also rescues her from an uncertain fate, although the narrator tells us that the prince and his wife looked forward to caring for her.[47] Not particularly predisposed to a father who has abandoned his child, Genji has further reason to feel inhospitable toward the prince who, having sided with the temporarily ascendant Kokiden faction, snubs him when he is exiled.

The series of intertwining incidents that lead to Murasaki's abduction are as follows. The nun returns to the city, but her death soon afterward leaves the child without support. After a visit to the Aoi Lady, cold and aloof as usual, Genji learns from Koremitsu of the prince's intention to reclaim the child. Knowing that if he waits until she is back with her father he will be criticized for having stolen away a daughter, he decides to act immediately: "Since he would be censured for frivolousness and impetuousness if people heard about it, he decided to bring her to Nijō" (1:325). The sudden turn of events answers in part the "question" posed at the end of "Kiritsubo": Who will Genji find to live with in his mother's old home? With the

Fujitsubo Consort now beyond reach, her niece must suffice and with proper teaching can be molded into a satisfying companion (as noted in the "rainy night critique"). The narrator even tells us that Genji begins "teaching her from that very moment" (the following day), explaining to her that "for women, it is best to be accommodating" (1:332).[48]

Materializing out of the pictures and calligraphic models Genji draws for her, the first postabduction poem appears, preceded by the following citation, which Genji writes on lavender paper to the "Musashi Plain," playing on "lavender" and links (*yukari*): "At the mention of Musashi Plain, I cannot help complaining." The line cites a *Kokin waka rokujō* poem:

> never have I been there　　yet the very mention of Musashi Plain
> 　　sets me to complaining;
> ah yes, it's all due to　　the *murasaki* I miss so much
> [siranedomo/musasino to iFeba/kakotarene/yosi ya sa koso Fa/
> murasaki no yuwe][49]

Genji then writes the following in "slightly smaller letters" (since it is his own composition):[50]

> though I have yet to see its roots [sleep with her]
> 　　still I am unbearably drawn to it,　　the link on Musashi Plain
> to those dew-drenched grasses　　I despair of stepping through
> [ne Fa minedo/aFare to zo omoFu/musasino no/tuyu wakewaburu/
> kusa no yukari wo]

The last poem, on the *"murasaki* link," suggests a fundamental ambivalence: the *murasaki*, which invokes the Fujitsubo Consort and completely colors his evaluations of women, is a source both of complaint and of unmitigated longing. The child is destined to stand forever in the shadow of that first obsession. As a Galatea who can be fashioned into a forgiving, talented, and trustworthy woman free of guile, she will eventually win his heart and supersede her aunt, but without the unquestioned royal standing enjoyed by the latter, her place will always be unstable and contingent, forever vulnerable to displacement.[51]

The final lines of the chapter reiterate that instability. The child, ignorant of her own father (as Genji was of his own mother), quickly warms to her "subsequent parent" (*noti no oya*). The narrating echoes the "rainy night critique" when it compares the child, who will be his "delightful playmate," to women whose "shrewd" ways only create mutual suspicion and resentment. If she were his real daughter, "he wouldn't be able to behave in such an uninhibited way, without restraint whether in bed or awake; she is an odd sort of treasure, he seems to be thinking" (1:336).[52] As in Tamakazura's case, their "unnatural" relationship displaces the "natural," and since it can progress at the present moment "naturally," it can become more natural, in fact, than the "natural" itself. The subject positions that the narrating constructs and participates in form a fluid space from which to explore continually the ambivalences constitutive of all seemingly central, dominant, or hegemonic notions—prior, natural, main, original, orthodox, and so forth—whether in the specific terms of imperial consorts, principal wives, sociopolitical rank and status, narrative story-lines, parent-sibling relationships, citations of poems, or rhetorical figures. The introduction of the Akashi Lady and the staging of the incident with Fujitsubo in a chapter ostensibly devoted to the narrating of Murasaki demonstrate how "narrating moments" fall into a physical "order" whose reading of necessity becomes directed toward specific intertexts (the *Ise* tale, Genji's mother and grandmother, an earlier encounter with Fujitsubo, and the "Haha-kigi" critique). The situation not only calls into question notions of "unity" and "narrative development" but places on the reader-listener the burden of making the links between those moments and pretexts. Readerly moments of interpretation then become iso-morphic to the narrating moments.

12

The Akashi Intertexts

As was suggested in Chapter 6 and as corroborated by the "critique of ranks," concerns of the *zuryō* class underwrite the *Genji* tale. When we reread the text in *zuryō* terms, we find Genji's actions and career converging with the interests of families from that class.[1] The most spectacular and ineluctable convergences, involving the eccentric and devout Akashi lay priest (*nyūdō*), span four generations and the broader genealogical ties and contribute to what are arguably the most important aesthetico-politico-genealogical configurations of the *Genji* tale.[2] The Akashi family narratings represent the ultimate "victory" of a *zuryō* family lineage in sociopolitical and aesthetic as well as "narrative" terms.

Readers will recall that the initial meetings between Genji and the Akashi Lady occur after the former's move from Suma to Akashi. Arising out of the topic of music and the priest's own narrations, the liaison, formed in the context of exile, produces a child who brings glory to the Akashi house: she becomes consort to the crown prince ("Fuji no uraha," Wisteria Leaves, 33), gives birth to a son ("Wakana I," New Herbs: Part One, 34) who is appointed crown prince, and is herself appointed empress (some time prior to "Minori," The Rites, 40). When the son becomes emperor, Genji assumes the most influential position in the land as maternal grandfather to a reigning emperor, precisely the position Fujiwara leaders had coveted. Crucial to the above moments is that the Akashi story, first and last, constructs a maternal link, through Genji and the surrogate mother Murasaki, to the imperial lineage. The further underside (*ura*) of that "marginal" story involves negative representations of the proud and talented Akashi Lady who is separated from her daughter and made vulnerable to often cruel and humiliating reminders of the humbleness of her station (*mi no hodo*). In the following I discuss narrating moments—bringing together the issues of narrating, poetry, substitutes, and (matrilineal) genealogy—devoted to the Akashi family.[3]

"Suma"

The narrating leads us to the Akashi "story" by means of an "incidental" moment, a conversation between the Akashi parents (a second "introduction" to the family after "Wakamurasaki," 5) toward the end of the "Suma" (12) chapter. The crucial kinship link is established again via Yoshikiyo: "Since the Akashi coast was a mere crawling distance away, Lord Yoshikiyo remembers the daughter of the lay priest and sends her letters, but she does not answer."[4] The father's surrogate reply asks for a meeting with Yoshikiyo, but the latter ignores the request, certain that the priest would never accede to a proposal of marriage. The priest, we are told, is

> an uncommonly prideful man, and although people in the province [Harima] praise the [present] governor and those related [*yukari*, including Yoshikiyo] to him as the only ones worthy of respect, that eccentric [the former governor] doesn't share those feelings in the least[5] and has thus passed the months and years; when he hears that this person (*kono kimi*) is living there in this manner (*kakute*), he says to the mother: "The shining one who is a Genji, born of the Kiritsubo Consort, is at Suma, having fallen out of public (*oFoyake no*) favor; emerging from our child's ties to a former existence (*kako no oFon-sukuse*), it is an unexpected event; let us find some way to take advantage of an occasion such as this (*kakaru tuide ni*) and offer our daughter to him."[6] (2:201–202)

Politics, narrating, and genealogy converge in the remarkable moment. The wife's apprehensive reply—"What an ill-suited match!" (*ana kataFa ya*) (2:202)—speaks to the discrepancy in social rank.[7] She recites rumors about Genji's affairs, including his misstep with the "emperor's wife" (i.e., Oborozukiyo)[8] and concludes that he would never seriously consider "strange mountain rustics" like themselves. The priest responds angrily that he has different matters in mind[9] and that he will eventually "contrive an occasion" (*tuide site*) to draw Genji to them. The full extent of the priest's intentions, here called "foolishly single-minded" (*katakunasiku*), are not revealed until "Wakana I." In its suggestion of unswerving devotion to a single idea, the comment echoes the hint dropped in "Kiritsubo" concerning Genji's grandfather,[10] and we eventually discover that Genji's maternal grandfather[11] is the Akashi priest's uncle, which makes the priest and Genji's mother first cousins and Genji and the Akashi Lady second cousins.[12]

The priest's wife continues to argue that Genji has been exiled for a serious offence (*tumi*) and reiterates that he wouldn't be interested, "even if in jest."[13] The priest's response invokes the kinship link and also reveals a *zuryō*-class attitude towards exile: "To meet with calamity (*tumi ni ataru*), whether in China or in our own courts, is what inevitably happens to those who are the most brilliant of their day, who far outstrip others; think of who he is; his late mother is the daughter of the Azechi major counselor, who was my uncle" (2:202–203). The comment recalls famous exiles like Minamoto no Takaakira and highlights the genealogical connections just noted: the candidate qualifies because he is both a Genji and a relative, and exile only enhances his brilliance. The priest then reveals knowledge of the circumstances behind Genji's mother's death and states how wonderful it is that she left "this person" behind. "Women," he concludes, "should prepare their hearts with pride and high ideals; I'm sure that he won't dismiss us just because he thinks I'm something of a bumpkin" (2:203). *Zuryō* conceit and faith in genealogical ties fill the priest with confidence.

The final moment suggests that the Akashi Lady has indeed inherited her father's pride: "Though she is not an outstanding beauty, she is of a gentle and elegant disposition and is quick-witted and sensitive, in no way inferior to women of high birth" (2:203). Realizing her own lot in life, "she thinks: a man of high rank would consider her/me insignificant, yet she/I would in no way countenance life with someone of her/our rank; if she/I lives long and is left behind by those that care for her/me, I/she intend to become a nun; I/she intend to jump into the sea; her father spares no expense as he looks after her with all his heart; he sends her twice a year to offer prayers at [the shrine at] Sumiyoshi and secretly places his hopes on the efficacious powers of the deity" (2:203).[14] The reference to throwing herself into the sea evokes the priest's admonition in "Wakamurasaki" and past texts like *Kojiki* and *Nihon shoki*,[15] as well as prefiguring the subsequent narration.

At the end of "Suma" and the beginning of "Akashi" (13) supernatural events bring Genji and the old man together. An apparition ("Suma") and the "late retired emperor [Kiritsubo]" ("Akashi") appear to Genji in separate dreams and urge him to leave Suma. The apparition materializes during a terrible storm that arises in the midst of purification rites performed for Genji. "Why," it asks, "when there is a summons from the palace (*miya*), do you not go?" Scholars disagree whether "palace" refers to the Heian capital, the underwater palace of the King of the Sea (whose dwelling is referred to as *miya* in *Nihon shoki*), or the dwelling of the Akashi priest. Genji takes it as a sign from the Dragon King of the Sea (who has an appetite for rare items) and decides in horror that he must leave Suma.[16] Actually, the narrating produces the "storm" out of Genji's poem:

> eight hundred and more all the myriad gods
>   must be deeply moved there being nothing at all
>   to call a sin committed
> [yaFoyorozu/kami mo aFare to/omoFuramu/okaseru tumi no/sore to nakereba]
>
> As he speaks, the wind suddenly begins to blow, and the sky darkens.
> (2:209)

The fierce storm, which arrives as Genji had floated out to sea a boat carrying an effigy (*Fitogata*, mentioned before) onto which his pollution had been ritually transferred, reinforces the "transgression" (*tumi*) that presumably caused his exile, even as it suggests its cleansing.[17] As commentators note, several levels of transgression (and alleged transgression) are implicated: Genji's affair with Oborozukiyo, his secret liaison with Fujitsubo,[18] as well as the historical examples of innocent men wrongfully exiled. Events recorded in the official chronicles in political terms (plots, for example, to contravene imperial successions) become transposed in the *Genji* text into sexual ones, into an eroticized reading that will yet have far-reaching political consequences. We can infer here that transgressions, alleged or not, have obverse aspects that can fashion completely unexpected successes and that *monogatari*, whose purpose the *Genji* narrating takes to be an exploration of those obverse aspects, can do them justice.

"Akashi"

The storm bridges "Suma" and "Akashi," the latter title reinforcing the crucial toponymic play: a place that will "clear the name" (see below) of the exiled figure when he is seduced by the Akashi daughter's poetic and musical skill at the dwelling by the bay (*ura*—also "underside"). When word comes from Murasaki of damage to the capital, Genji again protests his innocence and prays to the

Sumiyoshi god for help. His attendant's prayers include the phrase "having no guilt and being made to assume it" (*tumi nakute tumi ni atari*); the second half of the phrase, identical to the previous wording, suggests Genji's fundamental innocence as well as, I submit, that of other historical exiles. After lightning destroys part of his dwelling, his father appears to him and advises him to put his faith in the Sumiyoshi god and leave Suma. When Genji wishes he could end his life, his father replies, "That is out of the question; this is simply retribution for slight wrongs committed (*isasaka naru mono no mukuFi*)" (2:209).[19] The emperor reveals that though he himself was never guilty of misconduct (*ayamati*), he has been striving to redress unintended trespasses.[20] He then vanishes, saying that he must make a report to the palace, "taking advantage of an occasion like this" (*kakaru tuide ni*).[21] The moment recalls the Kiritsubo Emperor's vow, when his consort died, to oversee their son's success. As Tamagami states, such incidents in a tale in which supernatural occurrences are rare (actually, not only are they rare, but each incident is presented for a specific purpose) serves to "bring to light" (*akasi*, from *akasu*, "prove," "clear one's name") Genji's innocence— the Japanese term "pivoting" the name of the chapter, the seaside topos, and the priest's sobriquet—and also to construct, in incantatory fashion, a bond with the Akashi family.[22]

The next morning ("near dawn") a small boat appears bearing the priest, and Genji's relations with the family begin. Following instructions received in a dream, the priest prepared a boat and headed for Suma Bay, aided by a "marvelous wind" (*ayasiki kaze*) attributed to the Sumiyoshi god. It is the thirteenth, the same day as Genji's purification ceremony. Hearing news of the visitor, Genji reflects on his own dreams and not only receives the priest but seeks shelter in Akashi. The priest obliges, and the boat speeds back to Akashi, aided again by the "marvelous wind." Upon arrival, the priest offers a prayer of thanks to the Sumiyoshi god and feels "as if he has taken the light of the sun and moon in his hands" (2:224–225).[23] We are told that Akashi (light) is a much livelier place than Suma.

Genji and the priest, then, are brought together by the Sumiyoshi god and a direct intervention by the late Kiritsubo Emperor. Once at Akashi, the narrating gives us further information about the lay priest, noting his worldly concern (which compromises his admirable religious devotion) for his daughter.[24] He occasionally communicates that concern to Genji. The latter, remembering Yoshikiyo's comments (in "Wakamurasaki") about the "alluring" (*wokasi*) daughter, attributes the unexpected encounter to "effectual ties from a former life" (*sarubeki tigiri aru niya*).[25] Thoughts of Murasaki keep Genji at his own prayers, but he is curious. The priest prays even harder to the "gods and buddhas" that his wish (that Genji marry his daughter) come true. We then learn that he is

> around sixty, agreeably delicate in his old age, and grown thin from his devotions; no doubt due to an elegance deriving from his station [*Fito no Fodo*, i.e., descended from ministers], although he has an eccentric side and is a bit senile at times, he is well informed in ancient matters, is not at all crude, and combines cultivated attainments; for Genji, his accounts of past times and people help pass the idle moments; public and private life have left him little free time in recent years, and the priest brings up at his own grinding pace (*kudusiidete*) all sorts of ancient affairs[26] that he [Genji] had not heard about; among them are items of such great interest that he realizes how impoverished he would have been had he not seen this place or met this person. (2:228)

The priest, though a skilled storyteller well versed in "ancient matters," has difficulty broaching the subject of his daughter, and we are told that the latter, made all the more aware of her station (*mi no Fodo*) by Genji's presence, is even more miserable than before. Once again, we see enacted how stories, *monogatari*, can serve both to entertain and to instruct, and also to lure and to bond. We can only conjecture about those "ancient matters," but, given the references to illustrative precedents (*kozitu*), the reader-listener might be inclined to make the link once again, in the context of exile, to that famous *kojitsu* man Minamoto no Takaakira.

The narrating now effects a sexual-genealogical convergence in musical terms. First, Genji's skill on the seven-stringed koto entices a visit from the priest and inspires suggestive references: "lute-playing monks" (here, the priest),[27] Genji's "general" (and sensual) comment on the thirteen-stringed koto ("as for this one, it is most affecting when played in the spirit of a woman toying with your feelings, loosely strummed [*sidokenasi*]"),[28] and another citation of Emperor Daigo ("I [the priest] am the third generation of those who have received instructions on playing [the koto] directly from the hand of the Engi Emperor") (2:232). Then the priest slyly adds that his daughter has received that illustrious instruction, to which Genji, highly intrigued, remarks that the thirteen-stringed koto is especially suited to women, that its "illustrious line" (*sono oFonsudi*) had died out with the fifth daughter of Emperor Saga,[29] and that he would welcome the opportunity to hear the daughter play since present-day players only skim the surface of the technique.[30] Finally, the priest's own musical skill is linked to his storytelling prowess: he "tells stories (*oFonmonogatari*) omitting nothing" (2:234), and he "speaks—a story in unasked for fashion (*toFazugatari ni*)—about his daughter" (2:234).

Genji responds with amusement (at the priest's presumption) but finds himself uncontrollably moved at certain "moments" (*Fusi*). The priest then claims that Genji's arrival in Akashi is due to his prayers to the gods and buddhas, who have finallly taken pity on him:

> The reason is this: it's been eighteen years[31] since I began relying on the Sumiyoshi god; since she was a little girl I have had my reasons and have not failed to make a pilgrimage there twice each year, in spring and winter; at the six services during the day and night, I have sacrificed my own petitions for life on the lotus leaves [salvation] by praying with all my might that my hopes for this person would be granted. (2:234–235)

The priest tells of the decline, which he attributes to "adverse ties to a former life" (*saki no yo no tigiri no tutanasa*), of his own family fortunes following his parents' generation ("they had held on to the position of minister") and reiterates his longstanding ("since she was born") desire to marry off his daughter to a high-ranking person from the capital, a desire that "resulted in the resentment of many people due to our low station" (2:235). And, as Yoshikiyo had revealed in "Hahakigi," if he dies, the daughter is to throw herself into the sea. As he listens to the priest's story, Genji begins to realize (as does the reader-listener) that other factors may have led to his banishment: "Having wandered to this unexpected world, after being made to bear an unwarranted burden of sin, I have been anxious as to what sort of transgression was behind it;[32] I am deeply impressed, after hearing your story (*oFonmonogatari*), and putting it all together: it was due to a by no means shallow tie to a former life (*saki no yo no tigiri*)" (2:236). When Genji asks the priest to guide him, the latter responds with the following:

> to sleep alone   you now know its sadness;
>   lost in idle thoughts   as dawn comes to Akashi Bay,
>   we feel a desolation hidden to others
> [Fitorine Fa/kimi mo sirinu ya/turedure to/omoFi-akasi no/ura-sabisisa wo]

Genji replies,

> in these traveler's robes   lined with sadness,
>   I am reluctant to face the dawn;
> my pillow of grass   ties no dreamy knots
> [tabigoromo/ura-ganasisa ni/akasikane/kusa no makura Fa/yume mo
> musubazu]

The remarkable moment activates the full incantatory polysemy in the words "Akashi" (place name, stay up until dawn, gain light, clear one's sin) and *ura* (bay, behind/inside, lining of a robe, intention). The references to sleep (and sleeplessness) have powerful political (exile) and sexual overtones, and "tying dreamy knots" suggests sleeping with someone on those "traveler's robes," i.e., Genji's acceptance of the priest's proposal. *Ura*, which refers variously to Akashi Bay and the "intentions" of the old man (and his daughter) "hidden" there, can also mean "foretell the future" (cognate with "fortunetelling," *uranaFi*). In other words, the (imminent) obverse of the sadness expressed (the "we" in the priest's poem refers to the daughter) suggests the end of Genji's penance and heralds a new phase in his life. In the length and details of the particular moment devoted to the establishment of the ties between Genji and the Akashi priest, the pace of the narrating again insists on the significance of *zuryō* concerns. Before telling of Genji's wooing, the narrating reverses the mood: "The priest spoke on and on of countless matters, but it is too much of a bother [to write them all down]; since I have purposefully recorded it contrary (*Figagoto domo ni*) to how it happened, the intentions of our foolish and hardheaded priest surely will have been too much revealed" (2:237).[33]

An exchange of poems begins the wooing (and creation of a different bond). The priest answers for his daughter (incapacitated by diffidence and resistance in the face of eminence and by knowledge of her status [*waga mi no Fodo*]) the first poem from Genji and then persuades her to answer the second.[34]

> whether near or far,   unknown, those clouds,
>   to which I gaze in misery;
> I seek the tree tops   of a dwelling hinted at beneath the haze[35]
> [wotikoti mo/siranu kumowi ni/nagamewabi/kasumesi yado no/
> kozuwe wo zo toFu] (2:238)

Genji, duly impressed with the old man's calligraphic skill, tries again,

> choked up inside   pangs of sorrow
>   lie heavy in my heart;
> no one comes along to ask   say there, how do you fare?
> [ibuseku mo/kokoro ni mono wo/nayamu kana/yayo ya ika ni to/toFu
> Fito mo nami]
>
> It is difficult to talk of it [how I really feel since we haven't even met].[36]

The daughter finally replies,

> the extent of your heart   the ardor you seem to feel,
>   say there, how is it possible?
>   such distress only from rumors
>   of someone you have yet to see?
> [omoFuran/kokoro no Fodo ya/yayo ikani/mada minu Fito no/kiki ka
> nayamamu]
>
> The hand and what was written were of an elegance not at all inferior to
> the grandest ladies of the land.[37] (2:239–240)

The daughter deftly deflects Genji's phrase "say there, how do you fare?" into "say there, how is it possible?"[38]

The contrasts among the figures are effectively manipulated: the old man's seemingly blind ambition and joy at Genji's show of interest, Genji's amorous curiosity and almost unwitting seduction by poetic and calligraphic skill, and the daughter's irresolvable feelings of inferiority.[39] Not wanting to appear overly eager to meet a woman so below his station and also solicitous of Yoshikiyo, who had spoken of the daughter as his personal possession, Genji acts tentatively. Time passes as Genji and the woman, who we are told is far more prideful than the high-ranking court ladies, engage in a battle of wills (*kokoro kurabe*).

Before the actual meeting between Genji and the Akashi daughter, two sections defer the inevitable. The first tells of three moments: the Suzaku Emperor's dream of his father (the Kiritsubo Emperor) "on the thirteenth day of the Third Month" (2:241),[40] the death of the Kokiden Empress's father (the grand minister), and the ill health of the empress herself. When the emperor suggests a pardon for Genji —someone "who has sunk thus without having transgressed"—he is adamantly opposed by his mother, Genji being for her someone "who left the capital fearing [the consequences of] a transgression (*tumi ni odite*)" (2:242).[41] The second section begins with the narration of the daughter's feelings after Genji, unwilling to condescend to visiting the daughter himself, practically orders the priest to send her to him. The narrating modulates to and merges with her thoughts:

> It [visiting him] would in no way occur to the person in question [the daughter]; country persons of unfortunate rank (*kutiwosiki kiFa*)[42] might easily get involved that way, taken in by the sweet talk of a fellow down for a while from the capital; since he seems to think I am/she is of no consequence, I/she will certainly suffer greatly; my/her parents, too, who have their hearts set on an unobtainable goal, who are infatuated with their impossible hopes for my/her future . . . will end up with nothing but heartache.[43] (2:243)

Although she is perfectly content to exchange letters, hear his koto playing, and follow his daily habits from a distance, her parents, on the verge of seeing their prayers answered, fear Genji's ultimate rejection. Genji's arrogance abates, however, as he grows more eager for a meeting.

The actual encounter is staged again through music: Genji's desire to hear the daughter play the koto. The ever-confident priest, meanwhile, has made secret preparations. The day of the month (the thirteenth, with a brilliant moon in the sky) corresponds to that of those miraculous events recounted at the beginning of the chapter.[44] As he arrives at the daughter's quarters, after casting aside thoughts of Murasaki, the narrating very deliberately evokes the surroundings and emphasizes the daughter's feelings of resistance. The sound of a curtain cord brushing against a koto inspires Genji to recite,

> intimate words of longing: to speak of them with someone
>   is what I am wishing for
> that I might partly wake   from dreams afloat in a gloomy world
> [mutugoto wo/katari aFasemu/Fito mogana/ukiyo no yume mo/ nakaba samu ya to]

The daughter's reply is simply juxtaposed in the text (with no intermediary available),

> in this night never dawning   with only confusion
>   filling my heart
> how am I to distinguish   the part that is the dream?
> [akenu yo ni/yagate madoFeru/kokoro ni Fa/idure wo yume to/wakite kataramu]

> Her presence, which he perceives vaguely (*keFaFi*), strongly reminds him of the Ise Mother [the Rokujō Lady]. (2:246–247)

The daughter flees to another room and somehow bars the door. Genji does not exactly force his way in, "yet," the narrating asks, settling the matter with a rhetorical question, "how can he leave things as they are?" (2:247). After the initial encounter, Genji begins making occasional visits but now even brief periods of absence bring misery and regret.

The sudden link to the haunting Rokujō Lady,[45] also a skilled poet, invokes another family fallen on hard times. Not only is it the case, as Norma Field notes, that there are "parallels in family circumstance"[46] between her and the Akashi Lady—the Rokujō Lady, like the Akashi priest, is descended from a minister, and Genji's father and the Rokujō Lady's late husband are (step-) brothers—but the Rokujō Lady was married to a man (now deceased) who had once been appointed crown prince only to be deposed under circumstances only hinted at in the text.[47] Her father's aims no doubt resembled those of the priest. We can recall here with Field that the heads of the two families resemble other men who placed high hopes on daughters.[48]

Genji's thoughts of Nijō (and of Murasaki) and the woman's certainty that she will be abandoned (and thus will throw herself into the sea) lead the narrating to Genji's amnesty and his departure from Akashi. After a duet with the daughter, Genji leaves his koto as a memento, and he is reminded of Fujitsubo's musical skill: "He [Genji] had thought the sound produced by the princess nun [Fujitsubo] to be unequaled in the present era; splendid in a modern fashion, satisfying to anyone who heard it, enabling the listener to imagine the appearance of the performer, an unbounded skill indeed; hers [the Akashi Lady's] is a thoroughly flawless playing, a sound so fascinating, so superb as to arouse envy; even to Genji's well-versed heart it is so moving, arouses such affection" (2:255). First the Rokujō Lady, then Fujitsubo help further captivate Genji.

A final intertextual connection to earlier concerns—the darkness of a parent's confused heart—appears in a longer passage telling of Genji's imminent departure from Akashi. Several poem exchanges again reproduce a "poem-tale," further evidence of *zuryō* poetic skill. First the lady,

> the waves roll in   and break, as I cut and cut again the cloth
>   for these traveling robes;
> finding it soaked with briny tears   will he refrain from wearing it?
> [yoru *nami* ni/*tati*kasanetaru/tabigoromo/*siFodokesi* to ya/Fito no itoFamu][49]

Then Genji,

> here for you a memento   in exchange for one you offer,
>   for the time until we meet again,
> to count the days in between   a middle robe for middle days
> [katami ni zo/kaFubekarikeru/aFu koto no/Fikazu Fedaten/naka no
> koromo wo]

The robe Genji sends "is truly a memento that will add yet another layer [*FitoFe*, one layer of clothing] of intensity to the inevitable longing [*sinobu*, also 'keep secret' or 'forbear']; an indescribable robe bearing a wondrous scent: how could one's heart not be deeply colored [*simezaramu*, 'dyed']?"[50] The erotic nature of the exchange, interwoven with textile-based associative-words, has been noted,[51] but Genji's gift is, after all, a "middle robe," one worn between the outer and the innermost layers; it might help alleviate the lady's loneliness, but it also signals a deflection from absolute intimacy. The word plays, while emphasizing the relevance of such passages to the Akashi Lady, also focus narrative attention back upon itself (and upon its reciter-listeners). The priest's poem appears soon afterwards,

> weary of the world   I am now, by the sea, a body
>   thoroughly soaked with brine,
> no longer able to tear myself away   from these familiar shores
> [yo wo umi ni/kokora siFozimu/mi to narite/naFo kono kisi wo/e koso
> Fanarene][52]

> Now that I shall feel even more lost in the darkness of the heart, I shall
> only accompany you to the border.[53] (2:258–259)

Scholars note that the reference to "these familiar shores" suggests the priest's life at the near shore (in Buddhism, the unenlightened world, i.e., preoccupation with his daughter's welfare), in contrast to the far shore (the enlightened world). The section concludes with Genji's poem reassuring the priest of his devotion, the narrator's view of the daughter, the wife's continued anxiety, and the priest's supreme confidence—"Since there seem to be matters that he [Genji] cannot cast aside [the daughter is now pregnant], though he must leave us now, he no doubt has his own intentions" (2:260).

The narratings of the Akashi Lady include psychotextual evocations of the three most important female (mother) figures in the first two-thirds of the text: Murasaki (textual/sexual affinity, and surrogate mother to Genji's daughter by the Akashi Lady), the Fujitsubo nun (musical resemblance, and Genji's stepmother and mother of the Reizei Emperor), and the Rokujō Lady (resemblance in poetry and pride, and mother of Genji's adoptive daughter Akikonomu). The important "maternal" aspect that underwrites these relations intersects as always with aestheticogenealogical concerns, which directly involve the imperial line.[54] The private nature of the (often surrogate) ties turns out to have crucial consequences at the public level of imperial politics. As painterly skill bound Akikonomu to the Reizei Emperor, so koto skill (derivative of Emperor Daigo) lures, then binds, Genji to the Akashi Lady, whose low status in itself has nothing to recommend it—excepting perhaps the powerful promise of interest, as taught by the "rainy night critique." In the end, the close kinship ties between Genji and the Akashi family, strengthened by mutual poetic and musical inclination and talent (with the suggestion of Daigo's lineage and, within the context of exile, the fate of his son Takaakira), and a common link to the Sumiyoshi god, not only help Genji succumb to the Akashi daughter (and produce a future empress) but, assisted by the larger schemes of the father, even alter the balance of political power.

Inextricably caught up in the convergences of her father's schemes and Genji's fortunes, the daughter suffers for the family at practically every moment in the gradual but inevitable unfolding of the Akashi destiny. The more acute moments, which again indicate the care with which events concerning the family are constructed, include the following: (1) the birth of her daughter in "Miotsukushi"—the lady is in the throes of despair until Genji dispatches a nurse to Akashi; (2) the encounter with Genji's retinue when they happen to make a pilgrimage to the Sumiyoshi Shrine on the same day—she is made to "feel keenly her regrettable station" (*mi no Fodo kutiwosiku oboyu*) (2:293); (3) the painful departure from Akashi (and from her father) for the Ōi dwelling ("Matsukaze," The Wind in the Pines, 18)—the priest refuses to go along even to see them off and in a long speech sums up their fate, referring again to the "darkness in the heart" and ties to a former life; (4) the heart-rending separation from her daughter ("Usugumo," A Rack of Cloud, 19)—the Akashi Lady had refused to enter the capital proper, and Genji wanted to guarantee, by handing the child over to Murasaki (whom he himself has taught), that she would be properly groomed for entry into the imperial family;[55] (5) her grief when she cannot attend her daughter's coming-of-age ceremony ("Umegae," Branch of Plum, 32); and (6) the painful memories that attend the grandmother's revelation of the past to the daughter, now a senior consort ("Wakana I"). Genji does care for her, if only out of self-interest: we are occasionally told that Genji tries to be sensitive to her feelings, and she is installed in a wing (northwest-winter) of his Rokujō Mansion. She is also allowed to accompany her daughter when the latter enters the court of the crown prince ("Fuji no Uraha," Wisteria Leaves, 33).[56]

Given our earlier discussion of historical intertexts, especially the Daigo lineage, of particular interest is the reference in "Matsukaze" to the former owner of the Ōi dwelling where the Akashi Lady moves with her mother and her child when she refuses to live at Genji's newly renovated Eastern Mansion at Nijō. The place, we are told, once "belonged to the mother's grandfather, a Nakatsukasa prince, near the Ōi river" (2:388). Old commentaries offer two possible references: Prince Tomohira, son of Emperor Murakami and a relative of Murasaki Shikibu, and Prince Kaneakira (914–987), a brilliant statesman and man of letters.[57] The latter, like Takaakira, was a son of Emperor Daigo, and also like Takaakira, his mother was a *kōi*, Fujiwara no Yoshihime. He was ordered to take the Genji surname and rose to the rank of minister of the left but was reinstated as a prince in 977, when he began to pose a political threat to the Fujiwara hegemony. He left behind a poem in Chinese, "Tokyō no fu," to protest his unjust treatment and clear up matters to prevent misunderstanding for later generations. The reference further links the Akashi family to the Daigo lineage within the context of wrongful treatment by Fujiwara rulers and by fate.

Just before the Akashi Lady hands her daughter over to Genji, the narrating interweaves metonyms, poem-tale-like, with an exchange of poems between the Akashi woman and her daughter's nurse:

> As they spend the days in tears [after deciding to give up the child], it has become the Twelfth Month; with snow and hail more frequent, their loneliness grows more intense: "I am strangely destined, in various ways, to suffer painfully," she thinks and collapses in grief; she sits and stares at her child, stroking her with greater tenderness than usual; one morning when deep snowfall blankets the skies in darkness, she continues to think of everything that had happened and of all that was to come; it is not her custom to sit out near the veranda; she casts her gaze to the ice at the edge of the pond; wearing ample layers of soft white robes, her figure, her hair, and her profile from behind as she sits gazing out were precisely those of a lady of the highest ranks, her

attendants think; wiping away a tear, she says, looking helpless in her
grief, "How much more unsettled will I feel on days like this?":

in the deep snow   the path to the mountain
     will be clouded in darkness;
let the letters come and go,   never ceasing to leave their tracks
[yuki Fukami/miyama no miti Fa/Farezutomo/naFo Fumi kayoFe/ato
taFezusite]

The nurse's reply:

though I have to search my way   through the endless snowfalls
     on Yoshino Mountain
could the thoughts I send to you   ever cease to leave their tracks?
[yuki ma naki/yosino no yama wo/tadunete mo/kokoro no kayoFu/
ato taFeme yaFa] (2:422–424)

In the lady's poem, "snow" and "darkness," associated with the
Twelfth Month,[58] activate the sense of gazing in *Fukami* ("look
deeply/since it [the snow] is deep"). Both poems amplify "snow" by
adding the pivot-words "letters/step" (*Fumi*), "tracks/ink print" (*ato*),
and "visit repeatedly/exchange" (*kayoFu*), to the sense of distance in
"mountains" (*yama*, especially Yoshino Mountain). *FumikayoFe* can
mean "let letters be exchanged/let your letters keep coming" but also
"take steps to visit." The word for "snow" (*yuki*), moreover, is
homophonous with the word for "go," which adds a sense of
movement.[59]

Finally, when Genji comes for the child, the narrating combines
sorrow with equivocation: "She feels her breast shattered with sorrow (*mune utituburete*), knowing that no one else is to blame [but
herself for agreeing to it]; it's what I decided in my heart; if only I had
firmly refused [to hand her over]; how hopeless; still, she convinced
herself that it would seem much too frivolous [to change her mind
now]" (2:423).[60] The narrating then merges with Genji's thoughts of
"their ties from a former life (*Fito no sukuse*) difficult to take lightly"
(2:423) and follows it with other familiar references: "The confusion
of the heart (*kokoro no yami*) during those moments when her
thoughts are drawn to this child living with a stranger—it pains him
greatly to imagine it; he talks to her repeatedly to clear away (*akasu*)
her worries; 'what sadness is there if she can at least be looked after as
a person not from my unfortunate station (*kutiwosiki mi no Fodo*)?'"[61]
The text constructs an ambivalent interrelationship between the
lady's maternal feelings, tempered by keen awareness of her sociopolitical rank, and her gratitude—always complicated by pride—

toward Genji, whose interest in the lady, the narrating suggests, needs an occasional nudge. Here that nudge is provided by the child's beauty and a renewed sense of their mutual karma.

"Wakana I"

The Akashi story reaches a climax of sorts in "Wakana I" when the priest sends a final epistle to his daughter announcing his intention to sever ties with the mundane world. The two massive "Wakana" chapters (34 and 35 whose narrating takes up a tenth of the total space occupied by the fifty-four chapters) are filled with moments of remembrance, as the text signals both a regeneration ("new herbs," or shoots, signifying a new spring), for example, the marriage of the Third Princess to Genji and the birth to Genji's daughter of the Akashi great-grandson, and a degeneration with sinister signs of decay, exhibited in the Suzaku Emperor's senility, Genji's fortieth birthday celebrations,[62] the Akashi priest's decision to leave the world, Murasaki's illness and spirit possession, and Genji's "cuckolding" by Kashiwagi. The priest's epistle and such moments of remembrance shed new light on (and reconfigure) that textual past.

The chapter begins with a presumable focus: the retired Suzaku Emperor's illness and his wish to take vows as soon as he marries off his Third Princess, upon whom he has especially doted. The child's mother, known as Fujitsubo, is the daughter of a former (*sendai*) emperor. This Fujitsubo was made a "feminine Genji"[63] and entered the Rear Palace of the Suzaku Emperor while he was still crown prince. Talented enough to become empress, she lacked strong political backing; "her mother was an insignificant junior consort with no lineage (*sudi*) to speak of" (4:11–12); she suffered greatly at court, being completely overshadowed by Kokiden's younger sister, Oborozukiyo; and, when the emperor abdicated ("Miotsukushi"), her situation deteriorated further, and she eventually died a lonely death. The narrating recalls the situation of the Kiritsubo Consort, Fujitsubo, and Genji, perhaps to suggest a negative variation and to anticipate Kashiwagi's sexual transgression near the end of "Wakana II." Much of "Wakana I" narrates the emperor's (often foolish) decision making and Genji's acceptance of the childish Third Princess as his principal wife, a marriage that proves fatal to Murasaki.

Following the shift to another ostensible focus, Genji's fortieth birthday celebrations, the Akashi narrating begins. As they prepare for the birth of a great-grandson, Genji, who recalls Aoi's death, and the Akashi Lady, for whom the birth will determine the destiny (depending on the sex of the baby) of her family, exercise sharp vigilance. The impending birth brings a visit from the priest's wife, who narrates a "private" underside to the Akashi destiny: she reveals to the princess a past previously kept secret by the mother who feared that such knowledge would psychologically hinder her child's education and success. The princess realizes the role Murasaki's teaching has played in enabling her not only to cope with the resentment of other, higher-born women but, ignorant of her own birth, even to behave arrogantly herself. As if to reinforce the family's position, the moment ends with three poems by the three generations of Akashi women (the old nun, the Akashi Lady, and the soon-to-be-empress senior consort). The Akashi Lady's poem makes another reference to the "darkness of the heart" of a parent who worries about a child.[64]

> having given up the world   to go to Akashi Bay,
>   the person who resides there, he too
> knows a heart filled with a darkness
>   not easily cleared away
> [yo wo sutete/akasi no ura ni/sumu Fito mo/kokoro no yami Fa/
> Faruke simo sezi] (4:100)

When news of the birth (of a son) reaches the priest, he declares that he can "finally leave behind the border of this world (*yo no sakaFi*) with a peaceful heart," remakes his house into a temple, and sends a letter (included in the text) to his daughter. After complaining that difficult to read *hiragana* writings only sidetrack him from his devotions,[65] he reveals another Akashi underside by recounting a dream he had in the Second Month of the year the daughter was born:

> I am holding Mount Sumeru in my right hand, and from the right and left sides of the mountain, light from the sun and moon stream down, brilliantly illuminating the world; hidden in the shadows at the foot of the mountain, I am not in the light; the mountain is floating up out of a vast ocean, and I board a small boat and row westward—that's what I saw; I awoke from the dream, and from the following morning hopes for the future began to grow in me, a body of no consequence; I wondered, in any case, how I could possibly anticipate such glorious events; from the time that you began to swell inside your mother— since I found many instances of belief in dreams when I examined the

secular texts and consulted the heart of the inner teachings [Buddhist texts]—although we were poor, we were extremely grateful and raised you with great care; yet, unable to shake the feeling that our resources would not be adequate, I set out on this road [to Harima]. (4:106)

His decision to leave the capital, we now learn, was based on nothing more substantial than a dream. Incorporating associative poetic metonyms (sink [immerse], wave, rise up and return, bay) into his discourse, he continues:

I then *immersed* myself into the matters of this province and, abandoning all hope of *rising up and returning*, an old *wave*, to the capital, have spent the years at this *bay*, and in all that time I pinned my hopes only on you and offered many prayers with a single purpose; now the time has come when I can give thanks that things have turned out as I had hoped; during the reign when the youngster [i.e., the consort] becomes mother to the land [mother of the next emperor] and our hopes are fulfilled, go and give thanks to all the deities beginning with the Sumiyoshi Shrine. (4:106–107)

With his wish (that his granddaughter be empress) soon to be granted, the priest moves deep into the mountains to await the heavenly emissaries (*raigo*) who will escort him to the Western Paradise. His final poem:

that special dawn   when the light will pour forth
        has drawn near;
now, at this moment   I tell the tale of that dreamy night
[Fikari iden/akatuki tikaku/nari ni keri/ima zo misi yo no/yumegatari
suru] (4:107)

"Light" signifies the soon to be firmly established imperial connection and the subsequent Akashi family glory. In his instructions on how to deal with his death, the priest tells his daughter to consider herself a "transformed being" (*Fenge no mono*) as she performs the final rites. The letter comes in a box containing supplications to the Sumiyoshi Shrine.[66]

After telling us of the priest's many disciples, further proof of his spiritual power, the narrating effects a familiar temporal disjunction and returns to an earlier moment when the Akashi Lady, having heard about the letter, comes over from her daughter's quarters. The daughter realizes that her suffering was due to her father's reliance on that evanescent dream (*Fakanaki yume*). Recalling the priest's eccentric (contrary) spirit (*Figagokoro*), the nun's speech traces the deep ambivalences that constitute *zuryō* success: she had to abandon the capital, but she was still with her husband; when she was finally able to return to the capital, she had to leave her husband behind. Joy and glory, for their family especially, have been inextricably mixed with pathos and suffering. Her story ends with familiar references to fate and precedent: "If it should come about [that her great-grandson becomes crown prince], it will have been a destiny without precedent (*tamesi naki sukuse*)" (4:113).[67] The lady then gives the letter box to her daughter (the senior consort), delivering as she does so the equivalent of a testament: "Do not look lightly upon the kindnesses shown to you by the lady in the wing [Murasaki]; since I have come to realize that her deep feelings of affection and sympathy are of a kind rarely seen in the world, I hope that she outlives me" (4:115). She cites social status (*mi no Fodo*) as the reason for placing her daughter in Murasaki's care and mentions her later worries about entrusting her daughter to a stepmother.

Genji, who arrives before they can hide the letter, calls it a "testament" and marvels at their bonds from a former life: "As my years accumulate and I become more familiar with the ways of the world, I find myself strangely yearning for him; I am deeply moved that our relationship was governed by such deep ties" (4:119). When the Akashi Lady, apologizing for her father's bizarre scribbling (calling it *bonzi*, letters as unreadable as Sanskrit), mentions the "dream story," Genji makes a final revelation concerning the Akashi priest's father, whom we learned earlier had been a "minister":[68]

> It [the priest's hand] is superb, without a trace of senility; regarding everything, calligraphy and other matters, he was someone who should consciously be made a learned model (*iusoku*); it was simply that he lacked the worldly determination needed to succeed in official life; now take his ancestor the minister, his was a rare sort of presence with a wisdom he thoroughly employed in serving the court; during his tenure he met with misfortune, and people say that it was due to further retribution that his descendants have died out; yet, *though it is in terms of women*, you can't say that there are no successors at all; that too is no doubt the result of his unceasing prayers and devotions. (4:120)

The reference to "misfortune" has been read in the context of vengeful spirits who destroy family lines. The startling revelation of a crucial feminine role in genealogical succession may suggest a similar fate for the Akashi family but also intersects with the positions of the text's speakers and writers. Genji goes so far as to state that his marriage to the lady and even his exile were "all due to this singular man" (4:121). The narrating then modulates to other strands of the chapter—Genji's advice to the princess on Murasaki's role and his warning to the Akashi Lady to remain on good terms with Murasaki—before eventually returning to the Third Princess via the Akashi Lady's thoughts of her and Murasaki's and Genji's feelings for them both.[69]

When Genji's desire (aroused by the "rainy night critique") for women of the middle ranks is read in conjunction with the powerful (spiritualized and incantatory) force that emerges out of the Akashi lineage, we begin to see how that lineage (and the priest's obsessions) converges with the interests and rank of the tale's putative author (or authors),[70] at her particular historical moment.[71] Genji's relations with the Akashi man, who opted for provincial wealth over capital splendor, implicate historical connections among the *zuryō* class (and women writers), the modes and topics of learning, teaching and accomplishment, and the demoted or deposed "Genji." The Akashi family's ultimate success reconfigures the trials that Genji's mother endured so that the latter's death becomes only a temporary setback. Similarly, the priest's final letter forces a rereading (reconfiguration) of the foundations of Genji's rise to prominence: was he (Genji) simply an actor in the greater play orchestrated by that *zuryō* official? The priest's fateful dream, which convinced him to devote all his energies to his daughter's welfare, is revealed to be the force tying together various elements of the tale at the same time that it exposes the "private" aspect of life (including even a private appropriation of Buddhist notions—"ties from a former life," *sukuse*), a primary function of *monogatari* discussed in the *monogatari-ron*. In terms of gender, the Akashi women might be pawns in a larger, masculine game, but it is a game where success hinges on genealogical manipulation and accident, where the maternal side is all-important, as Fujiwara practices and Genji's comment on the ancestors of the Akashi priest attest. Genji himself, then, is rewritten as a pawn in the service of *zuryō* (political and narrating) interests. Those interests, intimately tied to Genji's political life, participate in complex relations involving economic, political, scholarly, and scriptive factors: They cannot be articulated by a discourse situated solely on the masculine side of the imperial, the Genji or the Fujiwara, a position that regards the feminine simply as victim; nor can they be conveyed by a discourse overly concerned with thematic interests that make it extremely difficult to articulate the "marginal" aspects, the "underside" of life. It is, as we have found, precisely the function of *monogatari* to narrate such a complexity of interests that other modes of discourse cannot effect.

Epilogue: Endings, Tellings, and Retellings

thus, indeed, has it been transmitted . . .
  "Kiritsubo"

or so the text seems to have it . . .
  "Yume no Ukihashi"

Readers of *The Tale of Genji* are well aware that there is no "ending" to the narrative (other than yet another instance of the narrating's explicit recuperation of the text in the second epigraph above), at least if we mean by ending a "resolution" of a story (or theme) in global or local terms. At the end of "Yume no Ukihashi" ("The Floating Bridge of Dreams," 54), the last of the so-called ten Uji chapters, the reader-listener is left hanging regarding the fate of Ukifune (ensconced at Ono in the northeastern edge of the capital) and Kaoru (anxious to reestablish contact after learning of her whereabouts). Readers in the West might be inclined to characterize the situation as a "lack," a negative aspect, something to be tolerated, perhaps, but not necessarily accepted or understood. The expectation of "resolutions" (and "conclusions") is deeply embedded in a particular (Western) tradition that has for several hundred years privileged such claims and manifestations of reason largely at the expense of other ways of configuring thoughts, language, and the world. Such privileging, furthermore, has been instituted in the wake of a long history of imperialistic ventures and conquests as a self-evident and universally valid modus operandi.

To read Heian Japanese texts and to grapple with their "otherness" is to confront a non-Western example of an alternative mode or modes of discourse, modes that demonstrate precisely such "other ways" of constructing the world. It is also, simultaneously, to confront the opportunity to explore the nature of that "otherness" and difference. One reason I embarked on the present study was to seize an opportunity that has often been missed and to examine the texts with an eye toward those aspects that effectively resist resolution or rationalization. I wanted to situate my own discourse at sites of resistance, contestation, convergence, and contradiction represented in the texts and to negotiate with terms and positions found in the volumes of criticism and commentary (and translation) that have arisen around them. I wanted to do so, moreover, in a manner that spoke to the need to preserve a certain contingency in my own positions of analysis. The problem that arose—the production of a book that satisfied readerly and institutional (disciplinary) demands for "unity " or "coherence" even as one of its aims was to contest traditional ways of appropriating non-Western texts, including sub-scription to such notions as "unity" or "coherence"—was not an easy one to resolve.

I decided to appeal to a strategy of integrations or "transpositions" that could enable the production of multivectored, polylogic readings of those aspects of the texts that in themselves required a replaying of the deferral of analytical closure. The strategy was to take readings and rewritings performed at one specific textual arena (the linguistic or "poetic," for example) not as final, controlling mechanisms of appropriation but as always and only preliminary to negotiations and rewritings performed at other arenas (the narrating "subject" posi-tions or the "prosaic," for example). My aim was to keep such negotiations situated as much as possible at textual "nodes" or thresholds where "resolutions" become difficult, if not impossible, to effect and where the specificity of a text can be reconstructed. By so doing I wanted to minimize (or at least be continually aware of) the interpretive violence (through acts of exclusion) that is necessarily concomitant to the establishment of all readerly moves and claims. The readings that resulted derive from an attempt to take such perceptions as the "lack" of "endings" (and also the problem of "beginnings"—one reason I discussed three *Genji* "beginnings," "Kiritsubo," "Hahakigi," and "Wakamurasaki," and closely exam-ined opening moments and movements of the other texts) as signal-ing discursive thresholds that could focus further investigation. I did not merely want to foreclose consideration of the *Genji* "ending" as a negative aspect, but I wanted to ask what would happen if we related it to other areas and arenas of the text and of Heian discourse in general.

I began, then, by attending to the Heian *hiragana* language and in particular to its obvious "tenselessness" and its powerful modal-aspect emphases. What are the larger implications, I wondered, of a narrating mode that privileged discernible moments of narrating that seemed to "tell" of events and, simultaneously, of its own processes, rather than to "show" them in some purportedly "unmediated" way. I then focused on such moments by using a term, "narrating moments," that could refer to the open-ended, topically oriented (and participatory) sections of narrating constitutive of all *hiragana* texts, whether "prose" narratives or the (always reconstructed) circumstances of poetic utterance (examples from the present study include sections involving the Myōbu ["Kiritsubo"], the Fujitsubo Consort ["Wakamurasaki"], the Akashi Lady ["Wakamurasaki"], the Murasaki Lady's death ["Minori"], the *Taketori* suitors, the *Kokinshū* and *Ise shū* prefatory notes, and the *Ise dan*). The interrelatedness of poetry and "prose" could then begin to be articulated in a way that implicitly questioned approaches that assumed generic (binary) distinctions between the two, although I also wanted to address the fact that poetic utterances were made to function in incantatory ways to create bonds among poets and between poets and their communal body, both in terms of "conventional" and "neomythical" constructions.

The "narrating moments" offered an entry into the obviously related questions of orality and contexts of utterance raised by Tamagami for the *Genji* text(s), questions that brought into the discussion the worldly circumstances (at least as far as we can surmise them, including the presence of painterly representations) in which *monogatari* were produced and received. Tamagami's groundbreaking assertions enabled me to reconnect the consistent narrating presence, marked conspicuously by such modal narrating suffixes as *ki* and *keri*, to the spaces ("salons") of women-in-waiting at the Heian palace and other locations. Those women who wrote or recited in their communal quarters were able to realize the extraordinary potential for narrative subject matter available in their own, their mistresses', and their sponsors' ever precarious positions. Not only were they allowed privileged glimpses of and easy access to the highly uncertain (since power rested greatly on accidents of birth) lives of the highest ranks of aristocracy, but their indispensable intermediary roles afforded them countless occasions for influencing (and critiquing) the course of their employers' daily lives. To follow the texts in terms of such socially situated linguistico-narrating movements meant, moreover, negotiating a discursive space where strict categories—whether of time (past versus present) or of subjectivity (I versus she or he)—were always put into question. The circumstances of narrating are also intimately related to the vexing question of variant texts, another way that contingency infringes on "content" analyses.

Consideration of those larger situations or contexts of utterance also necessitated the incorporation of configurations of genealogy, which I found to be an intertextual component kept operative by writer-reciters at all levels of Heian society and discourse. In the process I realized that not only must the genealogies of the represented and representing figures be mapped but, on a more complex level, to "genealogize" questions of "origins" was absolutely critical to the reading of Heian texts. Particularly relevant for the present study were the genealogical positions occupied by the larger Ki family (e.g., Haseo, Tsurayuki, and Aritsune) and their scholarly and political colleagues and sympathizers (e.g., Sugawara no Michizane, Prince Koretaka, and Minamoto no Tōru) with regard to the *Taketori*, *Kokinshū*, and *Ise monogatari* texts and the positions occupied by members of those lineages as well as the general class of middle-rank *zuryō* families in their relations with the "Genji" with regard to the *Ise shū* and *Genji monogatari* texts. I have noted that a man like Ki no Tsurayuki and a woman like Ise were accorded prominent positions in the *Genji* narrating and the *Kokinshū* seriate structure and that the stunning exile of a Michizane left an indelible imprint on the minds of lower-ranking officials and served as a metonym for other wrongly accused men like Minamoto no Takaakira and Narihira's father, Prince Abo. In the chapters dealing with the *Genji* text I tried to show just how the particular interests of *zuryō* class women underwrote, in what can too easily be perceived to be nothing more than an interesting leitmotif, the broader concerns of the tale and its "main" figures. Reading the moments of critique incorporated into the text further convinced me of the broader connections that needed to be made.

The last series of narrating moments I examined at the close of Part III, those moments dealing with the Akashi family, can lead us to a summation of the issues I have been raising and help us close the epilogue and this book. In general terms, the *Genji* narrating positions and moments (and their deictic anchors) participated in concerns that can be rewritten in terms of the positions of the women who served at the imperial palace (whether or not a particular woman, Murasaki Shikibu, produced all or part of the text). Genealogically, scholastically, artistically, and emotionally tied to personages who were active during the earlier periods, those women found in *hiragana* writing a means by which to reveal and recount a "private" side of life (the *ura*, or "underside," which I have mentioned on numerous occasions). As a space of contestation for both male and female writers, the *hiragana ura* was the site of a series of struggles that ranged from a native, private confrontation with Chinese public discourse in *Kokinshū*, one that made "public" the "private," to confrontations between such native modes as the *nikki* (diary) and the *monogatari* (tale) and their Chinese-language-based precedents and inspirations.

The following are among the configurations that I have rewritten. The ambivalences that form the "Genji" position, which presents an *ura* to the installed imperial line, become linked to the poetico-political ambivalences (noted particularly in the *Ise fūryū*) that are part of all Heian *hiragana* endeavors and form themselves an *ura* to Chinese discourse. Those ambivalences are "governed" from and by a stance locatable at *zuryō* sites that are inscribed by vast learning and often by traces of ancestral glory (and power, as in the case of the Ki family). It is not surprising that those "salon" intermediaries, women who had a hand in producing the *Genji* narrating, chose continually to negotiate in complex ways with what was "marginal" to life and, in particular, brought together two constituencies, the *zuryō* and the "Genji," in order to trace the problematic relations between those two marginal groups and the figures and families of the highest ranks of officialdom, the imperial household, and the always-changing networks of power. The many women who resist (in implicit and repeated gestures to figures like Kaguyahime, and women like Lady Ise) the main male figure of the *Genji* tale seem to present moments of feminine or *zuryō* consolidation that serve thoroughly to demystify Genji and prepare the reader-listener for the powerfully motivated Akashi assistance and ambition. To put it another way, the "fall" in the world of families and their individual members to *zuryō* and "Genji" positions becomes something like a fall into a constructed world of discourse in which (as in the *Genji* case) even moments of the narrating are marked by a concerted privileging of the "incidental" (a thematic and a narratological *ura*) over the possibilities for any "main" story (or theme). In short, the privileging of the Akashi family and the incantatory toponym *Akashi no ura* must then be read for the manner in which the narrator/narrating constructs an ineluctable "underside" to the delineation of Genji's life and also for the self-reflexive gestures in the Akashi narrating to a native poetic tradition (reconfigured, with *Kokinshū*, at the Heian capital) that incorporates by extension an appeal to the sense of a linguistico-spiritually based communality, one largely created by *zuryō* scholar-poets.

Undersides, of course, have their own undersides, and the Akashi "glory" is gained at great cost to the figures involved, including the narrating of its own "story," which must always remain an embedded one. As a site for the convergences in which a "Genji" transgression and exile stages a politics of sexual seduction enabled by a musicopoetics, the Akashi *ura* produces an eventual victory even as it prefigures the fact that victories can never be ultimate. It gives way in time to (is contingent upon) the separation of the Akashi father from his family and his abandoning of the world, and to Genji's desire to take Buddhist vows and his sudden disappearance from the tale. In his place emerge the "stories" revolving around another prime *zuryō* daughter, Ukifune, whose name embraces an incantatory verbal figure that underwrites the "Uji chapters": a figure "sadly" set "afloat" (*uki* = "gloomy" or "sad," and also "float"; *fune* = "boat") on a radically ambivalent path on which even death is no longer final but opens out onto a continual replay of transgression and deferral. On another level, the impressive and ongoing flow of modern-day *Genji* scholarship attests to the fact that a final word on the text will never be written. For that text and for the other Heian *hiragana* texts and their variants, "final words" are destined always to be inscribed as if on one of those "magic slates" whose traces serve to remind us only that we can and must perform the act of writing yet again.

Appendix:
Chapters in *The Tale of Genji*

Japanese Title	Translations by Seidensticker
1. Kiritsubo	The Paulownia Court
2. Hahakigi	The Broom Tree
3. Utsusemi	The Shell of the Locust
4. Yūgao	Evening Faces
5. Wakamurasaki	Lavender
6. Suetsumuhana	The Safflower
7. Momiji no ga	An Autumn Excursion
8. Hana no en	The Festival of the Cherry Blossoms
9. Aoi	Heartvine
10. Sakaki	The Sacred Tree
11. Hanachiru sato	The Orange Blossoms
12. Suma	Suma
13. Akashi	Akashi
14. Miotsukushi	Channel Buoys
15. Yomogiu	The Wormwood Patch
16. Sekiya	The Gatehouse
17. E-awase	A Picture Contest
18. Matsukaze	The Wind in the Pines
19. Usugumo	A Rack of Cloud
20. Asagao	The Morning Glory
21. Otome	The Maiden
22. Tamakazura	The Jeweled Chaplet
23. Hatsune	The First Warbler
24. Kochō	Butterflies
25. Hotaru	Fireflies
26. Tokonatsu	Wild Carnations
27. Kagaribi	Flares
28. Nowaki	The Typhoon
29. Miyuki	The Royal Outing
30. Fujibakama	Purple Trousers
31. Makibashira	The Cypress Pillar
32. Umegae	A Branch of Plum
33. Fuji no uraha	Wisteria Leaves

Notes

Introduction

1. See Richard Okada, "Unbound Texts: Narrative Discourse in Heian Japan."

2. By "poems" I refer to the thirty-one-syllable form generally known as *tanka* (short poem-song), forerunner of the even briefer form familiar to Western readers as haiku. I use the term "poem-song" to refer to the fact that *tanka* were recited or sung out loud.

3. Etymologically, *monogatari* relates to various types of verbal utterances from the babbling of babes to intimate exchanges, both verbal and physical, between lovers. *Mono* means variously "something tangible, a timeless presence, or (often frightening) spiritual energy" (the character for *oni*, "demon," for example, is sometimes read *mono*), something "vague" that results from the speaker's unwillingness to relate (specific) matters of a terrifying nature, and also refers to the "private" side of life. *Katari*, a form of the verb *kataru*, "talk, recount," suggests a possible cognate term, *kata*, "form or shape." Thus *monogatari* suggests the giving of (temporal) verbal shape to fixed (as by destiny) or undeniable occurrence. In the *Genji* text the term becomes relativized explicitly as a counter to Chinese writing and is employed strategically to articulate the seemingly "marginal" aspects of life. See also Mitani Kuniaki, "Monogatari to wa nanika," and the monumental study of *monogatari* by Fujii Sadakazu based on a thorough etymological examination of terms like *furukoto, katari,* and *monogatari: Monogatari bungaku seiritsu shi.*

4. Karatani Kōjin, *Nihon kindai bungaku no kigen,* 199–217.

5. The mid-Heian period, roughly from the mid-ninth to early eleventh centuries, is the focus of the present book.

6. I characterized the earlier study as "poetics," a conception, as Tzvetan Todorov states it, that takes language as its model. "A literary work does not have a form and a content, but a structure of significations whose relations must be apprehended." *The Poetics of Prose,* 41. Recent studies have looked at ways to politicize that relational structure.

7. The strong sense of the term derives from Julia Kristeva's reading of Mikhail Bakhtin. I take the term, which signals a problematic underlying the present study, as allowing us, among other things, to conceive of "history" not simply as "background"—an unimpeachable, validating "source" that can be appealed and "alluded" to—but as a constructed topos (or chronotope) that enables (or always already implies) the participation of other discursive representations or signifying practices in the very possibility of its

constructions. A recent study of narratology explains intertextuality in deceptively simple terms: "In its language every text harbors traces of culture and history." Steven Cohan and Linda M. Shires, *Telling Stories*, 50. In Kristeva's words, the term (together with a variant she prefers, "transposition") "specifies that the passage from one signifying system to another demands a new articulation of the thetic—of enunciative and denotative positionality." Bakhtin, whose politically motivated privileging of "novelistic" discourse makes it imperative that we exercise care in appropriating his insights, also makes it clear that issues larger than simple "allusion" to sources are involved.

> No living word relates to its object in a *singular* way: between the word and its object, between the word and the speaking subject, there exists an elastic environment of other, alien words about the same object, the same theme. . . . Indeed, any concrete discourse (utterance) finds the object at which it was directed already as it were overlain with qualifications, open to dispute, charged with value, already enveloped in an obscuring mist—or, on the contrary, by the "light" of alien words already spoken about it. . . . The word, directed towards its object, enters a dialogically agitated and tension-filled environment of alien words, value judgments and accents, weaves in and out of complex interrelationships, merges with some, recoils from others, intersects with yet a third group: and all this may crucially shape discourse, may leave a trace in all its semantic layers, may complicate its expression and influence its entire stylistic profile. (*Discourse in the Novel*, 276)

Cf. Roland Barthes: "Every text, being itself the intertext of another text, belongs to the intertextual, which must not be confused with a text's origins: to search for the 'sources of' and 'influence upon' a work is to satisfy the myth of filiation." "From Work to Text," 77. Cf. also "Intertextuality thus becomes less a name for a work's relation to particular prior texts than a designation of its participation in the discursive space of a culture: the relationship between a text and the various languages or signifying practices of a culture and its relation to those texts which articulate for it the possibilities of that culture." Jonathan Culler, *The Pursuit of Signs: Semiotics, Literature, Deconstruction*, 103. Finally, we must read the Bakhtinian chronotope and its basic dialogism against the movement of the Derridian nonconcept of the trace (or différance): "Whether in the order of spoken or written discourse, no element can function as a sign without referring to another element which itself is not simply present. This interweaving results in each 'element'—phoneme or grapheme—being constituted on the basis of the trace within it of other elements of the chain or system. This interweaving, this textile, is the *text* produced only in the transformation of another text. Nothing, neither among the elements nor within the system, is anywhere ever simply present or absent. There are only, everywhere, differences and traces of traces." *Positions*, 26.

8. Among the many studies I have found relevant are Michel Foucault, *Language, Counter-Memory, and Practice*, especially part two; Roland Barthes, *S/Z*; Edward Said, *Orientalism*, and his "Representing the Colonized: Anthro-

pology's Interlocutors"; Catherine Belsey, *Critical Practice*; Teresa de Lauretis, *Alice Doesn't: Feminism, Semiotics, Cinema*; Jacques Derrida, *Of Grammatology*; and Fredric Jameson, *The Political Unconscious*. I use the term
"signifying practice" in a manner similar to Wlad Godzich and Jeffrey Kittay
in their important study *The Emergence of Prose*, especially chapter 1, "Signifying Practice." "A signifying act is a mixture of types of communication. To
understand the communication process is to understand what kind of
mixture each act is and what fundamental differences exist between different
kinds of acts, different *signifying practices*. Insofar as it is the cultural sphere
that governs the behavior of individuals who belong within it, it is the
cultural sphere that puts into operation certain rules with respect to communication and signification. The signifying act is a shared, social act, an act of
social signification" (p. 3). I find the term useful inasmuch as it enables
analyses that can trace both a specificity and a communality.

    9. The notion of "new objects of knowledge" comes from Edward
Said. See, for example, "Orientalism Reconsidered," 225–226.

    10. On "worldly," see Edward Said, "Secular Criticism": "My position
is that texts are *worldly*, to some degree they are events, and, even when they
appear to deny it, they are nevertheless a part of the social world, human life,
and of course the historical moments in which they are located and interpreted" (p. 4, my emphasis). On the question "Who speaks?" see his
"Representing the Colonized." As Said notes in the latter essay, "narrative
was transformed from a formal pattern or type to an activity in which politics,
tradition, history, and interpretation converged" (p. 221).

    11. I use interchangeably the terms "narrator" and "narrating." The
latter term can become the subject of a sentence. The admittedly awkward
usage is intended to keep the reader mindful that Heian narrative is more a
matter of "positionality" or "perspective" than a clearly distinguishable I/he/
she subjectivity.

    12. As Stephen Heath suggests, "meaning is never a fixed essence
inherent in the text but is always constructed by the reader, the result of a
'circulation' between social formation, reader and text." Paraphrased in
Belsey, *Critical Practice*, 69.

    13. See Louis Althusser, *Lenin and Philosophy*, especially 170–186. "The
individual *is interpellated as a (free) subject in order that he shall submit freely to the
commandments of the Subject, i.e. in order that he shall (freely) accept his subjection*
(p. 182). Similarly, the concept of "hegemony," as articulated by Gramsci,
has been restated as follows: "[Hegemony names a] notion that a ruling class
does not 'impose' its ideology on the subordinate class but that the ideology
must be willingly accepted . . . dominance is not simply derived from the
oppressed's passive and helpless acceptance of ideology received blankly
and unquestioningly from the dominant though unnamed makers of ideology, but that dominance is created through a complex cultural interplay that
involves consent and willingness to move within the culture." Lennard J.
Davis, *Resisting Novels*, 39.

    14. See, for example, Stanley Fish, *Is There a Text in This Class?*, Wolf-

gang Iser, *The Act of Reading*, and Hans Robert Jauss, *Toward an Aesthetic of Reception*.

15. I have adopted a phrase, "inflected by historicity and contingency," used by Fraser and Nicholson in a recent essay that calls for the integration of postmodern and feminist perspectives. See Nancy Fraser and Linda Nicholson, "Social Criticism without Philosophy: An Enounter between Feminism and Postmodernism," 83–104.

16. John Barrell, *Poetry, Language and Politics*, 8–9; my emphasis.

17. Barrell, *Poetry, Language and Politics*, 4. Subsequent page numbers are given in the text. Cf. "The ideology of liberal humanism assumes a world of non-contradictory (and therefore fundamentally unalterable) individuals whose unfettered consciousness is the origin of meaning, knowledge, and action. It is in the interest of this ideology above all to suppress the role of language in the construction of the subject, and to present the individual as a free, unified, autonomous subjectivity" (Belsey, *Critical Practice*, 67). Cf. also Said's words: "Moreover they [our students] are taught that such fields as the humanities and such subfields as 'literature' exist in a relatively neutral political element, that they are to be appreciated and venerated, that they define the limits of what is acceptable, appropriate, and legitimate so far as culture is concerned" ("Secular Criticism," 21).

18. Cf. "Ideology interpellates concrete individuals as subjects, and bourgeois ideology in particular emphasizes the fixed identity of the individual" (Belsey, *Critical Practice*, 64).

19. See Fraser and Nicholson, "Social Criticism without Philosophy."

20. That some works fall out of favor while others previously ignored become canonized ought, Barrell suggests, to make writers question the notion that value lies in the "intrinsic nature of the text" and "ask what is it about their own historical situation that has encouraged them to develop the specific criteria of value embodied in practical criticism" (p. 3).

21. For a critique of "pluralism" see Tania Modleski, "Feminism and the Power of Interpretation: Some Critical Readings." The "ideology [of pluralism] insists on the sovereignty of the individual subject and on his right and ability to choose from among any number of viable alternatives. Whereas the pluralist tends to ignore or minimize the constraints on the individual's freedom, feminism, of course, stresses the way in which women's freedom has been curtailed, their right to choose severely restricted" (p. 122). See also Gayatri Chakravorty Spivak, "The Politics of Interpretations." "It is not too far from the truth to suggest that this freedom of choice by a freely choosing subject . . . is the ideology of free enterprise at work—recognizably a politics of interpretation" (p. 352).

22. See, in addition to the citations of Said, Spivak, and Modleski above, Teresa Ebert, "The Romance of Patriarchy: Ideology, Subjectivity, and Postmodern Feminist Cultural Theory." "If one is always situated in ideology ['There is no "outside" ideology, no unmediated direct access to the "real" or the "truth" from which to critique ideology'], then the only way to demystify these ideological operations of production and concealment—the only way to engage in ideology critique—is to occupy the interstices of contesting ideol-

ogies or to seek the disjunctures and opposing relations created within a single ideology by its own contradictions" (p. 27). See also the following: R. Radhakrishnan, "Ethnic Identity and Post-Structuralist Differance"; Toril Moi, *Sexual/Textual Politics: Feminist Literary Theory;* Harry Harootunian, *Things Seen and Unseen: Discourse and Ideology in Tokugawa Nativism;* Modleski, "Feminism and the Power of Interpretation"; Teresa de Lauretis, *Alice Doesn't;* and Renato Rosaldo, "Politics, Patriarchs, and Laughter."

23. *Die Krisis der europäischen Kultur,* quoted in Benjamin, *Illuminations,* 81. The notion of "primal elements of language itself" poses potential problems.

24. Benjamin, *Illuminations,* 80. We would do well to read Benjamin against Derrida's remark that the possibility of translation "practices the difference between signified and signifier. But if this difference is never pure, no more so is translation. . . . We will never have, and in fact have never had, to do with some 'transport' of pure signifieds from one language to another, or within one and the same language, that the signifying instrument would leave virgin and untouched." *Positions,* 20.

25. Gasché, *The Tain of the Mirror,* 263. Subsequent page numbers are given in the text. What makes Gasché's discussion of thematics especially important is its situating of critical discourse in the context of philosophical discourse.

26. The now familiar Derridian terms that appear in such analyses include "trace," "iteration," "différance," "hymen," "supplément," and "pharmakon." The trace, or the nonconcept of différance, marks the impossibility of pure beginnings at the same time that it proves that no beginning is possible without an essentializing moment. See Jacques Derrida, *Of Grammatology,* 44–65, and *Positions,* 17–36. For an accessible discussion of the term "deconstruction," see Derrida, "Letter to a Japanese Friend," 1–5.

27. As Alice Jardine states it, "Why this rejection [of 'parts or all of the conceptual apparatus we inherited from nineteenth-century Europe; including . . . certain elements and logics of the conceptual apparatuses based in traditional movements of human liberation; including, of course, feminism']? . . . Our ways of understanding in the West have been and continue to be complicitous with our ways of oppressing." "Opaque Texts and Transparent Contexts: The Political Difference of Julia Kristeva," 99.

28. "I am also far from averse to learning from the work of Western theorists, though I have learned to insist on marking their positionality as investigating subjects." Gayatri Chakravorty Spivak, "Can the Subaltern Speak?" 296.

29. See, for example, the special issue of *Kokubungaku: kaishaku to kyōzai* entitled "Taketori, Ise, Genji."

30. The *Taketori* princess or the Asagao Princess, on the one hand, and a male figure like Narihira or Genji on the other.

31. I am evoking the major statement on resistance by Paul de Man in the essay "Resistance to Theory": "The resistance to theory is a resistance to the use of language. It is therefore a resistance to language itself or to the possibility that language contains factors or functions that cannot be reduced

to intuition" (p. 13). And: "The resistance to theory is a resistance to the rhetorical or tropological dimension of language. . . . Since grammar as well as figuration is an integral part of reading, it follows that reading will be a negative process in which grammatical cognition is undone, at all times, by its rhetorical displacement" (p. 17). See *Resistance to Theory*, 3–20. The tension created by the necessity of (de-) reading both the figural (i.e., reading the figural "literally," so to speak, in contrast to our common practice, which amounts to reading the "literal" figuratively) and the consequent resistances immediately produced by it inform my own readings of mid-Heian texts. In terms of Japanese tropological moments, not to read the figural literally is to remain blind to the unintended irony of one's position. As a corrective to de Manian closed readings, I also have in mind (as in the epigraph) Edward Said's notion of resistance.

32. The Lady Ise attribution appears in the colophon to the Tempuku texts. Quoted in Fujioka Sakutarō's (1870–1910) influential *Kokubungaku zenshi: Heianchō hen*, 182.

33. I include the discussion of the *Genji* narrating in Chapter 6 for two reasons: first, the narrating perspectives, anchored in the mid-Heian "salons," warrant extended, particularized discussion; and second, I do not wish to privilege "narration" per se as the controlling factor over all the texts under examination.

34. Yamaguchi Nakami, "Heianchō bunshōshi kenkyū no ichi shiten." This section on the Heian language should only be taken as a heuristic prelude to the discussions of the texts and their scenes of utterance and narrating.

35. See Abe Akio et al., eds., *Genji monogatari, Nihon koten bungaku zenshū (NKBZ)*, 13, 14. See also Edward Seidensticker, trans., *The Tale of Genji*, 159.

36. Yamaguchi, "Shiten," 26.

37. In *Japanese Court Poetry*, the now classic study of waka that set the terms of waka study in the West, Robert Brower and Earl Miner refer to the "topics" of Japanese as one of its important features: "Japanese grammar employs topics as well as subjects. The difference between the two is primarily one of relative emphasis: topics are usually less explicit than subjects; they indicate involvement, but not necessarily participation, in an action or state. What would be a subject, an object, or even an adverbial phrase in English might be a topic in Japanese. Personal pronouns are apt to be treated as topics rather than subjects, although most often they are omitted altogether" (p. 7). The presence of "topics" in narrative discourse relates, I think, to the strong emphasis on poetic topics when composing in waka. The topics, say, of a poetry contest, often given out in advance, focus communal participation. Other factors—poetic moments, honorific language, and parabasis—also assist, of course, in maintaining an intelligible narrative line.

38. Cf. *The American Heritage Dictionary*, New College Edition: "A grammatical unit comprising a word or group of words that is *separate from any other grammatical construction* and usually consists of at least one subject with its

predicate and contains a finite verb or verb phrase" (emphasis added). It was not always so limiting. The *Oxford English Dictionary*, Compact Edition, gives such meanings as "way of thinking," "opinion," "quoted saying," and "an indefinite portion of a discourse or writing."

39. "Classical Japanese shares with classical Chinese a *concrete* particularity different from Western poetic language." Brower and Miner, *Japanese Court Poetry*, 6.

40. Ibid., 7; emphasis added. The discussion on language is found on pp. 6–12, with a couple of examples of the "delicacy of [verbal] distinctions" given on pp. 8–9.

41. By contrast standard references on English grammar distinguish three basic types of "mood": "indicative," "subjunctive," and "imperative." George O. Curme, *English Grammar*, 54–55. Yamaguchi's essay fails to account for the enunciative position. Based on the morphological situation, we can conclude that the dominant mood of the Heian *monogatari* discourse is some form of "surmise."

42. The author of a valuable study of the Heian language has characterized it in a manner that resembles Genette's analysis as a combination of the subjective and the objective. Watanabe Minoru, *Heian bunshōshi*, 188. Gérard Genette, *Narrative Discourse: An Essay on Method*, 219.

43. Brower and Miner's comment on the "confusion between narration and dialogue" in ancient Japanese songs remains relevant to the narrating situation I am constructing: "Another variety of problem in distinguishing between dialogue and narration grows, like many other problems, out of the confusion of the compilers of the chronicles as they attempted to combine the prose contexts and the earlier songs. Where today the logic and sense of a given series of lines seem to demand division into narrative and dialogue, the compilers attribute the whole to one of the speakers in the context or make divisions which seem to have little propriety. What is narrative usually becomes unlikely dialogue attributed to one of the characters in the prose narrative." *Japanese Court Poetry*, 61–62. The authors' desire for generic clarity and "propriety" teaches us that we should not expect a similar clarity of *monogatari* texts.

44. I discuss the last two in greater detail in Chapter 1.

45. In poetry collections the prefaces to poems that were written for screen paintings do not employ *keri*, but rather the suffix *tari*. In other words, the narration does not speak from "outside" the painting but from the perspective of the participants depicted in it. Narrative discourse appropriates the perspective. See Itoi Motohiro, "Monogatari no hyōgen," 83.

46. The burden placed on the narrator also becomes proportionately greater. Cf. "The present, in its so-called 'wholeness' (although it is, of course, never whole) is in essence and in principle inconclusive; by its very nature it demands continuation, it moves into the future, and the more actively and consciously it moves into the future the more tangible and indispensable its inconclusiveness becomes. Therefore, when the present becomes the center of human orientation in time and in the world, time and world lose their completedness as a whole as well as in each of their parts.

The temporal model of the world changes radically: it becomes a world where there is no first word (no ideal word), and the final word has not been spoken." Mikhail Bakhtin, "Epic and Novel," 30.

47. The "tone" of the Heian language is untranslatable as Brower and Miner note, but so is its "tenseless" feature, at least as we have seen it in the practice of the majority of translators working in English. See footnotes 17 and 49 (by the editor, Earl Miner) in Konishi Jin'ichi's *A History of Japanese Literature*, vol. 2, 256; 282–283.

48. Watanabe, *Bunshōshi*, 190.

49. Inasmuch as the Japanese language does not a priori posit transcendental "selves" so much as continually present interrelational subject positions (points at which any number of reading or writing "selves" can participate), the narrating constructs perspectives that are constantly alterable (marked by verbal, honorific morphemes to mark that alteration). The pronominal relativity inscribed in the discourse makes possible after-the-fact identifications.

50. The *Ise* variant on which most modern editions rely is the Tempuku text; the *Genji* variant normally used is the Ōshima text.

51. A member of the Nijō (Mikohidari) family of scholars, Teika spent much of his life comparing and collating Heian textual variants, and it is common to find some form of "Teika text" being used as a "base text" (*sokobon*) by modern scholars. Mitsuyuki was governor of Kawachi Province, from which comes the name used for his line of texts.

52. *NKBZ* 1:61.

53. Ibid., 65.

54. Twentieth-century scholars have discovered that texts considered to have been relatively "pure" Blue-Cover Texts contain contamination from Kawachi textual lines, and texts belonging to the "separate texts" line have been found to contain passages that predate both the Teika and Kawachi texts. Although the likelihood of a major reorganization of the current textual hierarchy is minimal at best, the very existence of much uncharted terrain demands that we preserve an attitude of contingency in dealing with Heian texts. The current efforts of Ii Haruki, one of the most prolific of modern textual scholars, to produce a new concordance of the *beppon* group of texts will be of value for future readers.

55. For example, the text belonging to the Tenri Library or the one owned by Isseidō Bookstore in Tokyo.

56. The Teika texts contain twenty-five poems not in the Hunter text.

57. Another type of text that presents a challenge to the Teika texts is the *Ise monogatari emaki* (Tale of Ise Picture Scroll). Alleged to resemble the Hunter text and also a manuscript attributed to Fujiwara no Tameuji (1222–1286), the text exhibits a marked difference from the Teika texts from *dan* 39 to 98. I discuss the possible relations between *Ise* texts and painting in Chapter 5. Even among texts related to the Teika line, discrepancies appear both in order and number of *dan*. The so-called expanded texts (*kōhon*), for example, are arranged similarly to the Teika texts until *dan* 71, from which point discrepancies increase, becoming extreme after *dan* 120. Moreover, Narihira's death

poem, which closes the Teika texts, does not appear at the end of the expanded texts.

58. Even *Taketori monogatari* names a sizable group of texts. Its extant versions have been divided into two major lines, "old" and "common," one line comprising three main classes, two of which are further divided into no less than six subclasses. Sakakura Atsuyoshi, ed., *Taketori monogatari*, 9–12. Besides quantity of variants, another formidable obstacle to reading Heian texts lies in the fact that the oldest extant texts are dated no earlier than the late Heian or early Kamakura periods, or approximately one to two hundred years after their appearance. In the case of the *Ise* text, the oldest available specimens date back no further than the early to mid-Muromachi period.

59. The celebrated calligrapher Fujiwara no Kōsei, for example.

60. See the discussion of Tamagami Takuya's "reading aloud" hypothesis in Chapter 6.

61. The following comment by Mitani Eiichi in an article on *Sagoromo monogatari* usefully relates the question of *monogatari* reception to the problem of variant texts: "Variant texts appeared because a reader's interpretation of a particular passage led to the creation of a new variant; reception (*kyōju*) also meant creation (*sōsaku*)." "Sagoromo monogatari no ihon seiritsu to sono jiki—maki ichi o chūshin to shite," 308. Mitani's study of the *Sagoromo* text demonstrates just how contingent the idea of "text" was during Heian times.

1   Languages of Narrating and *Bamboo-Cutter* Pretexts

1. Williams, "Writing," 1.

2. Tsukishima Hiroshi, *Kana*, 10.

3. Ibid., 11.

4. Ibid., 32.

5. The first text was *Kojiki. Nihon shoki*, another major Nara period text, appears in 720, but the two exhibit very different signifying practices. The Nara period is generally taken to end at 794, when the capital was moved to present-day Kyoto, but a temporary move to Nagaoka occurred in 784.

6. Page citations are to the *Kojiki* version edited by Nishimiya Kazutami, in vol. 1 of *Shinchō nihon koten shūsei* (*SNKS*), 1979.

7. Although most scholars believe Hieda was a man, some (e.g., Saigō Nobutsuna) believe the reciter was a woman.

8. I discuss sound and meaning in *Kokinshū* in Chapter 3.

9. See Saigō Nobutsuna, *Kojiki chūshaku*, 1:52–54.

10. The emphasis on orality might also have been related to *kotodama*, which signifies a spiritual power believed to reside in words, especially when formed into certain phrases and expressions as in song-poems, or pillow words. That power, moreover, could be transferred to others (such as imperial rulers) through recitation or at *utagaki* festivals when men and women courted each other by poem exchanges by which one appealed to (and possessed) the spirit of a potential lover. The necessary presence of poetic moments in texts relates as much to didactic or hegemonic concerns as

to their "literary" value. Origuchi Shinobu, *Zenshū*, vol. 7; also, Konishi Jin'ichi, *A History of Japanese Literature*, 1:103–110, and the discussion of the "incantatory" aspects of waka in the chapter on *Kokinshū* below.

11. I use the term "song-poem" when referring to early poetic utterances and the reverse, "poem-song," when referring to later waka.

12. So called because of the widespread usage of such graphs in the first great collection of Japanese poetry, the *Man'yōshū* (Collection of Ten Thousand Leaves, ca. 759). Parts of it have been translated into English. See Ian Hideo Levy, trans., *The Ten Thousand Leaves*, and Nippon Gakujutsu Shinkōkai, *The Man'yōshū*.

13. For a detailed explication of the opening lines of *Kojiki*, see David Pollack, *The Fracture of Meaning*, 28–31. Pollack's discussion in chapter 1 of the Japanese adaptation of Chinese script, valuable for its attempt to place the linguistic process into the broader context of cultural interchange, is occasionally weakened by a miscasting of language, meaning, and Derridean deconstruction. For one response to Pollack, see the article by Naoki Sakai, "Kindai no hihan: chūzetsu shita toki."

14. The Chinese themselves occasionally used characters primarily for sound value (in transcribing foreign names, for example). See Chapter 3 for a discussion of the "incantatory" aspect of waka.

15. In *Japanese Court Poetry* Brower and Miner note that the poem is probably of later origin: "Its prosodic regularity and form betray the hand of a later writer reshaping older materials and working within an established tradition of poetic form—as even the older Japanese commentators suspected" (p. 58).

16. The *Man'yōshū* edition used is that of Nakanishi Susumu. We must remember that Japanese, like Chinese, is read from top to bottom, right to left.

17. The modern term *ateji* signifies the same practice. *Ongana* (Sino-Japanese sound kana) are *kana* used for their Sino-Japanese sound values. A modern example: 良 pronounced *ra* (*ryō*); modern Chinese *liang*. *Seikun* (orthodox Japanese sound kana) signifies that both the Japanese pronunciation and the meaning of the graph correspond to the original semantic value of that graph (e.g., 花 modern Japanese *hana*, "flower"). For a discussion of all the various possibilities, see Tsukishima, *Kana*, chapter 1.

18. The exception is the special case of *Shinsen man'yōshū* (Newly Selected Man'yōshū), 893, believed to have been compiled by Sugawara no Michizane.

19. Compare the role of writing in China where a written text was readily intelligible to persons who spoke mutually unintelligible dialects.

20. In the following quote Brower and Miner are referring to ancient "mummers" (*wazaogi*), but their comments apply equally well to the present discussion: "Since the primitive songs were so closely related to social occasions, another important factor in establishing differing degrees of esthetic distance was the relation of a particular song to the occasion of its performance. . . . This kind of relation to the occasion of performance is perhaps more native to Japanese poetic practice, however, than to Western

traditions" (*Japanese Court Poetry*, 54). The "occasionality" of Japanese poetry (which cannot be emphasized enough) makes its colonization through Western terminology especially problematic.

21. For a critical discussion of "poem-prose" texts, referred to as versiprosa, see the study by Jeffrey Kittay and Wlad Godzich, *The Emergence of Prose*, chapter 4, 46–76. I share the authors' assumptions about discourse.

22. *Nihon koten bungaku taikei* (*NKBT*), 1:468–471.

23. See, for example, the notes in *NKBT* 1:470.

24. See, for example, Tsuchihashi Yutaka and Ikeda Yasaburō, eds., *Kayō I*, in vol. 4 of *Kanshō nihon koten bungaku* (*KNKB*), 1975, 168. The preceding section in both texts tells of a dragonfly that magically appears to devour a horsefly that was biting the emperor's arm. The incident is interpreted as a paean to the dragonfly.

25. The word appears frequently in *Nihon shoki* as well, but not with the rhythmical regularity of the *Kojiki* text. It must be remembered that since reading the latter text remains a supremely difficult task, different modern versions often provide divergent ways of reading a particular word or phrase. The text in the *SNKS* series is a good example of an alternative reading.

26. Kittay and Godzich, *Emergence of Prose*, 20. One of the first lessons taught to nonnative students of the Japanese language consists of just such words (e.g., *kore, sore, are, dore*).

27. Ibid., 19. The coauthors state further that for them, rather than "linking an instance of *langue* with its instantiation as utterance . . . it [deixis] will more broadly be the grounding of utterance or other particular signifying behavior in whatever coexisting or coextensive circumstances are necessary to empower it and give it meaning (and, of course, if those vary, its meaning varies)" (p. 21).

28. The perspective of the narrator in later texts exhibits similar tendencies. For example, the narrator in *Ise monogatari* uses *koko ni* to refer to the capital when speaking of Mt. Fuji. The *Taketori* narrator, too, often uses a verb that means "come" (toward me/us, the narrator/audience), where in English, for example, we would use "go," suggesting that the perspectival anchor is a deictically positioned "here." The *Genji* narrating represents the most extensive awareness of deictic moorings, including the use of honorific expressions. The presence of deictic markers in all types of Japanese discourse indicates that the extratextual situation-effect gestured to by the narrator (discourse) becomes the important, hidden aspect of the text. For later writings I connect the narrative deixis with its "coextensive circumstances," i.e., the historicopolitical and genealogical intertexts.

29. There were isolated instances where *keri* appeared in conversational passages in *kambun* texts. Donald Keene's rendition of the passage, "Many years ago there lived a man called the Old Bamboo Cutter," removes the emphasis on "now" and puts the discourse into the past tense. Keene's translation can be found in Thomas Rimer, *Modern Japanese Fiction and Its Traditions*, 273–305.

30. In the following discussion, *kana* refers to *hiragana*. As we shall note, traces of *kambun*, both syntactically and lexically, are found throughout the

Taketori text. "Historical" changes are acknowledged again from the Kamakura period (1185–1333) when distinctions between some Heian suffixes begin to collapse.

31. "Framed," as in Sakakura Atsuyoshi's characterization found in the influential early discussion of *keri* in the *Taketori* text. *NKBT* 9:5–24.

32. See the discussion of *ji no bun* in Chapter 6.

33. For English translations other than my own below, see Donald L. Philippi, *Kojiki*, and W. G. Aston, *Nihongi: Chronicles of Japan from the Earliest Times to A.D. 697.*

34. Kurano Kenji, ed., *Kojiki*, vol. 1 of *NKBT*, 147.

35. Ōno Susumu et al., eds., *Nihon shoki*, vol. 67 of *NKBT*, 180.

36. *Kojiki* and *Nihon shoki* again differ: the ostensibly "narrated" (or recited or intoned) text *Kojiki* is normally reconstituted into Japanese with far more *ki* suffixes than *Nihon shoki*, the ostensibly "Chinese" text compiled from written sources. Occurring at the beginning of accounts of imperial reigns phrases like the following are formulaic to *Kojiki*: OFosasagi no mikoto, naniFa no takatu no miya ni masimasite, ama no sita sirasimesi*ki* (The Honorable Ōsasagi took up residence at the Takatsu Palace in Naniwa and consolidated his rule) (*NKBT* 1:265). Or, "The Honorable Hondawake established his residence at the Akira Palace in Karushima and consolidated his rule" (*NKBT* 1:239).

37. The discussion below will offer further possibilities.

38. For example, mukasi okina ari*ki*.

39. Harada Yoshioki, "Jodōshi 'keri' no imi," *Kokugogaku—gengo to bungei* 28:27–31.

40. Chiyuki Kumakura, *The Narrative Time of Genji monogatari*, 56.

41. Ibid., 63.

42. See John Lyons, *Semantics* 2:707.

43. When the verb *ki* (the continuative form of the verb "to come" or "coming") combines with *ari* ("to exist" or "existing"), the vowels *i* and *a* contract to produce the vowel *e*. Likewise, the Heian suffix of visual conjecture *meri* derives from *mi* + *ari*. In early texts *keri* is represented either by *ongana* or by one of two single graphs (meaning "come" and "exist," respectively—the former being more frequent).

44. See also Mitani Eiichi's discussion of *keri* that ties it to expressions of communal affirmation like . . . *takke* found in Modern Japanese. *KNKB* 6:41–44.

45. See Ōno Susumu, *Nihongo no bumpō o kangaeru*, 140–142.

46. Takeoka Masao, "Jodōshi 'keri' no hongi to kinō—*Genji monogatari, Murasaki shikibu nikki, Makura no sōshi* o shiryō ni shite."

47. The remark is Kasuga Haruo's, cited in Itoi Motohiro, "Monogatari no hyōgen," 76. Itoi also mentions scholars like Mabuchi Kazuo who feel that *keri* and *ki* are neither oppositional morphemes nor markers of past tense or recollection.

48. Lyons, *Semantics* 2:811.

49. Kumakura, *Narrative Time*, 57.

50. Specific discussions of *ki* have also begun to pay attention to its close

connection with narrating moments and perspectives. First, Sakakura At-suyoshi's influential formulation: "Rather than past tense, *ki* is a complete-tive (*kanryō*) suffix that indicates a subjective attitude of recollection; *keri*, on the other hand, indicates an attitude that views the events a bit more objectively and always connects them to the present. . . . From there we can discern a kind of explanatory discursive attitude in *keri*" ("Kaisetsu," in *Taketori monogatari, NKBT* 9). Basing his discussion on Sakakura's remarks, Itoi Motohiro has claimed that the suffix *ki* signifies a "discursive present" (*jojutsu no genzai*), which can be divided into two types: the narrator's present (in which is included what is termed the "author"), and the present of the events being narrated (*monogatari no genzai*). Itoi's position posits an overall *keri* narrator and two *ki* narrators, and although it is not clear how the *keri* narrator is to be distinguished from the first *ki* narrator, Itoi rightly situates the discussion at the level of narrative perspective. Itoi Motohiro, *"Genji monogatari* no jodōshi 'ki.'"

51. Similar to what Lyotard terms "pragmatics of transmission": "What I am getting at is a pragmatics of popular narratives that is, so to speak, intrinsic to them. For example, a Cashinahua storyteller always begins his narration with a fixed formula: 'Here is the story of ——, as I've always heard it told. I will tell it to you in turn. Listen.' And he brings it to a close with another, also invariable, formula: 'Here ends the story of ——. The man who has told it to you is —— (Cashinahua name), or to the Whites —— (Spanish or Portuguese name).'" He then remarks, "The narrator's only claim to competence for telling the story is the fact that he has heard it himself. The current narratee gains potential access to the same authority simply by listening," and also that "the pragmatic rule illustrated by this example cannot . . . be universalized. But it gives insight into what is a generally recognized property of traditional knowledge. The narrative 'posts' (sender, addressee, hero) are so organized that the right to occupy the post of sender receives the following double grounding: it is based upon the fact of having occupied the post of addressee, and of having been recounted oneself, by virtue of the name one bears, by a previous narrative—in other words, having been positioned as the diegetic reference of other narrative events." Jean-François Lyotard, *The Postmodern Condition: A Report on Knowledge,* 20–21. In my reading *ki* and *keri,* when tied to the reception of *hiragana* discourse, are not unrelated to Lyotard's notion of "double grounding."

52. For a discussion of a wide variety of similar tales and legends, see Itō Shinji, *Kaguyahime no tanjō.*

53. In Japanese, monogatari no idekiFazime no oya. Tamakazura's and Ukifune's narrations are examples of a *Genji* "story" underwritten by the *Taketori* tale.

54. The awkwardness of the English is in part because I have followed the verbal suffixes and translated into nonpast when the suffix *ki* does not appear.

55. Only the *fudoki* from Izumo Province is complete. Parts of the Harima text are missing and certain, presumably important, sections of the *fudoki* of Hitachi, Toyogo, and Bizen have been handed down along with

various isolated sections from ten provinces. I have taken the present summary from "Ikago no woumi," in Akimoto Yoshirō, ed., *Fudoki, NKBT* 2:457–459. Subsequent page numbers will be included in the text.

56. A version of the "crane" tale is included in Noguchi Motohiro, ed., *Taketori monogatari*, 227–228.

57. *Fudoki, NKBT* 2:466–469.

58. The *Taketori* text will provide even more explicit names of characters.

59. The significance of the power latent in song-poems was not lost on those who seized control of the central government during the late seventh and eighth centuries. For example, in the compilation of *fudoki*, particular attention was paid to the gathering of the origins of place names (*meisho* or *nadokoro*, especially names of mountains, rivers, and plains) and tales told over generations by old storytellers. One reason for the interest in toponyms seems to be related to the belief that a regional spirit (*kunidama*) resided in a region's name, each geographical subdivision also harboring its own spirits (*seirei*). "Possession" of a toponym, then, meant authority over the spirits of that topos, and knowledge of the origin of a name (or of a deity) meant seizing its secret (i.e., its vulnerable spot) and thereby effectively subjugating it. A similar concern made it crucial for the government to gain knowledge of and to collect "poetic pillows" (*uta makura*) as well as the "origins" of the names themselves. Later sources show that rites associated with the accession of a new emperor included the intoning of song-poems and their toponyms and the commissioning of screen paintings based on regional topics—gestures toward a renewal of imperial hegemony based on the transferral of inherent spiritual power. The *Taketori* text will stage a similar movement of appropriation, but instead of founding acts by sacred deities, the terms (only the last instance, with Mt. Fuji, involves a place name) emerge, often in a comic reversal, out of poem-songs that sum up the behavior of the (definitely nonsacred) characters in the narrative.

60. We must keep in mind that studies of how the early Japanese reconstituted *kambun* texts are plagued by unresolved and in some cases unresolvable problems. An accurate discussion of some of those problems is found in Minegishi Akira, *Hentai kambun*, especially chapter 2.

61. Mitani Eiichi, ed., *Taketori monogatari, KNKB* 6:190.

62. The Nagu maiden's appeals can also be read as a commentary on certain social or political practices of the time. The mention of a "district office" might suggest the political status of the old man (village headman?) only interested in consolidating his wealth once he has gained a monopoly on sake.

63. That is the view taken by, among others, Mitani Eiichi. See his *Monogatari bungaku shiron*, 380–382.

64. The text cited is the one edited by Sakakura Atsuyoshi et al., *Konjaku monogatarishū, SNKS* 4:329–333.

65. The line can be restricted to a reading that would valorize the former (the emperor's act of abandonment), but the final verb form incorporates no honorific phoneme to warrant such a restriction.

66. I am indebted to Komine Kazuaki (in private conversation) for this comment.

67. Itō, *Kaguyahime no tanjō*, 154. The following summary is taken from the version in the *SNKS* 6:201–220. I offer the summary not to raise the question of "influence," but to call attention to the likelihood that educated men of the early Heian period were familiar with similar versions of the *Taketori* tale.

2 A Pivotal Narrative: *The Tale of the Bamboo Cutter*

1. Studies of narratology (dealing in particular with such notions as story, discourse, fabula, and narrating) I have found useful are Mieke Bal, *Narratology;* Gérard Genette, *Narrative Discourse;* Tzvetan Todorov, *The Poetics of Prose;* Wallace Martin, *Recent Theories of Narrative;* and Steven Cohan and Linda M. Shires, *Telling Stories.*

2. A useful discussion of fabula, which refers to what I have called "pretext and story," can be found in Mieke Bal, *Narratology*, part 1.

3. The accepted view is that the *Taketori* text was written by a man.

4. See the previous chapter. By "sections" I refer to passages signaled by a "tying up" of preceding verbal events.

5. The verbs are tukaFikeri, iFikeru, and arikeru. Japanese passages are taken from Katagiri Yōichi, ed., *Taketori monogatari, Kan'yaku nihon no koten* (*KYNK*) 10, 11. Subsequent page references are included in the text. Katagiri translates *keri* into modern Japanese with the phrase *no de aru*, which corresponds to the signification "the fact is" discussed earlier.

6. The play on *ko* prefigures the instances of word play that will appear later. In the *Konjaku* text *ko* appears twice, but the potential pivot-word is ignored. The significance of "names" in *Taketori* will be discussed below.

7. Keene does not mark the word play: "It must be you are meant to be my child." Donald Keene, trans., *Tale of the Bamboo Cutter*, 275.

8. On "diegesis," see Gérard Genette, "Frontiers of Narrative," in his *Figures of Literary Discourse*, 127–144.

9. Notice also the deictic positioning of the narrator in relation to the old man. He "brings" the child (here) instead of "taking" it (there) to a place away from the narrator. The narrator and the audience are both "here."

10. Taketori no okina, take wo toru ni, kono ko wo mitukete noti ni taketoru ni. . . .

11. Bamboo cutters belonged to a lower class of society known as *semmin*. Sight, knowledge, and possession will become importantly linked in later Heian narratives.

12. *Kamiage* and *moki/gi* were coming-of-age ceremonies comparable to *gempuku* for boys; hair that had been allowed to grow to the shoulders was tied up into a coiffure, and a train was attached above a woman's formal robes.

13. The Japanese text ends with the *keri* phrases "Faradatasiki koto mo nagusamikeri" and "ikiFoFi mau no mono in narinikeri."

14. For a useful discussion based on New Critical assumptions of the "images" connected with such figures, see Konishi Jin'ichi, "Genji monogatari no imejari," 217–231. The ability to soothe and comfort is precisely what Ki no Tsurayuki, in the "Kana Preface" to *Kokinshū*, claims for Japanese poetry (waka). I discuss the topic in relation to the incantatory aspects of poetry in Chapter 3 on *Kokinshū*.

15. The name inscribes a gesture to poetry as *nayotake no* functions as an originary pillow word (*makura kotoba*) for "shining."

16. The repetition of the number three (three *sun*, three months, three days) has been seen as a sign of the text's folkloric origins. See Mitani Eiichi, *Monogatarishi no kenkyū*, 329–336.

17. The end of the section reads: saru toki yori namu, yobaFi to Fa iFikeru.

18. The point is made by Mitani Eiichi in *Taketori monogatari, Utsuho monogatari*, 51.

19. I discuss such poetic figures as *kakekotoba* below and in Chapter 3.

20. On the rhetorical nature of language, see, for example, Genette, *Figures of Literary Discourse*, especially chapter 2. None of the discourses previously examined exhibited such a rhetorical dimension.

21. See the excellent discussion by Suzuki Hideo, "Monogatari seiritsushi oboegaki—kishu ryūri to irogonomi to—," 6–13. See also Mitani Eiichi, *Monogatarishi no kenkyū*, 384–393; and Takahashi Tōru, "Irogonomi," 50–51. The term does not appear in the *Konjaku* text.

22. Noguchi Motohiro, ed., *Taketori monogatari*, 11; all subsequent page references included in the text refer to this edition. Some texts give the name as Miyatsukomaro.

23. In most texts the man is listed as a shōshō (lesser captain), but here I follow Katagiri's emendation because shōshō represents a frequent miscopying of chūjō. Most commentators agree that the shōshō is the person who appears later as Tō no Chūjō.

24. *Nihon shoki, Nihon koten bungaku taikei (NKBT)*, 68:531–532.

25. Itō Shinji, *Kaguyahime no tanjō*, 78.

26. For information on the last two suitors I have relied on ibid., 76–81, and Mitani, ed., *Taketori monogatari, Utsuho monogatari*, 52–55. The argument concerning the last two names focuses on the possibility that they might have been called Prince Such-and-Such during their own lifetimes, but I prefer to emphasize that the *Taketori* text presents a riddle that any well-educated official living at the time the narrative was written could have deduced from the clues provided by the other three names.

27. The names appear as Tajihi no Mahito Shima and Fujiwara no Asomi Fuhito.

28. Katagiri, ed., *Taketori monogatari*, 12.

29. *Kojiki, NKBT* 1:186–187.

30. See Mitani, ed., *Taketori monogatari, Utsuho monogatari*, 22 and *Kojiki, NKBT* 6:174–175.

31. Mitani, ed., *Taketori monogatari, Utsuho monogatari*, 22.

32. When, for example, he confronts the alien beings who come to take Kaguyahime away.

33. See Mitani, ed., *Taketori monogatari, Utsuho monogatari*, 174–175.

34. See the discussions in ibid., 204–205, and 227–228. A situation involving a similar imperial messenger, Yugei no Myōbu, presents an important discursive threshold for the *Genji* text.

35. Katagiri, *Taketori monogatari*, 98–99.

36. Itō Shinji offers a convenient chart of the dates that have been surmised for *Taketori*, ranging from 806 to 956. He also lists possible authors. *Tanjō*, 81–88.

37. See the discussion in Mitani, ed., *Taketori monogatari, Utsuho monogatari*, 24–27.

38. Many of the objects that Kaguyahime demands appear in Chinese sources.

39. The minister of the right, Abe no Miushi, was, we remember, "a man of abundant wealth." See the important essay by Mitani Kuniaki on the politicoeconomic climate of the times, especially in regard to the fire-rat robe: "Taketori monogatari no hōhō to seiritsu jiki—'Hinezumi no kawagoromo'; aruiwa, aregori."

40. The received notion that the Heian Academy (or "University") was in decline by the early tenth century has been revised by Hisaki Yukio, who also notes that its prestige was still high in the eleventh century although sources of the time indicate highly ambivalent attitudes toward it. As government itself increasingly becomes a "privatized" (Fujiwara-run), *sekkan* affair, the earlier emphasis on the Academy as a training ground for government officials begins to weaken, and each of its departments becomes dominated by one or two families through hereditary succession. It remains, however, a viable institution into the twelfth century. See Hisaki Yukio, *Nihon kodai gakkō no kenkyū*, 168–186, 341–352. The standard study remains Momo Hiroyuki, *Jōdai gakusei no kenkyū*.

41. "The large number of conversational passages may be said to be a special characteristic of this narrative." Mitani, ed., *Taketori monogatari, Utsuho monogatari*, 61.

42. Narrative figures like Narihira, Hikaru Genji, Tō no Chūjō, Kaoru, Niou, and Prince Sagoromo all seek to discover women hidden away in remote areas.

43. TukiFi sugusu (the months and days pass).

44. I discuss the "feminine hand" (*onnade*) in Chapter 6.

45. AruiFa Fue wo Fuki, aruiFa uta wo utaFi, aruiFa syauga wo si, aruiFa uso wo Fuki, aFugi wo narasi nado suru ni.

46. Remember that the *Konjaku* text offered no names.

47. Recall that each of the five Chinese suitors also possessed certain characteristics. Narrative formulae through which the stories were told, however, did not change.

48. The poems in *Taketori* are far from easy or crude compositions as is often thought but inscribe a variety of rhetorical moves: pillow word (*makura kotoba*), poetic toponym (*uta makura*), pivot-word (*kakekotoba*), and associative-

word (*engo*). In addition to the "pivot-word," mentioned above, the other techniques also appear often in poems composed by the so-called Six Poetic Geniuses. See the discussion of such terms in Chapter 3.

49. Unfortunately Keene's translation does not. He erases the crucial poetic passages by incorporating them (he does designate some of them as "verse") into his text in prose paraphrase.

50. Keene's translation, here and later, conveys well the fact that word plays are at work (he cleverly turns "throwing away the bowl" into "being bowled over").

51. For an incisive reading of the section from a slightly different angle, see Takahashi Tōru, "Koto no ha o kazareru tama no eda."

52. The usual reading of the last etymology is *tamasakaru* (spirit having departed), but other possibilities have been offered: *tamasaka ni* ("rare, infrequent," i.e., the prince reappears on occasion after a long time) or *tamasaganasi* ("fake," referring to the prince's hoax).

53. Wang Ching. The name is written with the character 王 (king) and two kana for *kei*.

54. See Mitani Kuniaki, "Taketori monogatari no hōhō to seiritsu jiki."

55. As will be the case with all *monogatari*, discourse does not describe a journey so much as enunciate particular terms, here concerning the storm and the men's fears.

56. In *monogatari* for a woman to initiate a poetic exchange signals an extraordinary circumstance.

57. The situation is identical to the *Genji* opening, where we are told that Emperor Kiritsubo is infatuated with one consort, Genji's mother, thereby slighting his other women and engendering dire consequences for her. The *Taketori* telling of the loss of the imperial spirit and the neglect of his women is similarly radical as it constitutes scandalous behavior that would lead to the downfall of the country.

58. Texts like *Yamato monogatari* or *Konjaku monogatarishū*, in contrast, often provide a specific reign name or the name of a historical personage. The *Taketori* text, although it gives names to many of its figures, does not operate under the assumption that the events treated possess historical accuracy.

59. When the third suitor brings the fur robe, "the old woman thinks in her heart, 'This time she [Kaguyahime] will certainly be married,'" suggesting that the two princes' failures preceded the one in question.

60. For example, the second prince's citing of the particular day—about the tenth day of the Second Month—that he set out or the use of the twelfth and sixth months as a generic index, a hyperbolic gesture emphasizing the persistence of the suitors.

61. Perhaps because she can now be recognized as an alien creature. Katagiri, ed., *Taketori monogatari*, 48.

62. Later *monogatari* texts will make similar gestures. The ending of many of the *Genji* chapters are good examples.

63. *Dakuten* and *han'dakuten*.

64. Noguchi Motohiro, ed., *Taketori monogatari*, 105.

65. A process intimately related to the movement of the *Ise* text, as we shall see later.

66. See the *Kokinshū* discussion in Chapter 3.

67. We also noted the function of the Imube clan and its relation to the payment of tribute. As discussed in the Introduction, such moments may well be connected to the rise of variant texts.

3 Constructing a Capital "Poetics": *Kokin wakashū*

1. It is by no means certain which came first, the *Ise* tale (or parts of versions available today) or *Kokinshū*.

2. Usually referred to by its abbreviated title, *Kokinshū*.

3. Ki no Tsurayuki (d. 945), Tsurayuki's cousin Ki no Tomonori (d. 905?), Ōshikōchi no Mitsune (fl. 890–924), and Mibu no Tadamine (unknown).

4. Waka in Japan were almost never divorced from a compositional "occasion" at which "topics" (*dai*) were often issued by the sponsor of an event. The topic, selected to match the time of year and particular event, would immediately suggest appropriate words and phrases that enabled almost everyone to compose a passable poem.

5. According to section 20 of *Makura no sōshi*, most courtiers memorized only the most famous of the poems (still a considerable number). Matsuo Satoshi and Nagai Kazuko, eds., *Makura no sōshi, Nihon koten bungaku zenshū* (*NKBZ*) 11:84–91; Ivan Morris, trans., *The Pillow Book of Sei Shōnagon*, 18.

6. The advent of the *Kokin* collection also represents an important stage in the rise to prominence of *hiragana*, a script that made everyday writing a matter more conducive to exchange between men and women. See Nomura Seiichi, *Genji monogatari buntairon josetsu*, 87. I discuss the "feminine hand" in Chapter 6.

7. Furuhashi Nobuyoshi, "Kokinshū no bungakushi—oto no jusei kara," 41. See also his study of older poetry, *Kodai waka no hassei*, which is an extended call to take the "incantatory" aspects of song-poems into account. The article to which I have referred forms the last chapter of the book.

8. Laurel Rasplica Rodd, trans., with the poet Mary Catherine Henkenius, *Kokinshū: A Collection of Poems Ancient and Modern* (1984), and Helen C. McCullough, trans., *Kokin Wakashū: The First Imperial Anthology of Japanese Poetry (with "Tosa Nikki" and "Shinsen Waka")* (1985).

9. See McCullough's companion volume to her translation, *Brocade by Night: "Kokin Wakashū" and the Court Style in Japanese Classical Poetry*.

10. Edwin A. Cranston, "A Web in the Air." The work to which Cranston compares *Brocade by Night* is Konishi Jin'ichi, *A History of Japanese Literature*, vol. 1: *The Archaic and Ancient Ages*. See also my review of *Brocade by Night*, "Translation and Difference: A Review Article."

11. See Gary L. Ebersole, *Ritual Poetry and the Politics of Death in Early Japan*. Ebersole himself goes astray in his unquestioning attitude that the

significant "contexts" he finds are simply there for the privileged or informed researcher's taking. I find problematic, for example, such statements as the following: "Many of the poems in the *Man'yōshū*, *if used properly*, can serve historians and sociologists as *documents* demonstrating the figuration of early Japanese court society and the centripetal nature of the Court's power" (p. 50; my emphasis). The hidden valuation in the emphasized words further conceals the question of whether one can possess ultimate criteria, even within a given discourse, by which one can judge if a "document" is being "used properly."

12. Roy Andrew Miller, "No Time for Literature."

13. Ibid., 752–753.

14. See my discussion of similar issues in "Domesticating *The Tale of Genji.*" Science itself is coming under increased scrutiny from those scientists who are discovering that "objective" observations are just as fictional for their realm of endeavor.

15. That philology is Miller's prime interest in the review essay is evident from his concluding lines, where he calls for the incorporation of a "comprehensive philological approach both toward the texts and the language in which they are written" (p. 760).

16. One other important statement on waka is the article by Mark Morris, "Waka and Form, Waka and History." In his extremely wide-ranging and well-informed discussion that touches suggestively on, among other things, the phonological aspects of the poetry, antilinearity, and its 5/7 or 7/5 rhythms, Morris also elects not to include the *kotodama* problem. The same is true of Robert Brower and Earl Miner in *Japanese Court Poetry*.

17. One important example is Hyōdō Hiromi, "Waka hyōgen to seido."

18. See *Kokinshū*, vol. 2 of *Shimpojiumu nihon bungaku*.

19. Ibid., 17, and 37–42. *Hare no uta* is a term used in conjunction with its compliment, *ke no uta* (private [or quotidian, but also amatory] poems). Katagiri also states that high-ranking nobility almost never composed celebratory poems, which were relegated to lower-ranking officials, a relation similar to that obtaining between Hitomaro and the earlier emperors and empresses.

20. See such standard modern *Kokinshū* editions as the following: *Kokin wakashū*, Ozawa Masao, ed., *NKBZ*, 1971; *Kokin wakashū*, Saeki Umetomo, ed., *Nihon koten bungaku taikei* (*NKBT*), 1958; *Kokin wakashū zen hyōshaku*, Takeoka Masao, ed. (*ZHS*); and the two English translations by McCullough and Rodd-Henkenius cited earlier. Subsequent page citations will be to the *NKBZ* text.

21. As many have pointed out, although the "prefaces," one written in *hiragana* and another in Chinese, contain similar phrasing, they also show important differences. For the passage in question, the latter contains a phrase, "transforms the conduct of humankind," that the writer of the former omits. The omission can be read as an emblem for the Japanese attitude toward Chinese political practice in general; that is, the Chinese idea of the political function of poetry, as seen, for example, in the following passage from the major preface to *Shih ching*, did not take root in Japan: "The

former Kings used it [poetry] to ensure correct relations between husband and wife, to encourage filial piety, to foster upright conduct, to render moral instruction attractive, and to improve social relations" (McCullough, *Brocade by Night,* 304).

22. Masuda Shigeo's argument that the *Kokinshū* poem-songs show a distinct tendency towards deindividualizing the occasions of their production and his likening the result to "folksongs" (*min'yō*) support the claim I am making, although he does not speak directly of a political need to establish a communal body. See "*Kokinshū* no chokusensei—waka to seiji, shakai, rinri," *Kokin wakashū, Nihon bungaku kenkyū shiryō sōsho (NBKSS)*, 31–44.

23. Furuhashi, "Kokinshū no bungakushi," 46. The following remark by Hyōdō Hiromi is extremely suggestive in its political implication: "The foundation for the communal body of aristocratic society was appropriated by the state and was systematized in a one-dimensional manner under the name of the emperor" ("Waka hyōgen to seido," 62).

24. In an important article Suzuki Hideo argues that the point of the *Kokinshū* poems is to reconfigure what he calls "facts" (*jijitsu*) of nature, a process I am calling the reconstruction of reality. "Kokinshūteki hyōgen no keisei," 68.

25. The collection *Nōin utamakura* is a well-known example. On the role of toponyms in Japan, see Brower and Miner, *Japanese Court Poetry:* "Japanese is one of the world's few poetic traditions in which even nouns of place have connotative, semi-metaphorical significance" (p. 6). See also Katagiri Yōichi, "Uta makura no seiritsu," 22–23.

26. Tamagami Takuya, "Byōbu-e to uta to monogatari to," 11–12.

27. Genji's "journey" to Suma and Tamakazura's flight from Kyushu are prime examples.

28. An even more radical example is the following, *Kokinshū* 1041, cited by Furuhashi:

> for one who felt deeply for me   I did not feel the same,
>   is it now in retribution?
> the person for whom I feel deeply   does not feel the same for me
> [ware wo *omoFu*/Fito wo *omoFanu*/mukui ni ya/waga *omoFu* Fito no/ware wo *omoFanu*]

29. Position in the collection (another occasion) is crucial and should always be kept in mind when we analyze individual poems.

30. The mothers of the princes Koretaka and Tsuneyasu were Shizuko and Taneko, respectively, both daughters of Ki no Natora, and the princes would have been second cousins to Tsurayuki's father.

31. *Kokinshū* 76 is by the monk Sosei, who was also a member of the Urin Villa group; the next is another by Zōku, and the two after that are by Tsurayuki. The first poem in "Spring II" is *Kokinshū* 69.

32. *NKBZ* 7:85.

33. Ibid., 201.

34. The leaves from the two trees were worn in the hair and used to decorate ox-drawn carriages. There would be an obvious connection between

such festivals and the incantatory qualities of the words associated with them.

35. One of the recent English *Kokinshū* translations turns the last two sections into a rhetorical question that is not in the Japanese: "Shall I now abandon hope of a successful crossing?" McCullough, *Kokin Wakashū*, 141.

36. As one Western critic has put it, the frequent use of the pivot-word "shows the extent to which the 'Japanese mind' rejects linearity and the 'transparency' of the signifier which has dominated both Western thought and art since the eighteenth century." Noel Burch, *To the Distant Observer: Form and Meaning in the Japanese Cinema*, 47. See Mark Morris, "Waka and Form, Waka and History," for a discussion of what he refers to as "sentence," and also Hyōdō Hiromi, "Waka hyōgen to seido," for a discussion from a politicoritualistic perspective of the incantatory aspects of the poems. Hyōdō states, "It is not the case of there being first a sentiment for which a delineation of natural objects serves as its ornament" (p. 60).

37. I prefer the notion of originary enactment to Furuhashi's notion of *shigen* below.

38. Cf. Suzuki's discussion on the function of the occasion (*ba*) in "Kokinshūteki hyōgen no keisei." He emphasizes the role of the specific poet and notes that the formal constraints demanded by the occasion could allow any poet or reader to participate easily in the compositional process (p. 66). He also maintains, citing Kubota Utsubo, that the close relationship between the idea of immersing the self in literary pursuits and the Buddhist idea of impermanence, both resulting from the exclusionary sociopolitical (*uji-zoku*, clan-family) system operative at the time, needs further interrogation (p. 67).

39. The other poem is *Kokinshū* 556, by Abe no Kiyoyuki, from "Love II." The prefatory note tells us that Kiyoyuki sent the poem, based on words from a sermon by the monk Shinsei commemorating the death of an unnamed acquaintance, to Ono no Komachi:

> though I wrap them up out of sight   they spill out of my sleeves
>   these white jewels
> I find them to be tears   for one I do not see
> [tutumedomo/sode ni tamaranu/siratama Fa/Fito wo minu me no/namida narikeri]

To take tears or dew for jewels is a common metonym (*mitate*) by the mid-Heian period, but Kiyoyuki's poem situates the figure in a Buddhist ceremony and reworks a passage from *Lotus Sutra* in which a man sews a priceless jewel inside the garment of his friend, who doesn't realize it until much later (see Leon Hurvitz, trans., *Scripture of the Lotus Blossom of the Fine Dharma*, 164–165, 166). To the poet the jewels, which eventually bring comfort to the friend in the Buddhist scripture, are turned into tears for someone unseen. The tears in the poem, however, are not only for a person no longer living; they also become tears for a person not seen, i.e., Komachi. The poem further inscribes the "spirit" (the *tama* in *tamaranu* and *siratama*) of both figures.

40. See the article on *mitate* by Suzuki Hideo, "Kokinshū no mitate ni tsuite." He argues that the impulse to compare one "natural" reference with

another derives from Chinese poetry, especially of the Six Dynasties, and notes that the pivot-word as well as the associative-word merge a natural object with a human sentiment and thus are akin to the older pillow word and prefatory phrase (pp. 173–174).

41. The other three are *Kokinshū* 580, 623, and 779.

42. For discussions of the "preface" in English, see McCullough, *Brocade by Night;* John Timothy Wixted, "Chinese Influences on the *Kokinshū* Prefaces"; and E. B. Caedel, "The Two Prefaces to the Kokinshū." An overall list of such issues would include the following: authorship, date of composition in relation to the "Chinese Preface," points of difference between the latter and the *hiragana* "preface," the extent of reliance on Chinese precedents, what the preface is attempting to articulate about waka poetry (particularly regarding waka genealogy), its rhetorical nature (the so-called six styles, often referred to by the Sino-Japanese term *rikugi*), and the critical remarks about the so-called Six Poetic Geniuses (Rokkasen, a Kamakura-period term derived from the mention by Tsurayuki of six poets whose poetic skill was especially notable—see below).

43. *NKBZ* 7:54; *ZHS* 1:120–124.

44. The phrases used in the preface are actually "six rhetorical modes of songs" (*uta no sama mutu*) and "six varieties" (*mukusa*) of waka. The notion of "rhetorical mode" (*sama*) is a focus of attention throughout the "Kana Preface."

45. Takeoka Masao has actually found many correspondences with the poetics found in Kūkai's *Bunkyō hifuron.*

46. The English equivalents are from McCullough, *Brocade by Night,* 4–5. Compare Rodd-Henkenius: Suasive, Description, Comparison, Evocative Imagery, Elegantia, and Eulogies. Rodd, trans., *Kokinshū,* 37–39. The equivalents often mislead, as the following discussion will show.

47. Similarly, the English word "recite" can also mean "count."

48. Takeoka cites *Okugishō:* "not a matter of going alongside or using an illustrative example" (*ZHS* 1:102).

49. In her choice of "eulogistic," McCullough was no doubt evoking the older sense of eulogy meaning "to bless." The term "eulogy" carries the sense of words delivered to extol a deceased person, whereas "bless" is slightly more apposite, one of its meanings being "to confer well-being or prosperity upon" (*American Heritage Dictionary*).

50. *NKBZ* 7:55. The section does not appear in the "Chinese Preface." It is precisely at the level of rhetoricospiritual configurations where a major difference between the two prefaces lies.

51. A bit later we get a specific statement that "more than a hundred years and ten successions" have occurred since the Nara reign. Counting backwards from Daigo produces ten reigns at Heizei (r. 805–809) and more than a hundred years, if we place the time of the preface after the date of the imperial command in 905. Daigo reigned from 897 to 930. Heizei was Narihira's grandfather, a fact that will become important later.

52. In a famous remark Tsurayuki refers to Hitomaro as "the sage of poetry (*uta no hiziri*)."

53. Not simply "sincerity" or "truth," but always anchored in a specific, performative occasion.

54. Cf. "It is no more satisfying to read one of his poems than to fall in love with a woman in a picture" (McCullough, *Kokin Wakashū,* 7). My interpretation is closer to Takeoka (*ZHS* 1:183).

55. Sotohori-hime was the consort of the nineteenth emperor, Ingyō, and known, as was Komachi, for her beauty and her poetic skill.

56. Takeoka is uncharacteristically silent on Komachi (*ZHS* 1:184). The "Chinese Preface" uses the character for "illness."

57. In the case of Genji's mother, for example, psychological distress leads directly to physical distress.

58. I am grateful to Pamela Abee-Taulli for asking about the discrepancy.

59. As was the case with the previous section noted above, the present one is also absent from the "Chinese Preface."

60. Similar examples appear in *Man'yōshū.*

61. *ZHS* 1:226.

62. Kawaguchi Hisao, *Heianchō nihon kambungakushi no kenkyū,* quoted in *ZHS* 1:228–229.

63. See the discussion of Narihira and his associates in Chapter 5.

64. The particle *ya* also complicates matters since it can be read to mark a question, an exclamation, or a rhetorical question.

65. The terms "association" and "progression" derive from Konishi Jin'ichi. See Robert H. Brower and Earl Miner, trans., "Association and Progression: Principles of Integration in Anthologies and Sequences of Japanese Court Poetry, A.D. 900–1350."

66. One commentator attempts to keep operative the possibility by interpreting it as "the first day of spring is over." *Kokin wakashū,* Okumura Tsuneya, ed., *Shinchō nihon koten shūsei* (*SNKS* 1978), 10:28.

67. I sometimes use the term "foretext" for what is commonly referred to as a "headnote" because it speaks to the textuality of Heian discourse and forms a match with other terms like "pretext" and "intertext." See Chapter 5.

68. See the discussion of the poem in Chapter 5.

69. And "characters" as well. Later in the text the prior moment can be evoked by a mention of one of those metonyms to which new variations can be inscribed. The links between the instances relating to Yūgao and Tamakazura are perhaps the most spectacular example.

70. The passage is also one of the scenes depicted in the *Tale of Genji Picture Scroll* (*Genji monogatari emaki*). Page citations are to *Genji monogatari,* Abe Akio, et al., eds., *NKBZ* 16:490–492.

71. Seidensticker omits this line in his translation *The Tale of Genji,* p. 717.

72. Murasaki's poem, for example, echoes a famous line in the anonymous *Kokinshū* 694:

> on Miyagi Plain   stands the bush clover's sparse branches
>   each time they become heavy-laden with dewdrops,
> and await the passing wind   so will I be waiting for you

[miyagi no no/motoara no koFagi/tuyu wo omomi/kaze wo matu goto/ kimi wo koso mate]

The metonymic practices we have seen recall a characterization made by Milman Parry, paraphrased by Todorov, on the function of "epithets" in oral literature: "An epithet is attached to a substantive not in order to specify its meaning but because the two are traditionally associated; the metaphor is not there to increase the semantic density of the text, but because it belongs to the arsenal of poetic ornaments, and because, using it, the text signifies its adherence to literature or to one of its subdivisions." Tzvetan Todorov, *Introduction to Poetics*, 44. In our discussion, the text or poet does not signify an adherence to "literature" but to the reconstructed communal body. Furthermore, the relation is not one of "epithet" to "substantive" but of "epithet" to "epithet," which in my terminology becomes metonym to metonym. By evoking metonyms a poet sends a participatory signal to his or her reader-audience. No ultimate or overarching meaning is "specified" or pointed to, but, as one metonym calls forth another, the very process (similar to the one noted for the *Taketori* text) by which meaning can be made at all is reenacted. As Furuhashi argues, there is a danger in being too obsessed with "meaning," for it is constitutive of the associations themselves.

4 An Early Figure of Resistance: Lady Ise

1. Fujiwara no Kintō, *Shinsen zuinō*, 64. Poems cited from *Ise shū 3*, *Shikashū taisei* (*SST*), vol. 1.

2. Katagiri Yōichi, *Ise*, 212.

3. There is an example at the end of the "Utsusemi" chapter of *Genji:*

the dew that lies   on the fleeting cicada's wings
     hidden beneath thick leaves:
quietly, so quietly,   these sleeves, too, slowly dampen
[utusemi no/Fa ni oku tuyu no/kogakurete/sinobi sinobi ni/nururu sode kana] *Nihon koten bungaku zenshū* (*NKBZ*), 1:205.

Seidensticker notes: "It is very rare for a poem not by Murasaki Shikibu herself to be given in full" (*Tale of Genji*, 56).

4. *Kokin wakashū* (ca. 905–913), *Gosen wakashū* (ca. 951), and *Shūi wakashū*.

5. By contrast, Tsurayuki's poems number ninety-five, almost double those of the second-ranking Mitsune.

6. Konishi Jin'ichi has argued that later editors were inspired by the *Genji* opening. See his "Izure no ōntoki," 61–64, and the discussion of Ise and other women in Chapter 6.

7. Seven types of screen-painting poems (totaling seventy-one) by Ise remain. See Sekine Yoshiko, "Kōkyū bundan no senku toshite no Ise," 92–96.

8. I refer to the famous tale of Ikuta River. In the middle of the *Yamato* section, we are given a series of poems composed by palace attendants for a painting that depicts the story. See the discussion in the following chapter.

9. In Ban Nobutomo, *Hyōshō Ise nikki fushō*, 287–317. Nobutomo carried on Motoori Norinaga's work on textual criticism and was considered one of the four—with Hirata Atsutane, Tachibana Moribe, and Kagawa Kageki—greatest scholars of his time.

10. Further evidence that Katagiri is particularly aware of the fictive nature of the collection can be seen in his discussions of Ise's screen poems. Katagiri Yōichi, *Ise*, 139–156.

11. The "Kusuko Incident." I discuss the incident in Chapter 5.

12. See the discussion of *zuryō* in Chapter 6.

13. She was also believed to have been a woman of great beauty and was a first-rate musician as well.

14. Akiyama, *Ise*, 32–41. "Junior consort" translates *kōi; nyōgo* then becomes "senior consort." The standard translations are "junior consort" and "imperial concubine." See William H. and Helen C. McCullough, *A Tale of Flowering Fortunes*, 820.

15. The talented women assembled around the Fujiwara daughters formed important literary "salons," which provided the impetus for the institution of Heian cultural forms. See the discussion in Chapter 6.

16. The situation is a prime example of the value Heian society placed on "variation." The system of ranks and offices for both men and women provided the basic framework; with each generation new possibilities and combinations would be realized. Texts of the time show that writers and poets were ready to use the sometimes slight differences in much the same way that poets sought variation in waka that they accorded the status of originary conceptions.

17. Similar phrasing occurs in the "Wakamurasaki" chapter of *Genji*, for example, during the fateful meeting between Genji and Fujitsubo: "How did she manage it, I wonder?" (*ikaga tabakari-ken*), where only a short phrase is used to suggest the crucial incident.

18. For *fūryū* see Chapter 5.

19. In 891, when Ise's father was Governor of Yamato, Nakahira was seventeen and an *uemon no suke* (Assistant Commander of Gate Guards).

20. Katagiri, *Ise*, 53.

21. This poem, one of the oldest in *Kokinshū*, relates to legends surrounding Miwa Mountain—a "poetic pillow" (*uta makura*)—that tell of the relations between men and the female deity who inhabits the mountain and sometimes takes the form of a snake.

22. The issue becomes more complicated when we remember that imperial waka compilers often used personal collections as their main sources.

23. One obvious source for such a practice is the manner in which screen paintings were viewed and appreciated. Screen paintings depicted topics such as change of season, monthly celebration, and other felicitous occasions (more on this later).

24. Ise's intensity of feeling is emphasized in poem number 7 by a ploy also used in *Ise monogatari*, where a poem by Narihira so impresses those around him that they all fall silent.

25. Katagiri, *Ise*, 79–82.
26. See the discussion of Minamoto no Takaakira in Chapter 6.
27. In fact, most *hiragana* texts of the time (including the other main texts taken up in this study) are susceptible to such a reading.
28. The implied answer to the rhetorical question is "no, you wouldn't; that's why I sent you a quick reply."
29. She probably wrote her response directly on his letter.
30. The man's poem as it appears in *Heichū monogatari* replaces *miz-ukoFidori no* in the fourth phrase with *mitu ni Fitori no* (having taken a look, all alone). Shimizu Yoshiko, ed., *Heichū monogatari*, NKBZ 8:467.
31. Katagiri, *Ise*, 101–102.
32. Ibid., 126–127. The poem appears in *Kokinshū* (1000) and also in *Gosenshū* (1291) with a different prefatory note.
33. He was perhaps a model for the *Genji* figure.

5   Sexual/Textual Politics and *The Tale of Ise*

1. Takahashi Tōru, "Soshitsu to kaiko—uta monogatari no aironii," 122.
2. Ishida Jōji, ed., *Ise monogatari*, 266.
3. The first *dan* speaks of a "coming of age ceremony," and later *dan* suggest the exploits of someone who can be inferred to be Narihira, who then "grows" older and is referred to as an "old man," *okina*, and who finally leaves the famous death poem (*dan* 125 in the Tempuku texts). Only thirty or so of the more than two hundred poems in the *Ise* text are verifiable Narihira compositions.
4. See my discussion of textual variants in the Introduction.
5. See also the discussion of "seriality" below. The *Heichū* text does deal with a man who almost always fails at amorous conquest and thus represents an "other" to discourse by women.
6. The author of a commonly used English translation resorts to positivist methods to handle the difficulty. After telling us everything that *Ise* is not (not poetic anthology, not biography of Narihira, not unified, not historically accurate, no identifiable author), the author concludes: "It [*Ise*] can be *appreciated*, not in terms of preconceived notions about its theme or purpose, but as an *interesting combination of poetry and prose*, and as a *source of insights* into the psychology, values, and behavior of Heian society" (emphasis added). Helen C. McCullough, *Tales of Ise*, 65. The statement makes of *Ise* a (universalized) "document" for sociologists, historians, and psychologists.
7. Here I have in mind Barthes's distinction between "work" and "text." See Roland Barthes, "From Work to Text," 73–81. "The engendering of the perpetual signifier within the field of the text should not be identified with an organic process of maturation or a hermeneutic process of deepening, but rather with a serial movement of dislocations, overlappings, and variations" (p. 76), and "The Text . . . is read without the father's signa-

ture" (p. 78). See also the essay by Michel Foucault, "What Is an Author?" "In our culture (and doubtless in many others), discourse was not originally a product, a thing, a kind of goods; it was essentially an act—an act placed in the bipolar field of the sacred and the profane, the licit and the illicit, the religious and the blasphemous. Historically, it was a gesture fraught with risks before becoming goods caught up in a circuit of ownership" (p. 148).

8. The list is derived from solutions discussed in Ikeda Kikan, *Ise monogatari ni tsukite no kenkyū*, 521–570, and Fukui Teisuke, ed., *Ise monogatari*, 7–15.

9. The group of *dan* that allude to the Ise Virgin and those that tell of the Empress of the Third Ward (Fujiwara Takaiko, see below) are considered the two main thematic groupings in *Ise*.

10. Kenshō was a late Heian–early Kamakura period poet and critic and one of the systemizers of the Rokujō line of poetics. An often feisty participant in poetry contexts, he is especially well known as a writer of commentary and a collator of texts.

11. Kenshō cited in Ikeda, *Ise monogatari ni tsukite*, 522–523.

12. A medieval *Ise* commentary of unknown authorship attributed to Minamoto Tsunenobu. The author bases a discussion of the efficacy of poetry on the *Kokinshū* "Kana Preface" and recounts a visit to the Sumiyoshi Shrine when a man around one hundred years old appears to him and explains why *Ise monogatari* is so valuable for its insights into the way of poetry. The text identifies actual dates and personages for each *dan*, thus demonstrating a literal manner of textual reading also seen in the medieval *Genji* commentaries.

13. Cited in Ikeda, *Ise monogatari ni tsukite*, 534–535.

14. *Monogatari* titles were derived (often by later readers) from a main character in the text, as in *Genji*, from a poem in the text, as in *Sagoromo* and *Hamamatsu chūnagon*, or from a narrative topos, as in *Ochikubo monogatari*, *Utsuho monogatari*, or *Sumiyoshi monogatari*. The *Genji* text, careful in its usage of titles and names, gives the main character an all-important surname but tends otherwise to refer to characters by poetically derived metonyms: Aoi no ue (Heartvine Lady), Yūgao (Evening Faces), Hanachirusato (Village of Falling Blossoms), Tamakazura (Jeweled Chaplet), and so on.

15. See Fukui, *Ise monogatari*, 217–225.

16. Ikeda, *Ise monogatari ni tsukite*, 557.

17. Fujioka Sakutarō, *Kokubungaku zenshi*, vol. 1, 90. Fujioka also discusses the importance of humor in the *Ise* text.

18. The relations between the anonymous *Ise* "man" and Heian painting techniques will be discussed below.

19. The use of *keri* in a discourse spoken as if the events were happening right at that moment may also be intimately connected with painting.

20. We noted the "peeping" topos in *Taketori*. One of the most famous examples (see Chapter 11) is Genji's discovery of Murasaki in the "Wakamurasaki" chapter of the *Genji* tale. We must also remember the political intertext, which I discuss below. Page citations are to Fukui Teisuke, *Ise monogatari*, *Nihon koten bungaki zenshū* (*NKBZ*).

21. Or, depending on the variant, "acting like the adult he has become."

22. By "thing itself" I do not mean to endorse the following characterization of *Ise* poems: "Its prose passages . . . are designed *primarily* to provide settings for the poems—to serve as *black velvet cushions* against which the *gems* can flash and glow." McCullough, "Tales," 4; emphasis added.

23. Lead-in phrases can be of varying lengths, connecting with what follows either by syntactic, semantic, or phonological (and incantatory) links, which often turn on a pivot-word.

24. Like E. H. Gombrich's picture of the rabbit that magically turns into a duck. E. H. Gombrich, *Art and Illusion*, 5.

25. *To iFu uta no kokorobaFe nari*. Or, alternatively, "The sentiments are those found in this poem." The second poem, by Minamoto no Tōru, appears in *Kokinshū* (724) in an alternate form.

26. It has been suggested that the poem would not be a true *honkadori* because Narihira was only three years Tōru's junior. *Honkadori*, a term that comes into use during the Kamakura period, requires an old-new temporal distance for its full effect. Though such claims cannot be ignored, there is no evidence that the first poem is by Narihira.

27. The appearance of Tōru's poem and the added comment direct us to read *Ise* in terms of other texts. A similar textual moment appears in *dan* 41, where two sisters again form part of the foretext. Here a poem is sent along with another textile item, a "blue cloak." The last line of the *dan* tells us that it "most likely expresses the sentiments of the 'Musashino' poem" (*musasino no kokoro narubesi*), which also appears in *Kokinshū* as an anonymous poem (867).

28. The first poem appears in another collection, *Kokin waka rokujō*, but as an anonymous composition, headed only by the topic "robes with rubbed-on patterns" (*surigoromo*). It also appears in two collections of Narihira's poetry, but the collections probably took the poem from the *Ise* text. In *Shinkokinshū*, which also undoubtedly takes it from the *Ise* tale, it appears with the note "sent to a woman." The second poem, by the famous poet and eccentric Minamoto no Tōru (822–895), appears in *Kokinshū* with only the note "topic unknown" (*daisirazu*).

29. The word *kara ni*, as Mitani Eiichi has noted, appears in several of the most prominent *dan*. See "Ise monogatari no jidai," 263 ff.

30. An example mentioned before is the famous "meeting" in *dan* 25 between Narihira and Ono no Komachi. The two poems are simply listed successively in *Kokinshū*, and there is no evidence to suggest that the encounter ever took place. It is probably safe to extrapolate from the "meeting" here to other "encounters" (between the man and the Empress of the Second Ward or the Ise Virgin, for example) that have troubled positivist-minded scholars for centuries and to ask why the text's compilers felt compelled to suggest those particular meetings.

31. *Kogo jiten*.

32. *Kokubungaku daijiten*.

33. *Miyabi* has been taken to be the major "theme" of the *Ise* collection. I

would argue that it is not so much a "theme" as a metonym for a method of rewriting and the situating of that rewriting. Another term that sometimes takes on "thematic" proportions is *irogonomi* (lit., a predilection for color), which signifies the pursuit of amorous affairs, and its Sino-Japanese version, *kōshoku*. Takahashi Tōru suggestively links the term with imperial power and privilege, *ōken* (see "Soshitsu to Kaiko"). During the Heian period the term's signified can slide from the sense "action proper to and expected of a member of the ruling aristocracy" to a sense of "decadent behavior," when applied to a commoner or someone who has fallen from imperial grace. The most influential modern discussion of *irogonomi* is Origuchi Shinobu, *Zenshū*, vol. 1, 3–75 and vol. 14, part 2, chapter 3.

34. Some believe that he reedited the *Man'yō* collection while spending his lonely days at the old capital after the Kusuko Incident. Kanada Motohiko, "Arihara no Narihira to Ariwara shi to shinnōtachi," 289.

35. The low status of Genji's mother also determines her son's fate. As Murai Yoshihiko has found, Abo's mother was from the Katsui, a powerful regional clan of Korean descent. The clan produced families like the Sugawara and the Ōeda (later Ōe), whose members went on to achieve renown during the Heian period. "Ariwara no Narihira to sono shūhen—sotsuden no saikentō," 281.

36. The term used to refer to those royal sons who are granted surnames is *shisei genji*, the name "genji" commonly taken to refer to the general case. See Chapter 6.

37. See the discussion of Narihira in McCullough, *Tales*, 41–55.

38. The notion of "underside" will be a crucial one for reading the *Genji* text.

39. The prince appears in *dan* 82, 83, and 85.

40. Aritsune appears in *Ise* as does his nephew Toshiyuki. It has been suggested that another member of the larger Ki family, Tsurayuki, compiled the *Ise* text. For sources see Yoshikai Naoto, "Ariwara no Narihira to Ki shi," 313–314.

41. The Ki family historically had been victims of the relentless Fujiwara acquisition of power. Another of Natora's daughters, Taneko, was the consort of Emperor Nimmyō, and a son, Aritsune, was a talented official who served three emperors (see below). I discuss the position of the emperor's maternal grandfather in the discussion of the *Genji* tale.

42. The *Ise* text links Narihira with two figures: the Empress of the Second Ward, Fujiwara no Takaiko (842–910), who went on to become Emperor Seiwa's consort, and the Ise Virgin, Yasuko, who was the daughter of Emperor Montoku. On Princess Yasuko, see below. The situation recalls Genji's secret liaisons with Fujitsubo and Oborozukiyo and his open one with the Third Princess.

43. Several Fujiwara figures, including Yoshifusa, also appear in the *Ise* text. The one in *dan* 101 turns out to be Masachika (823–875), who belonged to one of the lesser branch houses and ended his career at low rank. The poem composed by Narihira in that *dan* can be read either as extolling the glory of the Fujiwara clan, especially the leader of the most powerful Northern

Branch (*hokke*), the previously mentioned Yoshifusa (804–872), or as suggesting that as a result of that glory the other court families had withered away. As previously noted, when historical figures are mentioned by name in the *Ise* text, they are inevitably outsiders to Fujiwara power. In *Ise*, therefore, political history (the specific "tradition" noted earlier) meets aestheticoliterary pose in the movement of *fūryū*.

44. The garden appears in *dan* 81.

45. For a discussion of the salons centered around men like Tōru, see Watanabe Minoru, *Heian bunshōshi*, 39–40; *Ise monogatari, Shinchō nihon koten shūsei* (*SNKS*), 9:204–219; and Katagiri Yōichi, *Ise monogatari no kenkyū*, 38, 47–49. I will discuss other salons in chapter 6.

46. Origuchi Shinobu, *Zenshū* 10:37.

47. See Jonathan Culler, *Structuralist Poetics*, 138. "To naturalize a text is to bring it into relation with a type of discourse or model which is already, in some sense, natural and legible." While *Ise* invites several types of naturalizing procedures, it also warns the reader that they may be misreadings.

48. It appears in *Kokinshū, Shinsen waka* (compiled by Tsurayuki), and *Kokinwaka rokujō*.

49. Cf. the lines "did you come to me, or did I go to you?" in *dan* 69.

50. Historically, the capital was moved from Nara to Nagaoka in 784 and then before the latter was finished to Heiankyō (roughly coterminous with present-day Kyoto) in 794.

51. The deictic term *kano* (modern Japanese *ano*, "that [person, thing] we all know about") is used, functioning as an appeal to the reader to participate in a textual situation still unclear at this point about a man everyone would recognize.

52. See *Ise monogatari, Yamato monogatari, Kanshō nihon koten bungaku* (*KNKB*), 5:47–49.

53. *Genji monogatari,* coincidentally, also sets its narrative fifty years or more prior to the alleged time of narration although, from the "narrating" perspective I am following, any "actual" past time becomes problematic.

54. It also heads the fifth book of *Kokinshū* "Love" poems.

55. See McCullough, *Tales*, 53 for four interpretations.

56. Perhaps the one modern scholar who has worked hardest at demystifying the relation between fact and fiction is Katagiri Yōichi. See Katagiri Yōichi, *Ise monogatari, Yamato monogatari*. Basing his stance firmly on thorough textual study and possessing a keen ear for the narrator's voice, Katagiri has labored tirelessly to keep critical attention focused on the fictive processes constitutive of the *Ise* text. Although his own critical voice at times gets caught up in the search for "origins," the Katagiri critical texts remain an indispensable adjunct to reading the *Ise* text. Also, his "three-stage" theory of how *Ise* developed has attracted wide scholarly attention and criticism. See Katagiri, *Ise monogatari no kenkyū*, and a summary in *KNKB* 5:15–19.

57. Katagiri makes the intriguing remark that the *dan* seems like a scene out of a Kabuki play. The same is true for passages in later *monogatari*, as we shall see. *KNKB* 5:55.

58. For a discussion of the three interpretative possibilities, see Takeoka

Masao, *Ise monogatari zenhyōshaku*, 1022–1024. Takeoka himself confuses fiction and fact and concludes that the Virgin, presumably still a child of ten or so, obeys her mother's command to care for the hunter but doesn't know enough to actually engage in a sexual encounter. Accordingly, the man ends up frustrated (p. 1024).

59. Shimizu Yoshiko focuses on such topoi (*bamen*) in most of the essays in her study *Genji monogatari no buntai to hōhō*.

60. The anonymous signifiers mark both a rise in emotions and an invitation for the audience to participate. The use of the topos as pretext for the famous meeting between Genji and Fujitsubo is discussed in Mitani Kuniaki, "Fujitsubo jiken no hyōgen kōzō: 'Wakamurasaki' no hōhō aruiwa 'pure-tekisuto' to shite no Ise monogatari."

61. Comparing the stylistic similarities between the poem and others by Narihira, Katagiri concludes that Narihira could very well have written the poem. *KNKB* 5:166–167.

62. *Dan* 10 of *Ise* is another example of the juxtaposition into a story of two anonymous poems.

63. That version of the poem is also found in several *Ise* texts.

64. As will be noted, there are those who believe that Genji and Fujitsubo only met once. Reader-listeners of the Genji-Fujitsubo tale would have readily recalled the *Ise* situation, another tale of apparent transgression.

65. McCullough breaks up the passage into four (past-tense) sentences, including certain extrapolations and one misreading: nothing in the Tempuku text corresponds to "as indeed was the Virgin [anxious to meet him]." McCullough, *Tales*, 117.

66. It would be a misreading to attempt to assign, in *monogatari* texts, any specific "point of view" or "consciousness" to a "narrator" or "character" as is customary in Western criticism. Heian *hiragana* discourse was a flexible signifying medium, interweaving action, "consciousness," citation, and poetry without "subjectively" changing register: it is marked by the *keri* (the situation is) mode, which constantly points to its enabling position of narrating.

67. It appears in *Kokinwaka rokujō—Kokka Taikan* no. 33775, with the appended topic *chigiru* (make vows).

68. The clandestine meeting between Narihira and Princess Yasuko is now considered to be purely fictitious. The princess's mother was Ki no Aritsune's daughter, whom Narihira is believed to have married. Aritsune is also thought to have been an important member of a *fūryū* "salon."

69. See the groundbreaking article by Masao Miyoshi, "Against the Native Grain: The Japanese Novel and the 'Postmodern' West," *South Atlantic Quarterly*. "Paratactic rather than syntactic, arithmetic rather than algebraic, the *shōsetsu* is the expression not of order and suppression, as the novel is, but of space, decentralization, and dispersal" (pp. 535–536).

70. Fukui, *Ise monogatari*, 193. The movement also recalls a comment by Roland Barthes: "The engendering of the perpetual signifier within the field of the text should not be identified with an organic process of maturation or a hermeneutic process of deepening, but rather with a serial movement of

dislocations, overlappings, and variations." Barthes, "From Work to Text," 76.

71. As noted in the discussion of *Kokinshū*, the incantatory aspect of all such "poetic toponyms" (*uta makura*) must always be kept in mind.

72. A bent verse is a kind of acrostic poem in which the poet takes the syllables of a given word, in this case *kakitubata* (iris, which just happen to be "blooming" at the swamp—we are given no indication of seasonal time), and, placing each syllable at the beginning of each segment, composes a *tanka* on a designated topic. In this case, the topic is feelings appropriate to a distant journey.

73. *KNKB* 5:75.

74. We noted the phenomenon in Chapter 3.

75. Their position each time is characterized by loss of clarity: they first lose their way, then the way is dark and narrow, and now they are in a boundary space. The vagueness of the interstices reflects the vagueness of the connecting links.

76. The poem appears in *Kokinshū* (411) under the topic "Travel." It is listed directly after the *karakoromo* poem. The phrase that follows the poem, which aids readerly interpretation, is omitted.

77. Fukui groups *Ise dan* according to thematic matter, which for him affords clues to the way the text "evolved." Fukui, *Ise monogatari*, 198–214. Katagiri calls the shorter *dan* that come after the longer ones *kōjitsu tan* (sequels). He thereby emphasizes (as I am doing) the notion of writing process over an arranging or "developmental" process. *KNKB* 5:172. The groupings also recall sections of the *Kokinshū* arrangement that tell shorter narratives within the larger series.

78. *KNKB* 5:130. Watanabe Minoru has also remarked that "[What *Ise* speaks] is, in a word, the external aspect of events *that can be seen with the eyes.*" Watanabe, "Heian bunshōshi," 37 (emphasis added).

79. Cited in KNKB 5:49–50. See also Tamagami Takuya's discussion of the relation between screens and poems presented at the *Daijōe* ceremony, where poets composed poems pretending to be the figures depicted on the screens. "It is fiction. It is called *daiei* [compositions on a topic]." Tamagami, "Byōbu-e to uta to monogatari to," 193.

80. The story is one of many legendary prefigurings of Ukifune's plight in *Genji*.

81. Takahashi Shōji, *Yamato monogatari*, 385.

82. Mitani Kuniaki is another scholar mindful of the relation between text and painting. The Ise text is, in his words, "literature of readerly identification" (*dōka no bungaku*). Following Shimizu Yoshiko, Mitani cites the passages (mentioned earlier) in *monogatari* when characters suddenly become referred to simply as "man" and "woman," the erasure of identity signaling an eroticized poetic exchange. Mitani compares the *Ise* signifiers to the manner that faces are drawn in the Genji scrolls: "slash for the eyes, hook for the nose" (*hikime kagibana*). The painted figures are also empty signs with which the reader can identify. Although Mitani's observation ties in well with the general movement of dissimulation that constitutes the *Ise* text, problems

arise when he attempts to preserve strict distinctions between the *katari* (what I have been calling diegesis) as a "past-tense mode" (*kakokei-shiki*) and waka as a "present-tense mode" (*genzaikei-shiki*) and when he further contends that waka represent a space where author, text, and reader "merge into one" (*dōka*), whereas the *katari* prevents that identification. "Dōka no bungaku," 119.

83. Such a narrative situation would explain, as discussed previously, the use of deictics like *koko* in *dan* 9 and 11, and *iFiokosekeru* in *dan* 10. I touch on the situation later in conjunction with the *Genji* text.

84. And the tendencies of the Heian language itself. In a narrative like *Genji*, such movements produce what I refer to as "narrating moments."

6 Situating the "Feminine Hand"

1. Normal practice would have dictated the appointment of a new Virgin (both Kamo and Ise) with each new emperor.

2. *Dai sai-in saki no gyoshū* (Collected Poems of the Former Great Kamo Priestess) and *Dai sai-in no gyoshū* (Collected Poems of the Great Kamo Priestess).

3. *Kakaishō*, edited by Ishida Jōji, 186–187. See also Ii Haruki, *Genji monogatari no nazo*, 4–12; and Mitamura Masako, "Josei tachi no saron—daisai-in saron o chūshin ni," 63–67. Fujiwara no Yukinari is believed to have perfected the *hiragana* calligraphic style. *Genji monogatari hyōshaku* (GMH) 3:203.

4. Similarly, although he takes a different tack, one of Fredric Jameson's goals is to radicalize the "modest claim, surely acceptable to everyone, that certain texts have social and historical—sometimes even political—resonance." *The Political Unconscious*, 17.

5. The other was *katakana*, a stiff, nonaesthetic style used in religious texts as sound markers to help reconstitute the Chinese texts into Japanese readings.

6. Sometimes called "Chinese written in an unorthodox style" (*hentai kambun*), that is, Chinese that would not necessarily be intelligible to a native reader of Chinese.

7. As previously noted a new capital was being built at Nagaoka before work was suddenly halted.

8. It cannot be emphasized too strongly that *hiragana* was used by *both* men and women and that I am not arguing for gender essentialism here.

9. These official histories were known as the *Six National Histories* (Rikkokushi). The last of the six was *The Actual Records of Three Reigns* (Sandai jitsuroku), begun in response to a command issued by Emperor Uda and completed in 901. Among its compilers were Minamoto no Yoshiari, Fujiwara no Tokihira, and Sugawara no Michizane.

10. Compare this statement by Richard Bowring: "This pressure [not to use Japanese], coupled with a Confucian-inspired distrust of fiction as an unworthy pursuit, served to divorce men from their tongue and condemn

them to working in a foreign language, which, of necessity, guided their thoughts and expression along non-native paths." "The Female Hand in Japan: A First Reading," 50.

11. I would translate its oft-quoted opening line as follows: "Though it is men they say who keep diaries, a woman will try her hand at it and keep one" (wotoko mo sunaru nik[k]i to iFu mono wo, wonna mo site mimu tote surunari).

12. *Tosa nikki, Kanshō nihon koten bungaku (KNKB)*, 10:321–322.

13. *KNKB* 10:302, 309. The latter passage does not refer to Narihira by name but cites his famous "mountain rim" poem (*Ise monogatari*, 82; also *Kokinshū*, 884):

> before we've seen enough leaving us wanting more
>   is the moon to disappear so soon?
> move away o mountain rim and do not let it set
> [akanakuni/madaki mo/tuki no/kakururu ka/yama no Fa nigete/irezu mo aranamu]

14. *Genji* commentaries are filled with surmises concerning the historical precedents and periods upon which the tale, especially the earlier chapters, is based. The Japanese term for such precedents is *junkyo*, which, as Tamagami Takuya warns, must not be mistaken for the search for "models" in modern fiction. See "Genji monogatari junkyo ron—Kakaishō so (II)," in *GMH*, supplement 1:402.

15. Ivan Morris notes, for example, that "the elaborate system of harems and eunuchs was never introduced from China" (*World of the Shining Prince*, 224), and harems in the Arab world were not noted for their cultural "production."

16. The women may have been oppressed in the larger scheme of things, but, on the one hand, their power to represent themselves and, on the other, the fragile nature of Fujiwara political practices rooted in genealogical imperatives that depended on the birth and education of particular offspring enabled their active engagement in transforming a society and politics based on a Chinese discursive ground to one based on a native one.

17. Catherine Stimpson, "Ad/d Feminam," 175. She had stated: "Regulating my interrogation is the conviction that women writers have had to overcome a devaluation of them as producers of public culture. Balancing this, as matter does antimatter, has been the pervasive insistence that women's primary work ought to be that of eros and of reproduction" (pp. 174–175).

18. The cultural, political, and genealogical role of what is referred to as *yūsoku kojitsu*, a term that covers everything from private customs and manners to official ranks and practices, needs thorough study.

19. See Bowring, *Female Hand*, 54.

20. See Takamure Itsue, *Nihon kon'inshi*, especially chapter 4. See also the comprehensive study by William H. McCullough, "Japanese Marriage Institutions in the Heian Period." It is useful to keep in mind McCullough's comment on the contingent nature of Heian marriage practices: "The rules

governing marriage were customary in kind, and they seem to have had little relation to the provisions of the court's legal code, with which they were often in conflict" (p. 147).

21. As Oka Kazuo states, "If Michinaga had not been married to Rinshi, the daughter of Minamoto no Masanobu, and to Meishi, the daughter of Minamoto no Takaakira and adopted daughter of Higashi Sanjō-in, he would not have been able, in all probability, to overwhelm Korechika, the minister of the palace (*naidaijin*), who had gained the complete confidence of Emperor Ichijō, and ascend to the glorious position of regent and chancellor." See Oka Kazuo, *Genji monogatari no kisoteki kenkyū*, 30. I discuss the terms regent and chancellor below.

22. As I shall note below, the *Gossamer Years* is far from "one long wail of jealousy by a woman in whom the emotion has attained hysterical proportions" (Morris, *World of the Shining Prince*, 244).

23. The now standard translations of Heian governmental terms, found in the appendices to *A Tale of Flowering Fortunes*, render both *sesshō* and *kampaku* as "Regent." William H. and Helen C. McCullough, *A Tale of Flowering Fortunes* 2:789–853. Although the terms—*sesshō* for a man who ruled in place of an infant or child emperor and *kampaku* for one who ruled after the emperor came of age—were sometimes used interchangeably, I have decided to keep "regent" as the translation for *sesshō* but to use "chancellor" to translate *kampaku*. Furthermore, I render the term for the highest minister, *dajōdaijin*, which the McCulloughs translate "chancellor," as "great minister," thus preserving the term "minister" for *daijin*, as in *sadaijin* (minister of the left), *udaijin* (minister of the right), and *naidaijin* (minister of the palace).

24. Since adoption means the naturalization of a fiction within genealogical succession, the Japanese would have been familiar and comfortable early on with such fictions, inscribed as they had to be into the Fujiwara hegemony in its very maintenance. The situation relates directly to the *Genji* tale where foster (parent-child) relationships play crucial roles.

25. Full-fledged members of royalty, of course, had no surnames. Genji (or Minamoto as the characters are also pronounced) was not the only name used in such cases, but it serves as a metonym for the act of demotion itself (*shisei genji*).

26. See Hashimoto Yoshihiko, *Heian kizoku* 13, 103–104; and Akagi Shizuko, *Sekkan jidai no shosō* 127–149.

27. Perhaps the most famous example of one who was able to return to royal status and eventually become emperor was Kōkō's son, who was given the Minamoto surname in 884. He was appointed crown prince in 887 and became Emperor Uda on the same day. Other examples are Kōnin, Kammu, and Kōkō (*Kakaishō*, 360). One recent *Genji* study makes much of this change in status, although I prefer to view the *Genji* title as a flexible signifier able to evoke the fate of "Genji" figures in general. See Norma Field, *The Splendor of Longing in The Tale of Genji*. The term "longing" in the title refers in part to such men, although Field, to my mind, makes too much of the "imperial" as "ontological" center.

28. Shimizu Yoshiko, *Genji monogatari no buntai to hōhō*, 284.

29. The famous incident where Genji places his son Yūgiri in the Academy, starting him out at the lowly sixth rather than the fourth rank usually accorded high-born courtiers, provides another moment of convergence between Genji and *zuryō* interests as well as an indirect valorization of the institution.

30. In one of the best recent books on feminist discourse, Toril Moi critiques keeping the "political" and the "aesthetic" separate: "If all readings are *also* in some sense political, it will hardly do to maintain the New Critics' binary opposition between reductive political readings on the one hand and rich aesthetic appraisal on the other. If aesthetics raises the question of whether (or how) the text works effectively with an audience, it obviously is bound up with the political: without an aesthetic effect there will be no political effect either. . . . As a political approach to criticism, feminism must be aware of the politics of aesthetic categories as well as of the implied aesthetics of political approaches to art." Toril Moi, *Sexual/Textual Politics*, 85–86.

31. See Chapter 1, note 59, and Mitani Eiichi, *Monogatarishi no kenkyū*, 363–393.

32. Morris, *World of the Shining Prince*, 227. The remark shows the dangers in "documentary" readings of Heian texts.

33. The importance of the incident to the *Genji* text has been emphasized recently by Suzuki Hideo and Fujii Sadakazu, the authors of an indispensable reference for the Heian period. See Suzuki and Fujii, *Nihon bungeishi, Kodai II*, 131. As Fujii writes, "It has become clear that the Anna Incident is a primary key to interpreting *The Tale of Genji*" (p. 130).

34. See Tanahashi Mitsuo, *Ōchō no shakai*, 43.

35. Kuroita Katsumi, ed., *Nihon kiryaku*, 110. For a description of an identical fate suffered, though for different reasons, by Sugawara no Michizane, see Robert Borgen, *Sugawara no Michizane and the Early Heian Court*, 278. Michizane is also cited as a possible "model" for the Genji figure. *Eiga monogatari* states the decree more clearly: "For the crime of having attempted to overturn the imperial line, we are appointing you provisional governor-general of the Dazaifu and sending you into exile." *Eiga monogatari*, Matsumura Hiroji and Yamanaka Yutaka, eds., 1:57; William and Helen McCullough, *Tale of Flowering Fortunes* 1:99–100, translation modified.

36. The incident and its immediate aftermath are recorded in Kuroita, ed., *Nihon kiryaku*, 110–111. It is also mentioned in *Eiga monogatari*, 56–59; William and Helen McCullough, *Tale of Flowering Fortunes* 1:99–101; *Ōkagami*, Tachibana Kenji, ed., 167–170; and the English translation, Helen Craig McCullough, *Ōkagami, The Great Mirror: Fujiwara Michinaga (966–1027) and His Times*, 129–131. Other discussions consulted include Tanahashi, *Ōchō no shakai*, 42–44; Murai Yasuhiko, *Heian kizoku no sekai* 1:89–94; Sakamoto Shōzō, *Sekkan jidai*, 193–203; Yamanaka Yutaka, *Heianchō bungaku no shiteki kenkyū*, 239–259; the same author's *Heian jidai no kokiroku to kizokubunka*; and Abe Takeshi, *Sekkan seiji*, 36–40.

37. Takaakira wrote a study of court practices (*yūsoku kojitsu*), *Saikyūki* (sometimes read *Seikyūki*).

38. The "numerous" consorts mentioned in the opening line of the *Genji* text, who resided at the Rear Palace of the Kiritsubo Emperor, loudly echo Murakami's situation.

39. The quarters, also known as the "Pear Garden" (Nashitsubo), were associated with the crown prince and could be taken as a future metonym for Tamehira. The ceremony, moreover, was based on the procedures followed at the time of Emperor Murakami's marriage to Anshi. Yamanaka, *Heianchō bungaku*, 243.

40. Kuroita, ed. *Nihon kiryaku*, 114. Morotada's death was thought by contemporaries to be the result of spiritual retribution. See also McCullough, *Ōkagami*, 268.

41. Kuroita, ed., *Nihon kiryaku*, 110. The reference is to the revolts of Taira no Masakado and Fujiwara no Sumitomo.

42. William and Helen McCullough, *Tale of Flowering Fortunes* 1:100; *Eiga monogatari* 1:58.

43. McCullough, *Ōkagami*, 129–130, translation modified; *Ōkagami* (Tachibana, ed.), 167–169.

44. *Nihon koten bungaku zenshū (NKBZ)* 20:206. For a freer translation of the present passage and the following, see Edward Seidensticker, *The Gossamer Years*, 72–73.

45. Seidensticker's translation of the *chōka* is found in *Gossamer Years*, 75–77.

46. Cited in Abe, *Sekkan seiji*, 39.

47. See, for example, Shimizu Yoshiko, *Genji monogatari-ron*, 115. Shimizu's study, which addresses the question of locating historical precedents and models for the *Genji* text, treats Takaakira at length. She takes up the problem again in *Buntai to hōhō*, 275–303. Learned women like Murasaki Shikibu would have been altogether familiar, a generation later, with an incident of such magnitude.

48. See, for example, Oka, *Kisoteki kenkyū*, 34–58. Itō Hiroshi surmises that since Tametoki was stationed in Harima when Takaakira was exiled, he might very well have witnessed the latter's party traveling through the province bound for exile. Tametoki is also believed to have been a student of Sugawara no Michizane's grandson, Fujitoki. *Genji monogatari no genten*, 43–44. The latter two men are known for certain to have graduated from the Heian Academy.

49. The untimely death of the empress's father, the powerful Fujiwara no Michitaka, enabled their family rival, Michinaga, to solidify his power through his daughter and Murasaki Shikibu's mistress, Akiko (whose own father, as noted, was a Minamoto). The fortunes of Murasaki Shikibu's father suddenly declined with the abdication of Emperor Kazan. Itō, *Genten*, 31.

50. Although I do not dwell on it here, the role of Buddhist (together with Shintō, Confucian, and Taoist) practices during the Heian period is vital to the texts. Any examination of Buddhism must, however, be wary of essentialist maneuvers that install it as a pure ground of discourse or interpretation. One question with which I intend to deal in the future is the particularly "private" appropriations of Buddhist practices by Heian court-

iers. The best sources for the topic are the works by Hayami Tasuku, especially *Heian kizoku shakai to bukkyō* and *Jōdo shinkō ron*, chapter 2 and supplementary chapter 1.

51. By "locking out" I refer not only to the physical resistance it signals but to the fact that such instances have proven resistant to Western analyses.

52. It should be noted that the *Gossamer* author is the only one among the women mentioned who was not a palace attendant. She was an *ie no josei*, a "woman of a private household," as opposed to a *miyazukai no josei*, "a woman who served at the palace." Suzuki and Fujii, *Nihon bungeishi*, 131–132.

53. The diary, well known for its alleged "third-person" narration, is also called *The Tale of Izumi Shikibu* (*Izumi shikibu monogatari*). The text sits at the convergence of personal poetry collection, diary, and narrative tale.

54. Richard Bowring, *Murasaki Shikibu: The Tale of Genji*, 3.

55. All of the above texts, except the *Ise Collection*, have been translated into English. See Donald Keene, trans., *The Tale of the Bamboo Cutter*; Helen C. McCullough, trans., *Tales of Ise*; Seidensticker, trans., *The Gossamer Years*; Edwin A. Cranston, trans., *The Izumi Shikibu Diary: A Romance of the Heian Court*; Ivan Morris, trans., *The Pillow Book of Sei Shōnagon*; Richard Bowring, trans., *Murasaki Shikibu: Her Diary and Poetic Memoirs*; and Edward Seidensticker, trans., *The Tale of Genji*.

56. See, for example, Mitani's essays collected in *Monogatari bungaku no hōhō*, chapters 5 and 6; Takahashi's in *Genji monogatari no tai'i hō*, chapters 2 and 9; Noguchi's *Shōsetsu no nihongo*; and Fujii Sadakazu, "Sōshiji no shomondai," *Kokubungaku: kenkyū to kyōzai*.

57. Two examples of *sōshiji*: (1) during the festivities accompanying the Reizei Emperor's visit to the retired Suzaku Emperor: "The occasion being a private one, among intimates, the wine ended up not flowing [being passed] to many persons; or is it that I have failed again to write them down?" (*NKBZ* 3:67; Seidensticker, *Tale of Genji*, 381); and (2) on the occasion of a wisteria (*Fuji*) viewing sponsored by the emperor in the chapter "The Ivy" ("Yadorigi," 49): "Imagining that, as usual, most of the poems would be awkward and old-fashioned, I will not write every one of them down" (*NKBZ* 5:471).

58. Enomoto Masazumi, *Genji monogatari no sōshiji*, 144. Sōgi's term is *sōshi no zi*. I am indebted to Enomoto's study for the following discussion of the history of the term.

59. Also known as *Kachō yojō*. The modern edition I have consulted is edited by Ii Haruki. See *Kachō yosei*, 28.

60. Enomoto, *Genji monogatari no sōshiji*, 145.

61. A woodblock printed edition was published in 1677. A handy modern edition has been published by Kōdansha. It is perhaps misleading to speak of "terminological consistency," since scholars to this day have not reached a consensus, strictly speaking, on what exactly constitutes a *sōshiji* passage.

62. Quoted in Enomoto, *Genji monogatari no sōshiji*, 151.

63. Translated also as "plain" or "standard narrative" in an informative essay on the narrative levels in *monogatari* by Noguchi Takehiko, who also

relies on Hagiwara. See Noguchi, "The Substratum Constituting Monogatari: Prose Structure and Narrative in the *Genji Monogatari*."

64. As Mieke Bal notes in her fine though formalistic study, *Narratology*
(pp. 129–130). Bal distinguishes between "narration" and "description."

65. Let us remember that the field of narratology as a specific subject of
study in the West is a relatively recent phenomenon: "During the past fifteen
years, the theory of narrative has displaced the theory of the novel as a topic
of central concern in literary study." Wallace Martin, *Recent Theories of
Narrative*, 15. Attitudes toward "narrative" began to change in the latter part
of the 1960s and the early 1970s. It was considered then (and still is
considered today) a "marginal" aspect of the marginal subject of "literature."
Among the precursors of the change were Northrop Frye and Wayne Booth,
who argued for the broadening of critical perspectives from the previously
valorized "realistic novel" to prose fiction in general (Frye), and for a closer
examination of the communicational, or "rhetorical," aspects of fictional
writing (Booth). With the work of writers like Roland Barthes, Tzvetan
Todorov, Gérard Genette, Seymour Chatman, Émile Benveniste, and the
Russian Formalists, discussions concerning the study of narrative and especially the issues surrounding narration became part of analytical frameworks
based on rewritings of scholars working in other disciplines: Ferdinand de
Saussure (one of the forefathers of the modern study of structuralist linguistics), Claude Lévi-Strauss (structuralist anthropology), and Vladimir Propp
(structural studies of folklore), among others. As noted in my introduction,
attitudes concerning narrative are moving away from a structuralist or
formalist projection and ways are being sought to refocus our attention on the
subjects of writing and enunciating within the context of such larger issues as
the construction (and suppression) of gender, race and ethnicity, class, and
nation. The notion of "narrative" ought to incorporate historical, imperialist,
epistemological, and gender-related issues and ought to be mindful of the
"worldliness" of the texts we study. The primary texts (there are many
others) are Roland Barthes, "Introduction to the Structural Analysis of
Narratives"; Tzvetan Todorov, *The Poetics of Prose;* Gérard Genette, *Figures of
Literary Discourse;* Émile Benveniste, *Problems in General Linguistics.* An important moment in the study of narrative comes with the Autumn 1980 and
Summer 1981 issues of *Critical Inquiry,* whose contributors included Hayden
White, Roy Schafer, Jacques Derrida, Frank Kermode, and Barbara Herrn-
stein Smith. The essays were later collected into a single volume, *On Narrative*
(edited by W. J. T. Mitchell). See also Fredric Jameson's elegant study of
structuralism and Russian Formalism, *The Prison House of Language.* Raymond
Williams provides an extremely useful summary of the issues in "Crisis in
English Studies," in his *Writing in Society,* 192–211. And many writers have
relied on the work of the linguist A. J. Greimas for narrative terms—Jameson
effectively utilizes Greimas's famous semiotic square or semantic rectangle.
See, for example, Jameson, *Prison House,* 163–168; Fredric Jameson, *The
Political Unconscious,* 254–257; and also Algirdas Julien Greimas, *On Meaning,*
especially Jameson's foreword, vi–xxii. Finally, one study still basically
within the area of "narratology" that nevertheless attempts to take into

consideration aspects of later poststructuralist and postimperialist problematics is Steven Cohan and Linda Shires, *Telling Stories*, especially chapters 5 and 6.

66. Tamagami Takuya, "Genji monogatari ondokuron josetsu," and "Genji monogatari no dokusha—monogatari ondokuron."

67. "Meiji people read *shōsetsu* and even newspapers out loud." Tamagami, "Josetsu," in *GMH* Suppl. 1: 147. Also referring to the Meiji period, Irokawa Daikichi, in private conversation, tells of his father reading the newspaper out loud each day. In a remark concerning the opening lines of chapter 2 of *Genji*, the "Hahakigi" (The Broom Tree) chapter, Tamagami explains the difference between reading out loud (which appeals to the ear) and reading silently (which appeals to the eye): "The passage [when read aloud] does not express an idea thought out in advance. . . . We must not look at all the words in the passage at once as a flat surface and attempt to dissect them. We must not attach too much importance to the material word and certainly not to the printed version of the material word. . . . When we listen to a text being read aloud, the word being uttered at each moment gains primacy; the others fade into memory, which in turn aligns them in order of proximity and distance; the words yet to be heard lie in the darkness of anticipation." In *GMH* 1:158.

68. Tamagami, "Josetsu," in *GMH* Suppl. 1:150. The primary audience, for Tamagami, are the princesses at the Rear Palace. One of Tamagami's examples of evaluative "comment" appears in the "Sakaki" (The Sacred Tree, 10) chapter, in the famous scene where the unrefined minister of the right discovers that Genji has spent the night with Oborozukiyo: "Indeed, it would be more proper for him [the minister] to speak after entering the room completely" (*NKBZ* 2:137).

69. Tamagami, "Josetsu," in *GMH* Suppl. 1:149.

70. Ibid., 153. Nakano Kōichi effectively argues that such an audience was much too limited and that the main *monogatari* audience was the composer's peers, i.e., other *nyōbō*. See "Kodai monogatari no dokusha no mondai," and *"Genji monogatari* no sōshiji to monogatari ondokuron."

71. Tamagami, "Josetsu," in *GMH* Suppl. 1:150.

72. Ibid., 152. The identity of the *Genji* narrator has been surmised, based on the discernible honorific level of the narrating and other matters, to be an old woman who had once been an attendant to Genji.

73. Tamagami identifies four written styles in circulation during the Heian period: texts written in Chinese by native Chinese, texts written in Chinese by Japanese (possibly with an eye toward Chinese readers), texts written in *manabun*, and texts written in *kanabun*. "Josetsu," in *GMH* Suppl. 1:145.

74. According to Tamagami, the case of the late-eleventh-century text *Sagoromo monogatari*, with its extraordinarily complicated textual lineages, demonstrates the fate that might have befallen *Genji* had it not been blessed (or cursed) by the collating activities of a Teika or a Mitsuyuki/Chikayuki. The situation accords with Mitani Eiichi's remark on the relation between the texts' reception and their variants.

75. Critics of the "proposal," notably Nakano Kōichi, have gone even further in their attempts to catalogue the *sōshiji*. See Nakano, *"Genji monogatari no sōshiji to monogatari ondokuron."*

76. Tamagami, "Josetsu," in *GMH* Suppl. 1:147. On Tamagami's valorization of orality, see below.

77. Such a stance cannot make visible the "difference" of *Genji* from other *monogatari*, a topic with which I deal in the sections of *Genji* itself.

78. As stated previously, the word in Japanese for "read" (*yomu*) inscribes, especially in regard to poetry, that very ambiguity between "reading" and "composing." Also, we have seen that calligraphic practice was one common way texts were appreciated, the act producing a techno-interpretive reading.

79. Tamagami, "Josetsu," in *GMH* Suppl. 1:147.

80. Ibid., emphasis added.

81. The scenes together with sections of written narration constitute the early-twelfth-century *Tale of Genji Picture Scroll* (*Genji monogatari emaki*), attributed to Fujiwara no Takayoshi.

82. I also use the term "narrator," although I do not intend by it any anthropomorphically determined personage but rather a "deictically" determinate position.

83. See Noel Burch, *To the Distant Observer: Form and Meaning in the Japanese Cinema*, chapter 7.

84. A recent study by Victor Mair provides further support for thinking the relationship between linguistic tense and picture and reinforces the necessity of reintroducing the pictorial element. Referring to the practice of "storytelling with pictures in ancient India," Mair cites such passages from the *Mahabhasya* of Patanjali as, "'He has Kamsa killed (i.e., he narrates the killing of Kamsa)' and 'He has Bali bound (i.e., he narrates the binding of Bali),'" and remarks that "it is proper to use the present tense, even though these events took place in the remote past, because the *saubhika* ('illusionists') and *granthika* (reciters) represent them as actually happening in front of the audience." He then includes a longer passage providing such comments as "[Here too the present is employed, for] in the pictures one sees the lifting of the arm and the falling of the blow as well as Kamsa being dragged about," and "while they delineate their destinies . . . from the beginning to end, they present the incidents as happening in the present time within the knowledge [of the audience]." Victor H. Mair, *Painting and Performance*, 17–18. For a brief discussion of *etoki*, including *kamishibai* (picture-card show), see also pp. 111–116. It can also be argued, as Fukuda Takashi has done, that the presence of explicit references in *Genji* to the visual proves that visual matters are irrelevant to it. *Genji monogatari no disukuuru*, 203–205.

85. Not in the sense of a heuristic plot that one reconstructs as the effect of the given narrative scheme but rather among the variations in textual lineages.

86. Gérard Genette, *Narrative Discourse*, 217.

87. Ibid., 218.

88. Ibid., 219. The notion of "transparency" is a problem Genette chooses to ignore.

89. Perhaps as in a No play or other stage performance. There are similarities between what I am describing and poststructuralist analyses of story and discourse. See, for example, Jonathan Culler's discussion in *The Pursuit of Signs: Semiotics, Literature, Deconstruction*, 169–187.

90. For example, Nakano Kōichi's articles, cited earlier, and Mitani Kuniaki, "Genji monogatari ni okeru ⟨katari⟩ no kōzō—⟨washa⟩ to ⟨katarite⟩ aruiwa 'sōshiji' ron hihan no tame no joshō."

91. For a study, which relies on Mitani's work, of "consciousness" in *Genji*, see Amanda Mayer Stinchecum, "Who Tells the Tale?—'Ukifune': A Study in Narrative Voice." An essay that follows Hagiwara and structuralist perspectives is Noguchi Takehiko's "The Substratum Constituting Mono-gatari." Mitani's work has depended on a conception of the Heian language as a *written* language, thereby tending to overlook the issue of orality. A representative essay by Mitani is "Monogatari to ⟨kaku koto⟩—monogatari bungaku no imi sayō aruiwa fuzai no bungaku."

92. Cf. "The process of reading is already not without consequences: two readings of a book are never identical. In reading, we trace a passive writing; we add and suppress, in the text read, and what we want or do not want to find there; reading is no longer immanent, once there is a reader." Tzvetan Todorov, *Introduction to Poetics*, 4.

93. Fujii, "Sōshiji no," 36.

94. See the discussion of themes in the Introduction.

95. See Richard Hideki Okada, "Domesticating *The Tale of Genji*."

7   Narrating the Private: "Kiritsubo"

1. *Nihon koten bungaku zenshū* (*NKBZ*), 1:93; unless otherwise noted references throughout the following chapters are to the *NKBZ* text and all translations are mine.

2. As it emphasizes each present moment of narrating, the tenseless *hiragana* narrating mode continually creates a sense of suspense, always keeping the reader-listener off balance, creating a constant sense of anticipation, a strong, "proleptic" sense, in Genette's useful term (*Narrative Discourse*, 40). The question, "Was it because she had to bear the brunt of all that rancor?" does precisely that. The reader-listener is kept guessing what direction the now-occurring, open-ended narrating will take. To the degree that the suggested possibilities are later realized, the mode may be thought of as constitutive of a "prophetic" quality that easily accommodates and reinforces passages of overt prediction and prophesy. That fact, I believe, is not unrelated to the movement we witnessed in *Ise monogatari*, a text I characterized as one that always begins. The final line of the passage quoted above incorporates precisely such a maneuver in its mention of "precedent."

3. The best discussion of this and of the opening chapter in general is Masuda Katsumi, *Kazan rettō no shisō*, chapter 8.

4. *Genji monogatari hyōshaku* (*GMH*), 1:33.

5. The Chinese emperor's obsession had disastrous consequences for the country. See the discussion below.

6. For a list of the emperor's consorts, see *Kakaishō*, 189–190, and Tamagami's corrections in *GMH*, suppl. 1:407–414.

7. The Engi era (901–922) came to signify a golden age, as the term *Engi no chi* (Glorious Engi Rule) suggests.

8. Edward G. Seidensticker, trans., *The Tale of Genji*, 3.

9. See also the celebrated translation by Arthur Waley, *The Tale of Genji*.

10. Such forces later reappear in the menacing form of a phenomenon known as *mono no ke*, a kind of spirit possession exemplified most consistently and terrifyingly by the figure of the Rokujō Lady. If what I have just stated seems an overreading, note the appearance of the word *mono*—which often suggests the darker side of the supernatural—in the phrase that appears following mention of the *kōi's* rapidly worsening condition: *mono-gokorobosoge ni*, which I have translated "apparently plagued by unaccountable feelings of despondency."

11. It forms an important part of the famous "defense of monogatari" (*monogatari-ron*) in the "Hotaru" chapter. Discrepancies of the type noted above appear often in Seidensticker's version. The normal tendency has been to brush aside such problems as an unavoidable feature of any task of translation and to do so especially with regard to the work of an experienced and (justly) celebrated interpreter. Most of the items discussed above surely could have been incorporated into the translation, with the addition whenever necessary of explanatory notes to guide the modern reader, but it would have required a radical departure from established practice. Building on Richard Bowring's groundbreaking efforts in his translation of *Murasaki Shikibu nikki*, translations of Japanese literature into other languages would benefit from more instances of experimental daring. See Bowring, *Murasaki Shikibu: Her Diary and Poetic Memoirs*. It is particularly important that narrational and tense constraints and other apparent anomalies be preserved, especially if they might allow readers to engage more of those areas of the text that are resistant to naturalizing impulses, which, as we are now learning, are accomplices of imperialist and patriarchal agendas.

12. Again, the movement of anticipation turns directly into completed action, i.e., a new state. We later learn that the *kōi's* father is kin to the Akashi priest.

13. For a discussion of the fact that Murasaki Shikibu's own mother seems to have died soon after she was born and her subsquent close relationship with her father, see Itō Hiroshi, *Genji monogatari no genten*, 31 ff.

14. Most all journeys in *Genji* are of a nondescriptive, nondiegetic variety. A character departs and arrives, but the middle is elided. Sometimes a character's departure is noted, but the narrating remains at a time prior to that point. A spectacular instance appears in the "Suma" chapter, where we are first told that Genji leaves the capital to go into exile and then, in an

exceptionally lengthy passage, the narrating reverts to a time prior to his departure to tell about his farewell visits to various women.

15. The third waka mode was called *nazuraFe uta*. See Chapter 3.

16. Tamagami makes the suggestive comment that, judging from her citations of Chinese texts (scholarship meaning competence in Chinese letters), the grandmother comes from a scholarly lineage. He also notes that citations of such texts appear frequently in *Genji* but that those by female characters are rare. *GMH* 1:68. In any case, Tamagami's observation connects the *kōi* with other women from scholarly families—Murasaki Shikibu, Sei Shōnagon, and Lady Ise—and she becomes thereby an excellent example of the kind of woman discussed in the "Hahakigi" (Broom Tree) chapter. The subversive effects of her being made consort would then take on a completely different cast.

17. The reference is to a poem cited frequently in the *Genji* text, a *Gosenshū* "Miscellaneous" poem (1103) by Fujiwara no Kanesuke, Murasaki Shikibu's great-grandfather:

> A parent's heart   resides not in darkness;
>   yet on the matter of the path
> on which to set forth a child   one has always lost one's way
> [Fito no oya no/kokoro Fa yami ni/aranedomo/ko wo omoFu miti ni/
> madoFinuru kana]

The specific reference is to the dilemma, a recurring one in *Genji*, of whether or not to send a child into court service. The sentiment would of course be understood immediately by the *Genji* audience, many of whose parents faced that very dilemma. The kinship tie between Murasaki Shikibu and the author of the poem has prompted one *Genji* scholar to conclude, given the rich poetic lineages involved, that the *Genji* text ought to be read as the creation of a family (a "house") rather than the view of a single person. See Oka Kazuo, *Genji monogatari no kisoteki kenkyū*, 35.

18. Seidensticker gives the opposite interpretation: "It was, he says, an intensity of passion such as to startle the world, and perhaps for that very reason it was fated to be brief" (*Tale of Genji*, 10).

19. Compare Seidensticker: "He cannot think of anything he has done to arouse such resentment, he says, and so he must live with resentment which seems without proper cause" (p. 10). The emperor is fully aware of the consequences of his actions.

20. In Seidensticker's version of the passage, not only does the prominence of his third-person narration obliterate the Myōbu's and the emperor's voices but his translation of the comment on a "former life" as "burden of guilt" conveys the wrong impression. The attribution of the inexplicable events in this life to bonds from a former life is a common *monogatari* response that doesn't necessarily imply guilt.

21. The word *Furu* can mean "fall" or "shake." It forms, in its latter meaning, an *engo* with "bell." "Bell crickets" are now called "pine crickets."

22. Two possible citations have been suggested. One is by Lady Ise, from the *Ise Collection*:

```
            this house of mine
                others will think it
                deep within the clouds
            the rain and the tears too      keep falling, falling
```
[waga yado ya/kumo no naka nimo/omoFuramu/ame mo namida mo/Furi
ni koso Fure]

The other is by Konoe no Kōi, from *Gosenshū,* "Autumn" (277):

```
            onto my sleeves       thoroughly drenched
                by the pounding showers of summer
            falls the heavy dew      of a desolate autumn
```
[samidare ni/nurenisi sode ni/itodosiku/tuyu okisoFuru/aki no wabisisa]

The second poem was apparently composed and offered to Emperor Daigo
when he paid a visit upon the death of the poet's mother.

23. Po Chü-i's poem "Song of Everlasting Sorrow," *Ch'ang hen ke* (J.
Chōgonka), tells of how T'ang Emperor Hsüan Tsung's love for a particular
consort, Yang Kuei-fei (J. Yōkihi), caused a country to collapse and eventually forced the emperor to witness her execution.

24. Po Chü-i's story of the T'ang emperor and his concubine is actually
set in an earlier time (of a "Han king," *han wang*) and considered to be a major
inspiration for the "Kiritsubo" chapter. Although it is difficult to speak of the
poem (or any other sources) as having "influenced" the *Genji* text or simply to
list similarities, a couple of aspects of Po Chü-i's poem held particular appeal
for the Heian reader: (1) the historical disjunction, which may have suggested
a similar strategy to the *Genji* author; (2) the degree to which the Han emperor
esteems beauty (*chung shih,* in the first line) over all else, an emphasis
underlying the Kiritsubo Emperor's actions; and (3) the emperor's grief over
his consort's death and his dispatching of a Taoist wizard to retrieve the spirit
of the dead person. We must also note the native channels through which the
emperor rereads the poem: illustrations by Emperor Uda and poems by
Tsurayuki and Ise. The Chinese text is included in Shimizu Yoshiko and
Ishida Jōji, *Genji monogatari, Shinchō nihon koten shūsei* (SNKS), 1:325–331.

25. See my "Domesticating *The Tale of Genji,*" 64–65, for a fuller discussion of the previous passage in the context of Shirane's reading of it. See also
Haruo Shirane, *The Bridge of Dreams: A Poetics of 'The Tale of Genji,'* 121.

26. We first learn of the Akashi family in the "Wakamurasaki" (Young
Lavender) chapter, but they and the lay priest are not fully introduced until
the "Akashi" chapter. Several other similar cases are mentioned in the text.

27. Genji himself is eventually accorded the status of Jun-Dajōtennō, a
sort of ad hoc retired emperor. Well known for his sponsorship of artistic
activities after he retired from office and took the tonsure, Emperor Uda
qualifies as a prime historical referent for the Kiritsubo Emperor.

28. Uda's mother was the daughter of Prince Nakano, the twelfth son of
Emperor Kammu. Michizane, himself appointed ambassador of a planned
mission, nevertheless led the opposition to the continued sending of envoys
(*kentōshi*) to China and was instrumental in having the practice abolished in
984. Regardless of why the mission was abandoned, its abandonment did in

fact contribute greatly to a renewed emphasis on native culture. See Tamagami's discussion in *GMH* 1:77–78. As noted previously, Michizane is also considered to have inspired the fictional Genji figure. For an informed discussion of the abandonment of the missions, see Robert Borgen, *Sugawara no Michizane and the early Heian Court*, 240–253.

29. The mention of "precedent" (*tamesi*) earlier in the first chapter is an underlying concern of the *Genji* narrator and is related, some believe, to the fact that the Kiritsubo Emperor is a fictional (and literal) descendant of the historical emperor. The "Testament" also recommends that Daigo seek the advice of Michizane and Ki no Haseo, among others. The *Genji* text, in fact, later mentions Uda's "admonitions" (see below). The Kiritsubo Emperor also leaves a testament for his son, the Suzaku Emperor. See the "Sakaki" chapter, *NKBZ* 2:96–97.

30. The *Yamato* text, believed to have been completed around the mid-tenth century, consists of sections of poetry and poetry-inspired legends. The first *Yamato* section also refers to Lady Ise (as Ise no go). *NKBZ* 8:269. Many of the sections, beginning with the first three, make reference to Daigo. Emperor Uda, then, becomes a point of convergence for the figures and issues addressed in this study.

31. Historically, the Kōrokan at the capital (one was also built in Dazaifu) ceased to be used some time after the last Korean visit to the capital in 928. See Bowring, *Murasaki Shikibu*, 20.

32. The identity of the former emperor is unclear from the *Genji* text. Tamagami's reconstruction (following previous commentators and generally accepted by later ones) of the lineage behind the text makes one of the Kiritsubo Emperor's older brothers, both of whom are sons of the emperor who reigned prior to the former emperor, the first retired emperor (*iti no win*). The latter term appears only once in *Genji*, in the "Momiji no Ga" (An Autumn Excursion, 7) chapter, where the narrator mentions the places to which Genji pays a New Year's visit. *GMH* 2:277–278; *NKBZ* 1:396; Seidensticker, *Tale of Genji*, 138. That would make Fujitsubo the Kiritsubo Emperor's niece and Genji's first cousin. *GMH* 1:123–124.

33. The brother will be mentioned later in "Wakamurasaki" as the Murasaki Lady's father.

34. I discuss the related question of "substitution" in Chapter 11.

35. Eleven by Western count.

36. Found in all of the texts discussed, juxtapositions are sites that demand readers to construct the possible links and associations from the given items.

37. See Norma Field, *The Splendor of Longing*, 168.

38. *Ise, dan* 69, *NKBZ* 8:191–193.

39. As scholars have pointed out, the Genji-Fujitsubo pairing also participates in the *onarigami* belief that the feminine half of a brother-sister pair is crucial to the governing of a country, precisely what happens later with Genji and Fujitsubo. The sister provides the spiritual power necessary for the establishment of political power. See Iha Fuyū, *Onarigami no shima*, and Fujii Sadakazu, *Monogatari no kekkon*, 135–150.

40. The emperor also encourages Genji to attend a gathering in "Hana no en" (The Festival of the Cherry Blossoms, 8), thus unwittingly putting him and Oborozukiyo together.

8 Feminine Representation and Critique: "Hahakigi"

1. *Nihon koten bungaku zenshū* (NKBZ), 1:129

2. The term *narabi no maki* appears in medieval commentaries beginning with *Kakaishō* (Shirane cites *Genji shaku*) and stands in contrast to the term *hon no maki* (main or root chapters). Scholars conceive of the difference in chapter clusters using terms and concepts such as orthodox line/heterodox line, Murasaki line/Tamakazura line, Kiritsubo line/Hahakigi line, extended *monogatari*/segmented *monogatari*, and main conception/auxiliary conception. Abe Akio's formulation of the "sixteen Kiritsubo chapters" and the "sixteen Hahakigi chapters" takes the latter group to be governed by the "rainy night critique" (*Genji monogatari kenkyū josetsu*, 939–1009). The *narabi* chapters are referred to as "ancillary" by Shirane and "minor" by Field. See Haruo Shirane, *The Bridge of Dreams: A Poetics of The Tale of Genji*, 87; Norma Field, *The Splendor of Longing in The Tale of Genji*, 87.

3. Shirane, *Bridge of Dreams*, 62.

4. See Chapter 9.

5. Mitani Kuniaki, "*Genji monogatari* ni okeru 'katari' no kōzō—'washa' to 'katarite' aruiwa 'sōshiji' ron hihan no tame no joshō," 188.

6. The *sōshiji* at the end of "Yūgao" (Evening Faces, 4) combines with the "Hahakigi" opening to constitute the "Hahakigi" group (*Hahakigi sanjō*). At the close of "Yūgao," the narrator remarks,

> Concerning such trivial matters, I empathized with the fact that he had taken great pains to keep them securely hidden and had refrained from letting any of it leak out; [I have revealed it] because there seem to be those who would interpret it as looking like made-up incidents (*tukurigoto mekite*) if even we who had been with him were wont to praise him just because he was the son of an emperor; I see no way of avoiding the crime (*tumi*) of having spoken too frankly. (1:269)

The comments touch on the storyteller's dilemma: to speak the truth is to reveal secrets for which the narrator will be subject to punishment; but not to do so and not to be taken seriously would be worse. Here we see again that *hiragana* writing often had to defend itself as a legitimate mode, as the transmitter of the obverse side (*ura*) of life. Another major *sōshiji* passage is the following, from "Takekawa" (Bamboo River, 44):

> The following, left as an unsolicited story by those mischievous and dull-headed gossips, still alive, who were among those in service at the residence of the succeeding grand minister [Higekuro] and thus distant from Genji and his family. It is nothing like the stories told by the women connected with Murasaki, though the former say that the inaccuracies in the account of Genji's descendants are due to the unrestrained babbling of

women older than themselves, who have grown senile—which is true, I wonder? (*NKBZ* 5:53)

7. *Genji monogatari hyōshaku* (*GMH*), 1:160.

8. Scholars are divided on the issue of a previous encounter, although most opinions, including those in older commentaries, read a previous encounter. Kifune Shigeaki, for example, argues that it is the first meeting. "Fujitsubo no miya zō shūfukuron—Wakamurasaki no maki no issetsu no saishin—," 41. Mitani Kuniaki, on the other hand, argues that it is not. "Fujitsubo jiken no hyōgen kōzō," 291.

9. Another indication of his coolness toward his "principal wife." Genji presumably lives at the palace and commutes to his wife's house.

10. See the discussion of *Ise dan* 1 in Chapter 5. The interplay between Narihira and Genji will continue throughout the chapters that tell of Genji's life.

11. Certain days were designated for abstinence. Factors (such as bad omens and dreams) could require additional days. Activities were proscribed, and everyone usually remained indoors with a sign on which was written the word *monoimi* hung on the gate.

12. Reference had already been made in the "Kiritsubo" chapter to a Kurōdo no Shōshō, who commentators believe is the same person. The irony in the characterization "born of a princess" becomes clear when we remember Genji's mother's low birth, which keeps problematic the emphasis both on the maternal lineage and on the deception behind appearances. I refer to Genji's companion as both Tō no Chūjō and the captain.

13. The figures of the Fujitsubo Consort and the Aoi Lady are hinted at throughout the discussion.

14. Such a woman is precisely what the Captain finds in the Ōmi Lady. As for parents doting on daughters and keeping their shortcomings a secret, Genji discovers one such parent (the Suzaku Emperor) when he decides to marry the Third Princess.

15. The so-called middle ranks are primarily the fourth and fifth ranks, although they sometimes extend into part of the sixth rank.

16. Seidensticker's interpretation, "The discussion progressed, and included a number of rather unconvincing points," dilutes the strategic thrust of *kikinikuki* (painful to hear, unworthy of listening to), a nodding disclaimer to the reader-listener designed to pique interest (*Tale of Genji*, 23).

17. It is not certain whether the first passage is spoken by Tō no Chūjō or Uma no Kami. While most commentators have taken it to be spoken by the latter, the revised edition of the Shōgakkan text attributes it to the former, which makes sense in that it appears to continue the response to Genji's question left suspended when the newcomers arrived.

18. Japanese scholarship on the "critique" derives from Hagiwara Hiromichi (Kōdō), whose *Genji monogatari hyōshaku* was a landmark publication. Major later treatments are Fujioka Sakutarō, *Kokubungaku zenshi: Heianchō hen*; Shimazu Hisamoto, *Taiyaku genji monogatari kōwa*; Abe Akio,

Genji monogatari kenkyū josetsu; and Fujii Sadakazu, "Amayo no shinasadame kara hotaru no maki no 'monogatari ron' e."

19. *NKBZ* 1:135. Most modern editions take the speaker to be the newly arrived director. I follow the most recent modern *Genji* text and take it to be a continuation of the captain's speech since it responds to Genji's question. See *Kan'yaku nihon no koten (KYNK)* 1:47.

20. The comments thus far already seem to be looking forward to the most prominent *zuryō* in the tale, the Akashi lay priest, who gains success for his family by carefully grooming his daughter and marrying her off to Genji.

21. It is important, I think, to note that the men are not simply discussing women *in general* but have in mind a specific purpose: marriage. Remember from Chapter 6 that Heian "marriages" were quite different from modern arrangements.

22. Teresa de Lauretis's essay "Desire in Narrative" is instructive here, especially her notion of a "twofold process of identification," the "masculine, active, identification with the "gaze" and the "passive, feminine identification with the image." *Alice Doesn't: Feminism, Semiotics, and Cinema,* 144.

23. *Kugyō* and *kandatime* designate the fourth and fifth ranks and sixth-rank *kurōdo* (chamberlains). *Tenjōbito* designates those of the third rank and above as well as the consultants. The *jige* were those of sixth rank and lower, who were not allowed to enter The Courtiers' Hall.

24. Cf. "The individual's exact niche in the social hierarchy was finally determined by a combination of rank and office." William H. and Helen C. McCullough, *A Tale of Flowering Fortunes* 2:794. The extent to which Genji's keeping Yūgiri at a low rank affected the latter's self-esteem and socio-sexual mobility is a negative case in point. See the "Otome" chapter in Seidensticker, *Tale of Genji,* 361–362.

25. A contraction of *sa (m)uma no kami,* head of the Left (Imperial) Stables.

26. The remark recalls the first *dan* of *Ise.* In *Genji* Yūgao will be just that sort of woman, as will the Murasaki Lady and many others, including the "Uji" women.

27. That is, without the divided skirt (*hakama*).

28. *GMH,* 180–181. Although Tamagami rejects the interpretation, it remains, nevertheless, an intriguing one.

29. Seidensticker, *Tale of Genji,* 24.

30. Other ambivalences include the Fujiwara (Tō no Chūjō)–Genji situation discussed before, the "foster" or "pseudo-kinship" relations, and the public-private nexus.

31. Genji's desire to train and teach Murasaki may derive from the instability of the mid-Heian social system that required the institution of personalized methods of teaching to insure the maintenance of family lines.

32. Commentators have noted that the director's narrating omits honorifics as if his remarks were of a general nature, closer to the position of the general narrating than a part of the immediate deictic arrangements of the characters. The omissions might also be due to male gendering.

33. A similar situation will occur when Genji discovers the Murasaki Lady.

34. Trustworthiness turns out to be valued more than birth or appearance.

35. There is disagreement among commentators whether the "person" in question is male (*NKBZ*) or female (see the *Genji* texts in *KYNK, Shinchō nihon koten shūsei* [*SNKS*, Shimizu Yoshiko and Ishida Jōji, eds., 8 vols. (1976–1985)], and Tamagami's *GMH* 1:197, or a general reference to either *NKBT* [Yamagishi Tokuhei, ed.]). See *GMH* 1:197. Since the Chūjo seems to be responding to the director's remarks and the latter was referring to the woman's position, it seems better to regard the "person" as male.

36. Tamagami cites passages like these to prove that tales were appreciated mainly by reading them aloud to others who looked at illustrations.

37. The *Genji* text is filled with references to *mukashi monogatari* that serve to distance *Genji* from them in an appeal for a different kind of narrating.

38. Seidensticker translates the captain's manner as containing "something slightly comical." Although humor pervades the narratings, the *monogatari* mode, revelatory of the underside of life, tells of that which cannot be expressed elsewhere.

39. As noted, the *Genji* narrator continually cites older *monogatari* to suggest a fundamental difference between those and hers.

40. Genji thinks she belongs to the lowest ranks, but she is actually the daughter of a high-ranking (third rank) middle captain who has fallen on hard times, thus putting her among the middle ranks. See *GMH* 1:485.

41. The common feeling that women are not supposed to show their expertise in Chinese learning lest they become the objects of ridicule appears from time to time in the *Genji* tale. That is not to say, of course, that the *Genji* narrator feels that Chinese learning is worthless or that women should refrain completely from acquiring it. Recall, for example, the *kōi's* mother's speech. A comment in "Otome" is also instructive: "I have abridged the account [of an occasion where Chinese poems were composed], since I would hate to be considered impudent for speaking of matters a woman can know nothing about" (*NKBZ* 3:21).

42. The *nadesiko* and the *tokonatu* (which appears in the second poem), translated as "wild pink" or "wild carnation," are believed to be the same flower. In the present context the first refers to the child (*nade* from *nadu*, "to pet," and *ko*, "child"), and the second, with its play on *toko* (bed), refers to the mother.

43. The poem contains the further play on *siku* (to lay out) to go along with the sexual implication in the word "bed."

44. The phrase is a citation of a *Kokinshū* "Summer" poem (167) by Ōshikōchi no Mitsune:

> I know not to let   even a speck of dust settle on our bed
>   where my beloved and I have slept
>   from the time our intimacy bloomed
> like the *tokonatsu* [bed/summer] flower

[tiri wo dani/suwezi to zo omoFu/sakisi yori/imo to waga nuru/tokonatu no Fana]

It is a pledge that the man's visits will be so frequent that no dust can settle on the marital bed.

45. Some read in the woman's verse a citation to an anonymous *Gosenshū* (230) "Autumn" poem:

> this bed   where the herd boy
>   spends nights those nights so rare;
> my sleeves used to wipe the dust away
>   are now damp with dewy tears
> [Fikobosi no/mare ni aFu yo no/tokonatu Fa/uti FaraFu sode mo/ tuyukekarikeri]

The poems employs the standard play on *aki* ("autumn" and "become tired of"). The "storm" refers to the threats from the captain's principal wife.

46. The *Genji katari*, then, can be read as reactivating the sense of *mono* and reenacting a mode that questions all *kata*, "prescribed forms," which the middle ranks consistently defy.

47. Genji, for example, manages to establish long-lasting liaisons with the Lavender Lady, the Orange Blossoms Lady, the Akashi Lady, and the Safflower Princess, but those "successes" are negated by his "failures" with Utsusemi, Yūgao, and Tamakazura, his unhappy marriage to the Aoi Lady, his rocky relationship with the Rokujō Lady, his ambivalent relationship with the Fujitsubo Consort, and a final disaster with the Third Princess. Even Genji's "successes" are marked by distinct difficulties and sorrows. Kaoru's situation will be even more tortuously complicated.

48. Whether similar object relations would have obtained had the text been written by men is difficult to say, given our temporal distance and relative paucity of sources. On the basis of the extant texts, it seems possible to conclude that women writers do seem to represent women in greater diversity than do men. I am aware of the risk of reifying the notion of "subject/enunciative positions," but I feel it is a necessary risk, as some have begun recently to argue. See Diana Fuss, *Essentially Speaking*, especially chapter 5.

49. Recent feminist writings, as I have noted, have been clarifying the notion of such constructions and their relation to power (patriarchy), and *Genji* scholarship would, I feel, benefit from an engagement with such perspectives.

50. The former are the *Shih chi, Han shu,* and *Hou han shu;* the latter are the *Shih ching, Li chi, Chun ch'iu, I ching,* and *Shu ching.*

51. The phrase is *kore ni,* referring presumably to the director's remarks. Some texts have *kore Fa,* "as for this/her," which would refer to the Fujitsubo Consort.

52. Here Genji's reaction can be read together with the comments in "Kiritsubo" as a strong indication that a sexual union had already taken place. That would make their encounter in "Wakamurasaki" the second such meeting.

53. As we also saw in the Myōbu section in "Kiritsubo."

9 A Figure of Narrating: Tamakazura

1. The property was originally the Rokujō Lady's and later inherited by Akikonomu. In terms of land rights, too, Genji is "extraneous" to it. See Fujii Sadakazu, *Genji monogatari no shigen to genzai*, chapter 8, "Hikaru Genji monogatari shudairon."

2. See the discussion in Haruo Shirane, *The Bridge of Dreams: A Poetics of 'The Tale of Genji,'* 28–30.

3. We learn of her father's rank and office in the "Yūgao" chapter (chapter 4). See *Nihon koten bungaku zenshū (NKBZ)*, 1:259, 261.

4. A *zuryō* connection is made explicitly in the "Yūgao" chapter. Tamakazura's attendants (she was not living with her mother at the time) are unaware of the mother's death, and Genji, wanting to keep matters quiet, forbids Ukon (Yūgao's closest attendant and daughter of her wet nurse— Ukon is the only one who was with the mother at the end) to report the death to the household and places her into Murasaki's service. The attendants at Tamakazura's residence remark, "Perhaps, it occurs to them, a womanizing son of a provincial governor, frightened by the captain (Tō no kimi), has taken her away with him directly to some far off region" (*NKBZ* 1:267).

5. She and her father, Tō no Chūjō, are the only two accorded that attribute in the tale.

6. Tamakazura is referred to by the bamboo planted inside Genji's hedge, and bamboo is one of the plants in the garden of Hanachirusato's quarter where Tamakazura is later placed.

7. The term *yūsoku*, as noted, is used for a variety of matters: the arts, scholarship, bureaucratic organization, precedent, ritual, and culture in general. Seidensticker's "ours is a good day for music" conveys one significa- tion of the term (*Tale of Genji*, 416).

8. Murai Yasuhiko notes that after the official histories (*Rikkokushi*) cease to be written, individual diaries written in Chinese take their place. The first of such diaries is *Uda tennō nikki*, written by Emperor Uda (he adds that in China emperors did not keep diaries), followed by the diaries of emperors Daigo and Murakami. It was believed that records of daily events could serve to instruct later generations. The latter two diaries became precisely such models of behavior. Murai also notes a general tendency during the late ninth and early tenth centuries for such dignitaries as Fujiwara no Tadahira and Morosuke to keep diaries, texts intended to serve as "mirrors" and "teach- ings" for a particular family, especially as public, political affairs become increasingly ritualized and privatized. It is at this time that there emerge *yūsoku*, or *yūsoku kojitsu*, texts designed for a particular family line. *Saikyūki* is one of the earliest and most representative of such texts. See Murai, *Ōchō bunka danshō*, 92–94.

9. The opening lines of the "Suetsumuhana" and "Tamakazura" chapters both pick up the reference to "dew" in Tō no Chūjō's narrating.

10. She was characterized as a "keepsake" (*katami*).

11. This is the only time in the *Genji* text when a female character is called by her surname.

12. For a discussion of the Lavender series, see Chapter 11. It is such

moments that deconstruct any clear binarism between a "Kiritsubo line" and a "Hahakigi line."

13. The element of competition with Tō no Chūjō also contributes to Genji's desire.

14. Since returning from exile to the mansion, built on grounds that used to belong to the Rokujō Lady, Genji has not engaged in any more affairs.

15. *NKBZ* 3:116.

16. See Chapter 7.

17. See Seidensticker, *Tale of Genji*, 359.

18. There is another "surplus" figure at Rokujō: Genji's daughter by the Akashi Lady, to whom Ukon compared Tamakazura at the beginning of the "Tamakazura" chapter (*NKBZ* 3:81). She is being cared for by her foster mother, the Murasaki Lady, even as her own mother occupies another quarter of the mansion. A comparison between that daughter and Tamakazura also implicitly constitutes much of the chapter.

19. *Monogatari ron—ron* meaning "argument," "exposition," "treatise," "opinion," or "discussion"—has been used to describe the conversations because common scholarly opinion holds that the putative *Genji* author, Murasaki Shikibu, is expounding her views of *monogatari* in the chapter.

20. Seidensticker's "Genji was famous" does not convey the power and stability suggested by the word (*Tale of Genji*, 430). Genji had been appointed grand minister (*dajōdaijin*) in the "Otome" (The Maiden) chapter.

21. *NKBZ* 3:187.

22. I.e., Tamakazura.

23. "Kochō" (Butterflies, 24).

24. Seidensticker's translation of Tamakazura as "Jeweled Chaplet" is apt in that "chaplet" signifies both a garland for the hair, and a string of beads. The notion of string fits well with the signification of *sudi*.

25. The verb used, *utiidu*, suggests revealing oneself, confession, and exposing one's true feelings.

26. The disjunction between the month and the prince's request suggests the extent of his ardor but also the *Genji* narrator's habit of constantly creating incongruous situations.

27. He is curious to see how such an accomplished man would go about his wooing (*midokoro arinamu kasi*). The situation is exactly the kind he hoped Tamakazura would create.

28. Genji, the narrating tells us, "is surely curious as to how the prince would respond" (*NKBZ* 3:189). As noted in the discussion of "Wakamurasaki," such women as Saishō were the tutors, nurses, guardians, and messengers who were indispensable to Heian society. Other important go-betweens who appear early on in the text include the attendant who recommended the Fujitsubo Consort, Yūgao's attendant Ukon, and Genji's male attendants Koremitsu and Yoshikiyo.

29. See, for example, *NKBZ* 3:190.

30. She would be carrying messages dictated by Genji, of course.

31. Or whether the bird sang out. The previous line goes, "One would most certainly have expected the *Fototogisu* to raise its cry [at a time like this]."

In other words, poems must have been composed by the prince and Tamakazura on the *hototogisu* (a summer bird), but the narrator did not bother to verify it. There is a play on the word *kiku* ("hear" and "ask"). The line could also mean that the bird's cries are bothersome (or poems on them overdone) so she didn't stay to listen for them.

32. Pretexts of the firefly incident include *Ise monogatari* (*dan* 39), *Utsuho monogatari* ("Hatsu aki" chapter), and *Yamato monogatari* (*dan* 40).

33. Seidensticker's interpretation is unwarranted: "He must be given credit for the fact that he held back from the final line" (p. 433). The text actually keeps the question suggestively open.

34. See Shimizu Yoshiko, "Genji monogatari no sakufū," *Kokugo kokubun*.

35. The phrasing is animated: "He both vivifies and murders [the prince] as he warns her" (3:195).

36. Not mentioned elsewhere.

37. This general will suddenly abduct Tamakazura prior to the beginning of the "Makibashira" (The Cypress Pillar, 31) chapter.

38. She wouldn't have seen such picture-tales in Tsukushi where she grew up. The word *sudi* resonates with the occurrences mentioned earlier, reinforcing her own textual line and function, as well as her "represented" line noted in the commentaries.

39. The extant version tells about an evil stepmother (a topic the *Genji* text continually gestures to) and about a Kazoe no Kami whom Tamakazura compares to Gen.

40. The comment recalls the director's remark in "Hahakigi" about a story that impressed him at first but that later seemed contrived; it also echoes sentiments discussed in the next chapter.

41. Genji's remark recalls the "Hahakigi" director (another male speaker) overhearing a story: For a discussion of the terms *ituFari, makoto,* and *soragoto,* see Abe Akio, "Hotaru no maki no monogatari-ron." According to Abe, *soragoto* refers to speech that is not grounded in real events and *ituFari* to speech that differs from someone else's speech. The latter is language based on language, whereas the former is based on a correspondence with life. Nihon bungaku kenkyū shiryō sōsho (*NBKSS* reprint, p. 294). The terms are not easy to keep distinct since "life" or "reality" is, to a crucial extent, also a verbal construct. The question of believability, whether or not a story is convincing, is the key quality being mentioned.

42. Referring to the six official histories (*Rikkokushi*), which were written in Chinese. Some scholars take it to refer to a particular text, *Nihon shoki* (The Chronicles of Japan).

43. "Hahakigi," *NKBZ* 1:13.

44. The gesture is not clearly stated in the text.

45. I.e., a father trying to seduce his daughter.

46. The phrase *kokoro nodokesi* is usually taken to mean either that Genji is not one to indulge in fleeting affairs or, more specifically, that he waited until the child Murasaki grew up before becoming sexually intimate with her. Seidensticker translates it as "the slow, plodding variety" (p. 438).

47. Here Seidensticker strays: "Genji might have been the hero of some rather more eccentric stories" (p. 438). The "uncommon variety" (*taguFi oFokaranu kotodomo*) results from the great differences among the middle ranks that we learned about in the Hahakigi "critique."

48. The phrase *na yomikikase tamaFiso* (do not have her listen to readings) suggests reading aloud. Genji is particularly concerned about the princess's education because he is grooming her, through Murasaki, to become an imperial consort.

49. She eventually goes to court, as Genji and the Murasaki Lady hope will happen to the Akashi Princess.

50. Genji's words serve to foretell the case of another "discovery," this time by Tō no Chūjō, of one of most comical figures in the tale, the Ōmi Lady. We discover her in the very next chapter, "Tokonatsu" (Wild Carnations, 26).

51. The question of intermediaries again becomes crucial. The narrator states that since the attendant whom Kashiwagi employs is undependable, he appeals his case to Yūgiri. We learned earlier that Tamakazura's servants leave much to be desired, and we will learn later that Kashiwagi is able to get a peep at the Third Princess because her attendants are also less than competent.

10 Aesthetics, Politics, and Genealogy

1. *Awase* literally means "match." The customary attitude that regarded the left as superior to the right often took precedence over any perceived superiority of entry, whether poem, tale, root, flower, or incense. An emperor's entry could further upset judgments.

2. Genji, who had acceded to the Rokujō Lady's request that he care for her daughter, has been acting as the daughter's guardian since the Lady's death in "Miotsukushi" (Channel Buoys, 14).

3. Gon Chūnagon, referred to here as the counselor.

4. Later in the chapter Genji singles out painting as the art form in which he most excelled.

5. The nickname, meaning "lover of autumn," derives from "Usugumo," when Genji asks if she prefers spring or autumn. See *Nihon koten bungaku zenshū* (NKBZ), 2:451–452.

6. Tamagami Takuya notes that the use of honorific language for the paintings shows that they are not ones that Genji himself collected but those handed down from his father, the Kiritsubo Emperor. *Genji monogatari hyōshaku* (GMH), 4:35. Genji's side presents old paintings with a decidedly lofty lineage; the counselor's side presents up-to-date ones.

7. One of the numerous consorts of the Han emperor Yuan-ti, Wang Chao-chün was forced to marry a barbarian king. The emperor had intended to select the ugliest of his women to present to his visitor. The emperor, however, knew of his (allegedly three thousand) women only on the basis of paintings done by artists heavily bribed by the women to make them look

beautiful. Wang Chao-chün, actually the most beautiful, did not resort to bribery, and therefore the artist depicted her in an ugly manner.

8. The famous reference to *Taketori* as the "parent of *monogatari*" appears here.

9. *GMH* 4:41.

10. For a note on the names, see *GMH* 4:41–42.

11. Tamagami notes that the first historical instance of a judge (*hanji*) occurs at the "Garden Contest" at the residence of Princess Kishi in the Third Year of Tenroku (972). *GMH* 4:45.

12. Genji and Fujitsubo discuss politics and Akikonomu at the end of "Miotsukushi" (Channel Buoys, 14).

13. The passage that follows again makes reference to historical personages.

14. Tamagami notes that reader-listeners of the time would have easily made the connection between the historical emperors and the *Genji* emperors: Daigo and his two sons, Suzaku and Murakami, are analogous to Kiritsubo and his two sons, Suzaku and Reizei. *GMH* 4:47. See also Richard Bowring, trans., *Murasaki Shikibu*, and Haruo Shirane, *The Bridge of Dreams*, 229.

15. Seidensticker's translation (*Tale of Genji*, 314). The McCulloughs give "Table Room" (*A Tale of Flowering Fortunes*, 843). The room was located in the emperor's private quarters, Seiryōden. Tamagami reasons suggestively that the location of the contest clearly shows that "picture contests" were considered a feminine activity and further that the narrator provides many details of the setting in order to evoke in the reader's mind the similarly arranged, precedent-setting "Tentoku Poetry Contest," held in 960 (Third Month, thirtieth day, of Tentoku 4) (*GMH* 4:50–51). The latter contest, sponsored by Emperor Uda, was a grand affair and the first waka contest held at the palace in which the major participants ("allies," *kata no Fito* or *kataudo*—depending on the contest such persons might be the actual composers of the poems or the gallery that debated the merits of the entries) were women. A Chinese poetry contest had been held at the palace the previous year. The extant records (one written by the emperor and one by a courtier, both in Chinese, and one in *hiragana*, of which there exist three variants) of the contest refer to it as "a contest of women-in-waiting" (*nyoubau uta awase*). Some of the names of women listed correspond to the names in the *Genji* chapter. Among the participants were celebrated figures like Minamoto no Shitagō, Nōin, Sakanoue no Mochiki, and Mibu no Tadami. The contest is included in *Uta awase shū*, Hagitani Boku and Taniyama Shigeru, eds., in *Nihon koten bungaku taikei* (*NKBT*), 74:78–104.

16. He is later known as Prince Hyōbu.

17. Seidensticker's "rather ordinary person" for *oremono* translates the modern Japanese *bonjin*, used by some commentators, rather than the Heian usage: a person whose mind is unfocused or is scatterbrained (*Tale of Genji*, 316).

18. Seidensticker chooses a slightly different emphasis: "Painting

seemed less study than play, something you let your brush have its way with when poetry had worn you out" (p. 316).

19. Modern commentators cite the reference in *Kakaishō* to the effect that "precedents are things that begin during the reigns of saintly rulers" (p. 348).

20. The notion of complementary engendering forces in the world, yin and yang, would have been familiar to Heian readers and writers, of course.

21. The discussions thus echo the context noted for the picture contest, the installation of Akikonomu (Genji's foster daughter) at the Reizei Emperor's court.

22. After giving the poem, the narrator adds a *sōshiji*: "Was that what was composed [what he composed]?" (*to ya arituramu*). The moment might even call for other possible replies from the audience. *NKBZ* 3:399.

23. Talented in all the arts, the prince, called Sochi no miya at the time, had previously acted as judge for the picture contest. The verb *sadamu* also appears frequently.

24. The *NKBZ* edition reads it as Genji testing the incense received from the Asagao Princess, but the term usually refers to a larger event that presents a fortuitous occasion for a revealing conversation. Yamagishi Tokuhei's interpretation in the *NKBT* edition accords with my view.

25. The *NKBZ*, *Shinchō nihon koten shūsei* (*SNKS*), and *GMH* texts do also, although their comments are tentative. *Kogetsushō*, as usual, cites lines from the old commentaries, of which only Norinaga's *Tama no ogushi* takes it to be a reference to the *Genji* Suzaku. The more convincing interpretation, in accordance with what we have discovered about the intertextual presence of Emperor Daigo in the *Genji* text, is to take the subject of the verb to be Daigo and the historical Suzaku.

26. Genji's comment probably refers in part to the prevalent belief that the world was entering the "latter age of the Buddhist Law" (*mappō* or *massei*).

27. The three geniuses of the native style, Ono no Michikaze, Fujiwara no Kōsei, and Fujiwara no Sukemasa, credited with raising *hiragana* writing to an art form, were active between the reigns of emperors Murakami and Ichijō.

28. Akikonomu's mother, the Rokujō Lady.

29. *GMH* 6:350. Commentators note that interwoven into Genji's discussion of calligraphic hands is an aestheticosexual summing up of his thoughts on the women in his life. The "underside-frontside" pattern emerges in a configuration different from the aestheticopolitical one mentioned earlier.

30. Seidensticker reads "among the ladies here to please us" for the phrase that refers to Murasaki, *koko ni to koso Fa* (and you who are right here). *Tale of Genji*, 517.

31. As previously noted, *katakana*, the other kana mode, never became the object of artistic interest.

32. Some commentators take the two terms to be one but most read them as two separate terms. "Reed hand" signified a style that merged

graphs with objects in a painting (making the letter for "a" in the shape of a crane, for example), a style that, having no determined forms, especially depended on an artist's innate skill. A "poem picture" was a painting that depicted the sentiment in a poem (a poem would also be written on it).

33. The phrases *sau no mo, tada no mo, wonna-de mo* have stumped all commentators. Tamagami takes *sau,* "grass," to refer to *man'yōgana* written in a cursive manner and *tada,* "usual," to refer to regular *hiragana (onna-de).* *GMH* 6:359–365. Problems arise since the narrator then mentions *wonna-de.* Is *onna-de* another variant style within hiragana (*SNKS* 4:269)? Or is the narrator saying "the grass and the usual, namely, the feminine style" (*NKBT* 3:171)? Seidensticker's "formal and cursive Chinese [reversing the two] and the more radically cursive Japanese 'ladies' hand'" is perhaps the best interpretation. It follows Tamagami but reads *tada* to refer not to *onna-de* but to a noncursive (*kaisho*) Chinese style. *Tale of Genji,* 518.

34. The word used is *sau,* which supports the interpretation given above.

35. Apparently a fixed style that Genji's creativity takes to new heights.

36. Seidensticker translates the last part "the bold abandon of which was such as to make the prince fear that all the other manuscripts must seem at best inoffensive" (p. 519). The prince is not making a judgment on the "other manuscripts"; he doesn't even look at them.

37. A title used at the time to distinguish the *Man'yōshū* text as we know it from poems in *Shinsen Man'yōshū,* believed to have been collected by Michizane.

38. Seidensticker's "The hand was very old-fashioned" places the passage into a negative register that is not necessarily present. *Tale of Genji,* 407. Since Genji is taken with it, and he also states a few lines later that he prefers the style, it seems better read in conjunction with the general valorization in *Genji* of the older against the modish and up-to-date.

39. Cf. Seidensticker: "Hers is a style which considers it mandatory to mention 'august company' whenever royalty is in the vicinity" (p. 407).

40. I follow the *NKBT* interpretation over the others, which take *sirabe,* as Seidensticker does, to refer to "formal concerts." *Sirabe* refers to the tunings of a musical instrument and emphasizes the ability, noted next, of the Japanese koto to blend in with other instruments.

41. "Native koto." Seidensticker, who seems uncertain what attitude to take, translates it "a crude domestic product," which makes the assessment too negative.

42. A brief reference to the Japanese koto appears in "Wakana II": "The *wa-gon* in particular, with its simple tunings and with no determined ways of playing it (*ato sadamaritaru koto nakute*), seems made to trip women up; as the sounds of koto in spring [concerts] comprise a chorus of instruments accommodating one another, Genji feels sorry for it" (4:179–180). Murasaki is the one who will play the instrument, as Seidensticker's version makes clear: "He [Genji] felt for Murasaki, whose responsibility it would be" (p. 600). The phrase "sounds of the koto in spring" (*Faru no koto no ne*) appears in other

texts as "that's how the sounds of the koto are" (*saru mono to koto no ne Fa*) or "that sort of koto sound" (*saru koto no ne*). The *wa-gon* was able to accommodate a variety of sounds but was extremely difficult to play well and was out of place in formal concerts. The latter aspects are most likely being emphasized in the present passage.

43. The meaning of the passage is not at all clear. For other possible interpretations, see *GMH* 5:377.

44. Another difficult passage: "the sounds of all instruments obey its sound" (*NKBZ* 4:189); "the sounds of various instruments reverberate obediently in the sound of the seven-stringed koto and blend with it" (*NKBT* 3:351); "following the sounds made by all the other instruments" (*SNKS* 5:181); "the sounds of all instruments follow the sounds of the *kin*" (*GMH* 7:363). Such textual difficulties, of which the passage is full, no doubt derive from the incomprehensibility of the mid-Heian musical traditions to later readers.

45. Ima Fa wosawosa tutaFuru Fito nasi to ya.

46. The underside to Genji's teaching of the Third Princess, of course, is the havoc the new configuration wreaks on Murasaki, a situation about which the latter complains only by way of periodic expressions of desire to take Buddhist orders, which Genji resolutely prohibits.

47. The Seidensticker version: "Let us think of the cabinetmaker. He shapes pieces as he feels like shaping them. They may be only playthings, *with no real plan or pattern.* They may all the same have a certain style for what they are—*they may take on a certain novelty as times change* and be very interesting. But when it comes to the genuine object, *something of such undeniable value that a man wants to have it always with him*—the perfection of the form announces that it is from the hand of a master" (pp. 26–27; emphasis added.) Among other things, the translation removes the crucial difference between crafting with and without preexisting forms.

48. Designated colors would later be added to the line sketch by apprentices and assistants. The scenes in the *Tale of Genji Scroll* were executed in just such a manner.

49. In the Seidensticker version the line "It is not with the things we know, mountains, streams, *houses near and like our own*" misses the clear reference to the position of painted houses. *Tale of Genji*, p. 27; emphasis added. The "houses near" are those "close to the eye," that is, in the foreground.

50. Like mountains found in Chinese landscape paintings.

51. Cf. Seidensticker: "It is here the master has his own power. There are details a lesser painter cannot imitate" (p. 27).

52. *GMH* 1:202. It is not clear whether, as Tamagami reads it, a clear distinction is being made between Chinese and Japanese painting. Form and subject matter are the foci of interest.

53. At this time the arts were commonly referred to as *hakanasi* (trivial, insubstantial, fleeting), as merely ornamental and marginal to life.

11   Substitutions and Incidental Narrating: "Wakamurasaki"

1. The "Tamakazura" line actually begins with "Hahakigi." For a list of the lines, see Jin'ichi Konishi, *A History of Japanese Literature*, vol. 2, *The Early Middle Ages*, 278, n.41. For a discussion of "Wakamurasaki" as the first *Genji* chapter written, see Ikeda Kazuomi, "Wakamurasaki maki no seiritsu."

2. The title "Wakamurasaki" has been read as a reference to the first *dan* of *Ise monogatari*. See, for example, *Genji monogatari hyōshaku* (GMH), 1:27, where Tamagami Takuya cites two "Miscellaneous" poems from *Gosenshū* that also refer to the *Ise dan*. The first, *Gosenshū* 1178:

through Musashi Plain   I made my way
      until my sleeves were drenched,
yet did I despair   of finding the Young Lavender
[musasino Fa/sode Fizu bakari/wakesikado/wakamurasaki Fa/
tadunewabiniki]

The second is *Gosenshū* 1278:

is it because   for a long time
      I have wished to dye my thoughts a deep hue
that I have asked after   the roots of the Young Lavender?
[madaki kara/omoFi koki iro ni/somemu to ya/wakamurasaki no/ne wo
tadunuramu]

The second poem in particular may suggest Genji's longstanding obsession with the Fujitsubo Consort.

3. "Would our little Murasaki (*wakamurasaki*) be in attendance by any chance?" Richard Bowring, trans., *Murasaki Shikibu: The Tale of Genji*, 91; *Nihon koten bungaku zenshū* (NKBZ), 18:201.

4. Edward G. Seidensticker, trans., *Tale of Genji*, 84.

5. *NKBZ* 1:273.

6. It seems that Genji went back to the cave to offer prayers himself.

7. Cf. Seidensticker: "Despite the sage's ministrations, which still continued, Genji feared a new seizure as the sun rose higher" (p. 86), a possible reading, although most commentaries read the passage as referring to Genji's actions. The speaker is not clear. A few read it to be the sage, but most take it to be Genji's attendants. The latter is likely since the narrator uses the humilific verb *kikoyu* for the speaker. Of course, the attendants night simply be transmitting the sage's words.

8. That is how most commentators interpret it. One exception is the edition by Shimizu and Ishida. See *Shinchō nihon koten shūsei* (SNKS), 1:185. Yamagishi, following *Kogetsushō*, reads the whole section, from the remarks about the treetops, as Genji's speech. *Nihon koten bungaku taikei* (NKBT), 1:179. Much of the chapter, indeed most of the *Genji* narrating, presents difficulties in distinguishing single speakers since the voice of what I have been calling the general narrator can always be heard.

9. The peak in question is undoubtedly Mt. Asama. Both mountains

appear in *dan* 9 of *Ise monogatari*, and they were famous as a pair. The *Ise dan* tells of the "man" going eastward to remove himself from the capital; the references to Akashi that follow, therefore, may be a prefiguring of Genji's later exile.

10. Son of the governor of Harima.

11. The reference to the Dragon King of the Sea recurs later, as does the mention of the daughter's throwing herself into the sea. See Chapter 12.

12. Cf. Seidensticker: "Ambition wide and deep as the sea" (p. 87).

13. There are a series of word plays on the sea and especially *mirume*, a kind of seaweed. A poetic play emphasizes the part of the passage dealing with the Akashi priest's plans for his daughter. Genji is unaware of its full import. His verbal play merges with the priest's political maneuver and demonstrates a poeticopolitical movement constitutive of the *Genji* text that I am tracing in this book.

14. As a result of the "Hahakigi" critique?

15. The full extent of his almost megalomaniacal plans is not made clear until the "Wakana I" chapter (34).

16. The reference to *mono no ke* recalls Yūgao's death in the previous chapter. The reader-listener learns much later that Genji often has been the target of such spirits.

17. The days would have gotten longer toward the end of the Third Month, just before the beginning of summer. Some texts have "with no one to keep him company," which would emphasize his solitary state but also imply his general condition (having lost Utsusemi and Yūgao and being unable to gain the Fujitsubo Consort).

18. The word *magiru* is cognate with *magiraFasu*, seen before. It can mean "hidden," but it also means "distracted," both in the sense of "take one's mind off of" and that of "be attracted by." Genji remembers, of course, the previous discovery of women nearby.

19. The fence had been mentioned previously (see above).

20. We must remember that he had ample opportunity to peep at ladies when he accompanied his father on visits to various consorts. The act of seeing often constitutes a powerful act of possession. See Mitani Kuniaki, "*Monogatari bungaku no 〈shisen〉,*" 89–108.

21. The "person he yearns for" is the Fujitsubo Consort. A similar adorable quality will mark a very different figure when Genji marries the Third Princess.

22. The *Ise* (49) poems are as follows:

> so young and fresh   an inviting place to sleep
>   this youthful grass;
> my only concern: that another will entwine with it
> [urawakami/neyoge ni miyuru/wakakusa wo/Fito no musubamu/koto wo
> si zo omoFu]
>
> like new grasses   the words you speak;
>   how strange indeed,
> my feelings toward you   have always been of the purest kind
> [Fatukusa no/nado medurasiki/koto no Fa zo/uranaku mono wo/
> omoFikeru kana]

23. The comment coincides with the "Hahakigi" opening that indicated that Genji must not be regarded as a common rake.

24. The emphasis on the child's lovable quality echoes the director's comment in the "rainy night critique" about women whom one can train to one's liking. See Chapter 8.

25. Genji is probably seventeen at this time, the Fujitsubo Consort around twenty-two. Since she entered the palace several years before Genji's *gempuku* at the age of eleven, she might have been twelve or thirteen, possibly only a year or so older than the child Genji has seen.

26. See Chapter 6.

27. The text placed the peeping at "twilight."

28. Add the Akashi priest to this company and we have a major narrative focus, as I am attempting to delineate it.

29. Besides the instances noted above, comments like "being curious as to how these young grasses (*wakakusa*) would grow up" (1:301), "I intend to teach her well" (1:312), "when he thus instructed her" (1:331), and "I shall teach you" (1:332) leave no doubt as to the focus of the narrating.

30. Akagi Shizuko, *Sekkan jidai no shosō*, 127–128.

31. The distincions are not hard and fast, and apply to almost any of the women (and men) that appear in the text. Norma Field makes the substitutive movements designated by the terms a central part of her study of the *Genji* "heroines." See the important article by Mitani Kuniaki, "Genji monogatari ni okeru disukuuru no hōhō: hampuku to saenka, aruiwa ⟨katashiro⟩ to ⟨yukari⟩."

32. Jacques Derrida, *Writing and Difference*, 213.

33. Jacques Derrida, *Dissemination*, 316.

34. Rodolphe Gasché, *Tain of the Mirror*, 212.

35. Gasché, *Tain*, 215.

36. I have discussed the mechanism of the "supplement" in the section on "Hotaru" and Tamakazura in Chapter 9.

37. Genji, we are told, does not remember his mother. What he sees in the Fujitsubo Consort, then, effects a reconstruction of that "original" figure.

38. Tamagami notes a distinct difference between the language of the previous sections and the language of the "Fujitsubo incident." *GMH* 1:101–102.

39. Tamagami notes that in the entire *Genji* text, this is the closest we get to the presentation of a sexual act. *GMH* 1:98.

40. Cf. Seidensticker: "And the tumult of thoughts and feelings that now assailed him—he would have liked to consign it to the Mountain of Obscurity" (p. 98). Genji does not want to forget his "thoughts and feelings" as much as he wants to tell the consort of the full extent of them. He wishes the night were longer so that he might attempt it (men arrived and left their women under cover of night).

41. The poem is constructed around the term *aFuyo* ("night of meeting" and "world where dreams can come true," both rare occurrences). The words *miru*, *aFu*, and *yume* are associative-words.

42. Cf. Seidensticker: "She had every right to be unhappy, and he was sad for her" (p. 99). The translation misses the powerful sense of propriety

displayed by the consort. It is not only (or particularly) Genji that is "sad for her" but rather the narrator's (and the reader-listener's) perspective that finds her behavior appropriate.

43. Fujii Sadakazu, "Tabuu to kekkon—Hikaru Genji monogatari no kōzō," 26–27.

44. He will later abduct a child who is the daughter of his (step-) mother-sister's older brother, who will fit into the genealogical pattern as his (foster) daughter (Genji tells her that he will become her mother), (foster) niece (i.e., niece to his "sister," the Fujitsubo Consort), (step-) cousin (i.e., daughter of his stepmother's brother), pupil, and, finally, wife.

45. As I have repeatedly emphasized, the Kiritsubo Emperor, even had he discovered the secret (and we don't know that he didn't), would probably not have been angry or surprised, given his encouragement of intimacy in the first place. We must also remember his promise to guarantee Genji's success to help atone for the Kiritsubo Consort's death. The incident bears a quite positive (private) facet that will govern Genji's future.

46. See also the earlier reference to the *Ise dan*. Mitani Kuniaki's reading of the relations between *Genji* and *Ise* skillfully traces the inversions at work, showing how the former, through its variations, forces a reinterpretation of the latter, thus demonstrating the inadequacy of simple observations of "allusion" or "influence." "Fujitsubo jiken no hyōgen kōzō."

47. The situation would have produced a "stepmother relationship," which is better avoided since it often results in cruel treatment of the stepdaughter. The *Genji* narrator takes particular care in telling of such relationships—they were, as we shall see, a focus of attention in the "Hotaru" discussion.

48. Cf. "'Young ladies should do as they are told.' And so the lessons began" (Seidensticker, *Tale of Genji*, 109). The sense of the Japanese (*kokoro yaFaraka naru*) is not so much of doing as one is told as of responding to kindness with like kindness, that is, without suspicion.

49. The poem recalls yet another famous poem, cited previously, on the *murasaki*, found in *Kokinshū* (867, "Miscellaneous"):

> thanks to a single *murasaki* stalk,   all of the grasses
>   on Musashi Plain,
> each and every one,   are unbearably dear to me
> [murasaki no/Fitomoto yuwe ni/musasino no/kusa Fa minagara/aFare to
> zo miru]

Genji cites the poem after the nun returns to the city; he wonders if he will be disappointed (if she proves inferior to the Fujitsubo Consort) when he sees the child close up.

50. I.e., instead of poem from the past (*Furu-uta*).

51. Though in time she becomes for all practical purposes Genji's principal wife, she is forever vulnerable to threats posed by other women (the Akashi Lady and the Third Princess being the two most prominent).

52. Genji's behavior does not include sex. Their sexual relations begin in the "Aoi" (Heartvine, 9) chapter.

12   The Akashi Intertexts

1. Members of such families include figures like Utsusemi, Suet-sumuhana, Tamakazura, and Ukifune. Yamanaka Yutaka remarks, for example: "That Utsusemi did not readily yield to Genji derives from the fact that the class to which the author herself belonged made her consciously portray women in the tale in such a manner." Yamanaka Yutaka, *Heianchō bungaku no shiteki kenkyū*, 144–145.

2. Abe Akio, for example, devotes almost four hundred pages to the Akashi family in his monumental study, *Genji monogatari kenkyū josetsu*. See pp. 549–938.

3. Discussions that touch on some of the issues I am raising also appear in Norma Field, *The Splendor of Longing in The Tale of Genji*, (64–85); and Haruo Shirane, *The Bridge of Dreams: A Poetics of 'The Tale of Genji,'* 13–84; see also Richard Bowring, trans., *Murasaki Shikibu: The Tale of Genji*, 22–45.

4. *Nihon koten bungaku zenshū* (NKBZ), 2:201.

5. Seidensticker keeps vague the force of *yukari*: "The incumbent governor was all-powerful in the province, but the eccentric old man had no wish to marry his daughter to such an upstart." Edward G. Seidensticker, trans., *Tale of Genji*, 242.

6. Seidensticker deflects the focus from the child's destiny: "What a rare stroke of luck—the chance we have been waiting for. We must offer our girl" (p. 242).

7. Seidensticker's "out of the question" (p. 242) emphasizes a personal response.

8. Oborozukiyo is principal handmaid (Naishi no Kami), not one of the higher consorts.

9. The reader-listener learns later that whereas her thoughts are only on the future of a daughter, his are on the larger family itself.

10. The situation of ambitious kin is later repeated with Fujitsubo's brother (Murasaki's father) and attendants, and Tamakazura's Tsukushi guardians, who want to marry her off to the Higo man.

11. Azechi major counselor, the same rank attained by Murasaki's grandfather. We have seen that wives are far more cautious than their husbands. The Kiritsubo *kōi*'s father, we remember, struck the first such note of fatherly ambition bringing misery to a daughter. His wife (Genji's grand-mother), we recall, was initially apprehensive about and later bitterly regret-ted having followed her husband's plan to make their daughter an imperial consort. Fujitsubo's mother, knowing the hardship the *kōi* experienced, had similar misgivings. The Akashi Lady's mother resists, also unsuccessfully, Genji's attempts to bring her and the daughter to the capital.

12. The arrangement is not unusual in Japan, where even first cousins marry. Genji and Fujitsubo seem to have been first cousins.

13. Seidensticker chooses a different focus: "It might just possibly be different if he were likely to look at her—but no. You must joking" (p. 242).

14. As I have indicated throughout, there is an easier slippage, aided by the use of suffixes, between first- and third-person narrating in Japanese than

in Seidensticker's translation: "No one among the great persons of the land was likely to think her worth a glance. The prospect of marrying someone nearer her station in life revolted her. If she was left behind by those on whom she depended, she would become a nun, or perhaps throw herself into the sea" (p. 246). The Sumiyoshi Shrine plays a major role in the fortunes of both the priest and Genji.

15. For discussions of mythic pretexts, see Field, *Splendor of Longing*, 67–68, and, especially, Shirane, *Bridge of Dreams*, 77–80. Shirane provides a useful summary of what he terms the myth of Yamasachi-hiko (The Luck of the Mountain), and his elder brother Umisachi-hiko (the Luck of the Sea) and its striking parallels with the Akashi story (p. 78). In the ancient texts the story actually concerns a dispute over a fish hook between two deities, Honosusori no mikoto, who is adept at fishing the "bounty of the sea" (*umi no sati*, also "tool for fishing"), and his younger brother, Hikohohodemi no mikoto, who is adept at hunting the "bounty of the hills" (*yama no sati*, also "tool for hunting"). *Nihon shoki, Nihon koten bungaku taikei (NKBT)*, 67:163–168. Although it would be a mistake, I feel, to make too much of the parallels, the pretexts do add a supernatural aura to the condition of exile and an impetus for Genji's move to Akashi and subsequent meeting with the family.

16. *Genji monogatari hyōshoku (GMH)*, 3:143–144. Tamagami suggests that since the ancient story makes the daughter of the Dragon King of the Sea the ancestor of the imperial line, an analogous circumstance faces Genji; however, the latter is "horrified by it," showing that political involvement is the farthest thing from his mind (*GMH* 3:144). Fleeing the overtly mythical, however, takes him right into the lair of the Akashi priest, thereby setting him on a course that will replay the larger structure of the myth.

17. Although it seems that Genji placed himself into exile, public perception has it (see the Akashi wife's comments above) that his exile was due to his affair with Oborozukiyo and that he was forced into it (by the Kokiden consort's faction). See Shimizu Yoshiko's influential argument that Genji voluntarily left the capital. *Genji monogatari-ron*, 220–230.

18. See headnote no. 14 in *NKBZ* 2:209.

19. Some commentators take the father's words to refer to Genji's liaison with Fujitsubo, but most read it as a reference to those wrongs a person commits in the normal course of life; the emperor himself makes a similar reference in the next passage.

20. The emperor's statement has been connected to a legend (regarding the rise of the Kitano Shrine) that Emperor Daigo was cast into hell for committing five sins. See *GMH* 3:162–163. The Kitano intertext provides yet further confirmation of the shadow of Daigo over the Kiritsubo Emperor.

21. We discover later that he appeared to the Suzaku Emperor.

22. *GMH* 3:161. The appropriation of poetry by *monogatari* here finds what can be called a polyvocally thematized example. In other words, the pivot-word operates at a thematico-incantatory level that nonetheless prevents univocal readings.

23. The narrator states specifically that the priest "feels as if he has taken the light of the sun and moon in his hands" (*te ni etatematuritaru kokoti site*), an

expression that he will use again in "Wakana I" when he refers to his granddaughter, now the empress, and his great-grandson, now the crown prince (4:106). Seidensticker translates it "as if the radiance of the sun and the moon had become his private property" (*Tale of Genji*, 252) which suggests a more active role than in Field's version, where it becomes, "He feels as if he basked in the 'light of the sun and light of the moon' at once." *Splendor of Longing*, 67.

24. The Eighth Prince faces a similar problem in the "Uji chapters." We can also read a reference to that major *Genji* intertext on the "darkness" of a parent's heart discussed with regard to the "Kiritsubo" chapter.

25. The Buddhist notion of ties to a former life, *sukuse*, is evoked whenever the unexpected occurs and is especially prominent in the sections devoted to the Akashi family. In the *Genji* text, where nothing happens that is not connected to another part of the tale, the notion does not simply bring together two otherwise unrelated matters, but compellingly reinforces other (i.e., political, genealogical, aesthetic, and sexual) ties. Here we have another case of the "privatization" of religious concerns.

26. A reference to "precedent and protocol" (*kozitu*) that we have seen before.

27. *Biwa Fousi*. It seems such monks, later to be important transmitters of the *Tale of Heike*, appeared around the time of Emperor Ichijō's court.

28. Many commentators take it as "for a woman to play this [instrument]," but my reading, similar to the one in NKBZ, reads Genji's comment as a trope, which the priest then misreads as a reference to his daughter: "He speaks in general terms but the lay priest breaks out incongruously in a smile" (2:232). The narrator calls the priest's smile "incongruous" (*ainasi*) because he takes Genji's words in a different direction. Of course, the narrator has created an ambiguous situation where Genji's intentions are also double.

29. A woman not listed in the koto genealogies; see headnote 14, NKBZ 2:232.

30. The comments recall our previous discussion of the arts: the current is often better than the old if the old is overly constricted by "form."

31. Commentators differ over the age of the daughter. Eighteen years, the reasoning goes, would make her nine in "Wakamurasaki," too young for the many suitors Yoshikiyo had mentioned. The priest himself may have had plans for her since she was born (below), but in regard to the Sumiyoshi pilgrimages, he simply states that he began them when she was still a little girl. She could easily have been twelve or thirteen in "Wakamurasaki" and therefore twenty-one or twenty-two at present. Field puts her age at twenty-two. *Splendor of Longing*, 68.

32. The world had believed Genji's "sin" to have been his affair with Oborozukiyo; Genji himself feels that it is his secret liaison with Fujitsubo; now the priest suggests another cause. As the NKBZ text notes, Genji's relationship with Fujitsubo converges with his ties to the Akashi family, the former showing, in a sense, a way to wipe clear the slate of transgression.

33. The narrator seems to mean either that her mistakes have made the

priest seem more of a fool than he is or that she intended to make him out to be that way but didn't intend to expose it all just yet. The phrase "write with conscious intent" (*kakinasitareba*) calls for the latter interpretation.

34. As Tamagami notes, etiquette required such a process of exchange even though the priest had gained Genji's assurance. *GMH* 3:203. Field also discusses this section. *Splendor of Longing*, 70–72.

35. There is some question whether Genji refers to looking at the clouds (the sky) or to being in the clouds (his remote dwelling at Akashi). I have tried to retain the ambiguity. The poem is called by Field, citing Fujii, "vacuous nonsense." *Splendor of Longing*, 70. After the poem the narrator utters the phrase "deep in thoughts too powerful," a citation of *Kokinshū* "Love" (503):

> deep in thoughts too powerful   I have lost the will
> to keep them safely hidden;
> so determined was I   not to let them show
> [omoFu ni Fa/sinoburu koto zo/makenikeru/iro ni Fa idezi to/omoFisi
> mono wo]

Genji, the narrator tells us, took great pains with his missive. He refers to his own misery (exile) and a desire that had been aroused by the priest's metonymic innuendo (the dwelling where the daughter lives—in the hills, away from the coast where Genji is staying). Genji is careful not to appear too forward, since news of the "dwelling" (daughter) had been offered by the father, but suggests at the same time, by means of the *Kokinshū* citation, the seriousness of his suit.

36. With no one to ask after him, Genji cannot relieve the sadness in his heart. A citation to a poem by Emperor Ichijō is noted in the commentary *Rōkashō* (ca. 1510), based on lectures by Sanjōnishi Sanetaka (1455–1537):

> though I am filled with longing,   to someone I have yet to meet
> it is difficult to speak of it
> the gloom hangs   heavy in my heart
> [koFisitomo/mada minu Fito no/iFigatami/kokoro ni mono no/mutukasiki
> kana]

37. Cf. "Consensus has it that the Akashi Lady is one of the finest poets in the tale" (Field, *Splendor of Longing*, 72), and "If we were to collect the poems recited in *Genji monogatari* and place them in the categories of an imperial collection, we would find that she is one character who is able to compose poems for the largest number of sections" (Suzuki Hideo, "Akashi no kimi," 18). That a *zuryō* writer (or writers) would show off her talents when dealing with a *zuryō* character further attests to the prominence of the family.

38. The narrating had informed us that the woman "found them [Genji's letters] marvelous but their social stations were not comparable (*nazuraFi naranu mi no Fodo*)" (2:239).

39. The daughter's resistance and pride and her concern for discerning genuine feelings evoke Kaguyahime's dilemma.

40. The same day as Genji's dream. The emperor is stricken by an eye ailment as a result of his father's gaze.

41. Some texts give "fallen into sin" (*tumi ni otite*). I prefer to sustain the ambivalence of the present version: Genji is the victim of the *perception* of transgression.

42. The term refers to the fact that the family has been the victim of unfortunate circumstances, not simply that the daughter is of low rank. Seidensticker glosses over the important words: "she knew that rustic maidens should come running at the slightest word from a city gentleman who happened to be briefly in the vicinity" (p. 260).

43. For two freer renditions, see Shirane, *Bridge of Dreams*, 80, and Seidensticker, *Tale of Genji*, 260.

44. Seidensticker omits the important date, rendering only "The moon was near full" (p. 261).

45. The sobriquet Ise no Miyasundokoro also referred to Lady Ise.

46. Field, *Splendor of Longing*, 64.

47. We get an inkling of the situation when the husband is mentioned in the "Aoi" (Heartvine, 9) chapter, indicating that the Rokujō Lady's possessing spirit has a dimension other than female jealousy. Deposed crown princes (*haitaishi*), according to some commentators, tend to turn into vengeful spirits. See, for example, Kawasaki Noboru, "Rokujō miyasundokoro," 13–23. For an opposing view, see Fujimoto Katsuyoshi, "Genji monogatari 'zenbō,'" 54–64.

48. *Splendor of Longing*, 65. Field also mentions Genji's grandfather and Tō no Chūjō. The similarities in circumstance might be a major reason that the Rokujō Lady's spirit does not attack Akashi family members.

49. The first segment is a lead-in for the pivot-word *tati*, "break" (waves) and "cut" (cloth). I have emphasized the associative-words *nami*, "wave" and "tears," and *siFodokesi*, "soaked with brine," "salty water, i.e., tears."

50. Seidensticker's version turns the narrator's more general comment into a personal one: "How could it fail to move her?" (p. 267).

51. *GMH* 3:243.

52. *Umi* points toward both "because it [the world] is gloomy" and "sea."

53. Akashi, in Harima Province, lies farther west than Suma, in Settsu Province, and so represents a different world. Even when his wife, daughter, and granddaughter leave for the capital, the priest remains within the Harima borders.

54. In contrast, Yūgiri, Genji's son by the Aoi Lady, remains the government official throughout, relating always at the Fujiwara level (i.e., Tō no Chūjō's family). The main "Uji" men, Niou and Kaoru, do not descend from Yūgiri. Niou is the son of the Akashi Empress and the "present emperor," and Kaoru is the putative child of Genji and the Third Princess (his real father is Kashiwagi).

55. The Akashi Lady doesn't enter the capital until Genji's Rokujō Mansion is completed, and even then she waits until well after the other three main women have moved in. As Suzuki Hideo points out, the narrator begins using honorifics when telling of the Akashi Lady from this point on, as if to

compensate for her anguish. "Akashi no kimi," 18. The separation, set in winter, is generally considered one of the best moments integrating a character's situation with poetic metonyms. See below and also Field, *Splendor of Longing*, 76, and Shirane, *Bridge of Dreams*, 83–84.

56. Seidensticker takes Murasaki to be the one who suggests that the lady accompany her daughter. Actually, the narrator first gives Genji's thoughts about the situation and then Murasaki's similar thoughts. Here is Seidensticker's version:

> It was assumed that Murasaki would go to court with the Akashi girl. She could not stay long, however, and she thought that the time had come for the girl's real mother to be with her. It was sad for them both, mother and daughter, that they had been kept apart for so long. The matter had been on Murasaki's conscience and she suspected that it had been troubling the girl as well. (p. 531).

My version:

> While such events [told in the preceding section] are going on, on the matter of [the Akashi Princess] entering the crown prince's entourage, Genji thinks: the principal wife [Murasaki] would be expected to accompany the child, but she wouldn't be able to stay with her for long; on this occasion, I would prefer to have that guardian [the Akashi Lady] with her; the lady [Murasaki] too thinks: it must happen sooner or later; to keep living apart like this will be unsatisfactory for her and a source of misery; the girl will soon be bothered by it as well and yearn to be with her mother; I'd hate to be despised by both sides. (3:440–441)

Murasaki then urges Genji to appoint the mother the princess's guardian at court.

57. *GMH* 4:70.

58. Winter will be the Akashi Lady's mark.

59. To further guarantee their bonds the nurse cites *Kokinshū* 1049, by Fujiwara no Tokihira:

> distant as Cathay   the mountains of Yoshino,
>   though you seclude yourself there
> I am not one who would think   of staying far behind
> [morokosi no/yosino no yama ni/komoru to mo/okuremu to omoFu/ware naranaku ni]

The poem also appears in the *Ise Collection*, where it is attributed to Tokihira's brother, Nakahira.

60. See Field, *Splendor of Longing*, 76–77, for a discussion of the preceding passage, which associates the lady with the season of winter.

61. Seidensticker's version, besides being typically distant in its third-person perspective, goes amiss on two counts, both of crucial importance. First, Seidensticker reads the *sukuse* reference as referring primarily to the child—"Yes, she was meant for unusual things, one could not deny it"—and then he ignores the reference to Kanesuke's *kokoro no yami* poem—"Genji could imagine the lady's anguish at sending her daughter off to a distant

foster mother"—a reference, we increasingly realize, always strategically placed. Seidensticker, *Tale of Genji*, 333.

62. Forty was considered the beginning of old age.

63. *Onna genji*, i.e., a woman made to take the Minamoto surname.

64. For a different view of the section, see Field, *Splendor of Longing*, 79–83. Field's attempt to keep the Akashi family situated within the context of a Genji whose "status as hero" must be protected from "the threatening contagion of Akashi prosperity" (p. 82) ultimately precludes attention to the remarkable and consistent Akashi underside to Genji's career and genealogy.

65. He is presumably accustomed to reading Buddhist scriptures written in Chinese.

66. The phrase no doubt gestures to *Taketori monogatari* and another child raised with great care.

67. Just prior to the nun's last comment, we are told of the Akashi Lady's return to her daughter's quarters; the narrating then backtracks and gives us comments by the nun and the lady before telling us again that the lady "has made her way back, having an attendant carry the letter box" (4:113). Seidensticker omits the second reference to the lady's departure: "The Akashi lady had someone take the letter box to the southeast quarter" (p. 576).

68. *Kano senzo no otodo*, mentioned in "Wakamurasaki" and again in "Akashi."

69. Later incidents involving the Akashi family appear in "Wakana II." Genji makes a pilgrimage to the Sumiyoshi Shrine to offer thanks, as directed by the priest's letter, and the grandson is appointed crown prince.

70. Interests that are also corroborated, as we have seen, by the narrative pacing in those often inordinately long sections and narrating moments devoted to the Akashi figures.

71. As Yamanaka Yutaka points out, during the time of Kaneie and Michitaka, for example, quite a few *zuryō* daughters were able to marry into *sekkan* families, further proof that such ambition would have been entirely justified. Yamanaka gives a few cases: a daughter (Moriko) of the governor of Musashi Province, Fujiwara Tsunekuni, married Fujiwara Morosuke and bore the prominent sons Korechika, Kanemichi, and Kane'ie; a daughter (Tokihime) of the governor of Settsu, Fujiwara no Nakatada, married Kaneie and bore Michitaka, Senshi, and Michinaga, among other children (Tokihime's granddaughter, Akiko, then becomes empress [*chūgū*] at Emperor Ichijō's court); similarly, a daughter (Takako) of Takashina no Naritada married the chancellor (*kampaku*) Fujiwara no Michitaka and her granddaughter, Sadako, also becomes Ichijō's empress. *Heianchō bungaku no shiteki kenkyū*, 142–143.

Bibliography

Works in Japanese

Abbreviations Used for Titles of Collections
GMH: Genji monogatari hyōshaku. Edited by Tamagami Takuya. 14 vols. Kadokawa shoten, 1964–1969.
IKIM: Issatsu no kōza Ise monogatari. Yūseidō, 1983.
KNKB: Kanshō nihon koten bungaku. 36 vols. Kadokawa shoten, 1975–1978.
KYNK: Kan'yaku nihon no koten. 60 vols. Shōgakkan, 1982–1988.
NBKSS: Nihon bungaku kenkyū shiryō sōsho. 50 vols. Yūseidō, 1970–1974.
NKBT: Nihon koten bungaku taikei. 102 vols. Iwanami shoten, 1957–1968.
NKBZ: Nihon koten bungaku zenshū. 51 vols. Shōgakkan. 1970–1978.
SNKS: Shinchō nihon koten shūsei. 85 vols. Shinchōsha, 1976–1989.
SST: Shikashū taisei. Vol. 1, *Chūko*. Meiji shoin, 1973.
ZHS: Kokin wakashū zen hyōshaku. 2 vols. Yūbun shoin, 1976.

Place of publication is Tokyo for all Japanese works.
Abe Akio. *Genji monogatari kenkyū josetsu*. Tokyo daigaku shuppankai, 1959.
———. "Hotaru no maki no monogatari-ron." *Jimbunkagaku kiyō*, vol. 24 (March 1961); later collected in *NBKSS, Genji monogatari* 4:285–299.
Abe Akio, et al., eds. *Genji monogatari*. Vols. 14–23 of *KYNK*. 1983–1988.
———. *Genji monogatari*. Vols. 12–17 of *NKBZ*. 1972–1975.
Abe Takeshi. *Sekkan seiji*. Vol. 4 of *Nihonshi*. Kyōikusha, 1977.
Akagi Shizuko. *Sekkan jidai no shosō*. Kondō shuppansha, 1988.
Akimoto Yoshirō. *Fudoki*. Vol. 2 of *NKBT*. 1958.
Akiyama Ken. *Ise*. Vol. 5 of *Ōchō no kajin*. Shūeisha, 1985.
Ban Nobutomo. *Hyōshō Ise nikki fushō*. Vol. 5 of *Ban Nobutomo zenshū*. Kokusho kankōkai, 1908.
Enomoto Masazumi. *Genji monogatari no sōshiji*. Kasama shoin, 1982.
Fujii Sadakazu. "Amayo no shinasadame kara hotaru no maki no 'monogatari ron' e." *Kyōritsu joshi tanki daigaku bunka kiyō*, no. 18 (December 1974), 34–46.
———. *Genji monogatari no shigen to genzai*. Tōjusha, 1980.
———. *Monogatari bungaku seiritsu shi*. Tōkyō daigaku shuppankai, 1987.
———. *Monogarati no kekkon*. Sōjusha, 1985.
———. "Sōshiji no shomondai." *Kokubungaku: kenkyū to kyōzai*, vol. 22 (January 1977), 36–42.
———. "Tabuu to kekkon—Hikaru Genji monogatari no kōzō." *Kokugo to kokubungaku*, vol. 55 (October 1978), 16–29.

Fujimoto Katsuyoshi. "Genji monogatari 'zenbō' 'kofu daijin no onryō' kō." *Nihon bungaku*, vol. 32, no. 8 (August 1983), 54–64.

Fujioka Sakutarō. *Kokubungaku zenshi: Heianchō hen*. Edited by Sugiyama Tomiko. 4 vols. Kōdansha, 1977.

Fujiwara Kintō. *Shinsen zuinō*. In *Nihon kagaku taikei*, edited by Sasaki Nobutsuna, 64–66. Kazama shobō, 1972.

Fukuda Takeshi. *Genji monogatari no disukuuru*. Shoshi kaze no bara, 1990.

Fukui Teisuke, ed. *Ise monogatari*. Vol. 8 of *NKBZ*. 1972.

Furuhashi Nobuyoshi. *Kodai waka no hassei*. Tōkyō daigaku shuppankai, 1988.

———. "Kokinshū no bungakushi—oto no jusei kara—." *Bungaku*, vol. 53, no. 12 (1985), 40–52.

Hagitani Boku and Taniyama Shigeru, eds. *Uta awaseshū*. Vol. 74 of *NKBT*. 1965.

Harada Yoshioki. "Jodōshi 'keri' no imi." *Kokugogaku—gengo to bungei*, vol. 6, no. 3 (May 1964), 27–31.

Hashimoto Yoshihiko. *Heian kizoku*. Heibonsha, 1986.

Hayami Tasuku. *Heian kizoku shakai to bukkyō*. Yoshikawa kōbunkan, 1975.

———. *Jōdo shinkō ron*. Yūzankaku, 1978.

Hisaki Yukio. *Nihon kodai gakkō no kenkyū*. Tamagawa daigaku shuppanbu, 1990.

Hyōdō Hiromi. "Waka hyōgen to seido." *Nihon bungaku*, vol. 34, no. 2 (February 1985), 54–68.

Iha Fuyū. *Onarigami no shima*. 2 vols. Heibonsha, 1973.

Ii Haruki. *Genji monogatari chūshakushi no kenkyū*. Ōfūsha, 1980.

———. *Genji monogatari no nazo*. Sanseidō, 1983.

Ikeda Kazuomi. "Wakamurasaki maki no seiritsu." In *Kōza genji monogatari no sekai*, edited by Akiyama Ken et al., 2:97–108. Yūhikaku, 1980.

Ikeda Kikan. *Ise monogatari ni tsukite no kenkyū*. Yūseidō, 1960.

Ishida Jōji, ed. *Ise monogatari*. Kadokawa shoten. 1979.

Itō Hiroshi. *Genji monogatari no genten*. Meiji shoin, 1980.

Itō Shinji. *Kaguyahime no tanjō*. Kōdansha gendai shinsho, 1973.

Itoi Motohiro. "Genji monogatari no jodōshi 'ki.'" In *Genji monogatari tankyū* 6:107–139. Kazama shobō, 1981.

———. "Monogatari no hyōgen." In *Taikei monogatari bungakushi*, edited by Mitani Eiichi, 2:75–92. Yūseidō, 1987.

Kachō yosei. Edited by Ii Haruki. Ōfūsha, 1978.

Kakaishō. Edited by Ishida Jōji. In *Shimeishō Kakaishō*, Tamagami Takuya, general ed. Kadokawa shoten, 1968.

Kanada Motohiko. "Arihara no Narihira to Ariwara shi to shinnōtachi." In *IKIM*, 286–292.

Karatani Kōjin. *Nihon kindai bungaku no kigen*. Kōdansha, 1978.

Katagiri Yōichi. *Ise*. Vol. 7 of *Nihon no sakka*. Shintensha, 1985.

———. *Ise monogatari no kenkyū*. Meiji shoin, 1963.

———. *Ise monogatari, Yamato monogatari*. Vol. 5 of *KNKB*. 1975.

———. "Uta makura no seiritsu—Kokinshū hyōgen kenkyū no ichibu to shite." *Kokugo to kokubungaku*, vol. 47 (April 1973), 22–33; later collected in *NBKSS, Kokinshū*, 256–266.

———, ed. *Taketori monogatari*. Vol 10 of *KYNK*. 1983.

Kawaguchi Hisao. *Heianchō nihon kambungakushi no kenkyū*. 2 vols. Meiji shoin, 1959–1961.

Kawasaki Noboru. "Rokujō miyasundokoro no shinkōteki haikei." *Kokugakuin zasshi*, vol. 68 (September 1967), 13–23.

Kifune Shigeaki. "Fujitsubo no miya zō shūfukuron—Wakamurasaki no maki no issetsu no saishin—." *Heian bungaku kenkyū*, vol. 43 (November 1969), 33–45.

Kitamura Kigin, ed. *Kogetsushō*. Revised and expanded by Mitani Eiichi. 3 vols. Meichō fukyūkai, 1979.

Kogo jiten. Iwanami shoten, 1974.

Kojima Noriyuki. *Honchō monzui (selections)*. Vol. 69 of *NKBT*. 1964.

———. et al., eds. *Man'yōshū*. Vols. 2–5 of *NKBZ*. 1971–1975.

Kokinshū. Vol. 2 of *Shimpojiumu nihon bungaku*. Gakuseisha, 1976.

Kokinwaka rokujō. In *Shimpan: Kokka taikan*. *Shisenshū-hen* 2:193–255. Kadokawa shoten, 1984.

Konishi Jin'ichi. "Genji monogatari no imejari." *Kokubungaku: kaishaku to kanshō*, vol. 30, no. 7 (June 1965), 217–231.

———. "Izure no ōntoki." *Kokugo to kokubungaku*, vol. 32 (March 1955), 61–64.

Kurano Kenji, ed. *Kojiki*. Vol. 1 of *NKBT*. 1958.

Masuda Katsumi. *Kazan rettō no shisō*. Chikuma shobō, 1968.

Masuda Shigeo. "Kokinshū no chokusensei—waka to seiji, shakai, rinri." *Baika joshi daigaku bungakubu kiyō*, no. 4 (December 1967), 15–40; later collected in *NBKSS, Kokin wakashū*, 31–44.

Matsumura Hiroji and Yamanaka Yutaka, eds. *Eiga monogatari*. Vols. 75–76 of *NKBT*. 1964–65.

Matsuo Satoshi and Nagai Kazuko, eds. *Makura no sōshi*. Vol. 11 of *NKBZ*. 1974.

Minegishi Akira. *Hentai kambun*. Tōkyōdō shuppan, 1986.

Mitamura Masako. "Josei tachi no saron—daisai-in saron o chūshin ni." *Kokubungaku: kaishaku to kyōzai no kenkyū*, vol. 34, no. 10 (August 1989), 63–67.

Mitani Eiichi. "Ise monogatari no jidai." In *IKIM*, 257–271.

———. *Monogatari bungaku shiron*. Revised edition. Yūseidō, 1976.

———. *Monogatarishi no kenkyū*. Yūseidō, 1979.

———. "Sagoromo monogatari no ihon seiritsu to sono jiki—maki ichi o chūshin to shite." *Kokugakuin daigaku kiyō*, no. 7 (1967), 277–309.

———, ed. *Taketori monogatari, Utsuho monogatari*. Vol. 6 of *KNKB*. 1975.

Mitani Kuniaki. "Dōka no bungaku." *Kokubungaku: kaishaku to kyōzai no kenkyū*, vol. 21 (January 1979), 115–122.

———. "Fujitsubo jiken no hyōgen kōzō: 'Wakamurasaki' no hōhō auriwa 'pure-tekisuto' to shite no *Ise monogatari*." *Monogatari, nikki bungaku to sono shūhen*, festschrift for Imai Takuji, 275–300. Ōfūsha, 1980.

———. "Genji monogatari ni okeru diskuuru no hōhō: hampuku no saenka, aruiwa ⟨katashiro⟩ to ⟨yukari⟩." *Nihon no bungaku* 5 (1989), 33–74.

———. "Genji monogatari ni okeru ⟨katari⟩ no kōzō—⟨washa⟩ to ⟨katarite⟩

aruiwa 'sōshiji' ron hihan no tame no joshō." *Nihon bungaku,* vol. 27 (November 1978), 182–196.

——. *Monogatari bungaku no hōhō.* 2 vols. Yūseidō, 1989.

——. "Monogatari bungaku no ⟨shiten⟩ miru koto no kinki aruiwa ⟨katari⟩ no kyōen." *Monogatari kenkyū* 2, 89–108. Shinjidaisha, 1988.

——. "Monogatari to ⟨kaku koto⟩—monogatari bungaku no imi sayō aruiwa fuzai no bungaku." *Nihon bungaku,* vol. 25, no. 10 (October 1976), 1–20; later collected in *Monogatari bungaku no hōhō,* 2 vols. (Yūseidō, 1989).

——. "Monogatari to wa nanika." In *Taketori monogatari, Utsuho monogatari,* edited by Mitani Eiichi, 379–388.

——. "Taketori monogatari no hōhō to seiritsu jiki—'Hinezumi no kawagoromo'; aruiwa, aregori." *Heianchō bungaku kenkyū* (May 1968); later collected in *Monogatari bungaku no hōhō* 1:201–221.

Momo Hiroyuki. *Jōdai gakusei no kenkyū.* Meguro shoten, 1967.

Motoori Norinaga. *Tama no ogushi.* In *Motoori Norinaga zenshū* 4:171–523. Chikuma shobō, 1968–1977.

Murai Yoshihiko. "Ariwara no Narihira to sono shūhen—sotsuden no saikentō." In *IKIM,* 277–285.

——. *Heian kizoku no sekai.* 2 vols. Tokuma shoten, 1986.

——. *Ōchō bunka danshō.* Kyōikusha, 1985.

Nakanishi Susumu. *Man'yōshū.* Kōdansha, 1984.

Nakano Kōichi. "Genji monogatari no sōshiji to monogatari ondokuron." *Gakugei kenkyū,* vol. 12 (February 1963); later collected in *NBKSS, Genji monogatari* 1:203–212.

——. "Monogatari dokusha no mondai." *Gakugei kenkyū,* vol. 13 (February 1964); later collected in *NBKSS, Genji monogatari* 1:194–202.

Nihon kiryaku. Edited by Kuroita Katsumi et al. Revised and expanded edition. Vol. 3 of *Kokushi taikei.* Yoshikawa kōbunkan, 1978.

Nihon kokugo daijiten. 20 vols. Shōgakkan, 1972–1976.

Nishimiya Kazutami. *Kojiki. SNKS.* 1979.

Noguchi Motohiro, ed. *Taketori monogatari. SNKS.* 1979.

Noguchi Takehiko. *Shōsetsu no nihongo.* Vol. 13 of *Nihongo no sekai.* Chūōkōronsha, 1980.

Nomura Seiichi. *Genji monogatari buntairon josetsu.* Yūseidō, 1970.

Oka Kazuo. *Genji monogatari no kisoteki kenkyū.* Revised edition. Tōkyōdō shuppan, 1967.

Ōno Susumu. *Nihongo no bumpō o kangaeru.* Iwanami shoten, 1978.

——, et al., eds. *Nihon shoki.* Vols. 67–68 of *NKBT.* 1965–1967.

Origuchi Shinobu. *Zenshū.* 32 vols. Chūōkōron, 1954–1968.

Ōtsu Yūichi and Tsukishima Hiroshi, eds. *Ise monogatari.* Vol. 9 of *NKBT.* 1957.

Ozawa Masao, ed. *Kokin wakashū.* Vol. 7 of *NKBZ.* 1971.

Saeki Umetomo, ed. *Kokin wakashū.* Vol. 8 of *NKBT.* 1958.

Saigō Nobutsuna. *Kojiki chūshaku.* Vol. 1. Heibonsha, 1975.

Sakai, Naoki. "Kindai no hihan: chūzetsu shita toki." *Gendai shisō,* vol. 15, no. 15 (1987), 189–207.

Sakakura Atsuyoshi, ed. *Taketori monogatari.* Vol. 9 of *NKBT.* 1957.

Sakamoto Shōzō. *Sekkan jidai.* Vol. 6 of *Nihon no rekishi.* Shōgakkan, 1974.

Sandai jitsuroku. Edited by Kuroita Katsumi et al. Revised and expanded edition. Vol. 4 of *Kokushi taikei.* Yoshikawa kōbunkan, 1966.

Sekine Yoshiko. "Kōkyū bundan no senku to shite no Ise." *Wakabungaku no sekai* 4:81–99. Kasama shoin, 1976.

Shimazu Hisamoto. *Taiyaku genji monogatari kōwa.* 6 vols. Yashima shobō, 1950–1957.

Shimizu Yoshiko. *Genji monogatari no buntai to hōhō.* Tōkyōdō shuppan, 1980.

———. "Genji monogatari no sakufū." *Kokugo kokubun,* vol. 22 (January 1953), 21–40.

———. *Genji monogatari ron.* Hanawa shobō, 1966.

———, ed. *Heichū monogatari.* Vol. 8 of *NKBZ.* 1972.

Shimizu Yoshiko and Ishida Jōji, eds. *Genji monogatari.* 8 vols. *SNKS.* 1976–1985.

Suzuki Hideo. "Akashi no kimi." In *Genji monogatari hikkei 2,* edited by Akiyama Ken, 15–20. *Bessatsu kokubungaku,* no. 13, 1982.

———. "Kokinshū no mitate ni tsuite." *Bungaku,* vol. 54, no. 2 (February 1986), 167–179.

———. "Kokinshūteki hyōgen no keisei." *Bungaku,* vol. 42, no. 5 (May 1974), 63–77.

———. "Monogatari seiritsushi oboegaki—kishu ryūri to irogonomi to—." In *Taketori monogatari, Ise monogatari hikkei,* 6–13. Gakutōsha, 1988.

Suzuki Hideo and Fujii Sadakazu, eds. *Nihon bungeishi, Kodai II.* Kawade shobō shinsha, 1986.

Tachibana Kenji, ed. *Ōkagami.* Vol. 20 of *NKBZ.* 1974.

Takahashi Shōji. *Yamato monogatari.* Vol. 8 of *NKBZ.* 1972.

Takahashi Tōru. *Genji monogatari no tai'i hō.* Tōkyō daigaku shuppankai, 1982.

———. "Irogonomi." *Kokubungaku: kaishaku to kyōzai no kenkyū,* vol. 30, no. 10 (September 1985), 50–51.

———. "Koto no ha o kazareru tama no eda." *Kokugo to kokubungaku,* vol. 61, no. 5 (May 1984), 1–13.

———."Soshitsu to kaiko—uta monogatari no aironii." *Kokubungaku: kaishaku to kyōzai no kenkyū,* vol. 24 (January 1979), 122–128.

Takamure Itsue. *Nihon kon'inshi.* Shibundō, 1963.

Takeoka Masao. *Ise monogatari zenhyōshaku.* 2 vols. Yūbunshoin, 1987.

———. "Jodōshi 'keri' no hongi to kinō—Genji monogatari, Murasaki shikibu nikki, Makura no sōshi o shiryō ni shite—." *Kokubungaku—gengo to bungei,* vol. 31 (1963), 2–15.

———, ed. *Kokin wakashū zenhyōshaku.* 2 vols. Yūbunshoin, 1983.

"Taketori, Ise, Genji." *Kokubungaku: kaishaku to kyōzai no kenkyū,* vol. 30, no. 8 (July 1985).

Tamagami Takuya. "Byōbu-e to uta to monogatari to." *Kokugo kokubun,* vol. 22 (January 1953), 1–20; later collected in supplemental vol. 1 of *GMH,* 183–207.

———. "Genji monogatari junkyo ron—Kakaishō so (II)." *Kokugo kokubun,* vol. 29 (November 1960), 1–15; later collected in supplemental vol. 1 of *GMH,* 402–419.

————. "Genji monogatari no dokusha—monogatari ondokuron." *Joshidai bungaku*, no. 7 (March 1955), 1–15; later collected in supplemental vol. 1 of *GMH*, 247–265.

————. "Genji monogatari ondokuron josetsu." *Kokugo kokubun*, vol. 19 (February 1950); later collected in supplemental vol. 1 of *GMH*, 143–155.

————. "Mukashi monogatari no kōsei." *Kokugo kokubun*, vol. 13, nos. 6, 8, and 9 (June, August, September 1943), 1–16, 40–53, and 16–26; later collected in supplemental vol. 1 of *GMH*, 109–142.

Tanahashi Mitsuo. *Ōchō no shakai*. Vol. 4 of *Taikei nihon no rekishi*. Shōgakkan, 1988.

Tsuchihashi Yutaka. *Kodai kayō no sekai*. Hanawa shobō, 1968.

Tsuchihashi Yutaka and Ikeda Yasaburō, eds. *Kayō I*. Vol. 4 of *KNKB*. 1975.

Tsukishima Hiroshi. *Kana*. Vol. 5 of *Nihongo no sekai*. Chūōkōronsha, 1981.

Watanabe Minoru. *Heian bunshōshi*. Tōkyō daigaku shuppankai, 1981.

————, ed. *Ise monogatari*. *SNKS*. 1976.

Yamagishi Tokuhei, ed. *Genji monogatari*. Vols. 14–18 of *NKBT*. 1958–1963.

Yamaguchi Nakami. "Heianchō bunshōshi kenkyū no ichi shiten." *Kokugogaku*, vol. 97 (September 1974), 16–34.

Yamanaka Yutaka. *Heianchō bungaku no shiteki kenkyū*. Yoshikawa kōbunkan, 1978.

————. *Heian jidai no kokiroku to kizoku bunka*. Shibunkaku shuppan, 1988.

Yoshikai Naoto. "Ariwara no Narihira to Ki shi." In *IKIM*, 309–314.

Works in Western Languages

Althusser, Louis. *Lenin and Philosophy: And Other Essays*. Monthly Review Press, 1971.

American Heritage Dictionary. New College Edition, 2nd edition. 1982.

Bakhtin, Mikhail. *The Dialogic Imagination*. Translated by Caryl Emerson and Michael Holquist. Texas, 1981.

————. "Discourse in the Novel." In Bakhtin, *The Dialogic Imagination*, 259–422.

————. "Epic and Novel." In Bakhtin, *The Dialogic Imagination*, 3–40.

Bal, Mieke. *Narratology*. Toronto, 1985.

Barrell, John. *Poetry, Language, and Politics*. Manchester, 1988.

Barthes, Roland. "From Work to Text." In *Textual Strategies*, edited by Josue V. Harari, 73–81. Cornell, 1979.

————. "Introduction to the Structural Analysis of Narratives." In *Image-Music-Text*. Translated by Stephen Heath. Hill and Wang, 1977.

————. *S/Z*. Translated by Richard Miller. Hill and Wang, 1974.

Belsey, Catherine. *Critical Practice*. Methuen, 1980.

Benjamin, Walter. *Illuminations*. Schocken Books, 1969.

Benveniste, Émile. *Problems in General Linguistics*. Miami, 1966.

Booth, Wayne. *The Rhetoric of Fiction*. Chicago, 1961.

Borgen, Robert. *Sugawara no Michizane and the Early Heian Court*. Harvard, 1986.

Bowring, Richard. "The Female Hand in Japan: A First Reading." In *The

Female Autograph: Theory and Practice of Autobiography from the Tenth to the Twentieth Century, edited by Domna C. Stanton, 49–56. Chicago, 1984.

——, trans. *Murasaki Shikibu: Her Diary and Poetic Memoirs.* Princeton, 1982.

——, trans. *Murasaki Shikibu: The Tale of Genji.* Cambridge, 1988.

Brower, Robert, and Earl Miner, trans. "Association and Progression: Principles of Integration in Anthologies and Sequences of Japanese Court Poetry, A.D. 900–1350." *Harvard Journal of Asiatic Studies,* vol. 21 (1958), 67–127.

——. *Japanese Court Poetry.* Stanford, 1961.

Burch, Noel. *To the Distant Observer: Form and Meaning in the Japanese Cinema.* Berkeley, 1979.

Caedel, E. B. "The Two Prefaces to the Kokinshū." *Asia Major* N.S., vol. 7 (1959), 40–51.

Cohan, Steven, and Linda M. Shires. *Telling Stories.* Routledge, 1988.

Cranston, Edwin A. "A Web in the Air." *Monumenta Nipponica,* vol. 43, no. 3 (Autumn 1988), 305–352.

——, trans. *The Izumi Shikibu Diary: A Romance of the Heian Court.* Harvard, 1969.

Culler, Jonathan. *The Pursuit of Signs: Semiotics, Literature, Deconstruction.* Cornell, 1981.

——. *Structuralist Poetics.* Cornell, 1975.

Curme, George O. *English Grammar.* Barnes and Noble, 1947.

Davis, Lennard J. *Resisting Novels.* Methuen, 1987.

De Lauretis, Teresa. *Alice Doesn't: Feminism, Semiotics, Cinema.* Indiana, 1984.

De Man, Paul. *Allegories of Reading: Figural Language in Rousseau, Nietzsche, Rilke, and Proust.* Yale, 1979.

——. *Resistance to Theory.* Minnesota, 1986.

Derrida, Jacques. *Dissemination.* Translated by Barbara Johnson. Chicago, 1981.

——. "Letter to a Japanese Friend." In *Derrida and Difference,* edited by David Wood and Robert Bernasconi, 1–5. Northwestern, 1988.

——. *Of Grammatology.* Translated by Gayatri Chakravorty Spivak. Johns Hopkins, 1976.

——. *Positions.* Translated by Alan Bass. Chicago, 1981.

——. *Writing and Difference.* Translated by Alan Bass. Chicago, 1978.

Ebersole, Gary L. *Ritual Poetry and the Politics of Death in Early Japan.* Princeton, 1989.

Ebert, Teresa. "The Romance of Patriarchy: Ideology, Subjectivity, and Postmodern Feminist Cultural Theory." *Cultural Critique,* no. 10 (Fall 1988), 19–57.

Field, Norma. *The Splendor of Longing in The Tale of Genji.* Princeton, 1987.

Fish, Stanley. *Is There a Text in This Class?* Harvard, 1980.

Foucault, Michel. *Language, Counter-Memory, and Practice.* Translated by Donald F. Bouchard and Sherry Simon. Cornell, 1977.

——. "What is an Author?" In *Textual Strategies,* edited by Josue V. Harari, 141–160. Cornell, 1979.

Fraser, Nancy, and Linda Nicholson. "Social Criticism without Philosophy:

An Encounter between Feminism and Postmodernism." In *Universal Abandon?*, edited by Andrew Ross, 83–104. Minnesota, 1988.

Frye, Northrop. *Anatomy of Criticism*. Princeton, 1957.

Fuss, Diana. *Essentially Speaking*. Routledge, Chapman, and Hall, 1989.

Gasché, Rodolphe. *The Tain of the Mirror*. Cambridge, 1986.

Genette, Gérard. *Figures of Literary Discourse*. Translated by Alan Sheridan. Columbia, 1982.

———. *Narrative Discourse*. Translated by Jane E. Lewin. Cornell, 1980.

Gombrich, E. H. *Art and Illusion*. Princeton, 1960.

Greimas, Algirdas Julien. *On Meaning*. Minnesota, 1987.

Harootunian, H. D. *Things Seen and Unseen: Discourse and Ideology in Tokugawa Nativism*. Chicago, 1988.

Hurvitz, Leon, trans. *Scripture of the Lotus Blossom of the Fine Dharma*. Columbia, 1976.

Iser, Wolfgang. *The Act of Reading*. Johns Hopkins, 1973.

Jameson, Fredric. *The Political Unconscious*. Cornell, 1981.

———. *The Prison House of Language*. Princeton, 1972.

Jardine, Alice. "Opaque Texts and Transparent Contexts: The Political Difference of Julia Kristeva." In *The Poetics of Gender*, edited by Nancy K. Miller, 96–115. Columbia, 1986.

Jauss, Hans Robert. *Toward an Aesthetic of Reception*. Translated by Timothy Bahti. Minneapolis, 1982.

Keene, Donald, trans. *The Tale of the Bamboo Cutter*. In Thomas Rimer, *Modern Japanese Fiction and Its Traditions*, 275–305. Princeton, 1978.

Kittay, Jeffrey, and Wlad Godzich. *The Emergence of Prose*. Minnesota, 1987.

Konishi Jin'ichi. *A History of Japanese Literature*, Vol. 1: *The Archaic and Ancient Ages*. Translated by Aileen Gatten and Nicholas Teele. Princeton, 1984.

———. *A History of Japanese Literature*, Vol. 2: *The Early Middle Ages*. Translated by Aileen Gatten. Princeton, 1986.

Kristeva, Julia. *Desire in Language*. Translated by Thomas Gora, Alice Jardine, and Leon S. Roudiez. Edited by Leon S. Roudiez. Columbia, 1980.

———. *Revolution in Poetic Language*. Translated by Margaret Waller. Columbia, 1984.

Kumakura, Chiyuki. "The Narrative Time of Genji monogatari." Ph.D. dissertation. Berkeley, 1979.

Levy, Ian Hideo, trans. *The Ten Thousand Leaves*. Princeton, 1981.

Lord, Albert B. *Singer of Tales*. Atheneum, 1971.

Lyons, John. *Semantics*. Vol. 2. Cambridge, 1977.

Lyotard, Jean-François. *The Postmodern Condition: A Report on Knowledge*. Translated by Geoff Bennington and Brian Massumi. Minnesota, 1984.

Mair, Victor H. *Painting and Performance*. Hawaii, 1988.

Martin, Wallace. *Recent Theories of Narrative*. Cornell, 1986.

McCullough, Helen C. *Brocade by Night: "Kokin Wakashū" and the Court Style in Japanese Classical Poetry*. Stanford, 1985.

———, trans. *Kokin Wakashū: The First Imperial Anthology of Japanese Poetry (with "Tosa Nikki" and "Shinsen Waka")*. Stanford, 1985.

————, trans. *Ōkagami, The Great Mirror: Fujiwara Michinaga (966–1027) and His Times*. Stanford, 1980.

————, trans. *Tales of Ise*. Stanford, 1968.

McCullough, William H. "Japanese Marriage Institutions in the Heian Period." *Harvard Journal of Asiatic Studies*, vol. 27 (1967), 103–167.

McCullough, William H., and Helen C. McCullough. *A Tale of Flowering Fortunes*. 2 vols. Stanford, 1980.

Miller, Roy Andrew. "No Time for Literature." *Journal of the American Oriental Society*, vol. 107, no. 4 (October–December 1987), 745–760.

Mitchell, W. J. T., ed. *On Narrative*. Chicago, 1980–81.

Miyoshi, Masao. *Accomplices of Silence*. California, 1974.

————. "Against the Native Grain: The Japanese Novel and the 'Postmodern' West." *South Atlantic Quarterly*, vol. 87, no. 3 (Summer 1988), 525–550.

————. "The 'Great Divide' Once Again: Problematics of the Novel and the Third World." *Culture & History 3* (Copenhagen, 1988), 7–22.

Modleski, Tania. "Feminism and the Power of Interpretation: Some Critical Readings." In *Feminist Studies/Critical Studies*, edited by Teresa de Lauretis, 121–138. Indiana, 1986.

Moi, Toril. *Sexual/Textual Politics*. Methuen, 1985.

Morris, Ivan, trans. *The Pillow Book of Sei Shonagon*. Vol. 1 of 2 vols. Columbia, 1967.

————. *World of the Shining Prince*. Knopf, 1964.

Morris, Mark. "Waka and Form, Waka and History." *Harvard Journal of Asiatic Studies*, vol. 46 (1986), 551–610.

Noguchi Takehiko. "The Substratum Constituting Monogatari: Prose Structure and Narrative in The Genji Monogatari." In *Principles of Classical Japanese Literature*, edited by Earl Miner, 130–150. Princeton, 1985.

Okada, Richard Hideki. "Domesticating The Tale of Genji." *Journal of the American Oriental Society*, vol. 110, no. 1 (January–March 1990), 60–70.

————. "Translation and Difference: A Review Article." *Journal of Asian Studies*, vol. 47, no. 1 (February 1988), 29–40.

————. "Unbound Texts: Narrative Discourse in Heian Japan." Ph.D. dissertation. Berkeley, 1985.

Oxford English Dictionary. Compact edition, 2 vols. 1972.

Pollack, David. *The Fracture of Meaning*. Princeton, 1986.

Radhakrishnan, R. "Ethnic Identity and Post-Structuralist Differance." *Cultural Critique*, no. 6 (Spring 1987), 199–220.

Rodd, Laurel Rasplica, trans., with the poet Mary Catherine Henkenius. *Kokinshū: A Collection of Poems Ancient and Modern*. Princeton, 1984.

Rosaldo, Renato. "Politics, Patriarchs, and Laughter." *Cultural Critique*, no. 6 (Spring 1987), 65–86.

Said, Edward. *Orientalism*. Vintage, 1978.

————. "Orientalism Reconsidered." In *Literature, Politics, and Theory*, edited by Francis Barker et al., 210–229. Methuen, 1986.

————. "Representing the Colonized: Anthropology's Interlocutors." *Critical Inquiry*, vol. 15, no. 2 (Winter 1989), 205–225.

————. "Secular Criticism." In Said, *The World, the Text and the Critic*, 1–30.

————. *The World, the Text and the Critic.* Harvard, 1983.

Seidensticker, Edward G., trans. *The Gossamer Years.* Charles E. Tuttle, 1964.

————. *The Tale of Genji.* Knopf, 1976.

Shirane, Haruo. *The Bridge of Dreams: A Poetics of 'The Tale of Genji.'* Stanford, 1987.

Spivak, Gayatri Chakravorty. "Can the Subaltern Speak?" In *Marxism and the Interpretation of Culture,* edited by Cary Nelson and Lawrence Grossberg, 271–313. Illinois, 1988.

————. *In Other Worlds: Essays in Cultural Politics.* Methuen, 1987.

————. "The Politics of Interpretations." In *The Politics of Interpretation,* edited by W. J. T. Mitchell, 347–366. Chicago, 1983.

Stimpson, Catharine R. "Ad/d Feminam." In *Literature and Society,* edited by Edward W. Said, 174–192. Johns Hopkins, 1980.

Stinchecum, Amanda Mayer. "Who Tells the Tale?—'Ukifune': A Study in Narrative Voice." *Monumenta Nipponica,* vol. 35, no. 4 (Winter 1980), 375–403.

Todorov, Tzvetan. *Introduction to Poetics.* Translated by Richard Howard. Theory and History of Literature, vol. 1. Minnesota, 1981.

————. *Mikhail Bakhtin: The Dialogical Principle.* Translated by Wlad Godzich. Minnesota, 1984.

————. *The Poetics of Prose.* Translated by Richard Howard. Cornell, 1977.

Waley, Arthur. *The Tale of Genji.* Doubleday, 1933.

Williams, Raymond. *The Country and the City.* Oxford, 1973.

————. *Writing in Society.* Verso, n.d.

Wixted, John Timothy. "Chinese Influences on the Kokinshū Prefaces." In *Kokinshū,* translated by Laurel Rodd, 387–402.

Index

About the Author

H. Richard Okada received his Ph.D. at the University of California, Berkeley. He taught at St. Pauls' School before going to Princeton University, where he is currently Associate Professor of Japanese literature in the Department of East Asian Studies.

Library of Congress Cataloging-in-Publication Data

Okada, H. Richard.
Figures of resistance : language, poetry, and narrating in the
tale of Genji and other mid-Heian texts / by H. Richard Okada.
p.   cm. — (Post-contemporary interventions)
Includes bibliographical references and index.
ISBN 0-8223-1185-2 (cloth). — ISBN 0-8223-1192-5 (paper)
1. Japanese literature—Heian period. 794-1185—History and
criticism.   I. Title.   II. Series.
PL726.2.O42 1992
895.6'090014—dc20   91-13312
                                                    CIP